The Beauty of Holiness

Phoebe Palmer As Theologian, Revivalist, Feminist, and Humanitarian

CHARLES EDWARD WHITE

WIPF & STOCK · Eugene, Oregon

Quotes and citations from the Methodist Episcopal Church Records are used by permission of The New York Conference of the United Methodist Church, 252 Bryant Avenue, White Plains, N.Y. 10605. The author also acknowledges the kind cooperation of The Rare Books and Manuscripts Division of The New York Public Library, Astor, Lenox, and Tilden Foundations.

Wipf and Stock Publishers
199 W 8th Ave, Suite 3
Eugene, OR 97401

Beauty of Holiness
Phoebe Palmer as Theologian, Revivalist, Feminist and Humanitarian
By White, Charles E.
Copyright©1986 by White, Charles E.
ISBN 13: 978-1-55635-801-2
Publication date 1/14/2008
Previously published by Zondervan, 1986

*This work is dedicated to my grandparents,
Dr. and Mrs. Clarence H. Snyder
and
Dr. and Mrs. Hugh A. White,
whose holy lives have helped me to understand
the lives of
Dr. and Mrs. Walter C. Palmer.*

Contents

	Foreword	vii
	Introduction	xv
	Acknowledgments	xviii
	Chronological Summary	xx
CHAPTER 1:	**Preparation for Ministry: 1807–37**	1
	Family Background; Childhood; Marriage; The Allen Street Revival; The Beginning of the Tuesday Meeting; Sanctification	
CHAPTER 2:	**Ministry in America: 1838–58**	27
	Preaching Holiness by Word; Preaching Holiness by Deed	
CHAPTER 3:	**Ministry in the British Isles: 1859–63**	67
	Britain's Preparation for Revival; 1859: Spying Out the Land; 1860: Quick Success and Obscure Labor; 1861: "I Am Content to Occupy a Small Space If God Be Glorified"; 1862: God Moves in a Mysterious Way; 1863: "Shaking the Dust Off Our Feet, We Will Go to the Gentiles"	
CHAPTER 4:	**The *Guide to Holiness* and More Camp Meetings: 1864–74**	91
	The *Guide to Holiness*; More Camp Meetings	
CHAPTER 5:	**Phoebe Palmer As Theologian**	105
	Theological Method; Influences; Entire Sanctification; Ecclesiology; Spirituality; Eschatology; The Importance of Phoebe Palmer's Theology	
CHAPTER 6:	**Phoebe Palmer As Revivalist**	161
	The Tuesday Meeting for the Promotion of Holiness; Theology of Revival; Methodology of Revival; Evaluation	

| CHAPTER | 7: | **Phoebe Palmer As Feminist** | 187 |

Background; Thought Expressed in *Promise of the Father*; Example and Influence; Evaluation; Conclusion

| CHAPTER | 8: | **Phoebe Palmer As Humanitarian** | 207 |

Motives; The Five Points Mission; Other Humanitarian Efforts; Evaluation

Conclusion	231
Appendix A: Camp Meetings and Revival Services: 1839–59	237
Appendix B: Revival Meetings in the British Isles: 1859–63	241
Appendix C: Camp Meetings and Revivals: 1863–74	243
Appendix D: Chronology of Controversy	245
Appendix E: A Covenant of Entire Consecration	247
Notes on the Sources	249
Notes	255
Primary Bibliography	307
Secondary Bibliography	314
Index	326

Foreword

At long last, one of the many scholars studying the life and public role of one of the nineteenth century's most prominent American women has produced a splendid biography. As wife, mother, and homemaker, Phoebe Palmer had a close involvement with Methodist perfectionism, and she exercised continuous influence over Methodist preachers and their wives and over the outstanding leaders in America's largest Protestant denomination for twenty-five years. This was evident not only in her helping them find and preach more clearly the Methodist doctrine of entire sanctification but also in her prodding them to numerous ventures on behalf of the poor. The latter included the founding of the first settlement house in America, called "the Five Points Mission," in New York, as well as several other activities to which Professor White devotes a chapter. She also became one of the nation's best-known religious writers and one of Methodism's most powerful public speakers, long before she acknowledged that what she called exhorting was tantamount to preaching. She then wrote a fine book on women's scriptural right to preach the gospel. Meanwhile, she had become editor of a widely circulated religious magazine and, through an evangelistic tour in England that lasted four years, made herself well known among Wesleyans in that country as well.

Professor White's fine book makes crystal clear that Phoebe Palmer's functioning as both a powerful writer and a revivalist, though not an ordained one, fit precisely the Wesleyan expectation that dedicated women would participate in the public aspects of evangelism. Despite the general assumption that Mrs. Palmer added a feminine touch hitherto missing, there is no question that she was following a Methodist tradition sanctioning women's leadership, not only in small class meetings but in public ways as well, that goes back to Wesley's own era. It was continued long after his death by persons such as Mary Fletcher and Hester Ann Rogers and was a generally accepted part of Methodist life in the middle of the nineteenth century.

For this reason, as Professor White's book demonstrates, Phoebe Palmer's feminism never needed to be aggressive. Her public participation, beginning with the sudden fame that her Tuesday Meeting for the Promotion of Holiness achieved in 1839, was entirely accepted by Methodist leaders (many of whom appeared in her parlors in the early years). She had instant and easy access to the columns of the largest Methodist newspaper in America, *The New York Christian Advocate*, and, whenever she wished, to those of what was then called *The Guide to Christian Perfection*. There never seems to have been a question raised about a woman's being responsible for such extensive "exhortation" as she gave in camp-meetings after 1841 and increasingly throughout the next two decades. That she (and her lay husband) should have become so famous by the 1850s as to conduct entire services by themselves simply displayed to the Methodists of that period what everyone knew was characteristic of that denomination's work in America: the important role it gave to laypersons in the very rapid spread of Methodism across the United States and Canada. Despite recent attempts to show that such women "feminized" the attitudes and doctrines taught by Congregationalist, Presbyterian, and Baptist ministers, that certainly is not what was happening in Methodism. There were no stronger or more decisive males in American public life, or in American Methodism, than some of those who were Mrs. Palmer's deepest admirers. Nathan Bangs, who presided at her meetings almost regularly in the 1850s, though never a bishop, was probably the most influential Methodist leader for the last twenty-five years of his half-century of ministry. A controversialist, and yet a notable historian, theologian, and biographer in the church, his devotion to many of the ideas and practices Phoebe Palmer supported was softened, not by the efforts of her womanly ways upon him, but by his earnest effort to apply what he believed the New Testament taught about compassion and perfect love.

So with the humanitarian work of Phoebe Palmer, which this volume describes fully. Although Professor White makes clear that her experience as a mother, whom death had deprived of her children, is never far out of sight, he shows her sober realism about poverty, economic interest of the privileged classes, and about the necessity of making the ethereal concept of Christian love effective in practice. Here is set forth her role in persuading her husband and many other Methodist men to provide funds, guidance, and participation in such activities as the Five Points Mission in New

York's red light district, perhaps America's first settlement house, as well as in direct ministries to the poor in deprived neighborhoods of the great cities of America. And although her public opposition to slavery did not lead her to abolitionism, her deep antipathy to that system was from the beginning powerful, as it was with Nathan Bangs, Abel Stevens, and Alfred Cookman. That all these leaders opposed radical abolition does not mean that they were pro-slavery. The long career of President Lincoln and other persons who, if they had to make a choice, cared more for the preservation of the Union than the abolition of slavery, makes this fact obvious.

Everywhere, in print and preaching, the central theme in Phoebe Palmer's ministry, like John Wesley's, was holiness of heart and life, the experience of perfect love and of the power of the blood of Christ to cleanse the Christian from the inward inclination to sin. John Wesley had taught generations of his followers to call this experience entire sanctification, or evangelical perfection.

Except for the extensive portion of her correspondence that appeared in 1872 in Richard Wheatley's *Life and Letters of Phoebe Palmer* and, usually without naming the recipient, in such of her own numerous books as *Present to My Christian Friend* and *The Way of Holiness*, no letters, no diary, and no personal records exist. This explains part of the reluctance of historians to undertake her biography. But in that published record, Mr. White believed, was an ample supply of evidence covering her adult life. Its general authenticity is verified in the few surviving letters that remain in the scattered manuscript collections and in the publications of her numerous correspondents. It covers in minutest detail the matters that made her important—her religious development in the 1830s, her thoughts on Scripture, faith, and holy living, and her methods of winning the adherence to Wesleyan theology of multitudes of earnest persons, including well-educated Christian thinkers, clergymen, and business and professional people. Using this evidence, Charles White has done what a theologian-historian was best prepared to do. He has analyzed her activities and her teachings both in the context of evangelical Christian America during the period of the Civil War and in the context of Methodist theology and spirituality since Wesley's time.

Especially useful are the early chapters, which chronicle her close adherence to the teaching of John Wesley, partly as mediated by a group of the aged Wesley's young associates. They reflected the power and clarity of the founder's preaching after the great revival of Christian holiness, which began in 1758. Among them was John Fletcher, whose works were published in three complete American editions before 1832 and whose explanation of Christian perfection had been joined in the popular mind with that of John Wesley; the English diarist Hester Ann Rogers, wife of an English Methodist preacher in the 1780s; and Adam Clarke, a notable Bible expositor.

White, therefore, treats her theological insights seriously, as they deserve to be treated. He knows, of course, that her theology was derivative rather than, as it is stylish to say, constructive. In this, however, she resembled John Wesley and all but a handful of the Methodists, as well as a multitude of other nineteenth-century Christians. That a woman without a great deal of formal education should have attained and expressed such widely approved theological insight reflects the clarity with which John Wesley's system of biblical theology was maintained during the hundred years following his death. It also bespoke the hunger of ordinary Americans for a faith in the grace of Christ to deliver them from both disobedience to God's will and what Wesley had called "inbred sin." All Christians believed that such original sin, such primal inclination to evil, remained imbedded in the hearts of those who had been "born again." Wesley's special contribution as a theologian was to gather up from many strands of biblical teaching and Christian thinking the idea that the love that had been "shed abroad" in Christians' hearts when they were converted could be, by the same faith, made perfect in this present life in an experience that he insisted again and again delivered believers from inbred sin.

Not just the responsiveness of prominent Methodist preachers and laymen to Phoebe Palmer's ministry, then, but the openness of people generally to the preaching of what later was called "the higher Christian life" was a moral event of greatest importance in nineteenth-century American culture.

Mr. White's book focuses these early chapters, then, on the ways in which Phoebe Palmer's activities and beliefs continued the course of John Wesley's revival. Like him and like her fellow Methodists (and, for that matter, like Moses and Jesus), she insisted that loving God with all your heart and loving your neighbor as yourself was the divine expectation. And she stressed, with them, that all holiness, like all salvation, was by grace, through faith, and not dependent in any way upon the works of human righteousness. She believed and taught throughout her public ministry, as Wesley did, that holy living was a *consequence*, rather than a cause, of the two great experiences of hallowing faith—regeneration and purity of heart. God's grace, extended to all who would receive it in the presence and sanctifying power of the Holy Spirit, promised to perfect our love for him and so enable Christians to keep the essence of the law. Moreover, with all Methodist preachers, she affirmed that human beings can be fully assured that such grace has come to them by the direct witness of the Holy Spirit to their own consciousness. Also with them, she affirmed that individuals are free to accept or reject that grace and, at any time after they have received it, free to turn aside from the high calling and fall back into the ways of sin. Human responsibility to trust and obey, then, she combined with a conviction of utter human dependence on the grace of God in Christ to enable one to trust and obey. This doctrine of personal moral accountability was central in everything Phoebe Palmer (and all other mid-nineteenth-century Methodist preachers) said or wrote.

Dr. White has had to come to terms, however, in the latter part of the book, with a large body of argument mounted by those Methodists who emerged after the Civil War as opponents of the doctrine of inward sanctification. Complicating this has been the work of numerous scholars who wrote in the last thirty years (including myself and John L. Peters) suggesting that Phoebe Palmer had departed in some significant ways from Wesley's theological and biblical ideas. Our principal charge was that she came to stress the exercise of faith for the attainment of the "second experience," while deemphasizing the idea that God granted the witness of the Holy Spirit to that attainment.

Mrs. Palmer developed, out of what everyone recognizes was an amateur's venture in scriptural exegesis, the notion that since the Hebrew Scriptures had declared that "the altar sanctifies the gift" laid upon it, if Christians would (as Wesley translated Hebrews 12:1) lay their whole selves in utter consecration to God's will on the divine altar, which she understood to be Christ, the altar sanctified the gift. Seekers not only had a right to believe that this was so but ought to rest their confidence on this promise until they were assured by the Holy Spirit and by the promised blossoming of perfect love in their lives that it was indeed so. When pressed by contemporary critics, including her beloved friend, the aging Nathan Bangs, as to whether she was substituting "naked" faith (that is, faith with no spiritual "evidence") for Wesley's "living faith," she denied it, at length and in public print, appealing to Wesley's many powerful descriptions of how believers are sanctified by faith. Her purpose in the use of the "altar" metaphor was, she said, two-fold. First, she wanted to stress the absolute necessity of full consecration to God's will. Second, she aimed to encouraged procrastinating seekers, as Wesley had in his famous sermon "Scripture Way of Salvation," to believe *now* for their sanctification, since it came by grace through faith, not by "works of righteousness."

Professor White argues here that Mrs. Palmer, in her effort to persuade persons of Calvinistic background that they did not have to spend a lifetime seeking inward holiness but might follow what she called, originally in a letter to a Presbyterian minister, "a shorter way," shifted slightly the emphasis Wesley had put upon the interdependence of progressive and instantaneous sanctification to a primary emphasis upon the "second blessing" alone. I think he underestimates at this point the great emphasis of Phoebe Palmer, even in her description of her own experience of perfect love, upon growth in holiness both before and after that moment.

He also lays out, in a long section of his chapter on her theology, numerous other points of small difference he thinks he observes between Phoebe Palmer's teaching and that of the founder of Methodism. Wesley scholars will quibble over these, as indeed I do. Several of the differences that White stresses may have been borrowed by her from Wesley and his contemporaries. For example, that Phoebe Palmer occasionally took a dream to have spiritual significance does not distinguish her from Wesley, nor from multitudes of other Christians. Frank Baker's new volumes of Wesley's letters for the 1750s contain a dozen or so in which he inquired of the most outstanding Methodists whether they had ever seen in their mind's eye a vision of three distinct persons of the Holy Trinity, and numbers of them professed to have had such a vision. That Mrs. Palmer, ninety years later, should have believed she had a similar "beatific vision" does not seem to me unWesleyan, nor an example of womanly credulity and romanticism, as some critics may have supposed.

The exciting point in Professor White's book, however, is the degree to which he demonstrates that, one hundred years later, even the details of Wesley's teachings were being so largely reproduced in the preaching and writing of a Methodist laywoman and popular exhorter. That the preachers of what was by then the largest Protestant denomination in America should have so willingly heard her messages and followed her spiritual directions is evidence enough that not only she, but they, had read Wesley's writings with care. Phoebe Palmer was not an exception but an example of the best in the founder's religion, I think. And for that reason she became, as one great minister noted at her death, "the Priscilla who taught many an Apollos the way of the Lord more perfectly."

The lesson I draw from this book and from Phoebe Palmer's life, then, is exactly the opposite of the one I have so often drawn from briefer studies of it. It is this: there was not a "holiness controversy" in the Methodist Episcopal Church, North, during the Civil War years. Mrs. Palmer herself rebuked the pioneers in the tiny Free Methodist secession of 1859 for their failure to understand how much Methodism remained committed to John Wesley's doctrines, particularly the doctrine of perfect love. As late as 1872, half of the Methodist bishops were well known as strong advocates of that experience; and all of them were close friends and admirers of Mrs. Palmer. White shows—as I have discovered in a two-year investigation of early Methodist preaching and publication in America—that the preaching of entire sanctification was far more pervasive in the early nineteenth century than I had once supposed. That doctrine, expressed in both Wesley's language of the Atonement and John Fletcher's language of Pentecost, was prevalent everywhere—among the earliest Methodists of Boston as among the Kentucky circuit riders.

The extensive controversy over the "second blessing" appeared only during the years *after* 1872, when certain prominent Methodists, in both the northern and southern wings of the church, abandoned a feeble effort to charge the proponents of sanctification with innovation and made a frontal assault on the whole idea of an immediate experience of entire sanctification. They knew that had been a central aspect of Methodist religion since Wesley's time, and they intended to change it. But the main body of Methodist folk continued to believe in the experience and at least down until 1900 remained convinced, as Wesley had taught them, that their mission was "to reform the nation, and to spread scriptural holiness over these lands."

Here, then, is an absorbing account that, despite the scholarly care with which it is written, deals clearly with matters so intrinsically interesting to Christian pastors and laypersons that thoughtful persons with any interest in American revivalism, feminism, and humanitarianism, particularly in the doctrine of entire sanctification, or perfect love, will find wonderfully instructive. Its publication fulfills my long dream that a competent biographer, who understands the religious importance of these issues, would produce a strong biography of this most powerful and influential Christian woman of the nineteenth century.

Timothy L. Smith
The Johns Hopkins University
Baltimore, Maryland

Introduction

In January of 1857 the editors of a national magazine published a portrait of an attractive young woman. Being honest men, they were forced to admit that their engraving was "not a perfect picture of the original; that is, she is not now so youthful and her features are not so artistically formed." They hastened to add, however, that the woman was actually more intelligent than she appeared in the picture.[1] Phoebe Palmer, the woman in the picture, probably was not offended by their comments. She was friends with the editors who had published her portrait, and shared their Wesleyan heritage of plain speaking. Anyway, physical beauty was unimportant to her; what mattered was the beauty of the soul. Mrs. Palmer believed that only one thing could make the soul beautiful: holiness. She spoke of the "beauty of . . . holiness" which empowered one to live a well-balanced or "symmetrical" life.[2]

This work will examine the career of Phoebe Palmer, and argue that her understanding of holiness gave her life both symmetry and power. The symmetry of her life is shown by her wide range of interests: She was a theologian, revivalist, feminist, and humanitarian. The power of her life is revealed in the significant contributions she made to American life in these four areas.

Phoebe Palmer was born in New York City in 1807 and died there in 1874. As a theologian she modified and popularized John Wesley's doctrine of Christian perfection. Her ideas became dominant within the Holiness movements of America and Britain, and from these movements were taken up into the Charismatic and Pentecostal movements of today. She spread her ideas through her eighteen books, and through a magazine called the *Guide to Holiness*, which at its peak had a circulation of 37,000.

Phoebe Palmer also taught her doctrines at camp meetings and revival services in the United States, Canada, and Great

Britain. Both Phoebe and her husband spoke at these gatherings, but it was generally agreed that she was the better speaker. Noted historian of revival, J. Edwin Orr, traces the origin of what he calls "The Second Evangelical Awakening" (1857–65) to the Palmers' ministry.[3] From 1840 to 1874, Mrs. Palmer was the central figure in the Tuesday Meeting for the Promotion of Holiness, which met in her home in New York City. This meeting was the focus of the early Holiness movement and by 1886 had spawned at least 238 similar weekly meetings in places as far away as India and New Zealand. To her parlors came such church leaders as Leonidas Hamline, Edmund Janes, and William Taylor, who became Methodist bishops; John Dempster, the "father of Methodist theological education"; John Inskip, leader of the National Camp Meeting Association for the Promotion of Holiness; Nathan Bangs, publishing agent for the Methodist Church; and Thomas Upham, internationally known philosopher. Upham professed entire sanctification under the ministry of Mrs. Palmer, as did B. T. Roberts, founder of the Free Methodist Church, and Frances Willard, leader of the Women's Christian Temperance Union.

Phoebe Palmer promoted the cause of feminism by example and argument. In an age when it was deemed unseemly for a woman to speak in public, she addressed thousands. In a day when men debated the capacity of a woman's mind for logic, she edited a popular magazine and wrote well-researched and closely reasoned books on Christian doctrine. In a day when women were often forbidden to speak in church, she urged on both female and male believers the duty of public testimony for their Lord. Mrs. Palmer defended her ministry, and the ministries of other women, in a lengthy book that is still in print.

Phoebe Palmer's theology of Christian perfection not only motivated her to write theology, to itinerate as an evangelist, and to promote women's rights; it also energized her to acts of benevolence. Beginning by distributing tracts from basement to garret in every building in her assigned section of the city, she went on to provide food and clothing when she found a need. Later she took in foster children and found permanent homes for them. Her commitment to the needy led her to resign from the comfortable Allen Street Methodist Episcopal Church to help plant a church in a poor neighborhood. As an officer of the Methodist Ladies' Home Missionary Society, she promoted the work of one of New York's first rescue missions. She also urged the establishment of foreign missions and helped to organize the sending of the first Methodist missionaries to China. While completing all of these tasks, Mrs. Palmer raised three children, all of whom entered some form of professional Christian service.

In Mrs. Palmer's funeral oration the eulogist said her name had become "a household word throughout the church"; but Phoebe Palmer is not commonly known today.[4] Besides the article on her in the *Guide to Holiness*, the only contemporary account of her life was a brief article in the *Ladies' Repository* in 1866.[5] Soon after Mrs. Palmer's death, Richard Wheatley published an exhaustive biography which included many excerpts from her diary and letters.[6] His work was followed by similar works on Mrs. Palmer's husband, Walter, and on her sister, Sarah Lankford Palmer.[7] Walter's biographer later wrote a volume on the Tuesday Meeting and then added a supplement to it on the *Guide to Holiness*.[8] Her life and work were also treated in the *Cyclopedia of Methodism*, where the article featured her portrait.[9] After the turn of the century, there seemed to be little interest in Mrs. Palmer. Various histories and dissertations about Methodism mentioned her only briefly until 1956, when John Peters explored her contribution to American Methodist theology.[10] Then in 1957 Earnest Wall wrote an article about her and Timothy Smith featured her in *Revivalism and Social Reform*.[11] Since then there has been an increase of interest in Phoebe Palmer's life and thought, but no full-length study of her career has yet appeared.

Perhaps those who would have written a complete biography were deterred by the inability to find her diary and letters. While many have searched for these documents, they have not been found. Happily, Mrs. Palmer's published works give us clear insight into her thought and a fairly detailed outline of both her inner and outer life. The lack of the unpublished sources is thus no barrier to a study of her career and thought. It may also be that Mrs. Palmer's contribution to American religion has been ignored because she was female, pious, and Methodist. Because she was female, perhaps the male-dominated scholarly community might have undervalued her contributions. Because she was pious, her cloying style might have put off more secular readers. Because she was Methodist, Reformed scholars might not have been as interested in her as in others of their own tradition. They may also have found her doctrine of entire sanctification absolutely incredible. Happily, today's renewed interest in the contributions of women, and the continued vitality of the Holiness, Pentecostal, and Charismatic movements have stimulated the study of Phoebe Palmer.

Acknowledgments

Most debts are pleasant to incur but painful to discharge. Not so with scholarly debts; they are only pleasant. I owe a debt of gratitude to several institutions: to the libraries and librarians at Harvard, Drew, and Boston Universities, as well as to those at Gordon-Conwell Theological Seminary, Garrett-Evangelical Theological Seminary, the Methodist Archives, and Spring Arbor College. The people at the New York Public Library and the library of the University of Michigan also provided helpful assistance. Spring Arbor College not only aided me through its library, but also provided secretarial help and other technical services. Timothy Smith got me started on this project with his stimulating work, *Revivalism and Social Reform,* and also provided gracious criticism of my work at several points. Melvin Dieter's work, *The Holiness Revival of the Nineteenth Century* (Scarecrow Press: 1980), provided essential background, and the man himself gave helpful encouragement. Professors Schoenalds and Maxwell guided me in their areas of expertise. Joe Allison and the staff at Zondervan did their work with alacrity.

Beth Rutledge, Norman Elliott Anderson, and Evelyn Mottweiler all aided in providing the illustrations. Donald Dayton exercised his bibliographic legerdemain to find what no one else had been able to locate, a copy of *Israel's Speedy Restoration,* and Catherine Clarke Kroeger provided me with a copy of *Mother's Gift.* Thomas Oden drew my attention to *Mary, or the Young Christian.* Anne Root and Delvin Covey smoothed out my prose. My two advisors at Boston University, C. Allyn Russell and Earl Kent Brown, saved me from numerous stylistic and factual pitfalls. In addition, Dr. Brown has been a friend, encouragement, and model over the four years we have worked together.

My parents and grandparents have provided financial support throughout five long years of doctoral study. Mike and Lisa Raskob gave Spring Arbor College a word processor for my use. I have nothing but praise for my Rainbow computer from Digital Equipment Corporation. It typed and retyped chapter after chapter, working any time of the day or night.

And, of course, there is the other woman in my life. Or rather women. Despite suffering the pains of thesis widowhood, Carol did not become jealous of the attention her husband paid to Phoebe Palmer. She shared the vision, criticized the chapters, and kept the household together. Miriam, Jana, and Sarah also sacrificed for Phoebe. Their daddy spent far more time with her than with them, especially in recent months. This is a situation I mean to correct.

Chronological Summary

1785		Henry Worrall converted
1792		Henry Worrall emigrates to United States
1804	Feb. 9	Walter Clarke Palmer born
1806	Apr. 23	Sarah A. Worrall born
1807	Dec. 18	Phoebe Worrall born
1827	Sept. 28	Marriage of Phoebe Worrall to Walter Palmer
1828	Sept. 28	Alexander H. Palmer born
1829	July 2	Alexander dies
1830	Apr. 29	Samuel M. Palmer born
	June 19	Samuel dies
1831		Marriage of Sarah Worrall to Thomas Lankford
1831–32		Revival at Allen Street Methodist Episcopal Church
1833	Apr. 11	Sarah Palmer born
1835	May 21	Sarah Lankford sanctified
	Aug.	Sarah Lankford involved in women's prayer meetings
	Aug. 28	Eliza Palmer born
1836	Feb.	Palmer and Lankford families move to 54 Rivington Street, New York City
	Feb. 9	First Tuesday Meeting held at 54 Rivington Street
	July 29	Eliza dies
1837	July 26	Phoebe Palmer sanctified
1838		Phoebe Palmer begins speaking at camp meetings
1839		Phoebe Palmer becomes first female Methodist class leader in New York
		Phoebe Palmer (daughter) born
		Guide to Holiness founded
		Men begin to attend Tuesday Meeting
1840		Phoebe Palmer takes leadership of the Tuesday Meeting
1842	Nov. 20	Walter Clarke Palmer, Jr., born
1843		*The Way of Holiness* published

1845		*Entire Devotion to God* published
1847?		Phoebe Palmer becomes officer in Ladies' Home Missionary Society
1848		*Faith and Its Effects* published
		Palmers leave Allen Street Church for Norfolk Street Church
1850		Five Points Mission established
1851–56		Controversy with Mattison occurs
1853		Palmers attend their first Canadian camp meeting
1855		*Incidental Illustrations* published
1856		Palmers return to Allen Street Church
1857	Feb.–Mar.	"A Laity for the Times" appears
	Oct.	Revival begins in Hamilton, Ontario
1859		*Promise of the Father* published
1859–63		Palmers lead revival services in Britain
1864		Palmers buy *Guide to Holiness* and Phoebe becomes editor
1865		Palmers move to 23 St. Mark's Place, New York City
1866		*Four Years in the Old World* and *Life and Letters of Hamline* published
1867		Palmers take trip down Mississippi River
1870		Palmers take trip to California
		Palmers move to 316 East Fifteenth Street, New York City
1872		Phoebe Palmer contracts nephritis
1873	Mar. 6	Thomas Lankford dies
1874	Nov. 2	Phoebe Palmer dies
1875		*Mother's Gift* published
1876	Mar. 18	Walter Palmer marries Sarah Lankford
1883	July 20	Walter Palmer dies
1896	Apr. 24	Sarah Lankford Palmer dies
1901		*Guide to Holiness* ceases publication with December issue

CHAPTER ONE:
Preparation for Ministry: 1807–37

FAMILY BACKGROUND

Early one morning in 1785 a teenage boy crept from his bed. Careful not to wake the rest of his Yorkshire household, he dressed and slipped away from the house. He was sure that his parents would disapprove of his plans. They were pious members of the Church of England and even had the local curate living in their home. Perhaps the boy was not satisfied with their religion, or maybe he was merely curious about the famous old preacher who had come to town. Either way, he did not want his family to know where he was going before 5:00 in the morning.

At 5:00 that morning John Wesley preached to the people of Bradford, Yorkshire. His text was probably one he had proclaimed hundreds of times before, John 3:7: "Ye must be born again." According to Mr. Wesley, nothing memorable happened that day. No record of that day appears in his printed journal or his diary. He had preached thousands of five o'clock sermons and would preach hundreds more.

But for thirteen-year-old Henry Worrall, the event was life-changing. He wanted to be born again, and he believed the Methodists could tell him how to do it. He did not record whether his parents discovered his early morning activities or not, but they must have noticed a change in him. From that day on he did his best to attend Mr. Wesley's meetings and later even joined the Methodist Society. He was proud to have received his membership ticket from the hand of Mr. Wesley himself.[1]

Not only was this a momentous day for Henry Worrall, it was

1

to become a momentous day for American Methodism. Seven years after Mr. Wesley gave him his membership ticket, Worrall left England for America.[2] There he married Dorothea Wade, and they both joined the Methodist Episcopal Church in New York City. They had sixteen children. Their fourth, Phoebe, became the most influential woman in the American Methodist church in her century.[3]

CHILDHOOD

Phoebe was born December 18, 1807. She had ten brothers and five sisters, but only eight of them reached maturity.[4] Henry and Dorothea Worrall brought their children up as God-fearing Methodists. Besides taking the children with them to the meetings of the Duane Street Methodist Episcopal Church, they trained them at home to serve the Lord.[5]

Each morning family prayers would be announced by an early bell, giving them all a half-hour to prepare themselves. With the ringing of the second bell, family worship commenced. They gathered in the sitting room, and then the father read from the Bible, explaining the verses as he went. Bible reading was followed by a song, and every child who could read had a hymnal. The family then sought God's blessing on the day in prayer. Once again in the evening the family gathered to worship the Lord as they had done in the morning. These were holy times, and the parents expected all the family to be present. Meals were another time for family worship. As they began, the family stood while they asked God's blessing on their food, and as the meal ended, they again rose while the father thanked God for his provision.[6]

This intense regimen had its desired effect, and most of the children professed faith while they were still young. Phoebe was an especially spiritually sensitive child.[7] A lie she told as a three year old caused her so much anguish that she still remembered it forty-two years later.[8] To avoid ever telling an untruth again, she always said, "I think so," rather than saying, "I know so." Such scrupulousness caused her siblings to tease her, and sometimes led her to troublesome excesses, but generally she was a model child.[9] She believed her parents' wishes to be the governing law of the household and at twenty could record in her diary, "I do not remember ever to have been willfully disobedient to any parental command."[10]

For the young Phoebe the only disadvantage in growing up in

such a devout home was that she never had a definite conversion experience. She had given her heart to Jesus at such an early age that she could never remember when she had done it. She felt that the Lord loved her, and that he was concerned about all her childish problems, but since she had never felt the deep conviction of sin, nor the sudden lifting of the load which others described, she wondered if she were really saved.[11] Once when she heard convicted sinners groaning for mercy at an altar of prayer, she went forward hoping that she would share their experience of burden and release. She was somewhat disappointed to find the only emotion she felt was a renewed sense of trust and hope in God.[12]

Through her teenage years and into her twenties she remained in this twilight state. She believed she was a child of God, but she lacked the assurance to cry, "Abba, Father." She wanted to trust unfailingly, but admitted, "my proneness to reason, and also the unwise propensity I had of measuring my experience by what I imagined [to be] the experience of others, gave the enemy advantage over me."[13] At one point she even wished she had been born before Christ so that under the dispensation of the Law she could have had tangible assurance that she was right with God:

> O had I lived in that day, how gladly would I have parted with every thing, however costly, and have purchased the best possible offering. All I would have to do, would be to lay it upon the altar, and know that it was accepted.[14]

Besides these spiritual experiences, we know little of Phoebe's childhood. Because her father was successful in the engineering business, the family was comfortably wealthy and probably socially well placed. The widely known Methodist leader Nathan Bangs taught Phoebe her catechism in 1817, and in 1818 the British Consul, George Buchanan, presented her with a New Testament.[15] Her writings tell us nothing of her formal education. We do have an early five-verse poem composed of pairs of rhyming couplets written on the fly-leaf of her Bible. It begins:

> This Revelation—holy, just, and true—
> Though oft I read, it seems forever new;
> While light from heaven upon its pages rest,
> I feel its power, and with it I am blest.

Note the sense of surprise that the Scripture is always new despite her long acquaintance with it. Phoebe felt this degree of familiarity with the Bible at the mature age of eleven.[16]

Besides the Bible, the biographies of famous Methodists formed her intellectual diet. She mentioned reading as a child the memoirs of William Bramwell, Mary Bosanquet Fletcher, Hester Ann Rogers, and Nancy Cutler. Her knowledge of the lives of John Fletcher, John Nelson, Lady Maxwell, William Carvosso, and Susanna Wesley probably also stemmed from her early reading. Of course she was well schooled in the details of John Wesley's life. When as an adult she visited Walsall, England, she reported that from childhood she knew that Wesley had been mobbed there in 1743.[17]

MARRIAGE

So careful was Phoebe to please her parents that as a teenager she discouraged several young men who sought her love. Her parents did not actively oppose any of these matches, but the absence of their explicit approval was enough for her. She carefully avoided contact with these suitors, and "resolved not to favor attentions I could not return."[18]

But in July 1826 she met one whose attentions she could return.[19] Walter Clarke Palmer was newly graduated from the Rutgers Medical College of Physicians and Surgeons in New York, and was establishing a practice in the city. Born in Middletown, New Jersey, on February 9, 1804, the son of Miles and Deborah Clarke Palmer, he had moved with his parents to New York in May of 1804. The elder Palmers were devout Methodists and held class meetings in their home. Walter was converted at thirteen and immediately set to work as a Sunday school teacher. He wondered whether he should prepare for the ministry, but then became convinced "that no calling on earth could be more Christlike, in its aims and purposes than that of a pious physician."[20] He completed his medical studies with honors and then embarked on three projects: establishing a medical practice, superintending the Sunday school at the Allen Street Methodist Episcopal Church, and wooing Phoebe Worrall.[21]

Walter's third project was crowned with success when on September 28, 1827, he was married to Phoebe in her father's home by Nicholas White of the Duane Street Methodist Episcopal Church.[22] On their thirteenth anniversary Phoebe recalled that day:

> Dear love! my tearful eye doth rest
> Upon a little scroll

> Which tells the day when we were blest,
> Tis here I see enrolled
> Your name with mine: my maiden name:
> I bade it then adieu,
> And from that joyous hour became
> One heart and soul with you.
> 'Twas then the lover's name was changed
> To husband! mine to wife,
> 'Twas not that love should be estranged,
> Sweet husband of my life;
> 'Twas but that those by God made one,
> By nature one in heart,
> Together through life's course should run,
> Some say, "Till death doth part."[23]

Their marriage displayed this remarkable unity of spirit as they worked together in speaking, writing, and publishing. So united did they feel that Phoebe signed both their names to many of her letters, and Walter continued to list her as co-editor of the *Guide to Holiness* for at least a year after her death.[24]

Even though the Worralls were pleased with their new son-in-law, they were sad to see the nineteen-year-old Phoebe leave home. She was the first one to break the family circle, and at the next day's time of family worship, her father mourned as if he had just been to a funeral instead of a wedding.[25] This sorrowing was short-lived, for after a brief honeymoon trip the newlyweds set up housekeeping a short distance away from Phoebe's girlhood home. Evidently the Palmer boys felt a strong attraction for the Worrall home, because Walter's brother Miles soon married Phoebe's sister Hannah.[26]

On their first wedding anniversary Phoebe gave birth to a son whom they named Alexander. She postponed having him baptized, because she was afraid to acknowledge that he really belonged to the Lord and not to her. As she spent hours carefully embroidering Alexander's baby clothes, she wondered whether God was pleased to have her spend so much time on something that was merely decorative. The baby was a sickly child and died eleven months later. Phoebe's grief was intense. She felt that while she was making up her mind about giving her child to God, the Lord forced the issue: "I felt that he was *taken* away—not *given* up—*torn* from my embrace—not a *free-will offering.*"[27] The next spring the Palmers again had a son, Samuel. Phoebe decided that God had given him to her to replace Alexander. She immediately curtailed all activities outside the home, saying, "Now that God has made up my loss, I will *live* for this one dear object—I will have done with those more extended expectations, and absorb my mind's energies in this beloved one."[28] Unfortunately, Samuel lived only seven short weeks.

Reflecting on these experiences on her wedding anniversary in 1830, Phoebe commented in her diary:

> I will not attempt to describe the pressure of the last crushing trial. Surely I needed it, or it would not have been given. God takes our treasure to heaven, that our hearts may be there also. The Lord has declared himself a jealous God. He will have no other Gods before him. After my loved ones were snatched away, I saw that I had concentrated my time and attentions far too exclusively, to the neglect of the religious activities demanded.[29]

As she tried to make sense out of these two heart-breaking tragedies, Phoebe came to believe that her affection for her children had displaced her love for God, and that the time she had spent needlessly fussing over them should have been devoted to the Lord's service. She had made idols out of her children, and the Lord had taken them. She hoped that she would never make that mistake again.[30]

THE ALLEN STREET REVIVAL

Less than a year after the death of little Samuel, the Palmers were involved in a revival that occurred in their home church. The pastor, Samuel Merwin, announced a series of preaching meetings initially scheduled to last for four days. He hoped that there would be enough interest to extend them for forty days. Walter and Phoebe were present at the first meeting at 10:30 Monday morning. When the preacher called those who desired a deeper work of grace to come to the altar, Walter led Phoebe to the place of prayer. She reported that she was "quickened in the divine life" and brought nearer to God, but Walter was even more greatly blessed. This new work of God in his life made Walter more active in the Lord's service.

While maintaining his medical practice, Dr. Palmer became deeply involved in the work of the revival. He attended so many services that Phoebe feared he would kill himself from overwork. His role was to wait until the preacher had finished the message and had invited seekers to come to the altar rail for prayer; there the leaders of the church would counsel and pray with them while the congregation remained seated in silent prayer. Walter was afraid to counsel those seeking grace at the altar, but he felt impelled by the Spirit to go about the congregation during the altar service, urging the young men to "come to Jesus." So many people responded to these revival services that they were extended beyond the four days, and even beyond the hoped-for forty days. They lasted more than a year. Phoebe recorded that during this time hundreds were saved, "scores" of them through the personal ministry of Walter Palmer.[31]

Although the revival energized Dr. Palmer as an evangelist and made Phoebe feel closer to God, she still was not satisfied with her spiritual life. As the revival services came to a close she wrote she was only "getting on feebly in the divine life." Her desires and plans were excellent, but she needed power to carry them out. She concluded, "I lack faith and courage."[32]

In April of 1833 Phoebe gave birth to her first daughter, Sarah. Unlike her brothers, she was a healthy baby. But her sister, Eliza, born in August 1835, was not. Phoebe was critically ill that summer, and both mother and daughter almost died. This brush with death gave her a new perspective on life. She had no fears about her eternal destiny, but she did not want to be saved "as by fire." She was conscious of "having done so little for him who had done so much for me." As she lay so close to death that she thought she could hear heaven's music, she hoped that she would not die so she could have more time to live for God. She recovered and resolved to continue writing religious poetry as one means of serving the Lord.[33]

After Phoebe and the baby recovered, the Palmers decided to move into a house at 54 Rivington Street, on New York's Lower East Side. Their home was located on the northwest corner of Rivington and Eldridge Streets, near what today is the Sara D. Roosevelt Parkway.[34]

They shared this house with Phoebe's elder sister, Sarah, who had married Thomas A. Lankford, an architect from Virginia, in 1831. Thus Phoebe and Sarah who were so close as children, and who, since the time of Sarah's marriage had lived within one hundred yards of each other, were now reunited in the same household.[35]

The happiness caused by the move and the health of the Palmers' two daughters was short-lived. One summer evening Phoebe put little Eliza to bed in her cradle. Eliza was dressed all in white; in the midst of the gauze festoonings hanging over the top of her cradle, she looked like a little angel. A friend came to visit, so Phoebe left the baby in the care of the nursemaid and went out of the room. A little while later the alcohol lamp the maid was using began to run out of fuel. Instead of blowing the lamp out, the maid tried to refill it while the wick was still burning. The lamp caught fire and burned her hands. Without thinking, the nurse threw the lamp away from her. It landed in the baby's cradle and sprayed burning alcohol all around. Phoebe heard the nurse's screams in time to run into the room and snatch the baby from the blaze. Eliza was still conscious, but she was so badly burned that she lived only a few hours.

Phoebe contained her anger at the foolish nursemaid and shut herself up alone to weep. In agony she walked the floor, wringing her hands and crying out, "O Lord, help! Help!" She took her Bible and asked God to show her why he had allowed such an awful thing to happen. She opened the Bible and saw the words, "O the depth of the wisdom and knowledge of God, how unsearchable are His judgments and His ways past finding out" (Rom. 11:33). That moment began a mystical experience that shaped the rest of her life. She felt the Holy Spirit whisper

> to my inmost soul, that if I would only look at the all-loving hand of my Heavenly Father, in this afflictive dispensation, and not at second causes, that just in *proportion* to the magnitude of the trial, in all its peculiarities, the result would be glorious.[36]

In the midst of her pain and anger, she felt God telling her to stop blaming the freakish circumstances for her daughter's death, to stop blaming herself for employing such a careless nurse, and to stop blaming the nurse for her horrible stupidity. If she could stop looking at second causes, and realize that this trial had come from God, and still trust his love and goodness, then she knew that good would result.[37]

Phoebe stopped crying and made a conscious choice to trust God's goodness and love: "From that hour, as a weaned child, I rested down and kissed the rod." She began to feel that the veil separating this world from heaven was almost lifted. She experienced a new closeness to her departed child and knew Eliza was in the presence of Jesus. Jesus himself seemed especially near. Earlier she had prayed the words of the hymn, "Nearer my God to Thee, nearer to Thee, Even though it be a cross that raiseth me," and now through the cross of her daughter's death she "apprehended as never before the deep significance of the apostle's words, 'Ye are come to Mount Zion, . . . to Jesus the Mediator of the New Covenant'" (Heb. 12:22–24).[38]

This newfound sense of close approach to Jesus gave her a corresponding sense of distance from the world. Things that had become important lost their significance. After being so close to Jesus, she was no longer jealous for her husband's professional preferment or her own worldly prosperity. As she explained it, "I have been weaned from the world." Along with this weaning came a new zeal to do Christ's work. She resolved that the time she would have spent caring for Eliza would be spent in helping to save souls. She would not allow herself to spend time "looking into the grave," and thus to "enfeeble our physical and mental energies." She thought of the day of Eliza's death as the beginning of her concern for evangelism. She later remarked, "In connection with the saving of souls, it was the beginning of days with me."[39]

THE BEGINNING OF THE TUESDAY MEETING

Sarah Lankford made an entire consecration of her life to God on May 21, 1835, at 2:30 in the afternoon. Converted at thirteen in 1819, she had been seeking the blessing of entire sanctification since 1821 when she read Wesley's *A Plain Account of Christian Perfection*. In 1825 she had read Timothy Merritt's *The Christian's Manual,* but it was not until 1835 that she found what she had sought.[40] That day she was reading *The Life of Hester Ann Rogers* and came across the passage, "Reckon yourself dead, indeed unto sin [Rom. 6:11] and thou art akin to God from this hour. O, begin, begin, to reckon now; fear not, believe, believe, and continue to believe; so shalt thou continue to feel." Sarah obeyed these instructions. She fell on her knees and cried, "Lord I will believe, help Thou my unbelief: . . . Yea, Lord from this hour, half-past two p.m., the 21st of May, 1835, I dare reckon myself dead, indeed unto sin."[41]

From that moment Sarah trusted that God had cleansed her and made her holy, even though she did not feel anything happen to her. For seven days she continued to trust without any emotional evidence. On the seventh day she met Timothy Merritt, who asked her if she had experienced holiness. She replied that she was not prepared to answer that question, but then went on to say, "I have dared to reckon myself dead indeed unto sin." Instantly all doubt vanished as "the baptism of the Holy Ghost then came in its glorious fullness."[42] She experienced such love that her "mortal powers could scarcely sustain [its] weight. I had such a deep consciousness of *purity* as is utterly inexpressible."[43]

The witness of the Spirit that she had been cleansed of all sin empowered Sarah for greater service to Christ. She had first become a Sunday school superintendent at fifteen and by 1835 was leading two women's prayer meetings in addition to working with various charitable societies. The first prayer meeting met at the Allen Street Methodist Episcopal Church on Monday afternoons, and the second met at the Mulberry Street Church on Wednesdays. Sarah wondered if she could use her time more wisely by combining the meetings and moving them to her home on Tuesdays. In February of 1836 she held the first meeting.[44]

Sarah was apprehensive about that first meeting and asked the Lord to bless it in a special way. She spent all of Tuesday morning in prayer. Forty women came that afternoon, including Mrs. Merritt, wife of Timothy Merritt. Although we know that Phoebe Palmer concurred with her sister's decision to hold the prayer meeting in their mutual home, no source tells us if Phoebe Palmer attended that first meeting.[45] After the opening exercises came the time for testimonies. One woman implored the others to pray for her. As they did, she jumped up from her knees exclaiming, "Wonderful, wonderful, *wonderful!*. . . Jesus is mine. He is my perfect Saviour!" One after another the women testified, "Jesus saves me this afternoon as never before." The high point of the afternoon occurred when Sister Merritt "prayed through," or felt she had received that for which she had been asking. She had been seeking full assurance of salvation for thirty years. She testified, "This afternoon Christ is *my* Saviour. Never before could I say it without fear. Now I rest down upon Christ as I do upon my chair, without fear of falling!" It was obvious to Sarah that the Lord had blessed her plans.[46]

SANCTIFICATION

Phoebe had not yet experienced sanctification and did not fully sympathize with her sister's experience or ways of serving Christ.[47] She did attend the Tuesday Meeting but did not have the same enthusiasm for it that Sarah had. Naturally Sarah wanted Phoebe to experience all the blessing she had been given, so she prayed for her sister constantly. One morning before breakfast Sarah piously announced that she had set the day aside to fast and pray for Phoebe's soul, and invited Phoebe to join her. Phoebe playfully replied, "I *must* have my breakfast; but I'll pray." Heartbroken at her sister's lightness, Sarah spent the day imploring God that Phoebe might see "the vanity of earthly joys and know a more spiritual life." In answer to Sarah's prayers, or perhaps in spite of them, in the afternoon Phoebe came to Sarah in tears, exclaiming, "Never did I see the vanity of earthly joys as today."[48]

Even before Sarah's sanctification, Phoebe had been seeking a deeper spiritual experience. Before Eliza died, Phoebe had been to a camp meeting at Sing Sing, New York, which gave her a great desire for heart purity.[49] But as in the past, the more she longed for sanctification, the more she doubted her justification. She decided that before she could go on spiritually she had to resolve this issue once and for all. She had been reading Philip's *Guides* and decided to follow his counsel about determining whether or not she was justified. Philip said all who knew themselves to have been led by God had a duty to believe themselves children of God (Rom. 8:14).[50]

When Phoebe resolved she would believe herself a Christian if she fulfilled the conditions stated in even this passage of Scripture, she suddenly remembered a long-forgotten dream. About five years previously she had dreamed that her spirit had left her body and gone to another world. Finding herself neither in heaven nor in hell, she was puzzled and asked, "Where am I?" "You are in the middle state," replied a voice. "But where am I going? What is to be my state?" she inquired. "Don't you know?" came the reply. "You have had the Bible, 'and by *this* you should have tried yourself, and have known what your state was before you came here; but . . . if you can think of but *one* passage by which to test yourself, you may just as well know what your state will be.'" Phoebe tried to think of an appropriate passage but could remember only the creeds of various denominations. So anxious did she become when no Bible verses came to her mind that she awoke. As she pondered the meaning of this dream she decided it was meant only to warn her that she would soon die. But after several months passed and she did not die, she forgot the dream. Only when she read Philip's suggestion that she test her state by Scripture did the recollection of the dream confirm her in following his method.[51]

As Phoebe resolved to test herself by the Scripture, two passages came to her mind: first, the one suggested by Philip, "As many as are led by the Spirit of God, they are the sons of God" (Rom. 8:14) and next, "Love is of God; and every one that loveth is born of God" (1 John 4:7). Realizing that she had been led by God and that she did love God, Phoebe concluded she must be justified, even if her emotions did not concur in this judgment. She resolved, "Whatever my feelings may be, I will believe God's immutable Word unwaveringly, irrespective of emotion."[52]

Much to Phoebe's surprise, when she determined to believe God's Word in spite of her emotions, then God's Spirit began to witness with her spirit that she was a child of God. She had been expecting the witness of the Spirit to be some overpowering emotion. Instead, God gave her the "still small voice of the Spirit, speaking through the naked word." She found "to just the degree I have *believed* God's Word, I have felt happy and assured." Previous to this she had been expecting "signs and wonders." Like Naaman (2 Kings 5) she wanted "some great thing."[53] Previously she had taken "the feelings and experience of others as a standard . . . instead of going to the word and the testimony."[54] This fault had been the greatest hindrance to her spiritual progress. Only when she gave up her demand that God assure her through an overwhelming experience, and became willing to accept the witness of the Spirit through the Word alone, was the question of her "adoption settled, and the witness given with the clearness of noonday."[55]

Soon after the question of Phoebe's salvation had been settled, Eliza's terrible death occurred. Despite the anguish it caused, Phoebe emerged from the experience more committed to the Lord and more determined to serve him. She recorded one opportunity for service in her diary on January 3, 1837. Like a good Methodist on New Year's Eve, she shunned those who ". . . pass the guilty night in reveling and frantic mirth,"[56] and planned to go to the church to renew her covenant with the Lord during the watch-night service. But when she realized that the activities of New Year's Day might distract her from the Lord's service, she was tempted to postpone renewing her covenant until after the holiday. She was afraid that all the holiday visits would cause her to waste time, spending it in frivolous chatter, rather than improving each conversation in the light of eternity.

Recognizing this suggestion as a temptation, she did renew her vow. As she did, a new confidence in God's ability to strengthen her filled her heart. This confidence was vindicated when the holiday arrived. She entertained over one hundred guests in her home, and yet did not feel distracted from her primary occupation of serving the Lord. She reported, "I do not think I ever felt, or manifested more cheerfulness, or was more successful in promoting the happiness of others, and yet I think no one left the house without thinking more of Jesus, and the interests of eternity." She realized that some of her friends would be disappointed that she had become as piously religious as Sarah, but her only concern was that she would be able to maintain this high level of spirituality.[57]

The following April she was asked to teach the Young Ladies' Bible Class in the Allen Street Sunday school. She did not like to speak in public, and her health was poor, but she consented in the hope that imparting grace to others would be a means of receiving grace herself.[58] This class became so popular that it constantly outgrew the rooms assigned to it. It finally stabilized at about sixty regular members, along with numerous visitors each week. The class began with the Old Testament, seeking to understand each section and to see what light the New Testament threw upon it. Phoebe ran the class as a discussion group and frequently reminded the members that they were the teachers as much as she was. During the week members of the class would gather in one of their homes to prepare discussion questions for the next week's session. The girls would give these discussion questions to Phoebe who had to study long and hard to be prepared for every session. Often she supplemented the members' questions with ones she wrote herself. Over the years she taught the class, she filled several large notebooks with these questions. She was so popular as a teacher that she led this class for eight years until her travels forced her to resign.[59]

Two months after beginning to teach the Sunday school class, Phoebe took another major step in her spiritual walk. Perhaps under the influence of Carvosso, in June 1837, she covenanted with God that she would be a "Bible Christian."[60] Believing that sanctification was such a high attainment that it was "almost beyond her reach," she sought "only to be *fully* conformed to the will of God, as recorded in his written *word*."[61] By this she meant that she would cease looking at the experience of others and take the Bible as her only standard for faith and conduct. Along with this resolve went the determination to perform every duty in the Lord's strength, no matter how inadequate she felt. She therefore began each day with a renewed solemn consecration of herself to the Lord.[62] Her goal was to give up her own will in all things, and to make "entire devotion of heart and life to God" the "sole principle of every future effort."[63]

Shortly after Phoebe made this decision, her pastor asked her to visit a woman who had recently been converted in the church. Phoebe did not know the woman and felt it was not proper to call on a stranger uninvited, but she consented to go. When she arrived at the home she found the woman herself to be soundly converted, but the woman's sister, who was also present, was not. In fact, this sister showed great displeasure during the whole conversation. Addressing herself to the unconverted sister, Phoebe inquired whether she did not feel the need for the same grace that her sister had just received. Rudely the sister exclaimed, "No!" Phoebe then warned her to be careful what she said before the Lord. God might punish her with death as he had Ananias and Sapphira when they lied to the Holy Spirit (Acts 5).

As Phoebe concluded the conversation, she began to wonder if she had said the right thing. Was it the Lord who led her to warn the woman, or was it her self, her pride, trying to hit back when someone had been rude to her? If it were her self, she had better abandon such efforts to serve the Lord. She felt paralyzed by this accusation and cried out in prayer, "What shall I do?" The still small voice she had come to trust whispered, "Stand still, and see the salvation of God" (2 Chron. 20:17). "What?" she thought. "Stand still and do nothing?" Another verse occurred to her and provided the answer, "Be steadfast and immovable, always abounding in the work of the Lord, forasmuch as ye know that your labor is not in vain in the Lord" (1 Cor. 15:58). Through this association of Bible verses, each mentioning standing still, she was sure God had spoken to her.[64]

From Paul's words to the Corinthians she realized the early Christians had the assurance that their labors were in the Lord, "and thus they enjoyed the heart-inspiring *confidence* that their labors were not *in vain*." If only she could have such confidence, how bold she would be in the Lord's work! How she longed to know that her labors were in the Lord and not from her self! If they were from her self, they would lead to failure, but if they were in the Lord then surely they would bring success.[65]

The only way to know her labors were in the Lord was to be conscious that the spring of every motive was pure. If she could be certain her motives were pure, she would know that nothing of self was vitiating her efforts to serve God. She had thought she had given herself up to God entirely, yet now there was reason for doubt. In the midst of trying to labor for God by warning the unconverted sister, self seemed very present. Thus she came to see "heart purity [is] an absolute *necessity* if I would be *useful*."[66]

During this time of her life she felt the "love which casteth out all fear [1 John 4:18], . . . had undisturbed possession of my breast," and she thought she was "enabled to reckon [herself] dead indeed to sin"; but she was not certain that her motives were pure. She later said, "I did not at the time have that *abiding*, lively consciousness of the seal of consecration on all my *powers*."[67] She thought she had probably done all that God required of her, but she wondered whether there might be some unknown defect in her that kept her consecration from being wholly acceptable to him. This uncertainty crippled her efforts to do the Lord's work.[68]

At the next Tuesday Meeting, Phoebe announced her purpose to have an absolutely pure heart. She had never spoken in the meeting before, and she had felt that her sister's description of the second blessing was a bit exaggerated, but now she rose to declare that the women's testimonies had convinced her. She now believed she could have the same full salvation from all inward sin which they claimed if she sought it by the same means that they had used. She then committed herself: "I purpose from this hour to leave no means unused that I may know the same grace."[69]

On the next day, July 26, during the evening, Phoebe felt led by the Spirit to determine that she would never rest, day or night, until she knew that even her motives were utterly cleansed. During her prayer time that morning she had been thanking God for Walter, when suddenly the thought occurred, "What if Walter should die? Would you shrink from that demand?" She thought of her three children already in heaven and her conviction that they had been taken because she had idolized them. She resolved to give Walter up to the Lord but then was interrupted in her devotions. This interruption caused her to be away from home all day, so it was not until evening that she resumed her prayers.[70]

Phoebe had believed she was entirely consecrated before, but now it seemed as if the Lord were showing her new areas of commitment. Just as Jesus had told the disciples, "I have yet many things to say unto you, but ye cannot bear them now," and then promised that the Holy Spirit would lead them into all truth (John 16:12–13), so Phoebe felt the Spirit was leading her beyond what she had ever known:

I felt that the Spirit was leading into a solemn, most sacred, and inviolable compact between God and the soul that came forth from Him, by which, in the sight of God, angels, and men, I was to be united in eternal oneness with the Lord my redeemer, requiring unquestioning allegiance on my part, and infinite love, and everlasting salvation, guidance, and protection, on the part of Him who had loved and redeemed me, so that from henceforth He might say to me, "I will betroth thee unto me for ever" (Hos. 2:19).[71]

She believed the Holy Spirit was leading her to solidify her commitment to God by making a solemn covenant with him. She wanted heaven and earth to witness her vows so that they never might be broken. In making this covenant Phoebe "reckon[ed] herself dead *indeed* unto sin," accounted herself permanently the Lord's, and thus "in verity no more at *her own* disposal, but *irrevocably the Lord's property*, for time and eternity," and "*count[ed] all things loss*" compared with knowing Christ (Phil. 3:7–10). Specifically she bound herself "to take the service of God as the absorbing business of life, and to regard heaven as her native home, and the accumulation of treasure in heaven the chief object of ambition."[72]

Phoebe then began to enumerate what she was giving up to the Lord in this covenant. She remembered her morning prayers and once again offered Walter to the Lord. She was renouncing all her rights to Walter, committing herself not to cling to him, not to object to anything the Lord might do with him, even if the Lord should take him. Many times before she had said, "My husband and child I surrender to Thee," but now for the first time she realized the depth of the commitment she was undertaking.[73] With the relinquishing of "the supreme object of my worldly affections," she felt "I was fully set apart for God, every tie that bound to earth was riven, and I could as easily have doubted my existence as I could have doubted that God was the supreme object of my affections."[74]

Phoebe now believed that her consecration to the Lord was finally "*entire, absolute,* and *unconditional.*"[75] But she returned to the old question of whether the Lord had received it. This question arose again because her experience was so different from what she had expected. Because her experience both before and after she made this final consecration was so different from that of others, she doubted that God really had accepted her.

She thought that before she could make an acceptable

consecration of herself to God she had to experience a crushing sense of inner corruption and guilt over a long time. Wesley had taught that a conviction of one's "deep corruption of [the] heart" was necessary before one could long for inner cleansing.[76] Fletcher spoke of an agonizing repentance, and Phoebe's sister Sarah had felt "overwhelmed" by her guilt eleven years prior to her sanctification.[77] But instead of this expected conviction of sin, Phoebe had been feeling she was "growing in grace daily." She believed that each hour "her heavenward progress seemed marked as by the finger of God."[78] True, that evening she did feel her "utter pollution and helplessness" in a new way, but this realization was not an hour old.[79] Thus she found it difficult to believe she had come to the place of entire consecration without first passing through the seemingly necessary slow stages of guilt and repentance.

The other consideration that caused her to doubt that the Lord had accepted her consecration was the absence of any emotion after she had given herself to the Lord. She expected some confirmation, some sign that the Lord received her. When none came, she wondered, *"How* may I know that the Lord *does* receive me?" Here, too, the Spirit replied through the Scripture, "It is written, *I WILL RECEIVE YOU"* (2 Cor. 6:17). But still Phoebe questioned, "Must I believe it, because it simply stands written, without any other *evidence* than the *Word of God?"*[80]

She was then led to see the absurdity of her position. She felt the Spirit say to her, "Suppose you should hear a voice, speaking in tones of thunder, from heaven, saying, *I will receive you,* would you not believe it then?" She had to admit that she would believe such a voice. But then she realized she had always professed to believe that the Bible was as much God's word as if she could hear God speaking in thunder from Mount Sinai. When she remembered, "The just shall live by faith" (Rom. 1:17), she determined that even if she lived to be a hundred "and never [had] any of those manifestations that others enjoy—never [had] anything but the naked Word of God upon which to rely," she would nevertheless trust God, and would say, "The foundation of my faith [is] Thy immutable Word."[81]

Determined she would believe God's word in the Bible as much as she would believe his word if she heard it from Sinai, Phoebe renounced her doubt that she was accepted by God: "In the strength of Omnipotence I laid hold on the WORD, 'I WILL RECEIVE YOU!' " God's word seemed "intensified to my mind as the *lively*, or living oracles—the voice of God to me." Thus she could no longer doubt that God had received her: "I *knew* that it could not be otherwise than that God did receive me."[82]

Even though she finally knew God accepted her, that night's spiritual battle was not yet over. Once again her experience disappointed her expectations. Others who had consecrated all and been accepted had burst out in praise when the transaction was complete. God's work in giving them a clean heart had imparted such joy that they had been "impelled" and "constrained" to express it in thanksgiving. Phoebe felt no such surge of joy. No "wonderful manifestation . . . at once [followed] as a reward of my faith." All she had was "faith—*naked faith in a naked promise.*" She certainly did not feel like rejoicing.[83]

In answer to these discouraging thoughts, Phoebe sensed the Holy Spirit's voice. Tenderly he inquired, "Through what power were you enabled to enter into the bonds of an everlasting covenant with God, yielding up that which was dearer to you than life?" She replied, "It was through the power of Omnipotence. I could no more have done it of myself than I could have created the world." "And upon whose WORD do you now rely?" asked the Spirit. "It is on the WORD of the immutable Jehovah," she responded. Through these questions Phoebe perceived that, with God leading her, she had not missed the way: "Through these reasonings I saw with the clearness of a sunbeam, that it was all from first to last the work of the Spirit."[84]

Because God had been directing her way and giving her the power to take each step, Phoebe could no longer doubt that the work had been done in her heart. She next reasoned that if God had done the work, then he deserved the praise:

> Now, that I so clearly apprehended that the power to will and to do, was all so manifestly of the Lord, I began to reason with myself thus: "Do I wait to thank a friend who does me a great favor, until I feel an *impelling* influence to do it? Do I not do it because it is a *duty?* And now, if the Lord has enabled me to make an unconditional and absolute surrender of all my redeemed powers and faculties, and has given his WORD, assuring me that He *does* receive me, shall I refuse to give Him the glory due to His name, till I feel constraining influences?"[85]

She felt ashamed of herself for being niggardly with praise when God had done so much for her. That she felt no overpowering emotion was no excuse to hold back what was due to the Lord. She had a duty to praise him.

Realizing her duty to praise God for what he had done for her, Phoebe began:

> Through Thy grace alone I have been enabled to give myself wholly and forever to Thee. Thou hast given Thy WORD, assuring me that Thou dost receive. I believe that WORD! Alleluia! the Lord God Omnipotent reigneth unrivaled in my heart. Glory be to the Father! Glory be to the Son! Glory be to the Holy Spirit forever![86]

While Phoebe was praising God only out of a sense of duty, the mystical experience she had just resigned herself to live without occurred. In the midst of glorifying the Trinity, "I felt in verity that the seal of consecration was set, and that God had proclaimed me by the testimony of his Spirit, entirely his."[87] She was ushered into a region of "light, glory, and purity."[88] She thought she was in heaven:

> [My soul] was permitted to pass through the veil of outward things, and return with all its tide of affections, and flow onward to its source, and to feel that nothing but a thin veil of mortality,—which seemed almost drawn aside,—prevented its coming into the full blaze of the presence of Him, "whose favor is better than life"; such was my sense of dwelling in God, and being surrounded by his presence and glory, that it seemed as though my spirit almost mingled in worship with those around the throne.[89]

So close did she feel to God that she could say, "My spirit returned consciously to its source, and rested in the embrace of God."[90] She was swallowed up in a sea of love: "I felt that I was but as a drop in the ocean of infinite LOVE, and Christ was All in All."[91]

As her view of Christ increased, her view of herself decreased. Aware that only through Christ's power had she come to this blessed experience, Phoebe lost her sense of her own importance. Although she previously had not often been tempted with pride, now she exclaimed, "Never before did I know the meaning of the word *humility*.... I saw I was not sufficient in myself to think a good thought, much less to perform a righteous action." This magnification of Christ and diminution of self led to an enlarged appreciation of the Atonement:

But amid these realizations of utter nothingness, I had such views of the unbounded efficacy of the atonement, that if the guilt of the universe had been concentrated and laid on my head,

> The stream of Jesus' precious blood,
> Would wash away the dreadful load.[92]

Phoebe continued exulting in God and what he had done for her. She rejoiced that he now reigned unrivaled in her heart, and proclaimed, "I am wholly thine! . . . now I am wholly, wholly thine!" While she was saying these words the Holy Spirit spoke again to her heart, "What! wholly the Lord's? Is not this the holiness that God requires?"[93] "Is not this *sanctification?*"[94] Phoebe saw her mistake in thinking sanctification was some difficult spiritual attainment, far beyond the reach of ordinary Christians. She had not been seeking sanctification, but had begun only by resolving to be a Bible Christian, and next sought only the conviction that her labors were in the Lord. From that stage the Lord had led her to a total consecration, and then to seek the assurance that her consecration was accepted. At the end of the process, she looked back and found that what she had experienced was sanctification. Instead of being an arcane religious experience, achieved at the end of an arduous spiritual exercise, it seemed so simple and reasonable:

> What more reasonable, thought I, now that I have been enabled through grace to resolve on being wholly the Lord's, than that he should set the seal of consecration, and proclaim me his own; and still further, that now, as I had set myself apart exclusively for his service, that he should take cognizance of the act, and ratify the engagements. So clear was the work, and so entirely apart from any thing like extravagance of feeling, that, as before said, as I had fixed my calculation on the performance of some great thing, such as an earnest struggle of spirit, or uncommon venturing of faith, &c. yet so unlike the simplicity of receiving it, to any of these preconceived views, that in the fullness of my heart, I almost exclaimed,—Why, it is hardly of faith, it is so simple and rational, and just as might have been expected, as the result of such exercise; it is all *here,*—I through the Spirit's influence, have given *all* for Christ, and he has revealed himself to me, and now he is my *all* in ALL.[95]

Once Phoebe realized she was sanctified, she knew "the blessing I had received was not imparted only for my own enjoyment." God called her to testify to it. This testimony would fulfill the scriptural requirement, "with the heart man believeth unto righteousness, and with the mouth confession is made unto salvation" (Rom. 10:9), and would encourage others to seek holiness. Public speaking terrified Phoebe, and dread of this obligation had hindered her spiritual progress for years. But now she felt that if she did not confess publicly what God had done for her, he would revoke the gift. Part of giving herself wholly to the Lord was yielding her tongue, and if she should "cease to comply with the terms in *being set apart for God*," naturally the covenant would be broken. Jesus seemed to ask, "Will you 'acknowledge what God [hath] wrought for [you], perhaps before hundreds?'" So complete was the conquest of grace in her heart, that Phoebe replied, "Yes, Lord Jesus, and before thousands too, if such be thy demand."[96]

After she had determined to confess publicly that God had sanctified her, she began to wonder whether she would be able to retain the blessing of holiness. She recalled her natural tendency to question rather than to trust, and then she realized that many others, seemingly more spiritually firm than she, had lost it. She remembered that even "the sainted Fletcher, of blessed memory," repeatedly did not maintain his sanctification. If Fletcher could not keep this blessing, how could she? Phoebe recognized that this line of questioning came from the Adversary, and she put it out of her mind. She determined she would not even consider his inquiries, because they were likely to lead her astray:

> In the strength of Omnipotence, I was enabled firmly to resolve rather to die than to doubt, or even reason with the enemy, assured that if I but ventured to parley, as in the case of the first transgression, his suggestions might soon assume the appearance of plausibility.[97]

Phoebe had thought she might be spending the night on her knees, but this season of prayer lasted only little more than an hour. Although she had anticipated a struggle like Jacob's, her victory was surprisingly quick. So, when some friends paid a late evening visit, she felt free to entertain them. Walter was away from home on a house call, so after the company left, Phoebe announced the good news to Sarah and then went to bed. Because God had so often communicated with her in dreams before, she hoped for "some glorious manifestation" of his presence while she slept. Instead, however, of renewed communion with God, she dreamed that a demon had entered the house. The demon was dressed like a Scotsman, with a white cloak poorly attempting to conceal his black kilt. His "countenance [was] fiendish in the extreme" and he demanded to see Dr. Palmer. Phoebe said her husband was in the next room, and when the demon moved toward the door, she began to scream for help. Trying to scream woke her up. Immediately she was tempted to question the reality of her sanctification. If God had really given her this blessing, why did she now seem more open to Satan's influence than before? She could not answer that question, but since "the deep tranquility of my spirit was not in the least disturbed," she repulsed it unanswered. She was soon deep in peaceful sleep.[98]

About an hour and a half later Phoebe had another spiritual visitor. This one claimed to be from the Lord, and said, "Behold, I, an *angel,* beseech you that you walk worthy of the vocation wherewith ye are called" (Eph. 4:1). Perhaps Phoebe's suspicions were aroused by the first dream, because she was cautious about accepting this spirit's credentials. She was put off by his misquotation of the Scripture.[99] With this she awoke to feel such a sense of God's glory and presence that she was "sweetly assured" that the second visitor had been sent by the Lord. Walter then returned from his house call to find Phoebe on her knees praising God for deliverance from the satanic temptation and for the assurance the angel brought. Because Walter had been sanctified several months previously, he was overjoyed to hear what the Lord had done for her and was particularly impressed by the angel's visit. Phoebe said she almost expected it, so close had been her communion with heaven.[100]

Thus ended the day Phoebe ever afterward called her "day of days,"[101] and whose yearly anniversary she celebrated even more joyfully than her wedding anniversary.[102] Although the great outpouring of God's grace into her life occurred on the evening of July 26, 1837, the aftershocks continued for two more weeks. During these weeks, this great upheaval of soul changed the contours of her life, opening new springs of energy which flowed into theology, revivalism, feminism, and humanitarianism.

Theology was the first area to be affected by the great change. While a full exposition of her theological thought will be given later, we may here trace the beginning of Phoebe's best-known contribution, her "altar theology." Phoebe had been sanctified on a Wednesday evening, and as she looked forward to the coming class meetings, worship services, and the Tuesday Meeting, she knew she would have to testify publicly about what God had done for her. She felt obliged to witness to the Lord's sanctifying grace, but when the opportunity came for her to speak, the Enemy attempted to weaken her assurance by "darken[ing] my evidence." She thought Satan was arguing that she believed she was sanctified without proper evidence, "that I believed merely because I would believe, without a reasonable foundation as the ground of my faith."[103] So powerful were these assaults of satanic doubt that "my whole frame was in feverish excitement." Phoebe pled with the Lord, asking for the witness of the Spirit in some "tangible" form. She had been relying on God's word, "I will receive you," and she had been experiencing great closeness to the Lord, but she wanted demonstrable evidence that she had a right to cling to that promise. She wanted objective, scriptural grounds for her belief that "I will receive you" applied to her: "What I wanted was a certain knowledge that would always be available, by which I might be enabled at any moment, to come at the precise ground of my belief."[104] God's answer to her prayers led to the formation of her altar theology.

On Tuesday, August 1, as Phoebe was praying for this assurance in order that she would be prepared to speak at the Tuesday Meeting, the Lord directed her mind to Romans 12:1: "I beseech you therefore, brethren, by the mercies of God, that ye present your bodies a living sacrifice, holy, acceptable unto God, which is your reasonable service."[105] Realizing that God had enabled her to present herself as a living, or *"continual,"* sacrifice, she deduced that Jesus cleansed the offering thus continuously presented from all unrighteousness:

> This [act of commitment], I was given to see, was in verity [the] placing all upon that altar that sanctifieth the gift [Matt. 23:19], and I felt that, so long as my heart assured me that I did thus offer all, that it was a solemn duty as well as a high and holy privilege, to believe that the blood of Jesus cleanseth at the present and each succeeding moment, so long as the offering is continued.[106]

Because she knew she was continually presenting herself to God as a living sacrifice, "lay[ing] all upon the altar," and because she knew that the altar sanctifies the gift, she could know with syllogistic certainty that she was sanctified. This scriptural logic put an end to her doubts and finally gave her the assurance she had sought so earnestly.

One other important spiritual event happened to Phoebe during these two weeks. On August 10 she awoke at four in the morning with a sense that God was about to impart a special blessing. For several days previously she had been urging the Lord not to let her stop short of any state of grace made possible for her by Christ's work. In the light of Ephesians 1:13, "Ye were sealed with that holy Spirit of promise, which is the earnest of our inheritance, until the redemption of the purchased possession," she cried out for two hours, *"Lord, seal me unto the day of redemption."* God graciously answered that prayer, and "sealed the truth on my heart." This sealing assured Phoebe that she "should be assimilated yet more and more to His own glorious likeness here on earth, and eventually reunited to Him forever." She felt that the Lord had made it clear that she would never fall from grace but would continue to increase in Christlikeness until she reached heaven. It was such a momentous experience that she exclaimed, "Surely it was to me a day to be remembered through the untold ages of eternity."[107]

Despite her estimate of the importance of the day of her sealing, she only mentioned it once in her published writings after she recorded it in *The Way of Holiness,* her first book. Perhaps as the years passed this experience was subsumed into the experience of sanctification, and the remembrance of the day of days served to recall both events. Despite the essential incompatibility of the assurance of final perseverance with Mrs. Palmer's Wesleyan-Arminian theology, she continued to hold to the doctrine. She believed that the sealing of the Spirit was a result of the believer's entire consecration, and that it empowered one for service by banishing doubt about one's final state.[108]

The details of Phoebe Palmer's sanctification are important because they reveal so many themes later developed in her theology. Both the method and the content of her theological thought reveal the imprint of her experience of sanctification. Mrs. Palmer's method, though nowhere clearly articulated, is the Wesleyan quadrilateral of Scripture, reason, experience, and tradition, if tradition may be defined as the teachings of the standard Methodist writers. All four elements came into play during her quest for holiness. The Bible was her most important authority, and she interpreted it as if it were a series of equally relevant theological propositions whose meaning becomes clear when reasonably arranged. The importance of reason is also shown by the scriptural syllogism which finally banished her doubt.

Despite decrying her early reliance on experience, Phoebe felt a mystical sense of union with God after she determined she would trust God's Word; this was an important confirmation that her reasoning about Scripture was correct. Finally, her reliance on the Wesleyan tradition is apparent from the very questions she set herself. Her expectations of the way God would deal with her soul arose from the Methodist theology and biography she imbibed with her mother's milk. The relative values of these four sources of religious authority, and the tensions among them adumbrated in her sanctification experience, become clear in her developed theological method.

Along with her method, much of the content of Phoebe Palmer's teaching is also foreshadowed in her sanctification experience. Over and over she insisted that holiness was not some high attainment, but rather was God's standard for every Christian. She continued to explain sanctification in terms of her altar imagery, developing its implications and finding more scriptural proof for it. She taught that the human part of sanctification began with entire consecration in which one renounced all one's rights before God and dedicated oneself to the Lord's service. She emphasized the importance of trusting the word of the Bible as much as one would trust the voice of God from Sinai. Because God had said, "The altar sanctifies the gift" and "I will receive you," the consecrated Christian had the duty to believe God had done his part, even if there was no further evidence of sanctification. The obligation to testify was another important element of Mrs. Palmer's theology, as was the expectation that assurance of sanctification would come if one fulfilled the obligations of believing God's Word in the heart and confessing God's grace with the mouth.

Besides shaping her theology, Phoebe Palmer's experience of sanctification gave her incredible energy as a revivalist, feminist, and humanitarian. The day of days had begun with her request to know that her labors were in the Lord, that they were not in vain. When this assurance came she felt both the obligation to work hard for God and the confidence that he would bless everything she attempted. As she described it,

> This assurance that all my powers are consecrated to holy service, gives me to feel the imperative necessity of being a laborer in the vineyard of the Lord, and this *knowledge* of consecration brings with it the cheering *certainty* that my labor

is not in vain. O! dear sister W., it would be impossible, even though time and space might admit, to describe to you how exceeding broad and high, deep and wide, in its bearing, this blessing has been in all my after experience, since its reception; eternity alone can disclose it.[109]

Little did Mrs. Palmer know when she wrote those words before 1840 how much more that blessing would come to mean to her. The next three chapters will attempt to record the labors that her experience of sanctification energized.

CHAPTER TWO:
Ministry in America: 1838-58

PREACHING HOLINESS BY WORD
Publications

God's gift of sanctification unstopped the springs of Phoebe Palmer's literary creativity. In June of 1837 she had given up her usual time for writing in order to concentrate on her own spiritual growth, but after she was sanctified she began to write once again.[1] Other than her childhood writing, most of her compositions had been occasional verses sung or recited at various public meetings. One of her earliest works of this sort was an ode written for Independence Day 1831, celebrating America's freedom from foreign domination, but lamenting America's enslavement of blacks, and warning that God would punish the country unless the slaves were freed. In 1833 Phoebe wrote the hymn for her local Sunday school convention, and the next year she achieved wider recognition by composing three hymns for the celebration of the semicentennial of American Methodism held in the John Street Church. In 1839 she composed four hymns for the New York meeting commemorating Methodism's first hundred years.[2] Some of these occasional poems were published in the Methodist newspapers: the *New York Christian Advocate and Journal* carried the hymn she wrote for the dedication of the second Wesleyan Chapel on Mulberry Street, and *Zion's Herald* in Boston reprinted her poem on the death of Methodist Bishop M'Kendree.[3] Many of these early poems appeared over the pseudonym, "Shepherdess."[4]

After her experience of sanctification Phoebe continued to

write occasional verse,[5] and at the urging of Timothy Merritt, consented to write about holiness for his newly founded *Guide to Christian Perfection*. Her first contribution to this periodical appeared in December 1839. It was an account of her sanctification experience published as a series of letters to a friend over the initials P. P. Because it was too long for one issue, it was published over the next few months.[6] She went on writing for the *Guide* until her death in 1874, and it was still publishing her work almost twenty years after she died.[7]

Phoebe Palmer's first book appeared in 1841. It was published anonymously and entitled *Mary; or, the Young Christian*. The work consisted of many excerpts from the diary of one of Mrs. Palmer's friends. Of course, this book reveals little of Phoebe's own theology.[8]

In 1842 Phoebe began a work that was serialized in the *New York Christian Advocate and Journal*. Entitled *The Way of Holiness*, it is a narrative of her religious experience, and it illustrates her theology of the Christian life. The idea of the work grew out of a conversation she had with a certain Dr. Bull, a Presbyterian elder. Wondering whether it were really necessary for one to struggle and wait for years before becoming holy, he remarked, "I have thought whether there is not a *shorter way* of getting into this way of holiness." Phoebe replied, "Yes, brother, THERE IS A SHORTER WAY!" She fell critically ill soon after this conversation, but still she felt the Lord leading her to present this "shorter way" to others. *The Way of Holiness* explained how she found that shorter way and told of some of the subsequent problems she overcame in her Christian life. Although it was her first major work, it presented all of her characteristic theological ideas: the centrality of holiness, the nature of faith, the image of the altar, and the necessity of testimony.[9]

In March 1843 the *Guide to Christian Perfection* began to reprint the series, and during that spring the work was first issued as a book.[10] The work received the endorsement of Leonidas Hamline, editor of *Ladies' Repository*, and was highly commended by Asa Mahan, the well-known president of Oberlin College. Mrs. Palmer's biographer reported that to many *The Way of Holiness* was "next in value to the Sacred Scriptures."[11] At first the work was issued anonymously because Phoebe did not think it seemly for a woman to become a public figure, but a walk through the Bowery persuaded her to let her name appear. She happened to pass the Bowery Theater and there noticed "a flaming placard announcing the play and the names of the players, of both sexes." "Here are the servants of Satan," she reasoned, "who are not afraid or ashamed to let their names appear. And should the servants of the heavenly king be less bold?"[12]

Phoebe's decision to let her name appear on the title page was momentous. Her books went hundreds of places where she could never go and helped to make her name well known.[13] Several editions appeared in England and at least three editions of *The Way of Holiness* were produced in Canada.[14] A missionary in France translated the work. He wrote to report that it had sold 1,600 copies in Paris during the first six months that it was available.[15] Wheatley reports that it was also translated into German.[16] From Liberia came a letter requesting 20 copies, and in Siam, Dr. Bradley and Mr. Caswell, two American missionaries, read *The Way of Holiness* and received "the gift of power."[17] In the United States 52,000 copies were ultimately sold, and world-wide sales were estimated at 100,000.[18]

Phoebe produced her third book in 1845. Originally titled *Present to My Christian Friend on Entire Devotion to God*, it is still in print as *Entire Devotion to God*. In twenty-one brief essays it explains the marrow of her theology and offers several testimonies of those who have received sanctifying grace. Like *The Way of Holiness, Present to My Christian Friend on Entire Devotion to God* was a popular work, with 25,000 copies printed by 1872.[19]

The year 1845 also marked the publication of the second of four biographies Mrs. Palmer wrote. Mrs. Lydia N. Cox, the subject of the biography, had been reestablished in the witness of holiness through Phoebe's ministry in 1840. Phoebe wrote her life story to show the way in which one could receive sanctification and live a holy life. The work dwells almost exclusively on the spiritual experiences of Mrs. Cox and was not as popular as Mrs. Palmer's other works.[20]

Despite the biography's lack of success, the demand for Mrs. Palmer's books was still high in 1848 when Phoebe published *Faith and Its Effects: or, Fragments from my Portfolio*. She composed this book by gathering fifty-five letters she had written to people who had inquired about holiness. These letters restate her doctrine of the Christian life and apply it to the specific situation of her correspondents. The book is not carefully edited and contains much repetition as she offers the same advice in response to similar questions from different people. Despite this redundancy, *Faith and Its Effects* became her second most popular work, appearing in an English edition in 1855, and selling 45,000 copies in the United States by 1872.[21]

Phoebe Palmer's next book was another biography. Mary Gardner was a sanctified woman whose endurance of suffering made her an example to many others whose lives were difficult. After being widowed and having her two small children die, she did not wallow in self-pity but got busy for God by organizing nine Sunday schools in her community. She then accepted a teaching post in a rough mountain settlement and there established another Sunday school along with her grammar school. She then lost her sight and so had to give up teaching. Because she could no longer live independently, she had to be cared for by various families. Even in these circumstances she continued to serve the Lord by visiting members of the Methodist classes in whatever town she happened to find herself and by exhorting in the Methodist meetings. Phoebe Palmer hoped Mrs. Gardner's determination to be useful to God in the midst of any situation would inspire others to do what they could to further God's kingdom. Like the biography of Mrs. Cox, this biography had a limited circulation, but it did sell "thousands" of copies.[22]

Phoebe's next book marked her only venture outside the theory or practice of the Christian life. It was a short tract on eschatology. In four brief letters to a clergyman friend, Mrs. Palmer urged the establishment of a Methodist mission to the Jews in Palestine. Spurred on by news of Jewish colonization, she searched her Bible for unfulfilled prophecy about the return of Abraham's seed to the Promised Land. In the Prophets she found promises that God would restore his people to their ancient homeland and would give them new hearts so they would worship him aright. She believed these prophecies were coming true and that Christians should aid in their fulfillment. She was pushing her friends in the Methodist hierarchy to send missionaries to Palestine, and published this work to enlist others in the cause. Neither the mission nor the twenty-page pamphlet was popular. The mission was never established, and the pamphlet soon went out of print. It was not advertised along with Mrs. Palmer's other works, and very few copies exist today.[23]

In 1855 the Palmers went into the publishing business. None of the published sources discusses this new venture, so we can only piece together part of the story from a few scraps of evidence. The first sign of the Palmers' publishing business is the appearance of books over the imprint "Foster & Palmer, Jr.," in 1855. Foster was the Reverend Elon Foster, who received a Doctorate of Divinity from the General Theological Seminary in 1855. He also became the Palmers' son-in-law that year by marrying their daughter Sarah. The Fosters pastored churches in the Troy Conference of the Methodist Episcopal Church. Exactly how Foster managed his involvement with the publishing company in New York City while pastoring in the Troy Conference is unclear. Even more unclear is how Walter Palmer, Jr., contributed to the family business. He was thirteen at the time when the partnership was formed. Perhaps the corporation was established in the names of the son and son-in-law, and managed by Dr. Palmer himself, or by someone he hired to do the work. The official partnership of Foster & Palmer, Jr., lasted until 1867. The last title bearing their imprint was *Sanctification Practical*, by J. Boynton, with two sections by Mrs. Palmer. In 1868 titles began to appear over the imprint "Walter C. Palmer, Jr.," with the announcement that this firm was the successor to Foster & Palmer, Jr.[24]

The first book published by the Palmer publishing company was *Incidental Illustrations of the Economy of Salvation, Its Doctrines and Duties*. This book is evidently material culled from Mrs. Palmer's correspondence and public speaking. It opens with an exhortation to express joy while singing, closes with a plan for watching over new converts, and presents a nearly four-hundred-page grab-bag of letters, anecdotes, exhortations, and reflections in between. Her goal in this book was to present old truths in new dress and to make them easier to understand. There is no logic to the arrangement of the one hundred seventy-two short chapters. This jumble of ideas betrays Phoebe's method of writing during this period. All through the 1850s she was extremely busy with humanitarian and revivalistic efforts, in addition to a ministry of hospitality. She wrote in odd moments here and there, rarely without interruption. Probably she tried to finish one chapter during each of these brief sessions. Thus her work gives little sense of flow and development of ideas, but the author's skill in storytelling and her pithy insight help to maintain the reader's interest.[25] The book sold seven thousand copies in 1855, the year of its publication, and eventually doubled that total.[26]

While it is true that Mrs. Palmer filled out her books with her correspondence, what is remarkable about these books is not that they contain some of her letters but that they contain anything else. During these years Phoebe was carrying on a world-wide correspondence. She received letters from missionaries in Liberia,

Argentina, Palestine, and China, as well as from ministers and laypeople from all over the United States.[27] In response she wrote thousands of letters, filling them with advice, encouragement, and occasional rebuke, in her neat handwriting. In 1848 she noted in her diary:

> Yet, perhaps, I may enumerate as among the most monopolizing demands upon my time the many letters which I am required to write. These, alone, are numerous enough to make volumes, yearly. I feel, in all these, that I serve the Lord Christ. It is enough.[28]

Many of these letters came from people she did not know, but they had heard her speak or had read one of her books. These people wrote to her about their spiritual experiences and questions. Typically they began:

> To my much respected Christian friend, Mrs. Palmer,
> My mind has often reverted to the short interview I had with you and the sweet, & holy influence it had subsequently, notwithstanding the unhallowed thoughts which at the time and since then *will* crowd in upon my mind. Your gentle and friendly manner leads me to think you will patiently peruse (what to most strangers would be uninteresting) a somewhat lengthy detail of my experiences and temptations, and will give in return (at some *convenient* time) your opinion of my present errors, & sins, or *whatever* stands in the way of the *perfect rest* of my soul in the bosom of Infinite Love.
> And first I suppose in order to judge correctly of what I am about to state, you should know something of the the [sic] temperament and habit of mind thus exercised. From a child I have been. . . .[29]

After filling pages with the details of the writer's spiritual struggles, Phoebe's correspondents would often ask for her advice about their Christian lives. Phoebe dutifully answered many of these unsolicited letters, and her response often prompted a series of exchanges which could go on for months, or even years.[30] By 1856 she had received about three thousand such letters.[31]

Just before the Palmers left for England in 1859, Phoebe's work on feminism appeared. The thesis for the book appeared in her journal for 1856: "The spirit of prophecy [has] fallen on women."[32] In *Promise of the Father; or, A Neglected Speciality of the Last Days*, she developed the argument that with the coming of the Holy Spirit at Pentecost came a new obligation for women to speak in public for the Lord. Just as the Spirit-filled prophets of the Old Testament had a duty to proclaim God's word, so today's Spirit-filled Christians, both men and women, have a responsibility to talk to others about the Lord. Women in New Testament times exercised this right and duty, but since those days the church has sinned by silencing their voices. This well-documented and closely reasoned work was different from the rest of Mrs. Palmer's books. Despite the difficulty of finding time to write, in *Promise of the Father* she displayed a skill in research and an ability in reasoning that were unnecessary in her other works.

Ranging from Justin Martyr to Queen Victoria, Mrs. Palmer defended her thesis by appealing to Hebrew and Greek etymology, the Old and New Testaments, the church fathers, the example of female leaders in early Methodism, and the evident blessing of God upon women's ministries in her own day. She exegeted each of the biblical passages treating the role of women in the church, contending that the prohibitions against female ministry were either misunderstood or culture-bound. In her eyes the villain in the story was the "Man of Sin," the Roman Catholic church, which ended the freedom of the primitive church with its man-made regulations.[33]

The book has recently come back into print and is important today both as one of the earliest statements in the struggle for women's rights and as a wide-ranging treatment of the biblical and historical evidence for the active role of women in Christian ministry. In its own day it was not as widely read as Mrs. Palmer's simpler books and by 1872 had sold only twelve thousand copies.[34]

Mrs. Palmer's nine other books were written after she left the United States for England in 1859 and will be discussed in the chapters dealing with the years in which they were published.

The Tuesday Meeting

The growth of American psychology and the expansion of Phoebe Palmer's ministry are linked in the person of Thomas C. Upham. Upham was the professor of mental and moral philosophy at Bowdoin College in Maine. In December 1839 he was in New York to supervise the republication of his seminal volume in American psychology, *A Philosophical and Practical Treatise on the Will*.[35] Mrs. Upham accompanied him to the city and was brought to the Tuesday Meeting by a friend.[36]

Mrs. Upham was a Congregationalist but had attended a

Methodist meeting in which she heard a woman profess entire sanctification. After an intense search of the Scriptures to see if the Methodists were right about this doctrine, Mrs. Upham was convinced of its truth and sought it earnestly. She found what she sought and attempted to share the news of her blessing with the members of her own church. She was informed that her experience was probably a trick of Satan, and that, even if she were right, a woman should not presume to speak in a church meeting. Among those who questioned her profession was her husband.[37]

Mrs. Upham had been praying for her husband's enlightenment for months and told her story at the Tuesday Meeting. After she heard the other women speak, she remarked to Sarah Lankford, "If my husband would come to this meeting and hear the testimonies that I have heard this afternoon, I am sure he would accept the truth of full salvation, and come into the light." Sarah decided that men should be allowed to attend the meeting and invited Mrs. Upham to bring the professor on the next Tuesday.[38]

But the women could not wait a full week to expose Professor Upham to the doctrine of holiness. Accordingly, Sarah Lankford entertained the Uphams on the next Thursday evening. Phoebe Palmer was also present and spent most of the evening answering the professor's questions about sanctification. The chief point at issue was faith: After he had consecrated himself, did Upham have scriptural grounds to believe that God had accepted his consecration? At the end of the three-hour session, he proclaimed himself intellectually convinced and even asked Phoebe to lead them in prayer as they parted, despite his former view that women should not pray in the presence of men.[39]

Upon retiring to her room, Phoebe spent the next hours in prayer. She cried out to the Lord for Upham's sanctification, realizing the great influence a man of his intellect and position could have. About midnight, she allowed herself to fall asleep, but that sleep was often broken by her prayerful longings. Waking early in the morning, she once again began to plead with God, asking that even at such an early hour the Lord would manifest himself to Professor Upham and give him "clear views of the simplicity of faith."[40]

On Saturday evening, Professor Upham returned to the Lankford-Palmer home and announced to the sisters that God had wrought the work in his heart. He had lain awake all night, and exactly at the moment when Phoebe had awakened and begun to pray for him again, he had offered himself wholly to the Lord. He had often done so in the past, but for the first time he now had the faith to believe God accepted his consecration. When he finally believed, "Christ gave Himself to me in all his offices." Upham said that he had previously had the faith of a servant, but now he had the faith of a son:

> For twenty-five years I have been determined to be a faithful servant, but I have been serving off in the kitchen, I would not let my Father take me into the parlor, and call me His dear child. But now it is *my* Father—my own *dear* Father![41]

The next Tuesday he gave his testimony, and from then on men were welcomed to the Tuesday Meeting. Because the meeting was held in the mid-afternoon of a week day, it is not surprising that many of the men who came to Phoebe Palmer's parlors were ministers.[42] Upham himself continued to attend whenever he visited the city, and his wife established a similar meeting in their home in Maine. When Professor Upham retired from teaching, he spent his winters in New York and regularly participated in the meetings in the Palmer home.[43]

The sanctification of Thomas Upham gave a fillip to Phoebe Palmer's influence. Professor Upham wrote two books on holiness in the next six years.[44] These books did not reveal that the author learned about holiness from Mrs. Palmer, but they clearly taught her doctrines. More importantly, Upham publicly identified himself with Mrs. Palmer's ministry through his attendance at her meetings. Doubtless the impact of the vision of the internationally known professor sitting at Mrs. Palmer's feet each week was not lost on the New York clergy.

During the next year, 1840, another major change occurred in the Tuesday Meeting. In April the Lankfords moved from the city to Caldwell-on-the-Hudson, about fifty miles away. The sisters' father, Henry Worrall, had been building a steam engine for a company there when the firm had gone bankrupt. Worrall bought the company and was thinking of asking Thomas Lankford to manage it for him. He thought it was a better business than Lankford's present occupation of building churches in New York but was reluctant to have his daughter and son-in-law live in a town where he could find not even one "professor of religion." Arguing that they could be missionaries, Sarah persuaded her father that they should go. Leaving Phoebe in charge of the Tuesday Meeting, they moved north and began a new congregation. Under Phoebe's careful leadership, the meetings continued to prosper. While Phoebe took responsibility for the meeting each week, Sarah often made the one-hundred-mile round trip to be present on Tuesday afternoons.⁴⁵

Besides the prestige of Thomas Upham, the presence of Nathan Bangs also contributed to the growth of the Tuesday Meeting. America's "Mr. Methodist," Bangs had been Methodist preacher, general conference delegate, book agent, editor of the *New York Christian Advocate and Journal*, editor of the *Methodist Quarterly Review*, chief founder of the denominational missionary society, and president of Wesleyan University. He was also an old friend of the Worrall family, and so it was natural that when he resigned the presidency of Wesleyan University and returned to the pastorate in New York City in 1842, he should be a guest in the Palmer home. He had been sanctified as a young man, and he delighted to attend the Tuesday Meeting to give his testimony and encourage others to seek this experience. His regular attendance at these gatherings added to their growing influence.⁴⁶

So popular were these gatherings that Phoebe reported in 1845 that the participants filled two parlors in her home. No exact attendance figures for this period are given, but Mrs. Palmer does note the presence of bishops, general conference delegates, missionaries, and ministers of various denominations.⁴⁷ The meetings continued to grow in popularity so that by 1857 the Palmer house was unable to accommodate all who wanted to attend. No more people could be crowded into the parlors, so the Palmers were forced to find places for them in the hall or on the stairs. This solution was only a temporary expedient. Because they wanted to keep the meeting in their home, the Palmers decided to spend about two thousand dollars to build an addition to the house to make room for all who wanted to come to the Tuesday Meeting.⁴⁸

Local Church Ministry

In addition to assuming responsibility for the Tuesday Meeting, Phoebe Palmer widened her sphere of activities in the Allen Street Methodist Episcopal Church. She began to speak about holiness in her own and other class meetings.⁴⁹ Walter had been leading the class which they both attended, but one evening in 1838 he was too ill to go, so Phoebe led the meeting in his place.⁵⁰ She also led the class several other times during the following year when medical emergencies called him away. In December of 1839 their pastor asked Phoebe to take a class of young converts on her own. She thus became the first woman to lead a Methodist class in New York City.[51] Walter continued to lead his class, with Phoebe filling in during his necessary absences. His class met on Thursday afternoons, and hers met in their home on Friday evenings. Their classes contained both women and men, and by 1845 Phoebe's class was larger than Walter's. They each led their classes until they were called away from the Allen Street Church in 1848.[52]

One of Mrs. Palmer's first activities outside her own local congregation after her sanctification was her attendance at various love feasts held in the city. By the early 1840s these love feasts were institutionalized as monthly "Family Gatherings" with Methodists coming from forty different churches.[53] Another area of service for Mrs. Palmer was the organization of the "Third Monday Evening Meeting for the Promotion of Holiness." This meeting was held each month in a different Methodist church in the city so that all New York Methodists would have a chance to hear about holiness whether or not their minister preached the doctrine. Timothy Merritt began these meetings but feared they would cease when he left the city. Phoebe agreed to take responsibility for them. She promoted them by arranging the schedule and distributing the publicity. Nathan Bangs presided over many of them, and they remained popular through at least 1848.[54]

Near the end of 1848 the Palmers resigned from their class leadership. They felt called to move their membership from the nearer, more prosperous Allen Street Methodist Episcopal Church to the feeble Norfolk Street charge in order to strengthen it. This transfer of membership by two respected lay leaders who had served the church for more than twenty years occasioned much misunderstanding and ill will. The minister at Allen Street, Bartholomew Creagh, naturally felt hurt that the Palmers were leaving, and the Palmers felt humiliated by his treatment of them as they departed. Fortunately, the ill feelings did not last long; explanations and apologies were offered and accepted. Within a few years the relative strengths of the two churches were reversed. The Norfolk Street Church was prospering and had paid off most of its debt, while the Allen Street Church languished because people were leaving it. Once again wanting to go to the place of greatest usefulness, the Palmers returned to Allen Street. The whole matter would not merit more than a footnote except that eight years after the event, the old wounds were reopened by Hiram Mattison in an attempt to discredit Mrs. Palmer's testimony and teaching.[55]

Camp Meetings

In 1838 Phoebe Palmer first began to travel to promote the Lord's work. At first traveling across town, she later would cross the continent and even the Atlantic in her efforts to promote holiness. With the exception of one year, during which she was so ill she almost died, every summer from 1840 until her death in 1874 found her at various camp meetings. When the camp meeting season was over, she attended love feasts, social meetings, revival services, and other gatherings in her zeal to spread scriptural holiness throughout the land.[56]

She attended two camp meetings during the summer of 1838, taking her family with her. Though their needs demanded much of her attention, she was able to organize some meetings and there speak for the Lord.[57] There is no account of her travels during the summer of 1839, but it is unlikely she ventured far from home because sometime during the year she gave birth to her second surviving child, a daughter named Phoebe.[58] In December of that year she journeyed to Williamsburg, Long Island, to attend a meeting for social worship in the home of Lydia Cox.[59] In 1840 she spoke in camp meetings at Rye, New York, and Williamsburg, on Long Island, as well as making a visit to Sarah Lankford's new home in Caldwell to help her in her evangelistic labors there.[60]

In August of 1840 the Lord gave Phoebe Palmer a vision of her future career which nerved her for many labors. So precious was this experience that she kept it secret until the last year of her life; only with the approach of death did she write it out for publication. For some time before this revelation, Phoebe had felt abandoned by God. She missed the sense of joy to which she was accustomed. The Adversary suggested God had forsaken her because of some sin, so she examined her heart and cried out to God to reveal any secret fault. When no answer came, she clung to her shield of faith, refusing to believe she had sinned unless God revealed it to her. As on the day of her sanctification, once again she felt "shut up to the exercise of naked faith in a naked promise." In the days that followed this struggle to maintain her trust in God's acceptance despite the absence of joy, God's Word seemed ever more penetrating, and she experienced "such piercing views of my utter nothingness" that she was almost crushed. One morning after a wakeful night, she took the Bible in hand and called on the God who had answered through the Urim and Thummim (Num. 27:21) to tell her through his Word what he was trying to teach her through this period of trial. As she opened the Bible her eyes fell on the words "I have chosen thee" (Hag. 2:23). At that instant

> the curtain of the future seemed uplifted. Yes! the Spirit took of the things to come, and revealed them to me. Perceptions of the great blessedness of the work to which the Lord might call me, in identification with the great fundamental truth of Christianity, "HOLINESS TO THE LORD," were granted, but with these glorious perceptions a view was also given of the trials I should be called to endure in connection with my open identification with TRUTH. "Yea," said the Spirit, "a sword shall pierce through thy own soul also, that the thoughts of many hearts may be revealed" (Luke 2:35).[61]

Not only did the Lord show her he would bless her ministry, he also revealed that like Mary she would receive this great blessing at the price of soul-piercing suffering.

In the strength of this insight, Mrs. Palmer continued her labors. During the summer and fall of 1841 she traveled in New York and New Jersey. She made the first of her many reports of the number of people influenced by her ministry when she reported that at the Hempstead Harbor camp meeting two hundred claimed to be saved and eighty professed to be sanctified.[62] Phoebe led a group which traveled to this meeting, and helped each person prepare for the event by holding a prayer meeting on the steamer while en route.[63] In November she left Walter with the children in New York and went to Burlington, New Jersey, where special meetings were in progress. Her role was to exhort and lead prayer meetings after the local ministers preached in the evening, and to lead love feasts, sanctification meetings, and home prayer meetings in the surrounding area during the day. Upon returning to New York in December she felt discouraged that her ministry did not show greater results. Invitations continued to arrive asking her help in revival meetings, and, because of her revelation the previous year, she felt as called to her work as Moses and Gideon had been to theirs. But God had not yet poured out the extraordinary blessing he had promised, which would validate her work in the eyes of others. She resigned herself to wait and to work.[64]

Early the next year, Mrs. Palmer received an urgent request from Bethlehem, Pennsylvania. Miss Frederica Böhler, granddaughter of Peter Böhler who had helped John Wesley to personal faith in Christ, wrote imploring Phoebe to come and help revive the backslidden Moravian community. Again leaving Walter to care for the children, Mrs. Palmer went and preached holiness with good success.[65]

Later in 1842 requests began to come in from other denominations. In August she traveled to Newburgh, New York, to speak to a Presbyterian congregation about holiness.[66] Mrs. Palmer was especially happy to minister outside Methodist circles because such meetings supported her contention that the doctrine of holiness brought true Christians together. How fond she was of repeating these lines:

> Names and sects and parties fall,
> And Christ alone is All in All.[67]

Walter was able to accompany her on some of these summer travels, as were her father and her sister Sarah.[68]

During the middle years of the decade Mrs. Palmer had several bouts with serious illness which curtailed her travels. In 1843 she attended only two camp meetings. She had given birth to her sixth child, Walter Clarke Palmer, Jr., the previous November.[69] Recovering from childbirth and caring for a newborn kept her close to home.

The next year, 1844, she was better and the baby was old enough to be left for short times. Beginning the year's travels in Boston, Phoebe spoke at ten different locations. She had to fit her meetings around general conference, which was held in New York during May and June. Mrs. Palmer served as hostess to at least seven delegates, including Leonidas Hamline who was elected bishop during the conference. Edmund Janes was also chosen for the episcopal office that year, and the presence of the two of them in the denomination's highest office strengthened Phoebe Palmer's influence. Both new bishops were advocates of holiness and both were close to the Palmers. Leonidas and Melinda Hamline were especially good friends of Walter and Phoebe Palmer. They often visited in the Palmer home and when separated kept in touch through letters. The women wrote each other frequently and included reports of their spiritual states along with other news. Mrs. Hamline's letters reveal that under Phoebe's influence she moved from being a doubter of holiness in 1844 to a defender of the doctrine in 1848. These two women kept up a correspondence that was ended only by death.[70]

Mrs. Palmer had an active year in 1844, but she was sick again in 1845 and 1846. Two meetings were all she could manage the first year and none at all during the second. The Palmers did, however, take a vacation trip to Saratoga Springs and Buffalo. At each stop of their journey they visited the local Methodist preacher and spoke to him about holiness.[71] Mrs. Palmer did not record the name of her disease, but the illness seems to have been brought on by overwork and exhaustion. She noted in her diary that there are laws of nature which people must obey if they wish to retain their health, and then commented, "I fear I have not been as attentive as I might have been, in observing these laws." Although she was so sick she expected to die, the relaxing excursion away from the city restored her strength.[72]

With the return of health came a resumption of labor. In 1847 Phoebe Palmer and Sarah Lankford traveled to Philadelphia where they organized a regular meeting for the promotion of holiness, modeled after the Tuesday Meeting. Later Phoebe took the train for Cape Cod where at the "Millennial Grove" she found a great response to her message. In 1848 she went to eight different places, finishing the year's travels in Baltimore where she attended a camp meeting with her mother-in-law. Phoebe was not scheduled to lead in this camp, so she planned to remain in the background. However, she felt impelled to speak in the general class meeting which was being held one morning. As she stood to speak she was recognized, and at the end of the meeting the leader called on her by name to close in prayer. After she finished praying, "scores" gathered around her. She had never met most of these people, but they knew her from her writings. The preacher in charge of the camp meeting asked her to lead a special meeting that evening, and Phoebe stayed up most of the night counseling with those who sought the Lord. About twenty said they were justified that evening, and several more testified to having received the witness of full salvation.[73]

Phoebe Palmer kept only scanty records in 1849. She stayed in New York City most of the summer. Perhaps the cholera epidemic which gripped the city that year limited her travels, either through a quarantine or through Dr. Palmer's increased work load.[74] One trip, however, which is not even mentioned in her published records for this year was to have a surprising result.

Sometime during the summer, she and Walter spoke in a

camp meeting in Collins, New York. Under her influence, B. T. Roberts, a Methodist preacher in his second year of ministry, professed sanctification. Roberts went on to become a leader in western New York holiness circles and headed a reform movement in the Genesee conference. When the reform movement failed, he was expelled from the Methodist church and then founded the Free Methodist denomination.[75] Although they taught the same doctrines as Mrs. Palmer, she was not entirely in sympathy with the Free Methodists. She felt they were untactful in the way they tried to promote the doctrine of entire sanctification. Such fanaticism discredited the doctrine of holiness in the eyes of more dignified folks.[76]

In 1850 Phoebe Palmer began to increase the number of meetings she held. Her three children were now seventeen, eleven, and eight years old, so they required less of their mother's attention. In March she participated in meetings in Boston's Broomfield Street and Hanover Street Methodist Episcopal churches. The high point of her visit was preaching to Boston's society people in two home meetings. Episcopalians, Presbyterians, and even Unitarians came to hear Phoebe speak for an hour and a half about entire consecration. Tears flowed as she spoke: and most of the listeners "in the most affectionate terms assured me of their hearty concurrence."[77]

Frederic Dan Huntington was probably one of the Unitarian who heard Mrs. Palmer speak. The first Plummer Professor of Christian Morals at Harvard College, Huntington was a doctrinally conservative Unitarian who, though he could not subscribe to the dogmatic rigors of homoousian trinitarianism, nevertheless accepted "special, supernatural redemption from sin, in Christ Jesus," the "eternally begotten Son of God," "the ever-living present Head of the Church and personal intercessor for his disciples."[78] He wrote to Phoebe Palmer during the summer of 1850 for her advice about how to be sanctified. In reply she took him to task for his unbelief, but not for his unbelief in the Trinity. Like so many others to whom she wrote, he refused to believe he was holy after he had made a complete consecration, unless he felt some change in his emotions. She told him to believe that the written Word was indeed "the voice of Christ speaking in his inmost heart." From what Huntington had written, Mrs. Palmer concluded that he had complied with the conditions of entire sanctification, and thus advised him to claim by faith what was rightfully his.[79]

No further record of their correspondence exists, but ten years later Huntington came to believe in the Trinity. He broke with the Unitarians, became an Episcopalian, and planted a church in Boston's newly reclaimed Back Bay. There, in his Sunday school, and in his mission chapel in the slums, he preached the authority of the Bible, the atonement of the incarnate Son, and the attainment of entire sanctification by faith.[80]

After leaving Boston, Mrs. Palmer spoke in at least nine other cities that year and in nine more in 1851.[81] The record for 1852 is vague again. Wheatley, who usually devotes pages to each individual year, reports the entire year in these words: "The Red Lion and Hillsdale, with other camp meetings were attended this year. Peace continued to flow like a river, and righteousness as the waves of the sea."[82]

In 1853 Phoebe Palmer reported her first trip to Canada. She went to Kingston, Ontario, where she was well-known because the local Methodist paper had serialized *Faith and Its Effects*. The camp meeting attracted the attention of the Kingston area; even the mayor and chamberlain attended the services. In all over five hundred professed conversion, and nearly as many claimed entire sanctification. The annual conference of the Methodist church reported an addition of six thousand members that year, mostly from the Kingston area. This meeting marked the beginning of many summers of productive labor by the Palmers in Canada. It also marked the beginning of Dr. Palmer's regular travels as an evangelist. During this summer he devoted his vacation month to traveling with Phoebe to speak in camp meetings. He continued this practice until he gave up medicine for full-time ministry in 1859. Of course, Phoebe kept on going to camp meetings and revivals throughout the year, and Walter joined her as his medical practice allowed.[83]

Bishop Matthew Simpson had spoken to Phoebe Palmer about his spiritual state during the spring of 1853. He had been dissatisfied with his spiritual state for a number of months and wanted her advice. She was surprised and concerned to learn that he had never experienced entire sanctification. In July she wrote him a follow-up letter reminding him that because he had set himself apart for God's service, all he needed to do was to believe the Bible and testify to his faith. Then he would be sure to get the witness which would assure him of his acceptability to God. For some reason, however, either he did not follow her advice, or her prescription did not work, and Simpson never did experience what

Mrs. Palmer promised. Although this failure did not rupture their friendship, it may account for the bishop's impatience with other holiness advocates and for the faint praise of Phoebe Palmer's theology in the introduction he wrote for her biography.[84] It may also be, however, that Simpson's coolness toward Mrs. Palmer's teaching came from another source. The bishop's wife was a striking woman and a fashionable dresser. She probably did not feel entirely comfortable with Phoebe Palmer's emphasis on the simple lifestyle as a requirement for holiness.[85]

In 1854 Phoebe spoke in eight camp meetings. During the summer Sarah Lankford went with her to Boston, and Walter joined them while the meetings were in progress. Unlike the Canadian visits, these sessions were not a great success. Phoebe was saddened by the evident worldliness of the Methodists in New England who were not ashamed of their ornate churches, rented pews, expensive clothes, and gaudy jewelry. Even more distressing was their resistance to the doctrine of entire sanctification.[86]

Late one evening as Walter, Phoebe, and Sarah were returning from Boston to New York, the boiler of their steamship exploded. Everyone assumed the boat was sinking. Amid the smoke and steam from the boiler and the wild confusion of the terrified passengers, there rose the clear tones of the songs, "We're Going Home to Die No More" and "How Do Thy Mercies Close Me Round." Without thinking, Phoebe had begun to sing, and Sarah and Walter soon joined in. "There are some Methodists here!" shouted one passenger, and the chaos subsided as the people prepared to meet God. Fortunately the ship did not sink, but Phoebe was proud to report the clear testimony that her family gave in the face of death.[87]

Phoebe Palmer spoke at about twenty camp meetings in 1855 and 1856. At many of these events she was accompanied by Walter who had taken a partner in his medical practice so he would have more than one month a year to devote to ministry.[88] Near the end of 1856 she held meetings at Victoria College, a Methodist undergraduate institution in Ontario. While there, she received a telegram reporting her mother's death. This news was announced at a college meeting, and the students rose as one to pray for her. As this happened Mrs. Palmer felt "a new baptism into the spirit of my work." She felt God had newly commissioned her for his service, and so she resolved to be even more diligent in reaching souls for Christ.[89]

In February and March of 1857 Phoebe Palmer wrote a series

of articles for the *New York Christian Advocate and Journal.* Entitled "A Laity for the Times," the series began with the report that the whole northern Methodist Episcopal Church gained only 896 members in an entire year.[90] Phoebe then pointed out that most lay-people do not feel a sense of responsibility for the unsaved around them. She urged ministers to mobilize their congregations for the work of evangelism. The Captain of our salvation has ordered each Christian to do her or his duty, she said, and in his authority the ministers must urge the troops into battle. Those who are weak must be trained "in the arts of holy warfare," and those who are reluctant must be mustered out of the ranks. Only through the efforts of every member will the church be free of bloodguiltiness. Mrs. Palmer was confident that if this plan were adopted, the church could expect 800,237 new members that year instead of the dismal 896. "Shall we have the greatest revival that has ever been witnessed, during this coming year?" she challenged.[91] So convinced was Mrs. Palmer of the rightness of her ideas that she had the articles published as a pamphlet and sent to three thousand Methodist ministers.[92]

As if in answer to her renewed consecration and as an imprimatur to her strategy for renewal, Mrs. Palmer saw greater blessing upon her labors during 1857 than any previous year. In July at Brighton, Ontario, she saw two hundred conversions.[93] At Millbrook, sixty to eighty persons crowded the altar each night seeking pardon or purity, and both Walter and Phoebe worked from six in the morning until midnight exhorting in the meetings and counseling with individuals.[94] Ten days of meetings in Roman Catholic Quebec saw 150 claim salvation.[95] In Spencertown the Holy Ghost fell so mightily upon the people that one hundred prostrated themselves in tears before God.[96] But these events were merely the prelude.

After attending these camp meetings in Canada, the Palmers started for home. Arriving in Hamilton one Thursday evening, they hoped to board the steamer and thus be prepared for the early morning departure for New York. But when they got to the boat they found they were too late to get on board and were told they would have to wait until the ship began boarding passengers the next morning. Because the Palmers had so many friends in the city, they were able to make hasty plans to spend the night there. Their hosts had been planning to go to prayer meeting, and the Palmers were eager to accompany them. Somehow the word got out that the Palmers were in town, so two other prayer meetings were combined with the one the Palmers were planning to attend. Phoebe was asked to speak and felt led to challenge the seventy people present to "bring all the tithes into the Lord's storehouse and prove Him therewith, that He would open the windows of heaven and pour out . . . a blessing" (Mal. 3:10). When she spoke about tithes she was talking not just about money, but about time, talents, and reputation. She told them that if they would consecrate themselves to the Lord and dedicate themselves to evangelism, God would pour out a revival. Thirty people solemnly raised their hands in promise that they would begin to work immediately, and the Palmers consented to present the gospel at a meeting the next night if the thirty would bring people to it. To everyone's surprise several hundred came to the Friday night meeting, and twenty-one claimed to be saved. The Palmers agreed to hold services over the weekend, and fifty-five more came to the Lord. Feeling sure that God was calling them to remain, the Palmers stayed in Hamilton almost three weeks. In that time five hundred professed salvation. Friends in London, seventy miles to the west, begged them to return there for meetings. The Palmers agreed, and two hundred people claimed justifying grace in less than two weeks.[97]

When she finally returned to New York, Phoebe Palmer looked back at an amazing season of blessing. She calculated that more than two thousand had been converted and one thousand sanctified.[98] Reporting her labors to the Hamlines, she says,

> Never have we witnessed such triumphs of the cross as during the past summer and fall. I think I should speak more than within bounds, were I to tell you that not less than two thousand have been gathered into the fold, at various meetings we have attended. Hundreds of believers have been sanctified wholly, and hundreds have received baptisms of the Holy Ghost, beyond any former experience. We feel that we are also ourselves getting nearer to the heart of Christ, and that all the sympathies of our being, are flowing out in unison with the world's Redeemer.[99]

She was confident God's blessing accompanied her because she preached sanctification and because she urged lay-people to join the work of evangelism. Clearly the Lord had "stamp[ed] our ideas of 'A Laity for the Times' with signal success."[100]

At the same time that the Palmers began their ministry in Hamilton during the first part of October, in New York a businessman named Jeremiah Lanphier began a daily noontime prayer meeting at the Fulton Street Dutch Reformed Church in New York City to pray for revival. Also during this time the financial panic of 1857 reached its peak and prostrated businesses everywhere. As the financial center of the nation, New York was particularly hard hit: People whose livings had been swept away began to search for other kinds of security. Thus the tinder was dry in New York; the fire was falling in Canada. Would the blaze spread across Lake Ontario?

One spark that helped to ignite revival fires in New York traveled across the water in a letter from Phoebe Palmer. On November 5 the *Christian Advocate and Journal* printed her letter recounting the Lord's triumphs in Hamilton under the headline "Revival Extraordinary; the Laity for the Times Exemplified" on the front page. Along with reporting the amazing numbers of the converted, Mrs. Palmer declared, "If the principles on which this revival *commenced*, and is now being carried out so wonderfully, is [sic] of God, where is there a place . . . but may not be favored with a revival *at once*?"[101] As hundreds of wistful Methodist pastors read her account, they must have wondered, "Why can't that happen here?" They determined by God's grace it would. As they preached revival and followed Mrs. Palmer's methods, more and more reports of God's special visitation appeared in the *Christian Advocate and Journal*. These in turn stimulated further effort, and the chain reaction spread. Unlike many other modern revivals, this awakening retained the emphasis on the laity which Phoebe Palmer gave it. It was a true grass-roots phenomenon, breaking out like a wind-swept fire in many locations at once, rather than following the path of a well-known preacher. As it turned out, Mrs. Palmer's prediction of 800,327 new Methodists in a single year proved too optimistic. In 1858 the northern church increased by only 136,036 members, but the contrast with the previous year in which total membership increased by 20,192 is obvious.[102] J. Edwin Orr, who traced the awakening touched off by Phoebe Palmer's ministry, reported that it ultimately brought a million converts into the American churches, and when it spread across the Atlantic, brought a million and a half into various churches in Britain.[103] Contemporary writers called the time between the fall of 1857 and the fall of 1858 *annus mirabilis*, the year of miracles.[104]

Upon their return to New York in November, Dr. Palmer had to give some attention to his medical practice, but Phoebe was free to promote the revival she had helped to start. After being home only a month, she reported meetings in more than five different cities.[105]

In March of 1858 Phoebe Palmer went to Oswego, New York, where she held four or five meetings every day. Besides being invited to speak in the Methodist church, she also addressed the Presbyterian, Congregational, and Baptist congregations.[106] Going next to Binghampton, she held services in which the great-granddaughter of Jonathan Edwards claimed to be sanctified.[107]

The summer meant another trip to Canada, but this time the Palmers headed for the Maritimes. They left the first week of August, planning to spend a couple of weeks at a camp meeting in Woodstock, New Brunswick. So great was the blessing that followed them, and so urgent were the calls for their assistance, that they once again prolonged their trip. When the Palmers finally returned home in December, they had held meetings in eight different locations and had seen more than twenty-one hundred people profess to receive justifying or sanctifying grace.[108]

In January 1859 the Palmers held two weeks of meetings in the church pastored by their son-in-law Elon Foster in Williston, Vermont.[109] Mrs. Palmer also led two series of meetings in Pennsylvania before leaving for England the first week of June.[110]

Visitation

So concerned was Phoebe Palmer for the salvation of souls that her efforts were not limited to speaking to those who attended church meetings. Soon after her sanctification, she began to distribute religious tracts in an effort to reach those who would never hear the gospel in a church. She evidently belonged to the New York City Methodist Tract Society which assigned her a section of the city and which met for prayer and mutual encouragement.[111]

Mrs. Palmer was zealous to visit every home in her assigned district. She reports how one afternoon she went from "cellar to garret" in several homes and gave tracts to fifty families.[112] Like a woman scouring her home in search of a lost coin, she searched her district for lost souls. One day she triumphantly reported the discovery and conversion of a family she had missed in earlier visits:

> If it had not been for tract visitation, which admits, or rather invites, and enforces ingress to the highways and hedges, these precious souls might not have been plucked as brands from the burning. They lived in the rear of an alley, and I had several times passed through my district, without even

suspecting that there was a dwelling there. But it has been my desire to explore my district thoroughly, and as far as time will allow, to hand the tract, myself, to each family, individually, whether in garret or cellar, believing that to do it by proxy, is not in general, the better way.[113]

During these visits Mrs. Palmer would not only give out tracts, she would also try to talk to people about their souls. Some rebuffed her attempts, but others listened. After talking with people about their souls, Phoebe's next step was to invite them to church. To make sure they got there, she would often return to their homes and collect them just before meeting time. Then they would all go to church together.[114]

From her description of her district with people living in cellars, garrets, and alleys, it is evident that her assigned area was not one of New York's more fashionable neighborhoods. Thus it must have been quite a sight to see Mrs. Palmer arrive at the church with her new friends in tow. Sometimes Phoebe provided proper clothing for her guests. She once visited a family lodged in a basement. The father was sleeping off the effects of the previous night's binge, and the eleven-year-old son sat listless in the corner. The mother was God-fearing but had been unable to interest her child in Sunday school. Seeing that the boy needed clothes, Phoebe promised to get him a coat if he would go to church. The boy brightened at the prospect, and before Mrs. Palmer left, "he seemed quite elated with the idea of attending Sabbath-school."[115] So eager was she to get people to church that at least once she paid a person to accompany her to the Lord's house. One twenty-year-old widow wanted to go with Phoebe but was reluctant to go to church because time in church was time away from her work. This young widow was attempting to support her three children and an invalid mother on her earnings as a cobbler. Because she was paid by the piece, each moment that she could work meant more food for her family. Phoebe calculated how much money the woman could earn in the time it would take her to go to church, and then paid the widow that amount to go to church with her.[116]

Church Planting

Seventeenth Street Church

Visiting people in poor neighborhoods and trying to get them to come to church with her probably showed Mrs. Palmer the need for churches in poor neighborhoods. Other women shared this burden, and in 1844 they formed the New York Ladies' Home Missionary Society of the Methodist Episcopal Church. Phoebe Palmer was an early officer of this group.[117] By 1847 they had persuaded the New York Annual Conference to appoint a missionary to plant a church at the lower end of First Avenue. The missionary would be a member of the Conference, but the women of the Home Missionary Society would pay his salary. After two or three years of effort, the work was not prospering, so the society considered abandoning it. Like the gardener pleading for more time for the barren fig tree, Phoebe Palmer urged the women to give the project one more year. Her words persuaded the ladies of the society, but the Conference refused to appoint a man to that charge. When Phoebe heard of the Conference's action, she took matters into her own hands. Visiting several members of the society's board, she convinced them to meet with the bishops of the church at the Methodist Book Room to discuss the matter. The bishops were impressed with the rightness of the women's cause, and after the meeting two of them went to dinner at the Palmers' nearby home. The minister whom the women had chosen to plant the new church also happened to be dining with the Palmers that day. Right there at the table the bishops appointed him to begin the new work. Having attained her first objective, Mrs. Palmer exclaimed, "Now Brother, we want a Church, and I will give you one hundred dollars, as my first subscription." Six months later, in 1850, they had begun construction of the building and were holding meetings in its basement. That was the beginning of the Hedding, or Seventeenth Street Methodist Episcopal Church. Within five years it was self-supporting.[118]

Messianic Synagogue

Phoebe Palmer's next attempt at church planting was not as successful. Believing that the Jews would be converted in the end-times, and that these end-times were near, Mrs. Palmer sought to establish a Jewish-Christian synagogue to call God's chosen people to faith in Messiah. To finance this venture she wrote to friends near and far, asking them to become one of a "Joint Company" for Jewish redemption by pledging one hundred dollars or more. The money would go toward employing a missionary and obtaining a building. The Palmers themselves put up five hundred dollars toward the goal. Enough people joined the effort so that Mrs. Palmer was able to engage the Reverend C. E. Harris as a missionary, but there was not enough for a building. The Palmers therefore opened their home. There every Tuesday night of the fall of 1855 and the winter of 1856 Harris held services for Jewish people. At first Phoebe was encouraged because a number of converted Jews attended, but as time went on their numbers did not increase, nor were non-Christian Jews interested in coming. Ten months after it had begun, Phoebe had to abandon the project.[119]

Norfolk Street Church

While not strictly an exercise in church planting, the Palmers' ministry in the Norfolk Street Methodist Episcopal Church helped to strengthen a feeble congregation. In 1848 the Norfolk Street Church sent a delegation to its sister church on Allen Street requesting help. The church asked Allen Street for money, members, and especially, class leaders. The leaders of Allen Street acknowledged the justice of the request, but not one of the church's one thousand members volunteered to transfer to the weaker church. Walter and Phoebe Palmer were both class leaders and wondered if they should change their membership. They had been members of the Allen Street Church for twenty years and held long-established leadership positions. Besides, the Allen Street Church was right in their neighborhood, and the Norfolk Street Church was farther away.[120]

As Phoebe was pondering their response and praying for guidance, one night she had a dream which gave her the direction she sought. In her dream she was in a large glass house at noon. Sunlight flooded every inch of the dwelling, illuminating it brilliantly. In her hand was an oil lamp. Someone asked her, "Does your lamp shine?" When she looked closely at the lamp, Phoebe could see that it was indeed lit, but the flame was almost invisible in the strong light of day. "Y-e-s my light shines," she replied, "and if you will *shut out the sun you will see it.*" When she woke up she realized God was leading them to be lights in a dark place by moving from the large and wealthy church to the weak one. On the first Sunday they attended their new church the Lord began a revival there, and within a few years the Norfolk Street Church was strong and well established. The Palmers remained in the church for eight years and then moved back to Allen Street when that society began to lose members.[121]

Prison Ministry

Mrs. Palmer's quest for souls took her not only to the cellars, garrets, and alleys of New York, but also to the Tombs. Officially known as the New York House of Detention but called the Tombs because of some early suicides inside it, this jail was among the worst in the nation.[122] Nine prisoners were sometimes crowded into cells made for one, and the stench could make one vomit. Mr. Lewis Dwight, secretary of the Prison Discipline Society, reported, "I have been fifteen years engaged in visiting Prisons, and I have never seen human beings in a more filthy, neglected, and insufferable condition, than in [this prison]." He continued, "Where are the philanthropists of the city? where the intelligent and humane editors? where the Christian ministers? *'I was in Prison, and ye visited me not.'*"[123]

Perhaps in response to Mr. Dwight's words, the ladies of the Moral Reform Society began to provide "pious matrons" to take care of the female inmates in the Tombs and began to hold religious services there twice each week. Phoebe Palmer went to such a service in 1844 and was asked to speak to the women. These visits became a regular practice, and Mrs. Palmer often took her sister or the wives of visiting dignitaries with her to her Sunday afternoon prison meetings. She felt great sympathy for the female inmates, mindful that many of them had been trained from infancy for a life of crime. Their state before God would contrast favorably with that of children from religious homes who for years had resisted the Holy Spirit, or with that of many "Gospel-hardened sinners" who regularly attended the fine city churches.[124] Mrs. Palmer and her friends visited the jail at some personal risk. Jail fever was an ever-present danger. It was extremely contagious, often fatal. Yet each week Mrs. Palmer was there in the jail, telling the women of Jesus' love.[125]

Controversies

As Phoebe Palmer's ideas became well-known through her travels and books, they inevitably provoked comment. Generally these comments were positive: Besides the endorsements of Mahan and Hamline already noted, her early books were favorably reviewed by the *New York Evangelist*, the *Wesleyan Methodist Magazine*, *Zion's Herald*, and the *London Quarterly*.[126] But by 1848 the opposition her revelation had led her to expect began to arise.[127] This opposition crystallized around Hiram Mattison.

Mattison was a Methodist elder and professor of astronomy and natural philosophy in Falley Seminary in upstate New York. He later served as pastor of the John Street Church in New York City and as assistant editor of the *Northern Independent,* an unofficial Methodist newspaper. In addition to tangling with Mrs. Palmer, he also published polemical works aimed at (in alphabetical order): Annihilationists, Arians, Presbyterians, Roman Catholics, Seventh-day Baptists, Spiritualists, Unitarians, Universalists, and worldly Methodists.[128]

Mattison began to write about Mrs. Palmer's theology in 1851. Most of the articles were carried by the *New York Christian Advocate and Journal,* but others were scattered in different periodicals. Mrs. Palmer replied directly to Mattison only three times, but several others came to her defense.[129] Unfortunately for the historian, these writers usually used now-impenetrable pen names. After the first round in the winter of 1851–52, the controversy died down only to be stirred up again in 1855. The dispute reached its peak (or nadir) in 1856 with the publication of several anti- and pro-Palmer tracts. These tracts were printed and distributed at the expense of the disputants when the editors of the various papers which had been printing the polemics lost their stomach for the prolonged and increasingly bitter controversy. At this point in the debate Mrs. Palmer did not write in response to Mattison's charges, but another Methodist minister, J. H. Perry, stated her case for her. His replies to Mattison were written with the help of the Palmers and printed at their expense. The pamphlets of 1856 marked the last stage of the printed debate, but in the last sermon he ever preached, Mattison warned against Mrs. Palmer's theology.[130]

Mattison believed Phoebe Palmer's teaching was erroneous and divisive. In the beginning of the dispute there were eight propositions which he affirmed about Mrs. Palmer's teachings, and which the Palmers and Perry denied:

1. Mrs. Palmer's "sanctification" is mere consecration, or being set apart for God, like the consecration of a church, or of a bullock laid upon a Jewish altar. The *essential* change in the purification of the heart by the Holy Spirit is almost wholly ignored.

2. Consequently, according to Mrs. Palmer, all *feeling* and *consciousness*—all *fruits* or results as evidence of the fact—are repudiated. We must believe it *is* so because it is assumed that it [must] be so.

3. Mrs. Palmer believes that the faith by which we are to be sanctified is to believe that we *are* sanctified.
4. Mrs. Palmer teaches one must publicly profess entire sanctification, or backslide from that state of grace; and the stronger one's doubts are, the more strong and decisive must be one's professions.
5. Mrs. Palmer teaches no minister should preach "holiness" unless he himself is wholly sanctified.
6. Mrs. Palmer teaches the ministry and membership should be classified into "sanctified" and "unsanctified," and everything arranged accordingly in the Church.
7. Mrs. Palmer teaches the preaching of God's word, the love feasts, and prayer and class meetings in the M.E. Church, are *not* for the promotion of holiness; therefore separate meetings must be got up for this purpose, under the auspices of the "sanctified," even though they lead, as they have done in several instances already, to ruinous divisions in the churches.
8. Mrs. Palmer's entire theory—the "altar," the *faith,* and the *sanctification*—is *purely ideal* and imaginary—a theory utterly unknown in Methodism, except as advocated by George Bell and Maxfield—at variance with the Holy Scriptures, and calculated to promote fanaticism, and strife, and division, and every evil work.[131]

Later as the controversy went on, the indictment against Mrs. Palmer and her allies grew to twenty-two counts. Even a casual reading of the list will show just how far afield the debate wandered and the disgraceful tone it took. Summing up his case, Professor Mattison asserted he had proved:

1. That Dr. Perry did make a retraction, and that I obtained it from him; and that I only allowed my name to be coupled with his, [sic] to relieve him from pain and embarrassment.
2. That I stated nothing but the naked truth in the alleged "stultification;" that the events occurred just as I narrated them; and that they are perfectly consistent with each other.
3. That Dr. Perry makes "concessions" on very small points, when clearly made out against him, leaving unnoticed the more important ones to which he cannot reply.

4. That the alleged untruth about the "Jewish altar" is an honest truth, and perfectly consistent with all I have ever written upon the subject.
5. That Mrs. Palmer did assail Brother Creagh, her pastor, writing him at least one very severe letter, and finally Dr. and Mrs. Palmer left his church, because he did not preach the "shorter way" doctrine that consecration is sanctification.
6. That the most dishonorable and cruel measures were resorted to by Dr. Perry and Dr. and Mrs. Palmer, to make the widow of a Methodist minister certify in print what she knew and told them was not true! And all this, in order to convict me of impropriety, meanness, and falsehood, or "for the promotion of holiness."
7. That the alleged "reckless assertion," that "neither Wesley, Watson, Benson, Clarke, Asbury, Fisk, Olin, nor any of our deceased bishops ever professed entire sanctification, so far as it appears," and is strictly true in its obvious and necessary import; that is, they never professed it orally, and publicly, and before "promiscuous assemblies;" and that Bishop Hedding, though allowed to have been wholly sanctified even by Mrs. Palmer herself, absolutely declined making any such profession even upon his bed of death, and with only his Christian brethren around him, though urged to do so by "The Author of the Way of Holiness."
8. That I never agreed to discuss the whole eight propositions in a single article, as Dr. Perry incorrectly alleges.
9. That I never agreed to use no personalities in reference to Dr. Perry in the discussion with him, he himself being witness; and that what I wrote would not have been a breach of such an agreement even if it had already existed.
10. That Mrs. Palmer has been in the habit of assailing Methodist preachers in the public prints for years past; that without provocation she has made no less than *six* such attacks since 1839, one on Rev. Wm. Roberts, two on Dr. Foster, one on Rev. Tobias Spicer, and two on myself, besides the epistolary assault upon Rev. B. Creagh.
11. That I have never assailed Mrs. Palmer in any instance, and have never used the least undue severity in noticing her doctrines or labors, except in one article of November

19th, in which case I was betrayed into an allusion to her "household arrangements" by following Dr. Palmer himself, and that I voluntarily recalled that allusion at the first opportunity.

12. That the alleged attempt at "speculation" is a "myth," without shadow of foundation in fact.

13. That the story of my having "annoyed generally the editors of our periodicals with my communications on this subject" till they closed their columns against me, is equally fabulous.

14. That the late lamented Dr. Olin *did not* approve of Mrs. Palmer's particular views, but *disapproved* of them, and lamented the circulation and effect of her books, at least during the last years of his life.

15. That Dr. Perry has stultified himself most effectually in several respects in assigning his reasons for engaging in the controversy.

16. That all that Dr. Perry says about the character of my *Review*, the use of epithets, his unwillingness to reply, his sympathy for me, &c., is sadly at variance with the facts in the case, both as respects the *Review* and the doctor's subsequent conduct.

17. That I did not misrepresent Mrs. Palmer in the quotation from *"Entire Devotion,"* but that Dr. Perry misrepresented me sadly, though perhaps unintentionally, in all he wrote upon that subject.

18. That Dr. Perry is silenced upon several important issues that have arisen, and unable to make any further answer whatever.

19. That the fruits of this new style of "holiness," so called, is the division of churches, censoriousness, fanaticism, the ejection of God's ministers from their pulpits, and every evil work.

20. That Mrs. Palmer is in the habit of sending "very singular" epistles to laymen as well as ministers, if they happen to oppose her views and measures.

21. That Dr. Palmer is compassing sea and land, paying out money freely, and scattering Dr. Perry's pamphlet all over the country, to accomplish by detraction what Dr. Perry failed to do in argument, namely, seal my mouth by the ruin of my character.

22. That from the first to last Dr. Perry has failed on every point he has attempted to establish against me, though he has made every possible effort to accomplish his purpose; and that he stands before the public in the light of a vanquished assailant, smarting under the mortification of defeat, and sorry he ever made the assault.[132]

From the evidence presented by both sides, it is impossible to determine the validity of each separate charge. Leaving aside the personal issues dealing with agreements, misquotations, forced statements, and unkind letters, the gravamen of Mattison's contention was that Mrs. Palmer so lowered the standard of sanctification that those who were merely justified could claim to have attained the height of sanctification. When these misled saints began to enforce their views on their brethren in a manner which gave the lie to their claims, the peace of the church was destroyed. Mattison believed that such ill effects were the inevitable result of Mrs. Palmer's erroneous teaching about a "shorter way" of sanctification. For their part, Mrs. Palmer and her defenders never admitted that division and strife followed in her wake, and they claimed that her teachings were nothing other than the good old Methodist doctrine, which was really the good old biblical doctrine.

An evaluation of these rival claims must await the chapter on theology, but it may be noted here that the controversy seems to have had little lasting effect.[133] True, it did weary the contestants and consume their savings. It also caused Mrs. Palmer a great deal of emotional anguish. While the controversy with Mattison was simmering during the fall of 1855, but before his first direct attack on her ministry, Mrs. Palmer had a nightmare in which she was chased by wild beasts and attacked by a furious lion. She later saw the dream as a warning of the coming attack from Mattison.[134] As disturbing as the conflict was to the disputants, its larger effect was negligible. Phoebe Palmer's great success in Canada and the revival she sparked made Mattison's questions about her theology seem like mere cavils. Mattison himself found he had other battles to fight. A few years after his controversy with Mrs. Palmer, he withdrew from the Methodist church because it had not taken a firmer stand against slavery. He founded the Independent Methodist Church, but later was reconciled to his former denomination after the United States government settled the slavery question.[135] Even before the combatants moved on to other things, the Methodist public lost interest in their debate. Evidently many people responded to the paper war between Mattison and the Palmers as did one I. Winner who wrote to the editors of the *Advocate* saying that the paper should not waste its readers' time with rival theories of holiness, but should give them practical help in living holy lives.[136]

PREACHING HOLINESS BY DEED

Family

During these years of active ministry Phoebe Palmer raised three children. After Eliza's death she bore a girl and a boy who, along with their elder sister Sarah, grew to maturity.

Sarah had been born in 1833. Sometime in 1847 she professed conversion.[137] She later graduated from Rutgers College and married the Reverend Elon Foster, who became involved in the family publishing business. Reverend Foster died in 1898, while Sarah lived until 1918.[138]

The Palmers' second surviving child, Phoebe, was born in 1839. In 1855 she married Joseph Fairchild Knapp, one of the founders of the Metropolitan Life Insurance Company of New York. This marriage was to bring her into the highest social circles. Presidents Grant, Cleveland, and Harrison were guests in her home.[139] Besides entertaining presidents of the United States, the younger Phoebe also wrote lyrics and music for various hymns. She is best known for composing the tune to Fanny Crosby's "Blessed Assurance, Jesus Is Mine!" She wrote the tune and took it over to the blind writer's home. There she played it for her and asked, "Fanny, what does that tune say to you?" Fanny thought a few moments and then replied, "Blessed assurance, Jesus is mine!" Encouraged by Phoebe's positive response to this suggestion, Fanny Crosby went on to write the rest of this well-known gospel song. In addition to her ministry of writing songs, Phoebe Palmer Knapp participated actively in the holiness camp meetings at Ocean Grove, New Jersey. Joseph Knapp died in 1891 but, being a prudent insurance man, left his wife an annuity of fifty thousand dollars. Most likely Mrs. Knapp used some of this income to keep the *Guide to Holiness* afloat through 1901. She died in 1908.[140]

Walter Clarke Palmer, Jr., was born November 20, 1842.[141] Before 1852 he was converted after an avuncular chat on the knee of Bishop Hamline.[142] He married Mary Gorham, daughter of the former editor of the *Guide to Holiness*, sometime before 1868, and was publication and circulation manager for the *Guide* when his parents were the editors.¹⁴³ As late as the spring of 1874 he was unable to profess entire sanctification, although his mother hoped that the loss of two daughters within one week would drive him closer to Christ as the death of her children had done for her.¹⁴⁴ Walter became disabled and had to give up his publishing duties prior to 1883, and died in 1885.¹⁴⁵

Personal Benevolence

Visiting the poor and imprisoned to meet their spiritual need for salvation helped to make Phoebe Palmer aware of their other needs as well. Her diary mentions taking food to a destitute family and her correspondence contains thank-you letters from people to whom the Palmers had given money.¹⁴⁶ Walter Palmer often gave his medical care free of charge to his poor patients, and more than once left them money for food and medicine.¹⁴⁷ Once the Palmers even adopted a boy who needed their aid. Phoebe became acquainted with the case of Leopold Soloman on a visit to the Tombs. He was a Jewish lad who had embraced Christianity. Leopold had been disowned by his parents and then jailed as a vagrant with no means of support. The Palmers officially adopted him, and he came to live with them for a short time. They later sent him to a boarding school, but when he returned to the city during the vacation his natural parents, "by . . . various deceptions, . . . enticed him to return to their home." There he was persuaded to forsake his Christianity, and the Palmers never heard from him again.¹⁴⁸

The extent of the Palmers' personal benevolence is hard to measure. Mrs. Palmer did not note every meal she took to the sick or every garment she gave to the poor. Nor do we have a systematic record of those who were encouraged and challenged at the Palmers' dinner table, those who used the Palmer home as a hotel during Methodist conferences, nor of those who used it as a hospital while the Palmers nursed them back to health.¹⁴⁹ We do not even have a full record of the orphan children she took in and for whom she later found homes.¹⁵⁰

While we are not able to calculate the amount of time or money the Palmers gave individually to aid the needy, we can gain some idea of Mrs. Palmer's contribution to various benevolent organizations.

Colonization

Even before her experience of sanctification, Phoebe Palmer was moved by the plight of the slave. The American Society for Colonizing the Free People of Color of the United States had been founded in 1816. Its goal was to return freed slaves to Africa. Although rejected by many blacks in its own day and universally disparaged in our own, many people of good faith thought of it as the only realistic hope of bettering the lot of the slave. By 1824 it had been cautiously endorsed by the Methodist Episcopal Church, and by the early 1830s the New York Annual Conference was vigorously promoting its program.[151] Phoebe contributed to the colonization cause by writing at least three poems in its support, one possibly as early as 1828. This poem, "Redemption of Africa," was sung at the ninth anniversary meeting of the New York State Colonization Society.[152] Her "Ode for the Fourth of July" in 1831 was probably read at a special Methodist service for the benefit of the Colonization Society. The annual conferences regularly urged the local Methodist societies to hold such meetings and to take special collections for the cause.[153]

From the sentiments expressed in Mrs. Palmer's colonization poems, it is evident that her motives in supporting the colonization society were not compromised, as were the motives of some. The main themes of these poems are justice and redemption. Nowhere is the slightest hint that the black is unfit for American life or that the slave is inferior in any way. Rather, justice demands the return of those stolen by the slaver and will visit America with the sword unless the blacks "live unoppressed, live joyous, free."[154] After the slaves have been freed, and won to Christ, they may return to their homeland with the message of redemption. Then the world will see "Redeemed, enlightened, Afric [sic] rise."[155] Although the scheme she endorsed did not bring justice to the slaves or redemption to Africa, at least Phoebe Palmer's motives in supporting the Colonization Society in the 1830s were pure.

Relief Ministries

Allen Street Church Benevolent Society

Sometime during the 1830s the Palmers took up leadership in the Benevolent Society of the Allen Street Methodist Episcopal Church. While only a part of its records has survived, we do know that Walter served as its treasurer from 1838 to 1842, and that its

Board of Managers met in the Palmer home for seventeen years. The society administered the church's fund for the relief of the poor.[156]

Committee for Promoting National Education

In 1845 Phoebe received a letter from Catharine Beecher, asking her to join in an effort to promote popular education on the frontier by sending young women there as missionary teachers. These women would promote education by holding school five days a week and would promote religion by teaching Sunday school on the seventh. Miss Beecher had three other goals in mind. First, she hoped that her organization would encourage female solidarity by providing jobs for women. Working-class women could thus escape from the economic exploitation of the clothing industry, and upper-class women would be released from the social pressures which forbade useful employment. Second, these pioneer teachers would elevate the moral tone of the frontier, and third, they would unite the nation by training "the whole rising generation in common moral principles."[157]

Mrs. Hamline, wife of the newly elected Methodist bishop, had recommended Phoebe Palmer to Miss Beecher. Catharine Beecher wrote that she had read *The Way of Holiness* "with deepest interest and profit" and suggested that Mrs. Palmer might like to meet her sister, Harriet Beecher Stowe, who was then in New York. Like Phoebe Palmer, Mrs. Stowe had lately been led into the "Way of Holiness" by the "Bible method." In this letter Catharine Beecher also invited Phoebe Palmer to join the managing committee. Her second request was that Mrs. Palmer engage in a bit of benevolent chain mail, copying the letter and sending it to three friends in different cities.[158]

Evidently Phoebe Palmer complied with these requests, for six weeks later Miss Beecher wrote again, thanking her for her role in the project and asking her to use her influence to publicize it among the Methodists. Phoebe continued to be involved for at least the next fourteen months, probably helping to recruit teachers and teacher supervisors as well as raising funds and introducing Methodists to the project.[159]

Female Assistance Society

Mrs. Palmer did not just visit poor families to give them tracts. In the late 1840s and through the 1850s she combined her work for the tract society with service under the aegis of the New

York Female Assistance Society for the Relief and Religious Instruction of the Sick Poor. Phoebe Palmer was a life member of this organization and served as its corresponding secretary, writing its annual report from 1847 until she left for England in 1859.[160] Besides publicizing the society through writing its reports, Phoebe's duties included collecting money for it, and then distributing food, fuel, and clothing to the poor in her assigned district. Her diary reported that much of her time had been taken up in visiting the sick poor, and that she thought five of those she visited had been converted.[161] While there is no way of determining exactly how many people Phoebe Palmer visited during the years she worked for the society, information does exist to permit a rough estimate. In 1836 her sister Sarah was one of the society's twenty-three officers and managers. The women made a total of 4,340 visits, or an average of 187 each.[162] If these figures are representative, and if Phoebe carried her share of the visiting load, they give an indication of the magnitude of her labor. She does seem to have done a better job in her visiting and writing for the society than in her collecting for it. The report for 1851 lists her as seventeenth out of the twenty-one women who received donations for the society. She collected only eight dollars of the $2,500 raised that year.[163]

American Female Guardian Society

During these years Mrs. Palmer made time to serve with yet another benevolent organization. The American Female Guardian Society had been founded as the American Female Moral Reform Society in an effort to redeem prostitutes and wipe out their profession. Its efforts led it to the conclusion that prostitution was just one aspect of a bigger problem, the male domination of women. It therefore added to its purpose the achievement of female emancipation. By 1848, when Phoebe Palmer first mentioned the group, it had changed its name and undertaken yet one more task, that of caring for friendless women and children in the city.[164] The society had established the "Guardian Home for the Friendless," and Phoebe had become one of its managers. As a manager, she raised funds for the organization. Besides raising money, Mrs. Palmer also endeavored to find homes for the orphan children the home took in, and even provided foster care in her own home while the adoption process was going on.[165]

Five Points Mission

In the 1840s New York's Broadway, near the city hospital, was a center of fashion and wealth.[166] Elegant stores were filled with costly goods; handsome carriages brought shoppers with no regard for money; and well-dressed people crowded the streets in their pursuit of wealth and happiness. But less than a minute's walk away from that spot on Broadway, five streets came together to form an intersection known as the Five Points. The area now is known as Foley Square in the heart of the Civic Center, but then basement rooms were filled with as many as twenty-six residents, quarrels broke out between criminals who had no regard for life, and sordid children roamed the alleys in pursuit of entertainment and food.[167]

Charles Dickens traveled to New York in 1842 and visited Five Points one evening. He found it a dirty place filled with dangerous people.

> This is the place, these narrow ways, diverging to the right and to the left and reeking everywhere with dirt and filth. . . . Debauchery has made the very houses prematurely old. See how the rotten beams are tumbling down, and how the patched and broken windows seem to scowl dimly, like eyes that have been hurt in drunken frays. Many . . . pigs live here. Do they ever wonder why their masters walk upright in lieu of going on all fours? and why they talk instead of grunting? . . . What place is this to which the squalid street conducts us? A kind of square of leprous houses, some of which are attainable only by crazy wooden stairs . . . . Here, too, are lanes and alleys, paved with mud knee-deep, underground chambers, where they dance and game; . . . ruined houses, open to the street, whence, through wide gaps in the walls, other ruins loom upon the eye, as though the world of vice and misery had nothing else to show; hideous tenements which take their name from robbery and murder: all that is loathsome, drooping, and decayed is here.

Even more powerful than Dickens's account of the decaying buildings and lives is his admission that before he entered the Five Points that evening, he made sure he had two tough policemen to go with him.[168]

Where Charles Dickens required two tough policemen, Phoebe Palmer went alone. Up and down those rickety stairs, in and out of those foul-smelling rooms, back and forth through those dangerous passageways, she and the other ladies of the Home

Missionary Society went in search of children for the school, women for the workroom, drunkards for the wagon, and, above all else, souls for the Lord. Phoebe Palmer originated the idea of planting an outpost of God's love in the heart of Satan's territory. Her father had died in 1847, and Phoebe resolved to make his home-going the occasion of renewed labor for the Lord. He was to be buried in the Greenwood Cemetery. As the funeral cortege made its way to the graveyard, Phoebe was following her father's coffin, but her mind was not on her own sorrow. During that trip she conceived the idea of a mission at Five Points. Her purpose in selecting this location was to prove the power of Christianity to elevate the most degraded.[169]

Other officers of the Ladies' Home Missionary Society were reluctant to try to establish a mission in so unpromising a location as Five Points. The Presbyterians had begun a work there in 1830, but it had come to nought.[170] Phoebe kept up the agitation for three years until it finally looked as if she would gain her objective. But when she again presented the project to the society's board in 1850, one of the women spoke out against it saying,

> I will give ten dollars toward the sustainment of another German mission, but not one dollar will I give toward the sustainment of one at Five Points, for it will be money thrown away; many attempts have been made, but none have [sic] succeeded, and none can succeed.

Her negative feelings were echoed by another; and still another said she was unwilling to give one cent to Five Points, but she was willing to give thirty dollars to the German mission. The discussion shifted to the German mission, and it looked as if the society would again do nothing about Five Points that year. Seeing the way the meeting was going, Phoebe burst out: "I will give one hundred dollars toward a mission at Five Points." This commitment rallied those on the board who shared her concern for the mission, and the matter carried. They hired a missionary and began the work that year.[171] So successful was the work at Five Points that it came to overshadow all the society's other projects. For the next quarter of a century the Ladies' Home Missionary Society and the Five Points Mission were virtually identical.[172]

One of the characteristics of the work at Five Points was the involvement of the women of the society in its daily work. They did not pay a missionary to go places they would not go and do things they would not do, but rather they worked alongside him in their efforts to reach the people of Five Points. Dr. and Mrs. Palmer had gone over the neighborhood a number of times in an early effort to secure a place to begin the mission, and it is likely that she was one of the women who tamed the children in the Sunday school, visited nearly every one of the one hundred houses, and called on almost every one of the five thousand residents of Five Points during the mission's first year of operation.[173] As the demands of Phoebe Palmer's travel schedule increased, she was not able to be as involved in its ministry as before, but until 1864 she was listed as second directress of the society.[174]

Foreign Missions

Besides trying to win people to Christ in America, Phoebe Palmer was also interested in reaching people in other lands. Shortly after their marriage, Walter had talked with her about the possibility that he might be called to foreign missionary service. Phoebe was not sanctified at this time and entertained the hope that he was mistaken. Because she feared, however, that God would kill her rather than let her stand in Walter's way, she said nothing. Walter understood the meaning of her silence and let the matter drop.

About ten years later, in 1837, when she had grown in her commitment to the Lord, the call to missionary service came once again. This time the need was for missionary physicians to go to China. Unlike the previous occasion, this time Phoebe did not flinch from the path of duty. Counting the cost of leaving home and friends, she determined to serve the Lord in China. After making this commitment, she felt the Spirit calling her to remain where she was but to work as hard for the Lord as if she had gone to China. God then promised her that, if she would obey, she would do more for missions by staying home than by going overseas.[175]

China Mission

A few years later Mrs. Palmer's commitment to foreign missions began to bear fruit. She had been urging upon the Methodist bishops, and especially Bishop Janes, as well as the board of managers of the General Missionary Society of the Methodist Episcopal Church, the duty of sending Methodist missionaries to China. But the reply had always been that the missionary work in China was so hard that years would pass before there would be any results, and so the board would not even attempt it. Unwilling to take no for an answer, Phoebe one day suggested that she and Walter pledge five hundred dollars toward the establishment of a mission, if they could get twenty others to do so also. The pledges would be paid over a ten-year period. Walter replied that they should give twice that amount, and Phoebe urged him to make the challenge public at the next meeting of the Missionary Society. He did so, and the required number of pledges was soon reached. The board sensed the leading of the Lord and by 1847 had appointed five Methodist missionaries for China.[176]

Palestine Mission

The Palmers later employed the same strategy to get the mission board to send Methodist missionaries to Palestine. In 1853 they wrote to the secretary of the board urging the establishment of such a mission and offered the same pledge of one thousand dollars if nineteen more donors could be found. Dr. Palmer added that he had already obtained some of that number and that each had promised that these pledges would be over and above all other giving. The Palmers then went in person to press their cause home to the missionary secretary. Although he admitted all the Palmers said about the needs in Palestine was true, once again the response was no because of the difficulty of the field. The Palmers continued to lobby for the Palestine mission in person and in print through *Israel's Speedy Restoration*. Mrs. Palmer tells us she was not ashamed to add tears to her appeals. Finally the board voted five thousand dollars to begin a trial ministry in Jerusalem, but other difficulties intervened and the trial was never carried out.[177]

CHAPTER THREE:
Ministry in the British Isles: 1859-63

BRITAIN'S PREPARATION FOR REVIVAL

The news of the American *annus mirabilis* rapidly spread to England. Transplanted Britons wrote about their experience of the revival to the folks back home. British publishers searched American newspapers for revival intelligence and reprinted it in their church papers and in tracts. Americans who happened to be in Britain became instant experts on the revival, as did travelers newly returned from the States. By the summer of 1858 most British Evangelicals were well informed about the American events, and by 1859 Americans were going to Britain to explain and expand the revival.[1]

Walter and Phoebe Palmer were two of the Americans who took ship for England during this period. Twice previously they had been forced to cancel plans for an English trip, but in 1859 they gave way to the pressure of repeated invitations from friends in Britain, as well as to the desire to see the homeland of their biological and spiritual fathers.[2]

The interconnections between British and American Evangelicals were numerous and strong, especially among the Methodists.[3] Many Americans besides Phoebe Palmer had ancestors who traced their conversions to John Wesley. In addition, British Methodism had supplied many of the preachers who rode the American circuits, as well as most of the literature these preachers gave to their congregations.[4] Americans contributed to the sense of unity by sending official representatives to the British Annual Conferences, and also supplied them with a steady flow of unofficial fraternal delegations.⁵ As the safety and speed of the Atlantic crossing improved, the British Isles seemed even closer. One Methodist preacher in Georgia said that taking a ship to England was likely to be faster and more comfortable than riding a horse to the other side of his own conference.⁶

The Palmers found the British fields white unto harvest. Six years before their arrival, the dismal results of a religious census had stimulated new efforts in evangelism in many denominations. These efforts were increasing when, in December of 1857, a recession occurred. As in America, the economic downturn was the occasion for people to turn heavenward for help and security, and religious services became more popular. Then the news of the American revival began to arrive. American-style revival services sprang up all over the islands, and other American revivalists preceded the Palmers to British shores.⁷ James Caughey and Charles Finney both returned to England to further the incipient revival. Caughey, whose six years of itinerating in Britain between 1841 and 1847 had produced twenty thousand conversions, went back in 1857 to the scene of his previous triumphs.⁸ Finney had preached in England between 1849 and 1851, and his *Lectures on Revival* was widely read there. The appearance of a Welsh translation of his book had led to a powerful revival in Wales. Although his colleagues at Oberlin tried to keep him home, Mrs. Finney was sure they should return to England, and in December 1858 they sailed for Liverpool.⁹ Besides the expectation of revival, and the presence of other American evangelists, the Palmers were also aided by the publication of Phoebe's account of the revival in Hamilton. In the places where they were to hold meetings, the local Methodists reprinted her article from the *Christian Advocate and Journal*, and distributed it as a tract. The local promoters would then add the specific information about the dates and times of the Palmers' upcoming meetings to Mrs. Palmer's report of the Canadian revival.¹⁰

1859: SPYING OUT THE LAND

Dr. and Mrs. Palmer departed for Liverpool on June 4, 1859, on board the steamer *City of Baltimore*.¹¹ Accompanying them was their sixteen-year-old son, Walter, Jr.¹² The ship's crossing was easy and, unlike those who saw the voyage as time for recreation, the Palmers redeemed the twelve days at sea. On the first Sabbath they endured the morning prayers of the Church of England read by the captain and the ship's physician, neither of whom was "a man of evangelical piety." Later that afternoon, Walter and Phoebe left their first-class cabin and went down among the steerage passengers where they found several "disciples of Jesus." Encouraged to find so many like-minded souls, the Palmers proposed holding a worship service in the second-class cabin that very afternoon. After opening the service with singing and prayer, both the Palmers spoke and then invited testimony. Several took the opportunity to tell of God's goodness to them. As she heard their words, Phoebe felt she was among "heaven's nobility." Later, when she reflected on the day, she congratulated herself that she had obeyed the scriptural admonition, "Mind not high things, but condescend to men of low estate" (Rom. 12:16).[13]

Unfortunately, Mrs. Palmer was not similarly impressed with the piety of the ministers on board. Though several ministers of different denominations were present, it was Mrs. Palmer who organized a daily prayer meeting in the dining salon. To make matters worse, some of the ministers actually played board games with the other passengers. One of these ministers, a well-known professor from Union Theological Seminary, defended his actions when Phoebe took him aside. She had pointed out that the games were often accompanied by gambling and drinking. The professor admitted that some games could lead to dissipation, but argued that others were harmless. He himself drew the line at cards because of the association with gambling. Phoebe wondered how he could possibly play a board game to the glory of God or be an example to the flock if he was engaged in such a questionable activity.[14]

Arriving in England on June 15, 1859, the Palmers spent the summer months visiting friends and holding a few brief meetings in various locations. They also got up to Ulster to share in the Irish revival before beginning their first serious evangelistic campaign in September. They seem not to have had a definite itinerary, nor even firm plans about when they would return to America. What they did have was a handful of open-ended invitations to hold meetings in various places and a number of wealthy friends who had asked them to visit if ever they came to Britain. They also had a firm belief that God was leading them to the Old World to spread the revival begun in the New and that he would provide specific guidance when it was needed.[15]

When their boat docked in Liverpool, they found the Reverend Thornelow, a Wesleyan minister, awaiting their arrival.

The Palmers did not know Thornelow, but he knew them through Phoebe's writings. He had read of their trip in the *Guide to Holiness*, and had come to welcome them to England. His greeting was particularly cheering to Phoebe, who had prayed that God would give them a token of his good favor by leading someone to meet them as they disembarked.[16]

From Liverpool they traveled by rail to London, where they stayed in turn at the estates of two wealthy friends. Besides seeing the sights of London, they also made a pilgrimage to Wesley's City Road Chapel, where, at the grave of John Wesley, Walter and Phoebe renewed their covenant to give themselves to promoting holiness. While in London they promoted the cause of holiness by holding parlor meetings in the homes of their hosts and friends.[17]

From London the Palmers moved north to Bowden, near Manchester. There they stayed with a couple they had never previously met, but with whom they had corresponded for the last two years. Walter and Phoebe led some revival services in Bowden and its neighbor, Altringham. More than twenty professed conversion, and several others claimed entire sanctification. Phoebe was tempted to be disappointed at this meager response but felt the Lord was impressing her with the value of a single soul.[18]

The response to the Palmers' ministry in Belfast was much more exciting. All of northern Ireland was ablaze with revival fires, and Phoebe hoped that the reign of the "Man of Sin" might soon be coming to an end.[19] While in Belfast the Palmers stayed in the home of the brother-in-law of the mayor. They held meetings in the Wesleyan chapels in Donegal Square and Frederick Street. Between twenty and forty professed conversion each day, and many others claimed entire sanctification. The awakening had earlier been accompanied with modest physical manifestations, notably fainting. People fainted under Mrs. Palmer's ministry also, but, as she commented in reporting one such episode, "[It] made little confusion, and tended only to deepen the impressive solemnity of the service."[20]

The Palmers spent August back in England, again visiting friends and attending some revival meetings. September found them in Newcastle, after holding meetings in Walsingham and St. John's Chapel along the river Wear in Durham.[21] They came to Newcastle at the invitation of the Reverend Robert Young, chairman of the Newcastle district of the Wesleyan church. Phoebe had read his *Suggestions for the World's Conversion* with great profit and was eager to work alongside him. Young, for his part, had a great appreciation for Mrs. Palmer's ministry and had prepared his people for her coming by preaching from various New Testament passages emphasizing the role of women in the church.[22] The meetings in Newcastle opened on Wednesday, September 14, 1859. Young had engaged the Brunswick Chapel, the largest building available, and had posted bills throughout the town announcing the services. Four services were scheduled for each day, and five ministers were present to assist the Palmers. Two thousand people filled the chapel each night. Three hundred professed salvation the first week, and the revival continued on into October. By the time the Palmers bid adieu to Newcastle thirty-five days later, the secretaries had recorded the names of thirteen hundred who had sought God at the altar. Phoebe said she had seen revivals in America and in Ireland, but that she could not remember a more glorious work of the Spirit.[23] The news of the revival in hard-bitten Newcastle spread throughout the land. The *British Standard* in London carried reports, and even secular newspapers noted this movement which claimed to have converted one percent of Newcastle's population. New invitations began coming to the Palmers daily, urging them to come and help in other cities.[24]

Not content to harvest a ripe field and then move on, the Palmers did what they could to see that the revival continued after they had departed. Besides urging the unconverted to come to Christ, and believers to go on to perfection, Walter and Phoebe also promoted the formation of "Vigilance Bands" to carry on the work of the revival. One such group was formed in Newcastle soon after the Palmers left. Composed mainly of young men converted in the recent services, its sixty members led thirteen prayer meetings weekly in various parts of the city. They also visited homes and passed out tracts. In the group's first eight months its members visited six thousand families and handed out twenty thousand tracts.[25]

Besides bringing more than thirteen hundred to "pardon or purity," and gaining national attention for the Palmers, their time at Newcastle had brought them to the attention of William and Catherine Booth, who later founded the Salvation Army. William had been converted under James Caughey, and preached the same brand of holiness as did his spiritual father and the Palmers.[26] The Booths had not attended the Palmers' services, but they were deeply interested in their ministry because they preached holiness and because Mrs. Palmer spoke in mixed gatherings. In December

1859 Catherine Booth learned of a pamphlet written by a local minister, Arthur Rees, attacking the ministry of Phoebe Palmer because she was a woman. Various people published defenses of her ministry, but these did not satisfy Mrs. Booth. "They make so many uncalled-for *admissions* that I would almost as soon answer her *defenders* as her opponent," she wrote to her mother. William, as he had in the past, urged Catherine to speak in public and answer Rees. Too shy to do so, Mrs. Booth began to compose a pamphlet in defense of Mrs. Palmer and other women who spoke in public. Working on the pamphlet wiped away the last vestige of Catherine Booth's reticence; writing to convince others, she convinced herself that she had not only the right, but the duty to speak out for the Lord. Soon thereafter she gave the first of a lifetime of strong and effective messages.[27]

The Palmers' last service in Newcastle was Friday night, October 14. After resting on Saturday, they began a series of meetings in nearby Sunderland on Sunday afternoon. Phoebe had doubts about whether there would be as great a response as the one she had seen in Newcastle, but her faith was strengthened when she saw the leaders of the church seeking God's power in the first meeting. Her faith soon changed to sight as three thousand people crowded into the chapel each night, and an average of one hundred seekers each day professed themselves converted. The revival embraced both children and the elderly. So profound was its effect upon the community that the secular press linked it with a "maiden session" in the local court, that is, one in which no criminal cases were presented. Such a session occurred about once in a century and was celebrated by giving the judge a pair of white gloves. Thirty days into the meetings the secretaries had recorded the names of 2,011 persons who had presented themselves at the altar for prayer. Many of these were nominal church members, but they felt no assurance that they were really justified. Phoebe called those who received this assurance "converts" and estimated that two hundred of those who came forward sought and professed to have found entire sanctification.[28]

After thirty-five days in Sunderland the Palmers returned to the home of friends outside Newcastle for a week of rest. Then they traveled down the Tyne to North Shields. Once again their meetings met with great success. A band of one hundred women and men volunteered to visit the homes of the community and to talk to people in the streets to invite them to the revival meetings. Despite the cold and snow, people filled the chapel each night so that even the standing room was gone. Dr. and Mrs. Palmer had planned to remain at North Shields for two weeks, but the response was so great that they were persuaded to stay for one week more. Not everyone in the town greeted this extension with delight. The pub keeper said their stay had already hurt his trade, and the theater owner, who had shut his doors because of the scanty attendance, angrily claimed that another week of the Palmers would put him out of business. As she sat in Wesley's study to write on Christmas Eve, Phoebe Palmer had much for which to praise God.[29] In four months she and Walter had led successful campaigns in three different cities. Each series of revival services had influenced all levels of society, and had included people of several different denominations. By this time she had received the final tabulation from Sunderland, and so she was able to record that in the fifteen weeks since she and Walter had begun their labors 4,345 people had presented themselves at the altar as seekers and then professed to have obtained the blessing they sought.[30]

The Palmers spent Christmas week resting at East Jarrow. They made the trip over to West Jarrow where the Venerable Bede had lived. Phoebe commented that the monks of that day were "perhaps better monks than live in our day, though no doubt, mistaken men."[31]

1860: QUICK SUCCESS AND OBSCURE LABOR

From Jarrow the Palmers went north to Scotland. Others had tried to dissuade them from going there. The Methodists had been losing ground, and Phoebe remembered the remark of a doughty Scot as reported to John Wesley: "The doctrine of Perfection is not calculated for the meridian of Edinburgh."[32] But, because they had been invited, and even implored, by the minister and official board of the John Street Wesleyan Chapel, the Palmers went to Glasgow.[33]

There they found that the arrangement of the church hampered their effectiveness. There was no altar at which to hold a prayer meeting with the seekers after the preaching service. Walter tried to make do the first evening by asking all those who felt the need of the full baptism of the Spirit to rise, but Phoebe knew that they needed the closer personal contact and opportunities for counseling which an altar service would afford. When she raised the question with the church leaders after the service, they said it would probably take a week to get permission from the trustees to modify the building. Pointing out that they were in a spiritual war, and that delay in battle leads to defeat, she persuaded them to order the changes on their own responsibility. The carpenters arrived at four the next morning, and by the beginning of the afternoon service at three in the afternoon, the transformation was complete. Instead of the enclosed pews which had stood beneath the high pulpit, there now stood an altar enclosing a large carpeted area. This newly created space was crowded with seekers that very afternoon, and, with the fortifications in order, the Palmers pressed the battle into Satan's camp.[34]

People from many denominations attended the meetings. As had happened in Sunderland, many whose membership in a church had been only perfunctory now felt themselves to be living members in the body of Christ. Others sensed the perfect love of sanctification. The Palmers resisted the temptation to calculate their doctrine for the meridian of Glasgow and found the more they emphasized Christian perfection, the greater were the numbers of those professing salvation and sanctification. Phoebe wrote, "The more definite and uncompromising we have been in presenting these cardinal doctrines of the cross, the more manifestly has truth triumphed in the conversion of sinners and the sanctification of believers."[35]

At the final meeting of the Glasgow crusade, the presiding minister asked all those who wished the Palmers to return to the city to indicate it by raising a hand. Unexpectedly the crowded church rose to its feet as one person, and many stood with both arms upraised. Walter turned to Phoebe and whispered, "What shall we do?" Thinking quickly, Phoebe told him to say, "If three hundred will obligate to subscribe to the rules of the Christian Vigilance Band, and engage to labor at least one half-hour daily in specific effort to save souls, it will be my pleasure to encourage the people to anticipate our return."

When this proposition was repeated to the congregation, over three hundred took the vow to spend thirty minutes each day trying to save souls, and to meet with others in the band to hold one another accountable to keep the pledge. The Palmers left the next day for Edinburgh, but the revival went on. Of course the secretaries had to close their list because the fruits were being gathered in many different churches, but not before they had recorded thirteen hundred recipients of grace, of whom probably one thousand claimed to have been born again. Three months after the Palmers left, a minister from the John Street Chapel reported that very few of those converted had backslidden, and that he had more people wanting to distribute evangelistic tracts than he had tracts to give them.[36]

Edinburgh was a place of refreshment after the weeks of hard labor in Glasgow. The Palmers spent almost three weeks there before returning to England for a stay of five weeks in Carlisle. There 450 individuals claimed to have been saved.[37]

Again hoping for a rest, they went to Penrith, where they rested by holding only one meeting each day. The response to these meetings was enormous, and their number was gradually increased until one day the Palmers held four meetings. Not only did they increase the number of meetings each day, but they also lengthened their stay through the end of April. In the town of 6,000 inhabitants, 700 persons presented themselves at the altar during the Palmers' meetings. Of that number, 100 claimed entire sanctification.[38]

Before leaving Penrith, the Palmers toured one of the castles of the Earl of Lonsdale. The earl usually spent only a few weeks each year in residence, so the place was empty except for the staff of servants. Phoebe noted the six-hundred-acre park surrounding the dwelling, the unused library served by a librarian employed at the cost of two hundred pounds sterling a year, and the bathroom fixtures fashioned from pure gold. As they recorded their names in the guest book in the porter's lodge, Phoebe added these verses of Scripture for the edification of the earl or any other readers: "Godliness with contentment is great gain. For we brought nothing into this world, and it is certain we can carry nothing out. And having food and raiment let us be therewith content" (1 Tim. 6:6–8); and "How hardly shall they that have riches enter into the kingdom of God!" (Mark 10:23).[39] In May and the first week of June, Walter and Phoebe Palmer preached at Gateshead, just across the Tyne from Newcastle. Here they stayed with the daughter and son-in-law of the mayor of the city. So many people from different denominations were blessed by the services that the meetings were called "The Evangelical Alliance Revival." Between five and six hundred persons professed to be converted.[40]

Once more needing rest, the Palmers remained in Gateshead after the close of their special meetings. During this time Walter took their son and some other friends on a trip to the continent while Phoebe stayed behind to regain her strength through a total rest. This total rest included helping in the formation of a Female

Vigilance Band in Gateshead and leading a series of meetings which began as a seaside holiday. Mrs. Palmer's hostess had persuaded her to go to Tynemouth for a few refreshing days at the beach. On Sunday they went to the local chapel, and Phoebe was asked to conduct the Sunday night service. The response to this service was so good that a meeting was called for Monday night, and then for Tuesday, and so on through the week. Recent converts came over from North Shields and Newcastle to aid in the meetings. By the weekend the secretary's list contained one hundred names. When her husband and son returned from their trip, the Palmer family took ship from Gateshead bound for London.[41]

Sometime after the Palmers left the North, friends of Mrs. Palmer published a series of letters she and others had written describing the work she had just completed. The work, *Some Account of the Recent Revival in the North of England and Glasgow*, was designed to promote the cause of revival generally, and the Palmers' labors specifically. Evidently it achieved at least some of its desired result, because after its publication the Palmers begin to speak of having to choose between various invitations to hold services.[42]

Passing through London, the Palmers arrived on the Isle of Wight at the height of the holiday season. They spent some of their time visiting the beaches and seeing the royal palaces. Queen Victoria was in residence at the time, and Mrs. Palmer took the opportunity to present her with a copy of her book, *Promise of the Father*. Her Majesty was not able to accept the gift in person but did so through her private secretary. A few weeks later Mrs. Palmer felt moved by the Lord to communicate with Queen Victoria again. In a carefully worded and respectful letter, Phoebe warned the queen that patronizing the theater and the race course, as well as breaking the Sabbath by cruising on the royal yacht, imperiled her immortal soul. While Her Majesty had instructed a courtier to write to Mrs. Palmer of the queen's gracious acceptance of the book, no such response came in reply to the letter.[43]

Spending most of July and August on Wight, the Palmers held meetings in the Wesleyan chapels of the various towns. As in previous services, many who came to the altar were already church or chapel attenders. One old man told Mrs. Palmer, "I have been going to 'the Church' and partaken of the sacrament, but it seems not to have done me any good; and now I have come here hoping to get my heart right."[44] In Newport, however, the situation was different. One hundred fifty names were recorded as professing salvation, and all but ten of those had never regularly attended any church. In all about six hundred people professed salvation during the Palmers' weeks of ministry on Wight.[45]

Poole on the Dorset coast was the scene of the Palmers' next labors. Here they faced a crisis in their ministry. The services had opened on Sunday night; on Monday morning they received an anonymous note informing them that the man who served as circuit steward and Sunday school superintendent also ran the town's biggest liquor establishment. Finding that the information was correct, they felt that this was a sin far worse than Achan's (Josh. 7) which would certainly prevent God from blessing their meetings. Thus they begged leave from the Wesleyan circuit superintendent to finish the week of meetings and quietly slip away, rather than to labor under these impossible circumstances. The superintendent was unwilling for the Palmers to go, but he was also unwilling to discipline the chapel's leading layman. No decision was made, and as the week went on, Phoebe's conviction grew that if they did not here take a stand against "the great god Bacchus" God would withdraw his blessing from all their efforts. Previously they had spoken against alcohol despite the stony response from lay-people and ministers, but they had never before taken an uncompromising position.[46] Now Phoebe felt compelled to force the issue, and so she refused to hold any more services until the evil was put away from Israel. The circuit superintendent bowed to her pressure and called on the liquor dealer. Either he must renounce his sin or resign his membership. The man unwisely chose to enjoy the pleasures of sin for a season and resigned from the society. Walter and Phoebe Palmer resumed their revival meetings, and that evening they reported "twenty souls were born into the Kingdom." From that night on, the work began to prosper.[47]

While they were holding meetings every evening in Poole, some Anglican friends invited them to come to Swanage to speak one afternoon. Dr. and Mrs. Palmer took the ferry across the harbor, and then dined at the rectory before the afternoon meeting. The church was being repaired, so the meeting was held in the rectory barn, which had been remodeled for divine service. All the ministers from the various denominations in the town were present, and the congregation was so large that many had to remain outside and listen through the open doors and windows. Dr. Palmer spoke about the baptism of the Spirit from the second chapter of Acts, and then Mrs. Palmer exhorted the gathering. No record of the number of conversions exists for that particular meeting, but during the three weeks the Palmers spent in and around Poole during September three hundred people became "joyful witnesses of God's saving mercy."[48]

Following Wesley's maxim "that we are not only to go to those who want us, but to those who *need* us MOST," the Palmers turned down invitations from several larger and more influential circuits to go to Stroud, a town of six thousand people thirty miles northwest of Bristol. There in two weeks 250 individuals claimed pardon or purity.[49] From Stroud they crossed the country to Norfolk to hold meetings in King's Lynn. There three hundred people professed salvation in two weeks.[50]

Exhausted by the labors of the last few months and battling severe colds, Walter and Phoebe went back east to Royal Leamington Spa in Warwick, where they took the waters. After a week of rest, they began to preach in the Wesleyan chapel on November 14. Late one night the Palmers held a special service for a group of people who rarely came to church. The church women prepared a midnight supper, and the town's prostitutes were invited to the meal. A number came, and as she ate with these women Phoebe wondered, "Who maketh thee to differ?" (1 Cor. 4:7). Phoebe talked to them "tenderly as sisters," and was encouraged to see some of them rising from the table with the promise to forsake their old ways through the power of God, and to seek Christ as Savior. Besides these women, three hundred individuals claimed conversion during the Palmers' three weeks of ministry in Royal Leamington Spa. After the Palmers left, the Anglican vicar invited all converts who did not plan to unite with the Wesleyans to join a prayer band that he was organizing. About fifty responded. When the churches held a dinner for the new converts, three hundred came. The usual price for such a meal was one shilling, but this one was free. The sponsors paid for the evening by selling pictures of Walter and Phoebe Palmer. They made enough to cover the cost of the dinner and even made a small profit.[51]

The Palmers closed the year's labors abruptly at Banbury in Oxfordshire. Imitating the early Methodists, they held prayer meetings between five and seven o'clock each morning, along with one at noon. The meetings were going well. Beginning December 2, more than five hundred persons sought Christ during the first eleven days. One night, however, an intoxicated man came to the altar. Try as she might, Phoebe could not persuade him to renounce his evil habit. As she counseled with the man, Satan seemed to resist her efforts, arguing that it was unfair to belabor this poor man about drink, when so many British Methodists drank liquor every day. So depressed was Phoebe at this thought that she almost was unable to close the meeting. She spent a sleepless night and got up ill in the morning. By evening her mood had changed, and she felt great power as she exhorted the crowded chapel. She gave the invitation, but instead of people rushing to the altar, no one came. There was a long, embarrassing period before even one person came forward for prayer. Phoebe sensed that the Lord had departed, saying, "Neither will I be with you any more, except ye destroy the accursed from among you" (Josh. 7:12). After another sleepless night, Phoebe spoke to the issue at the next midday prayer meeting. She asserted that the revival had ended and that they would see no more of the Lord's power until they purified themselves by renouncing all involvement with alcohol. Many church leaders who drank heard this message, along with one of the town brewers, who served on the official board of the chapel, led a class, and superintended the Sunday school. The society did not heed Phoebe's words: Only a few took the temperance pledge, and no disciplinary action was taken against the brewer. Thus, the Palmers departed, fearing that Christ's little ones might be offended by the example of the leaders and that the blood of the unsaved would be upon those leaders' hands (Matt. 18:6; Ezek. 3:18).[52]

Around Christmas the Palmers left Banbury for Oxford, where they were the guests of the Reverend and Mrs. Rowley. Mrs. Rowley was the daughter of Adam Clarke, the great Methodist commentator. A visit to Oxford meant a visit to the landmarks of Wesley, and so a pilgrimage to Lincoln College was one of the first items on the agenda. While they were not permitted to go inside Wesley's rooms, they could stand in the courtyard and gaze at the windows. As Phoebe stood there looking up, she contemplated the mighty work of God which had its start behind those mullions. Less an object of adoration than Wesley's windows was the bishop's throne in the Oxford cathedral. Samuel Wilberforce was the incumbent, and his days of defending the Scripture against the assaults of the liberals were yet to come. All Mrs. Palmer knew of him was that he had permitted the cathedral to be decked out with popish furnishings. She stood amazed that so close to the very spot where "the martyr-spirits, Cranmer, Ridley, and Latimer ascended to heaven amid burning fagots" that the "degenerate son of the venerated philanthropist, Wilberforce," aided by Dr. Pusey, should be leading Oxford back to Rome.[53]

1861: "I AM CONTENT TO OCCUPY A SMALL SPACE IF GOD BE GLORIFIED"

On New Year's Eve the Palmers began twelve days of services at nearby Maidenhead in Berkshire. Perhaps because the response was small, Mrs. Palmer reports no numbers from those meetings. As she and Walter traveled down the Thames, Windsor was their next stop. Once again the royal family was in residence, and once again they received Mrs. Palmer's disapproval. This time the object of her criticism was their luxury. Upon seeing Prince Albert's hunting pack, she commented that it cost more each year to feed one of the royal hounds than "to preserve in good condition many a half-famished child who seldom gets a piece of meat from one month's end to another."[54]

Walter and Phoebe Palmer found much opposition in "Wicked Windsor." The Anglicans were decidedly high-church; one of their clergymen warned the poor that if they visited the Methodist chapel their public assistance would be cut off. The minister at the Independent chapel spoke against the Palmers' meetings. To make matters worse, the Wesleyans usually could muster only thirty hearers for Sunday preaching, and most of those were servants in other people's homes. Because most of the Wesleyans were domestics, they had little time to promote the revival as the Methodists had done in other places the Palmers had visited.

Phoebe Palmer believed it was always God's will for the church to be triumphant and thought that when it was not, there must be sin in the camp. Seeing the low state of evangelical religion in Windsor, she concluded something must be wrong. Day and night she asked the Lord to reveal the hidden sin that crippled his power. That prayer was answered on the first Sunday afternoon as Phoebe walked around at the rear of the chapel and discovered a hidden basement. "I do wonder what is in that basement," she said to her hostess, as she "lingered gazing at the suspicious premises." Her friend replied, "Oh, never mind what is in that basement! it is time we were hastening homeward." This guilty response reminded Phoebe of the poem,

> There's a spirit below, and a spirit above,—
> The spirit of hate, and the spirit of love;

> The spirit above is the spirit divine;
> The spirit below is the spirit of wine.

Because she did not know for sure that liquor was being stored in the basement, Phoebe let the matter drop, but the next evening all became clear. The congregation was unusually large because many people had come from London on the evening train. On the same train were several hogsheads of liquor which were to be stored in the chapel. The congregation got to the chapel first because the drayman had to unload the barrels from the train and put them on his wagon. Evidently he sampled some of his cargo, because he arrived at the chapel in no state to do careful work. As Phoebe was speaking about the Lord to the congregation above, there suddenly came from the basement a loud crash which seemed to shake the foundations of the building. Instead of rolling the hogsheads quietly into the cellar, the drayman was letting them drop to the floor from above. The presiding minister hastened out to investigate, and Mrs. Palmer announced his embarrassed report to the assembled throng. She then called for the desecration to be removed. It came out that the decision to store the liquor had not been made by the people now responsible for the chapel, and early the next morning the minister took the first steps to cleanse the temple. From that time on the revival went forward, and some two hundred people professed to be saved or sanctified. Mrs. Palmer wrote that the victory at Windsor alone was well worth the trip across the Atlantic.[55]

After getting the better of Bacchus, Phoebe Palmer once again reproved the queen for breaking the Sabbath. Among the converts from the revival meetings were some musicians in the queen's band. They were required to perform each day at dinner and on Sundays as well. It was the queen's custom to make an appearance on the castle grounds on Sunday to hear the band play. Many weekend revelers took the train out from London to see their sovereign, hear the band, and enjoy the country around Windsor. Some of the newly saved musicians came to Mrs. Palmer for advice. What should they do since they were "required to break the Lord's Day by ministering to the gratification of those thus profaning the Sabbath, and this by the command of their sovereign?" Mrs. Palmer does not record what advice she gave the musicians, but she does report that she wrote to Queen Victoria, pointing out her responsibility before God to set a good example for her people. Surprisingly, the queen's secretary sent Mrs.

Palmer a "respectful" note indicating that the letter had been received. As for the bandsmen, they were saved from a cruel dilemma by the illness of the royal mother, the Duchess of Kent. Under the solemn circumstances they were not required to perform and were soon transferred to London where the bishop forbade such Sabbath activities.[56]

After Windsor, the Palmers made a quick trip back to Poole. Their stand against alcohol had so encouraged the local "friends of temperance" that they were building a temperance hall and wished to have the Palmers help them lay the cornerstone. This trip also gave Walter and Phoebe the chance to inspect the renovated Wesleyan chapel, which after the Palmers' meetings was enlarged to seat an additional three hundred people. On the way back to Lancashire they paused at Bristol and rode out to Ashley Down to see George Müller at his orphanage.[57] Birmingham was next, with a visit to the grave of Hester Ann Rogers. Then they passed through Manchester on their way to Rochdale, eleven miles to the northwest. The train from Manchester was buffeted by gale winds which threatened to rip the cars from their tracks. Never had Phoebe seen such a storm.[58]

Perhaps the storm which opposed their travel to Rochdale presaged the storm which was rising to oppose their travels generally. This storm, however, would not blow in nature, but among the Wesleyans alienated by the Palmers' uncompromising stand against alcohol. While at Rochdale Phoebe first noticed some efforts to close Wesleyan chapels against their ministry. These efforts were not at first successful, but a cloud the size of a man's hand had appeared on the horizon.[59]

The gathering storm did not hinder the Palmers' labors in Rochdale. In five weeks of ministry 374 people claimed to be converted, and 167 others professed entire sanctification. Of the almost four hundred new converts, three hundred presented themselves to the Wesleyan society as trial members.[60] Next the Palmers crossed the country to arrive in Great Grimsby on the North Sea coast at the mouth of the Humber. During the last two weeks of March they held revival services in which four hundred individuals sought salvation or sanctification.[61]

While they were in Grimsby, a delegation came from Boston to request the Palmers to labor there next. They declined this opportunity in the flourishing city to go to the obscure town of Loughborough in Leicester but promised to return to Boston soon. In Loughborough they ministered from April 7 to April 21 and helped between two and three hundred people seek "pardon or purity." May found them in Macclesfield. Here they visited the birthplace of Hester Ann Rogers and the grave of Nancy Cutler. As a result of the Palmers' meetings, 321 persons professed conversion, and 85, sanctification. Moving north, they visited Bradford, where Phoebe's father had heard John Wesley preach. As May ended, the Palmers began their ministry in Epworth.[62]

As the birthplace of the Wesleys, Epworth held a special attraction for the Palmers. During the day they visited the church, graveyard, and rectory, as well as reviewed all the references to Epworth in Wesley's *Journal*. In the evenings they held special meetings, but these were less successful than in other places. Besides drawing sinners to Christ, the circuit trustees who had invited them hoped that the Palmers would draw the saints to an "organ-tea." This meal, at which the Palmers spoke, was held to raise funds for building a new organ. Everyone present had to pay to get in, so naturally those with little sympathy for the church stayed away. Even though it was only one meeting, Phoebe felt that the pecuniary aspect of their visit drew the people's attention away from the work God wanted to do. As was usual when the response was disappointing, she reported no statistics from their week of meetings, saying only, "We saw a few souls saved."[63]

Keeping their promise to return to the east of England, the Palmers traveled to Boston in June. There they held meetings for three weeks which saw some three hundred people confess Christ as Savior. Next they turned north, going to Darlington in Durham. In a month there, 370 persons professed justification. August found them at Barnard Castle. So popular were their meetings that special trains had to be scheduled to bring into town all the people who wanted to get to the revival services. In thirty days, 303 adults claimed conversion, along with about 40 children.[64]

At Berwick-upon-Tweed during the first two weeks of September, the Palmers found only twenty-seven members in the Wesleyan society. Yet so many people from the town came to the revival services that the Exchange Building was rented for the meetings. Some evenings fifteen hundred were present, and one evening between two and three hundred stayed after the preaching for special prayer. Unfortunately, no exact records were kept during these meetings, probably because they became so large they outstripped the organizational resources of the tiny local Wesleyan society.

Once again many of the seekers were church or chapel goers

who felt no assurance of the Spirit that they were born of God. The Palmers' witness that one could know that one was a child of God met a ready response in many hearts. The meetings undoubtedly would have gone on beyond the two weeks, but the chronic cold which had hampered Walter for the last few months suddenly worsened, causing him to retire from the field of battle. Retreating to Edinburgh, the Palmers sought seclusion and rest for the doctor. While Dr. Palmer was mending, however, Mrs. Palmer was holding various ladies' meetings among the Presbyterians during the day and speaking to different groups every night.[65]

Although Dr. Palmer had not made a full recovery, he and Phoebe went down to Liverpool, intending to hold meetings there as soon as his health would allow. He was still not well by October 5, but so urgently did the Palmers and their hosts feel the need to continue the work that Mrs. Palmer and a local pastor began a series of meetings without him. When Walter grew stronger he resumed his role of leader in the revival meetings. The Palmers' services went on with great success despite the Trent Affair, which enraged much of Britain against the Union.[66] Phoebe, too, saw things from the British perspective and wrote home amazed that Lincoln had not apologized sooner. Walter and Phoebe remained in Liverpool until the end of the year, and 1,125 adults professed to have been born again due to their labors. After the Palmers left, the revival continued, adding 900 more to the total.[67]

1862: GOD MOVES IN A MYSTERIOUS WAY

South Wales was the first scheduled stop for the Palmers in the new year, but on the way down from Liverpool the train stopped in Shrewsbury just fifteen miles from Madely.[68] Not knowing when they would have another chance to visit the place where John and Mary Bosanquet Fletcher labored, Dr. and Mrs. Palmer decided to interrupt their journey for a brief visit to the village. They had previously written to the Wesleyan superintendent of the Madely circuit, saying that they might call on him, but when they arrived they found that he lived in an out-of-the-way place. Because they had already visited the Fletchers' church, rectory, and gravesite, they were tempted to forego the call and spend the night in an inn near the railway station. As they considered this plan, Phoebe thought, "Did [I] not pray for divine direction when [I] wrote . . . ?" and wondered if they changed their plans, would their yea be yea (Matt. 5:37)?

In obedience to Phoebe's scrupulous conscience, she and Dr. Palmer traveled out to the superintendent's home. There they learned that many had been praying that they would hold services in Madely; their host urged them to remain. Evidently the arrangements with their Welsh friends were flexible, so after receiving their permission, the Palmers consented to lead some revival meetings in Madely. The Anglican rector from the village enthusiastically supported the services. He knew Mrs. Palmer from her books, having read *The Way of Holiness, Faith and Its Effects,* and *Promise of the Father.*[69]

After one week of meetings in Madely, the Palmers moved a mile to Madely Woods where they held services for another week. Then they went to tiny Dawley for the last week of revival meetings. The response to these three weeks of services was the best the Palmers had seen in England. The meetings were packed, and people came to them from all around. Some even made the trip over from Birmingham, and Banbury, seventy miles away. The secretaries recorded the names of 895 converts during the three weeks the Palmers were there, but they admitted that they could not get all the names of the people who crowded the altar. After the Palmers left, the revival spread to nearby towns. As a result, the societies in the Madely circuit of the Wesleyan connexion received 900 new members, and the adjoining circuit of Wellington received 400. Uncounted others recommitted themselves to the Established Church, especially in those areas where the rectors led revival meetings.[70]

After spending three unscheduled weeks in Madely, the Palmers resumed their journey to Wales. They were going there in response to the repeated invitations of the Reverend E. Russell. When the Palmers would decline his invitation, pleading a previous commitment, he would simply invite them for another date. After several such exchanges, Mrs. Palmer at last sent him her final answer, "repeating in the most emphatic manner our utter inability to come." The Palmers felt it was time to return to America and wanted no further commitments. Refusing to acknowledge that this was her ultimatum, Russell once again wrote back and pled that the Welsh believers had faith that they would come: "And now, if you do not come, what will become of our faith?" Part of Phoebe said that she must be true to her own sense of the Spirit's leading and not answerable to the impressions of others, but the other part of her feared to trifle with the faith of a fellow disciple. In the end she gave way to his plea and fit the trip to Wales into the schedule. This trip provided the opportunity to stop in Madely. The victories won in that campaign, as well as those the Lord was to win in Wales later, convinced her that the Welsh believers' faith had been of God.[71]

From February to June the Palmers ministered in the towns and villages of Wales. They had good results in Bridgend, Cowbridge, and Cardiff. By April 15 they had seen over one thousand people seek Christ. Then they went to Merthyr Tyvdil. After speaking to fifteen hundred people a night in the crowded Charles Street Wesleyan Chapel in Cardiff, speaking to the forty members of the Wesleyan society in Merthyr was a real discouragement. Besides being few, the people of the village were resistant. So poor was the response that both Walter and Phoebe had to make a conscious effort to believe that God had led them there.

The circumstances told them they had made a mistake in leaving responsive Cardiff and coming to resistant Merthyr, but this conclusion was inadmissible. For them to be in the wrong place meant either that the Lord had withheld his guidance or that they had not followed his leading. Their doctrine of the faithfulness of God made the first conclusion impossible, and their doctrine of the sanctification of the believer made the second conclusion unthinkable. Because God is faithful, he will guide the believer who asks for his direction. Because the believer is sanctified, that believer will do God's will as long as all is on the altar. Because the Palmers had not willfully removed anything from the altar, they must be doing God's will and following his leading. Therefore they were in the right place in Merthyr.[72]

With their confidence renewed, the Palmers pressed on in Merthyr. They preached holiness night after night until the leaders of the society were convinced that they needed it and that God would supply it. After the preachers and class leaders bowed at the altar seeking purity, sinners began to come there for pardon. In the two weeks Walter and Phoebe spent in the village, 32 were listed as sanctified and 194 gave their names to the secretaries as those who were converted.[73]

In leaving Merthyr for Abergavenny the Palmers chose to go to a situation even less promising than the one which they had just left. So bitter were the feelings among the fifty Wesleyans in the town that the society had not held a love feast for more than a year. If ever a place needed a revival, this was it. As usual Walter and Phoebe began by preaching to believers about the necessity and possibility of present holiness. Perfect love for God brought holy love for his people; under conviction from the Lord, the members began to settle their differences. When the believers began to act like Christians, the nonbelievers began to be interested in the gospel. After sixteen nights of the Palmers' preaching, 250 professed conversion. From Abergavenny the Palmers journeyed to Baina and Aberdare where more than 232 people claimed justifying grace.[74]

After the work in Wales the Palmers sailed to the Isle of Man for a few days of rest. Their host suggested that they hold some services on the island. He thought that if the meetings were held in a nondenominational building, they would reach more people than if they were held in a church, so he rented a hall at his own expense. The Palmers held a week of meetings and were about to leave to preach in Ireland when they were presented with a petition signed by two hundred people asking them to remain. They delayed their departure for three days to hold more meetings. During the whole of their brief visit, "sinners have been awakened, backsliders reclaimed, mourners comforted, believers justified [sic], and doubting and struggling souls sanctified."[75]

The Wesleyans were holding an American-style camp meeting in Enniskillen, Ireland, from July 3 to July 17. About five thousand people came to the services; Walter and Phoebe Palmer joined them halfway through the meetings. Also arriving at about the same time was the circus. As the workers began to pitch tents near the revival tent, Phoebe remarked, "The Adversary is now going to make an effort to revive his work, and the servants of sin are pitching their tents." Despite this frontal assault, God's work went on, and very few went to the circus performances. By the next day the circus tents were gone.[76]

Before the Palmers arrived at the camp meeting, there were no secretaries to take the names of those who came forward for prayer. Phoebe thought this a dangerous practice: the various local societies would not be able to follow up the seekers and conserve the gains made, and people who were not at the camp would not be able to see the real magnitude of the work the Lord was doing in the meetings. After the secretaries were appointed, they reported that in the second half of the camp meeting five hundred people professed either to be saved or sanctified.[77]

After the close of the camp meeting, the Palmers held services in Portadown. There was a good response, but Phoebe lamented that no one kept records of the people's names. Next they moved to Londonderry where they planned to hold a week of meetings.

Here Mrs. Palmer became seriously ill and had to be taken back to England for medical care suited to Dr. Palmer's standards. Despite this medical care she grew rapidly worse and flickered between life and death for several days. As she faced death her only regret was that she might be removed from the field of labor when there still seemed to be so much for her to do. She lay dangerously sick with congestive fever for three weeks but then gradually began to gain strength. As she improved, Dr. Palmer moved her to the suburbs of London where she could continue to recuperate in the home of a friend during October and November.[78]

Back in July, while the Palmers were ministering in Ireland, the Wesleyan Annual Conference voted to prohibit its societies from sponsoring meetings led by people who were not part of the Wesleyan connexion. The Palmers were an obvious target of this legislation, but so were the native evangelists Richard Weaver and William Booth. Weaver was stirring up trouble with his attacks on religious formalism, and Booth's challenging preaching could lead to emotional excess. The Palmers had made enemies by their strong stand against alcohol and formalism. In addition, some objected to their ideas about entire sanctification. In taking its action, the conference recalled the trouble which Americans James Caughey and Lorenzo Dow had caused in the past. It decided to kill four birds with one stone by banning all revivalists who were not Wesleyans. Soon after this decision, the Primitive Methodist Conference took a similar action.[79]

By December Mrs. Palmer's health had improved enough to allow her to return to the revival circuit. She and the doctor traveled to Leeds in Yorkshire. They visited James Sigston, biographer of William Bramwell, whose work had greatly influenced Mrs. Palmer. Then they visited Bramwell's grave and called on his daughter. Next they toured Cross Hall where Mary Bosanquet and Sarah Ryan had once run a school and orphanage.[80]

The Palmers found Leeds a stronghold of Methodism. No less than twenty-two chapels were there, built by the various Methodist denominations. Although the Wesleyan and the Primitive chapels were closed to the Palmers, the United Free-Church Methodists and the New-Connexion Methodists welcomed them. In this friendly environment, Mrs. Palmer was strong enough to hold three meetings every day, and in the first few days 170 adults testified to having received saving or sanctifying grace. The meetings were crowded and were so well received that after two weeks of labor in one of the city's chapels, another invited the

Palmers to come there for eight days. Mrs. Palmer wrote glowingly of their success in Leeds but reported no figures other than the preliminary total of 170.[81]

From Leeds the Palmers moved west to Runcorn in Cheshire. During the last week of December, one hundred individuals claimed to be born again and many others to be sanctified. The Palmers would have continued in Runcorn, but they had promised to return to Liverpool as soon as Richmond Hall, where they had held meetings, became vacant. The hall was open during the first part of January, so the Palmers returned to the city.[82]

Sometime during 1862 Mrs. Palmer published another book. It was a biography (more properly, a thanatography) entitled, *Sweet Mary; or, A Bride Made Ready for her Lord*. It told of the death of a woman who had been converted under Mrs. Palmer's ministry in England. The concern of the book is entirely with Mary's spiritual life; such unimportant details as her last name or where or when she lived are not included. What are included are the letters Mary wrote to Mrs. Palmer for spiritual guidance. While only letters from Mary were printed, and none of Mrs. Palmer's replies, each of Mary's letters repeats so much of Phoebe's response to the previous one that the series explicates much of Phoebe Palmer's theology of the Christian life. Evidently this work was successful, because it went through at least five English editions and was also published in America.[83]

1863: "SHAKING THE DUST OFF OUR FEET, WE WILL GO TO THE GENTILES"

In mid-January the Palmers began a campaign of the Midlands which lasted twelve weeks. They held services in Walsall, Wolverhampton, and Birmingham, as well as in some other locations, before returning to Liverpool in April. In most of these places the ban of the Wesleyans and Primitives did not hamper their effectiveness. While the conference could order its superintendents to keep the Palmers out of Wesleyan chapels, it could do nothing to keep the Wesleyans out of the Palmers' meetings. Nor could it keep Wesleyan preachers from working alongside the Americans.[84] Upon her return to Liverpool, Phoebe totaled up the numbers from their three months of work: 1,327 people professed to have been saved, and 273 claimed entire sanctification.[85]

Two weeks after Mrs. Palmer reported the results of their

crusade, the Palmers were preaching in Manchester. They divided their stay of five weeks in April and May between three chapels and saw five hundred people listed as having been saved and one hundred sanctified. They spent June in Nottingham where 510 persons claimed pardon and 130 claimed purity. By July they were in Southport on the Irish Sea. Nightly the altar was surrounded, but no secretary was appointed, so Mrs. Palmer could not report the number of people helped. Once again they went to Enniskillen for an Irish camp meeting in August. One Sunday a hundred people testified to being blessed with pardon or purity. In September they worked at Lough in Lincolnshire for three weeks, but Mrs. Palmer did not include any statistics in her report of their visit.[86]

Mrs. Palmer's health once again began to fail, so she and Walter decided to bring their British labors to a close. They returned to Manchester in October to await a steamer back to New York. While they waited they spent a few evenings at the Independent chapel and there led fifty or sixty people to a deeper knowledge of God. Even on board ship their work continued. One man, a class leader among the Primitive Methodists, died at sea. Mrs. Palmer repeatedly visited his widow to console her. During one of these visits she found that the man had died with all their money in his pocket, and someone had stolen the money from his dead body. Because his widow had no money to travel the two hundred miles overland to her relative's home at the end of the voyage, Mrs. Palmer took a collection for the woman. Having thus been useful wherever they went, the Palmers arrived back in New York on October 19, 1863.[87]

CHAPTER FOUR:

The Guide to Holiness and More Camp Meetings: 1864–74

Within two hours of the time Walter and Phoebe Palmer crossed the threshold of their home on October 19, 1863, a delegation arrived to ask them to hold revival services in the Allen Street Church. The Palmers consented and thus began the itinerant ministry to which they would devote the next eleven years of their lives. Walter did not resume his medical practice which he had given up to make the trip to England, but devoted himself entirely to ministry. Phoebe no longer had children to care for and had given up her offices in humanitarian organizations. She had relied on Sarah Lankford to lead the Tuesday Meetings while she was in Britain, and she knew she could continue to rely on her sister to fill in for her when necessary; thus Phoebe also felt free to go whenever and wherever the Lord led.[1] Income from the sale of Mrs. Palmer's publications made the Palmers financially independent, so they could go where they thought they were needed most. They never received a fee for their services and did not mention Mrs. Palmer's writings in the meetings. Sometimes they even returned the money they were given for traveling expenses.[2]

In addition to traveling to various revival services and camp meetings, the Palmers also furthered the cause of holiness by writing and publishing. During these last eleven years of her life, Mrs. Palmer wrote or helped to write seven books. Besides writing books, upon her return from Britain she assumed the editorship of the *Guide to Holiness* and helped that magazine grow to national influence.

THE *GUIDE TO HOLINESS*

The Palmers Buy the *Guide to Holiness*

Mrs. Palmer's association with the *Guide to Holiness* went back to its inception in 1839. Its founder, Timothy Merritt, was then the associate editor of the *New York Christian Advocate and Journal*. He and Mrs. Lankford were returning from a love feast at the Mulberry Street Methodist Episcopal Church to the Lankford-Palmer home where he was a guest. Merritt wondered aloud if it would be valuable to have a publication to print the kind of testimonies of entire sanctification which they had heard that evening to give them a wider circulation. When he and Sarah Lankford reached the house, they discussed the idea with Phoebe Palmer. She encouraged Merritt to pursue the idea and promised to write for the magazine.[3] Over the years Phoebe continued to write for the *Guide*, working with several different editors. Her early articles often used personal experience to illustrate doctrinal truths. As she began to speak in revival services and camp meetings, the *Guide* carried reports of her work, usually in the form of letters. Sometimes these letters were written to the magazine's editors, and other times they were to Sarah Lankford, who passed them on for publication.

In 1857 the *Guide to Holiness* did a feature article on Mrs. Palmer. Later the same year and into 1858 it gave publicity to her involvement in the ongoing revival. When the Palmers went to Britain it reported their results from time to time during the first two years, and then in 1862 and 1863 carried a report from the Palmers in almost every issue.

By the time the Palmers returned from abroad, the *Guide to Holiness* had established itself as a noteworthy magazine. In the early 1850s its circulation was between three and five thousand. This figure towers above the few hundreds on the lists of many religious periodicals and compares favorably with the probably inflated average circulation of 7,400 reported for all American magazines.[4] The revival of 1857 and 1858 gave a great lift to the popularity of the *Guide*. In the wake of Phoebe Palmer's revival meetings, its circulation rose to more than twelve thousand. Ontario, the scene of Mrs. Palmer's most successful labors, led all other regions in the number of subscribers, with New York a close second and Massachusetts a distant third.[5] One should not suppose, however, that the *Guide* was read only where the Palmers had preached. The subscription list also contained the names of nearly five hundred readers in Mississippi and thirty-one in the far-off Hawaiian Isles.[6] By 1860 four thousand additional subscribers had been added to the list, bringing the total to sixteen thousand.[7]

The coming of the Civil War hurt the *Guide to Holiness* just as it hurt all magazines. Those five hundred subscribers in Mississippi could no longer get their magazine, any more than could any other Southern reader. Interest in the war between the states eclipsed interest in the war between the spirits; and the winds of war were "blowing paper higher than a kite—to wit, more than a hundred per cent above its usual price."[8] Under these conditions, by 1863 the *Guide* lost at least three thousand subscribers from its circulation list and even more from its list of subscribers who were not in arrears paying for their subscriptions.[9]

Thus when Walter and Phoebe Palmer returned from Britain, they found a strong magazine, but one that had recently fallen on hard times. The Palmers decided to buy the *Guide to Holiness* and to install Mrs. Palmer as managing editor, with help from her son-in-law Dr. Foster as assistant editor. The Fosters then gave up the pastoral ministry and moved to Brooklyn where Elon could give his attention full time to the publishing business.[10] The Palmers also bought *Beauty of Holiness and Sabbath Miscellany*, which was being published in Cincinnati by their friends the Reverend and Mrs. A. M. French, merging the two magazines so there would be no rivalry between these leading holiness publications. The Palmers paid $13,000 for the *Guide*, one dollar for every name on the subscription list. This was a generous price, because at the time, less than seven thousand of the people on that list had paid for their subscriptions. Although the price of paper continued to rise after the war to a level three times that in 1860, the Palmers increased the price of the *Guide* only twenty-five cents, so that in 1864 it cost one dollar a year. As a cost-cutting measure, they reduced the size of the magazine 25 percent, from thirty-two pages to twenty-four.[11]

For the *Guide to Holiness* merely to have survived during the postwar period was a significant achievement. Hundreds of periodicals were launched in those days, and hundreds failed. The average life of a magazine was four years. In this difficult climate, Mrs. Palmer's *Guide* not only survived, but it also more than doubled its circulation, reaching a peak of 37,000 in 1870 and sustaining that number through 1873. In addition to subscribers in the United States and Canada, the *Guide* claimed readers in England, Africa, India, and Australia.[12]

This circulation made the *Guide to Holiness* one of the major magazines of its day. If it were not exactly in the same league with *Godey's Lady's Book*, whose circulation in 1865 was 100,000, still the *Guide* probably had a larger circulation than 90 percent of all the magazines published in the United States. It very likely was one of the top 10 of the 400 religious periodicals. None of the religious reviews ran much beyond 10,000 copies; by 1870 the circulation of the *Guide* exceeded that of the *Ladies' Repository* and equaled that of the *New York Christian Advocate and Journal*, the self-proclaimed "most widely circulated Methodist weekly Journal in the world."[13]

The last year of Mrs. Palmer's life saw the influence of the *Guide to Holiness* decline. Other holiness papers were founded, and these siphoned off subscribers. In their travels the Palmers found people who were surprised to hear that the *Guide* was still in business. These people had been told that it had been suspended or merged with another periodical. After Mrs. Palmer's death, her husband Walter assumed all the editorial responsibilities. When he married Sarah Lankford, she joined him as editor of the *Guide* and carried on the work with George Hughes after Walter's death. The magazine was sold in 1901 to the Pepper Publishing Company in Philadelphia, which installed Clarence B. Strouse as editor. They published four issues under the title *The Consecrated Life and Guide to Holiness* and then discontinued the periodical.[14]

Other Publications

After returning from Britain the Palmers published an account of their labors called *Four Years in the Old World*. This work consisted mainly of the letters Mrs. Palmer had written to her family while she was away. Besides reporting the places and results of their labors, Mrs. Palmer also included many stories of people who were converted in the meetings. In addition to these spiritual elements, there were long sections, usually in the first letter from a new location, giving her impressions of the scenery and of British life. Mrs. Palmer thought the British countryside beautiful but disliked the dirt of the smoky cities. With a few notable exceptions, she found the Established Church and its ministers corrupt. With no exceptions, she found the British aristocracy effete and sunk in sinful luxury. Queen Victoria and Prince Albert won her faint praise as upright rulers but did not impress her as examples of "experimental piety."[15]

The unstated purpose of *Four Years in the Old World* seemed to be to vindicate Mrs. Palmer's theories about revival. It told how the Palmers conducted revival services and how the Lord blessed their ministry. It also showed how, even after the Palmers left an area, others who followed their methods continued to experience success. Its clear message was, "If you want to experience a revival as the Palmers did, use the same methods as the Palmers did." Very likely many people wanted to have a revival like the one the Palmers had, for by 1872 eighteen thousand people bought copies of the book.[16]

The Palmers published another work in 1866. Walter was listed as the author, but both he and Phoebe worked together on the book. Called *Life and Letters of Leonidas L. Hamline, D.D., Late One of the Bishops of the Methodist Episcopal Church*, it celebrates their close friend who died in 1865. The work is an edifying volume in the tradition of Eusebius, publishing page after page of original sources with a minimum of editorial interference or discernment. The work reveals Hamline as an ardent proponent of entire sanctification and an intimate companion of the Palmers. Besides being a fitting tribute to a friend who had labored hard for the gospel, this work was helpful in promoting scriptural holiness. Spreading the knowledge of the achievements of this episcopal champion of sanctification would strike a blow for the "old Methodist doctrine," and the reflected glory of the departed bishop would brighten Mrs. Palmer's image. The Palmer publishing company did not publish this book, so we do not know how popular it was. There is, however, no evidence that it went through more than one edition.[17]

In 1867 Mrs. Palmer wrote an introduction and an appendix to *Sanctification Practical* by J. Boynton. In these she restates her ideas of how one may attain holiness. The next year, 1868, saw the publication of *Pioneer Experiences; or, The Gift of Power Received by Faith*. In this work Mrs. Palmer presented the testimonies of many individuals who were sanctified by following the method she prescribed. Not all of them were sanctified under her ministry, but they all were examples of the truth of her teaching. Mrs. Palmer published two new books in 1869. The first was a synopsis of her teaching about sanctification and of her rules for living a victorious Christian life. As they left an area after holding services, the Palmers distributed *The Parting Gift to Fellow Laborers and Young Converts* to help the converts continue to walk with Christ and promote the work of revival. The second work published in 1869 was a condensation of *Promise of the Father*, called *The Tongue of Fire on the Daughters of the Lord*. *Promise of the Father* had not sold as well as had most of Mrs. Palmer's books, so she evidently hoped that making its main points available in a smaller and cheaper format would promote its message.[18]

Phoebe Palmer's final work, *Mother's Gift*, was published posthumously. It was a collection of poems written over the course of her lifetime. While not quite as awful as the sixteen-stress verse written by James Thurber's Ohio Methodist great-aunt Lou, its chief value today is to reveal what Mrs. Palmer thought about various topics which she mentions only briefly in her other writings. Her interest in colonization is explicated by her poems, as is her interest in temperance and foreign missions. The subject, however, about which she writes more than any other in the poems is death. Many of her poems are designed to console those who have lost loved ones. Sometimes she writes about heaven, and other times she presents the idea that the dead in Christ become angels and minister to those who remain alive.[19]

MORE CAMP MEETINGS

In the years between 1863 and 1869 the Palmers ministered in some of the locations they had visited in the forties and fifties, but they also extended their travels into the West. The nation's rail network was expanding, enabling the Palmers to take the message of full salvation farther and farther away from home. Beginning in their home church on Allen Street in October, the Palmers then journeyed to Troy, New York, where they finished the old year and began the new. In the spring of 1864 they were on their way home from meetings in Lawrence, Massachusetts, and had a brief layover in Boston. They agreed to hold two meetings during the day at Tremont Temple before they took ship for New York that evening. The two meetings were so well attended that Walter and Phoebe consented to delay their departure for twenty-four hours. The delay of one day soon became two, and then three, and so on until the Palmers had concluded ten days of meetings. Members from all of the Evangelical denominations in Boston participated in the meetings: Phoebe reported that people said Boston had not seen such a visitation of the Spirit for years. Other labors in New England, New York, and Canada, along with a series of meetings in far-off Iowa, filled the rest of the year.[20]

During August of 1864, Phoebe Palmer spoke at a camp

meeting in Sing Sing, New York. There Martha Inskip, wife of the rising young Methodist pastor, John Inskip, received the blessing of entire sanctification, which she had been seeking for some time. Her husband was not entirely pleased with his wife's actions. Earlier that year Mrs. Inskip had attended the Tuesday Meeting. Going to the Palmers' made her late for a dinner she and John had planned to attend. When she eventually arrived, everyone wanted to know where she had been. She was reluctant to tell them, but they pressed her to know. She then admitted she had been at the Tuesday Meeting. They all looked amazed and exclaimed, "*You* have been to Dr. Palmer's meeting!" "Yes," she replied defensively, "and I say to you that they have something there that I have not, and I mean to have it, by the blessing of God."[21]

John Inskip was even more "afflicted and mortified" when his wife professed sanctification, but as the days went by, his feeling changed to admiration. Nine days after her profession, at the close of his morning sermon, he called his people to join him at the altar to receive perfect love. He then began attending the Tuesday Meeting at the Palmers' himself and asked them to come lead revival meetings in his church. Inskip later became a leader in the National Camp Meeting Association for the Promotion of Holiness, and he and Martha followed the Palmers' example, traveling together to promote the cause.[22]

The Palmers spent most of 1865 preparing *Four Years in the Old World* and the *Life and Letters* of Bishop Hamline for publication, so they were limited to a few camp meetings in Canada that summer. After they published both books in 1866 they resumed the familiar revival trail in New York, New England, and Canada, but they broke new ground with a trip to Chicago. They held meetings on the way out to Chicago and on the way back to New York. At one of these meetings near Jackson, Michigan, they met Asa Mahan and discussed his forthcoming book on the baptism of the Holy Spirit, which they were to publish. Before traveling on to Chicago, they went back east to Ann Arbor where they spoke in a camp meeting and spent the night with their old friends Dr. and Mrs. Gilbert Haven. Dr. Haven was the president of the University of Michigan, where he spread scriptural Christianity through his weekly sermons in the university chapel.[23]

The Palmers' meetings in the Chicago area were attended by a young school teacher, Frances Willard. Miss Willard had become a friend of Melinda Hamline, widow of the Methodist bishop, who talked and prayed with her about holiness. In addition, she gave

Frances several books on entire sanctification and some issues of the *Guide to Holiness*. When Mrs. Hamline's close friend Phoebe Palmer came to town, Frances was sure to be in the meeting. After Mrs. Palmer spoke, Frances Willard knelt at the altar to reconsecrate herself to God. She wanted to confess important sins like "a speculative mind, a hasty temper, a too ready tongue, and a purpose to become a celebrated person," but was humiliated to find that her modest jewelry "came up to me as the separating cause between my spirit and my Saviour." Yielding to Christ even in this trivial matter, she felt a great peace and joy come into her soul. She intuitively knew the will of God in even daily matters and flew to do it. As time went on, however, others discouraged her profession of holiness, and as she later admitted, "I kept still until I had nothing in particular to keep still about." Frances Willard went on to become president of the Women's Christian Temperance Union and a leading crusader for women's rights, but as she confessed in 1887, "that sweet pervasiveness, that heaven in the soul, of which I came to know in Mrs. Palmer's meeting, I do not feel."[24]

The year 1867 featured a trip down the Mississippi River from St. Louis to New Orleans between January and March. On the way down, Mrs. Palmer wondered if the Lord might want them to hold some revival meetings in the South. The Southern Methodists did not respond as Phoebe had hoped they would. Perhaps they regarded her as a Yankee carpetbagger and did not even come to hear her speak, or perhaps they were repelled after the first hearing. It would be no surprise that the South did not welcome her if she even hinted publicly what she had written privately about the recent war. To Mrs. Hamline she had explained her views on the cause of the conflict:

> The want of perfect love caused their disasters. So we think. I have always thought that the separation of the M.E.C., North and South, was the entering wedge, and in part through political intrigue, preparatory to a bolder step—the separation of the States. What a pity that the ministers of the church South do not see their error. But though they mourn their desolations, I fear that they are not yet sufficiently humble to learn the lessons that infinite wisdom would teach.[25]

If Mrs. Palmer tried to enforce the need for Southern sanctification by telling Southern Methodists that its lack was the cause of the war and their defeat, the wonder is not that they did not pack her meetings but that they did not lynch her. Even if she kept her thoughts about the war to herself, her condescending attitude must have angered them.

In New Orleans the Palmers met Dr. and Mrs. Newman, missionaries from the Northern Methodist Church. With them they visited a biblical institute for blacks and rejoiced to hear the former slaves testify to their "twofold liberty." Later in the week the Palmers went to a black church. Here Dr. Palmer spoke to the fifteen hundred people in the congregation about heaven. He reminded his listeners that God is no respecter of persons and that the Lord will seat his servants at his throne and will reign with them there forever and ever. To Mrs. Palmer the most impressive thing about the black congregation was its giving. The congregation had already built the large sanctuary and now was engaged in building a school. Instead of having ushers pass plates, the whole assembly lined up to bring its gifts to the front. Phoebe was thrilled as she saw these former slaves

> come with hearts divinely stirred, and spirits made nobly willing, and give of their earnings—probably all beyond their actual needs,—not only for church-expenses, but, as they are eager to learn, for building schoolhouses. . . .

She felt this display of generosity showed maturity and responsibility, and asked, "Who will, in the presence of such facts, dare to repeat that such a people cannot take care of themselves?"[26]

Among whites, the Palmers did not have such a good reception as they had had among the blacks. True, in Natchez, Mississippi, the Southern Methodist minister had told the Palmers he wished his people were more spiritual, but evidently he did not press his suit strongly enough for the Palmers to interrupt their schedule and hold a few days of meetings. In Baton Rouge some members of the Southern church entertained them cordially, but they did not urge the Palmers to remain and lead revival services as had happened so often in the North and in England. In New Orleans itself the Palmers worked in the Northern church for a week, but only "some of the more devoted" members of the Southern church attended.[27]

The summer of 1867 was filled with the usual camp meetings in the North. Near the end of the year the Palmers held ten days of services in Washington, D.C. Nine months earlier they had been in Cincinnati. There Mrs. Palmer had called on the mother and sister of General Grant. These Methodist women urged Phoebe to hold meetings in the nation's capital and assured her that the general undoubtedly would attend. Unfortunately for Grant and for the rest of the country, which would suffer under his corrupt administration, the general escaped capture by the Lord at the hands of Phoebe Palmer.[28]

In 1868 and 1869 the Palmers continued to hold revival services throughout the northern United States and Canada. In the latter year alone, Mrs. Palmer recorded more than twelve thousand miles of travel to promote holiness.[29] They generally had good success but found it difficult to labor in regions tainted with Free Methodism. From Utica, New York, Mrs. Palmer wrote that it was difficult to preach holiness because the presiding elder in the district thought it synonymous with Free Methodism. From Illinois she wrote that the Free Methodists had done the cause of holiness much harm by their "factious and schismatic proceedings."[30] It is ironic that Mrs. Palmer should feel her ministry so greatly hampered by the Free Methodists in upstate New York and in Illinois. Back in 1849 at a camp meeting she held in upstate New York, B. T. Roberts, the leader of the eastern Free Methodists, professed entire sanctification. In Illinois the Free Methodists were led by J. W. Redfield, who, like Roberts, claimed sanctification at one of Phoebe Palmer's camp meetings.[31] Thus two of the people who made the most trouble for her had been brought to Christian perfection as a result of her ministry!

In 1870 Walter and Phoebe Palmer added a missionary trip to California to their regular itinerary. In between the thousands of miles of travel Mrs. Palmer had to find time to move to a new house. This was the second time they had moved in the last six years. Although the house at 54 Rivington Street had been expanded in an attempt to hold all those who wished to attend the Tuesday Meeting, it had proved inadequate. In 1865 the Palmers had moved to 23 St. Mark's Place, near what is now Thompkins Square, giving their old house free of charge to a pastor friend to use for the ministry. Mrs. Palmer was reluctant to move again. She had a "rooted aversion to change," and she also feared that a move to a nicer location would smack of the conspicuous consumption which was beginning to typify the Gilded Age. She was persuaded to move, however, as more and more immigrant Germans moved into her neighborhood, bringing their beer gardens with them. The area was fast becoming one in which it was unfit for a woman of piety to live. At last she consented and moved to 316 East Fifteenth Street, right across from Stuyvesant Park, where St. Mary's

Church is located today. Twenty ministers attended the dedication of the house, and Phoebe wrote a hymn to celebrate the occasion.[32]

The last four years of Mrs. Palmer's life, 1871–74, continued to be filled with travel to promote the doctrine of entire sanctification. She was limited to seven camp meetings in 1872 because she contracted Bright's disease, or nephritis.[33] From the day her condition was diagnosed, Mrs. Palmer knew her time was limited. Rarely did a day pass without pain or even prostration, but the next year she held a month of meetings in Toronto, along with leading services in thirteen other locations.[34] Besides her speaking, she felt a special burden to publish an autobiography which would show how God had led her through life.[35]

In the midst of her busy travel schedule and her writing responsibilities, Mrs. Palmer had to keep up with her correspondence and be available to visitors who called on her. She recorded in her diary for March 1 of this year that she "mailed nearly a dozen letters to-day" and reported her frustration that "the demands of my correspondents are far beyond my ability to meet, either in time or physical endurance." She was likewise frustrated by the demands of visitors. Feeling she had an obligation to speak to anyone who called on her, she would drop what she was doing to attend to them: "I seem to have done so little to-day, while a pressure of things demanding attention has been turned aside, by callers requiring my attention in the parlor," she wrote in her diary on September 12.[36]

During the final years of her life Phoebe Palmer saw a fluctuation of interest in holiness which stood in marked contrast to the continued rising tide she had experienced between 1857 and 1863. As early as 1864 one minister reported that her labors in Troy, New York, had been ineffective. "Lectures, skating parties, minstrels, glass-blowers, and dancing parties have the inside track," he wrote. "The age does not incline to the severe religion of . . . John Wesley."[37] In 1869 Mrs. Palmer wrote that there seemed to be less interest in holiness in eastern Canada than there had been in 1857, and in 1873 she criticized the officials who ran the Sing Sing camp meeting for not promoting sanctification vigorously enough. They had scheduled only one holiness meeting a day and had put it in a side tent away from the main tabernacle.[38] Another sign of declining interest was Phoebe Palmer's defense of the camp meeting. In 1865 and again in 1873 she editorialized in the *Guide* against those who said camp meetings were ineffective or that they were not worth the sacrifice of time and money they required.[39]

Despite these discouraging trends, Phoebe Palmer also saw causes for rejoicing. Chief among them was that with proper preaching the interest in holiness could be revived. A postscript to Phoebe Palmer's letter about the Canadian lack of interest in holiness states that "a remarkable revival of holiness has succeeded the time referred to."[40] Another encouraging sign was the establishment and success of the National Camp Meeting for the Promotion of Holiness, announced in the pages of the *Guide to Holiness* in June of 1867 and chronicled therein through special supplements.[41]

Whether the interest in holiness was waxing or waning, Phoebe Palmer kept busy promoting the cause. From January through August of 1874, the last year of her life, she traveled to speak in revival services or camp meetings in Canada, New York, Connecticut, Ohio, and Illinois. She and Walter also made a trip to Florida for some much-needed rest in a healthier climate.[42] They returned from all their travels to New York in August, 1874, knowing that Phoebe was dying. Breathing became difficult and she could no longer write. Her sleep was broken, she suffered a heart attack, and then became blind. The blindness was a special trial to her because it made her feel so lonely. On September 8 she felt death was near, so she called all her family to her bedside. Husband, children, grandchildren, sisters, and brothers all gathered around her. Like Jacob, she blessed each of them, and admonished each individual to follow the Lord.[43]

After this farewell she lingered eight more weeks. Her pain increased, making her fear she would not bear the trial bravely: "Do remember," she said, "if I should say or do anything that is not just right; it is not myself, it is only the effect of the disease." Despite this fear, she bore the suffering nobly, not even deigning to groan. Instead, when the pain was greatest, she would cry out, "Alleluia, Alleluia, Alleluia! Precious Jesus, Precious Jesus," and "Thy will is best; Thy will, not mine, be done." Conscious that the ability of the Christian to endure suffering and to face death calmly was thought to be strong evidence for the truth of Christianity, she testified:

> I want to say that my teachings have been correct, and I am now testing them in this hour of extreme suffering, and find that I am fully saved; not a shadow of a doubt. The altar is a beautiful type; it is a Scriptural figure, and I am resting upon it. And the altar, which is Christ, sanctifies the gift. The blood of Christ cleanses me from all unrighteousness. Glory, Glory![44]

Mrs. Palmer died in her husband's arms at 2:30 Monday afternoon, November 2, 1874. Sixteen months after her death, Walter married Phoebe's sister Sarah Lankford, who had been a widow for three years. They lived together for seven years, and then he died in 1883. Sarah Lankford Palmer continued the work of the Tuesday Meeting and the *Guide to Holiness* into the 1890s and died the day after her ninetieth birthday, April 24, 1896.[45]

CHAPTER FIVE:
Phoebe Palmer As Theologian

Phoebe Palmer never thought of herself as a theologian. She did not like "theology": to her it signified a complex, man-made substitute for God's simple truth. Theology was the province of the profound, of the adept, of those who wrote imposing books of argumentation which proved unapproachable by the masses. Theology kept people from understanding God's Word:

> I was, for years, hindered in spiritual progress by theological hair-splittings and technicalities, and it was not until I resolved to let all these things alone, and take the simple, naked word of God, . . . that the steady light of truth beamed upon my heart.[1]

Mrs. Palmer loved to picture herself as a simple believer in contrast to the erudite theologians. She said, "It has been my aim to avoid most carefully every thing like a display of theological technicalities. . . . I have aimed to follow the simple Bible mode of teaching."[2] She did not waste her time in abstruse or futile discussions, but simply obeyed Christ by witnessing to the truth:

> We have never felt it [our] duty to sermonize in any way, by dividing and sub-dividing with metaphysical hair-splittings in theology. We have nothing to do more than Mary, when by the command of the Head of the Church, she proclaimed a risen Jesus to her brethren—[John 20:17–18].[3]

Despite these disclaimers, Phoebe Palmer was a theologian. If her narrow range of theological interest disqualifies her from being considered a systematic theologian like Calvin, an occasional theologian like Luther, or even a "folk" theologian like Wesley, still she was a popular teacher of biblical truth, whose various ideas may be fitted into a consistent pattern.[4] That pattern may not qualify as academic theology, but Mrs. Palmer and thousands of her followers found it adequate to explain their faith.

Phoebe Palmer and her hearers assumed the cardinal doctrines of orthodox Christianity, so she rarely discussed the classical issues in systematics. She never specifically addressed such important areas as theology proper, christology, or anthropology, because her interests lay in other areas. Like John Wesley, Phoebe made the Christian life her main subject of theological concern. Thus her interests lay in the doctrines of entire sanctification, ecclesiology, spirituality, and eschatology. This treatment of her theology will focus on those areas, but will begin with an account of her theological method.

THEOLOGICAL METHOD

Mrs. Palmer never published an analysis of how she arrived at theological formulations, but scattered through her writings are many comments about the various ways to discover God's truth. From these occasional remarks, one may induce the method of her theology. Not surprisingly for one who was a Methodist from birth, her method turns out to be the Wesleyan quadrilateral of Scripture, reason, experience, and tradition.

Scripture

Phoebe Palmer's theology began with the Bible. As an eleven-year-old child, she had written a poem claiming God's guidance through his word;[5] she returned to this theme in the introduction to her first book. There she asserted that "the BIBLE was the all-commanding chart by which the propriety of each successive step [in her spiritual journey] was determined."[6]

Authority

Phoebe could trust the Bible as her chart through life because it was the authoritative word of God. The foundational tenet of her theology was that when the Bible speaks, God speaks. She said that human language failed to express how deeply she was convinced that "the Bible is the living voice of the living God."[7] Mrs. Palmer believed that "the Bible was as much the WORD OF GOD as though she could hear him speaking in tones of loudest thunder every moment, or as though she could see it written in a sign arching the heavens."[8]

Phoebe was fond of repeating, "The voice of the Scriptures is the voice of the Holy Ghost."[9] Actually, Mrs. Palmer thought the voice of the Holy Spirit in the Scriptures was even more reliable than a heavenly voice. She pointed out that Peter heard the heavenly voice at the Transfiguration, and yet called the Scripture "the more *sure word of prophecy*" (2 Peter 1:17–19, her italics).[10] To her, the word of God in its inscripturated form was as valid as if "the Word were again made flesh and dwelt among us" (John 1:14).[11] Every word in the Bible was given at the "express dictation of the Holy Spirit," and thus the Scripture was "the One Infallible standard" to which believers must subject "our own and all human opinions."[12]

Perspicuity

Not only did Mrs. Palmer assert the authority of the inerrant Word of God, she also taught its perspicuity. "Everything in religion is exceedingly simple," she once wrote to an inquirer. She went on to admonish him that he was confused because "You have been looking too high. You have overlooked the simplicity of the way."[13] Religious matters were essentially simple; only when one turned from God's Word to man's theology did confusion result. She wrote to another correspondent that he was perplexed because he had been studying theology instead of reading the Bible: "I fear that my dear Christian friend has been hindered, in his Christian course, by an undue attention to technicalities in theology. The Bible is a wonderfully simple book."[14] Because the Bible is a simple book, it is easy to understand. No one need "wade through . . . many theological works" to find its meaning. Anyone who really wants to understand the Bible need only to resolve to obey it, and then its teachings will become clear: "All its doctrines are easy to be understood to those who, with humility and decision, resolve on obedience to its precepts."[15]

Phoebe was convinced that William Carvosso was one who resolved to obey the Scripture, and she used his example to make her point. He was a plain, simple man who had no time for the "fine-spun webs" of theological discussion. While all the well-meaning theologues were weaving fabrics for the nicer sort of people, Carvosso went to the naked Word and there learned truths so powerful that hundreds were converted through his ministry.[16]

Hermeneutic

Mrs. Palmer's method of understanding the Bible grows out of her doctrine of inspiration. Because the Holy Spirit is the author of Scripture, he is also its interpreter: "The same Spirit that indited the Holy Scripture is given to open its meaning to the humble believer."[17] Mrs. Palmer says that when she is puzzled by something she has read in the Bible, she takes "the naked, unadorned word upon my knees in the presence of God" and asks the Holy Spirit for "direct and special illumination" about its meaning. Then she checks her impression of the Holy Spirit's response by consulting "every available human resource," such as works by various commentators, examining the context of the passage in question, and finally comparing Scripture with Scripture. She has confidence that by using this method the most humble believer, with the Holy Spirit for a teacher, may skillfully wield the sword of the Spirit, and "make [a] way through every conceivable difficulty."[18]

The key to receiving the help of the Spirit in understanding the Scripture is the willingness to obey its teaching. Phoebe Palmer's fundamental hermeneutic principle is John 7:17, "If any man will do his will, he shall know of the doctrine."[19] This verse epitomizes her teaching on hermeneutics because it explains her idea and exemplifies its weakness. Her idea is that the Holy Spirit will make the meaning of the Scripture clear to any believer who is willing to obey it. God is not interested in having the believer speculate about his truth; he is interested in having the believer live that truth. Thus Phoebe taught that the debating hall was worthless as a place to understand God's Word. Only in the prayer closet does one learn the mind of God:

> I keenly feel the absurdity of speculation on hallowed subjects, by those who rejoice alone in the victory of opinion. The closet is the place, and deep, long continued communion with God [is] the source for the solving of all difficulties.[20]

Mrs. Palmer felt that her hermeneutical principle applied especially to the doctrine of entire sanctification. She believed that the doctrine was so little understood because the Scriptures teaching it were so little obeyed. In answer to the question, "How is it that so many good people differ on a theme so momentous?" she replied:

"If any man will do his will, he shall know of the doctrine, whether it be of God" [John 7:17]. Was there ever any one, either of the ministry or laity, who resolved to know of the doctrine of holiness *experimentally,* and brought it to God's *time,* NOW, but has proved the faithfulness of God, and [has been sanctified entirely]?[21]

Phoebe Palmer asserted that all differences of opinion about sanctification arise because some people want to speculate about it instead of experiencing it. She urged her readers, "Enter into the bonds of an everlasting covenant to *live* in the entire devotion of all your powers.... [Then]," she promised, "you will immediately find what you thought to be the mystery of faith simplified."[22]

She once drove home her point by telling the story of a man who did not know whether or not he was wholly sanctified. Phoebe told him he should be sure about so momentous a question and challenged the man not to. sleep until he knew that he was sanctified. He replied that he was afraid to make such a pledge because he might never be sure of his state. She responded that he should trust God's promise to sanctify the believer and to assure him that the work had been done. The man realized he had never really believed that promise before. He confessed his unbelief, and, at Phoebe's urging, "made the venture" to trust God to sanctify him that instant. In that moment he was "save[d] to the uttermost" and found clear assurance that "the blood of Jesus cleanseth from all sin." Mrs. Palmer concluded the story by pointing to its lesson: "How soon was he saved from his doctrinal perplexities on resolving that he would not rest until he experimentally *knew* the doctrine!"[23]

Phoebe Palmer's hermeneutic stands firmly in the mainstream of Christian tradition. She taught that the Holy Spirit will reveal the meaning of the Scripture even to the simplest believer who wishes to understand the Bible in order to obey it. That believer will ask God for understanding, read each Scripture in its context, test all insights by the analogy of Scripture, and make use of every available human aid to understanding. In laying down these rules for interpreting the Bible, she was restating the common wisdom of the church, written down as early as Augustine's *On Christian Doctrine.*[24]

Like Augustine, however, Mrs. Palmer sometimes goes astray when she forgets the rules she has laid down. The most common violation is to forget the context of the Scripture, and thus to apply it in situations very different from the one to which it was originally addressed. When Phoebe Palmer forgets to consider the context, she often falls into the fallacy of equivocation, judging two situations analogous merely because the same word may describe them. For example, when she uses Psalm 81:10, ". . . open thy mouth wide, and I will fill it," to encourage those who do not know what to say in a testimony meeting to begin to speak anyway, she is misled by equivocation. The context reveals that the psalmist means that God will fill the people's mouths with food, but Mrs. Palmer thinks that the Lord will fill the people's mouths with words.[25] Her favorite hermeneutical text, John 7:17, is another example of the weakness of Phoebe Palmer's interpretation of Scripture. Once again Mrs. Palmer errs in her understanding of Scripture when she neglects the context. In this text Jesus is arguing with his opponents about the origin of his teaching. He says that if anyone really wants to do God's will, that one will realize that his "doctrine," that is, the content of his teaching, comes from God, and not merely from himself. Phoebe picks out the word "doctrine" and applies it not to the whole of Jesus' teachings, but to one specific element of Christian theology, usually the "doctrine" of entire sanctification. Jesus tells his opponents that those who choose to do God's will can recognize the divine origin and authority of his message; Phoebe uses his words to argue that all who are completely surrendered to the Lord will agree on Christian doctrine, especially the doctrine of entire sanctification. Her argument is an unwarranted application of the Lord's words, caused by inattention to the context and a misunderstanding of the equivocal word "doctrine."

Reason

Although Phoebe Palmer did not always practice her own hermeneutical rules perfectly, the existence of those rules revealed her faith in reason as a means of discovering theological truth. The proper way to learn how to think and act was first to ask the Holy Spirit to teach through the Scripture, and then to use rational hermeneutical rules to interpret that Scripture. Only the Bible, reasonably interpreted, could be trusted to confirm or deny one's impressions of the Holy Spirit's leading. Nothing which was absurd or unreasonable could be part of God's truth, so people should use their common sense when trying to determine the Bible's meaning: "There are no . . . inconsistencies in the Bible, and sensible people are not required to go beyond their senses and believe there are."[26] God is not unreasonable, so he never contradicts himself or commands people to do what is impossible.[27] Because God is reasonable, and because he is the source of the believer's mind, Christians may trust their regenerated intellects:

> I saw that the God of nature, as the giver of every good gift, had given me judgment, the power to perceive, through a sanctified medium, whatsoever things were pure and lovely. That grace did not take away my power to reason, but turned it into a more refined, *sanctified* channel, and then required the full use of a renovated intellect.[28]

Experience

Discovering theological truth by examining one's own spiritual experiences and learning from those of others was the third part of Phoebe Palmer's theological method. She revealed her own convictions about the value of experience in a paragraph she and Walter wrote about Bishop Hamline: "Lastly, Mr. H[amline] was convinced that to know anything satisfactory of religion we must *experience it*. To speculate upon it is like laboring to ascertain the flavor of a fruit without tasting it."[29] She taught that the things that people learn from experience are "more deeply written on the heart than what is learned by mere precept."[30] Phoebe wrote books relating her own spiritual experience and edited a volume that collected the experiences of others because "[theological] difficulties, in many minds, may be met by observing how other minds, similarly constituted, were helped out of difficulties."[31]

Even more than her comments about the value of experience, or the books she published about it, the existence of the Tuesday Meeting for the Promotion of Holiness shows the value Phoebe Palmer placed on experience as a teacher of theological truth. After singing, prayer, and some brief introductory remarks, the meeting was opened for anyone there to relate her or his spiritual experience. Sometimes seekers told of their uncompleted search for holiness and requested those present to pray for them. At other times, the sanctified would explain how they had received the blessing and tell about the difference it made in their lives. Often the simple testimony of one who found full salvation would cut through the clouds of perplexity that surrounded others. Mrs. Palmer related the story of "a teacher in Israel of some celebrity, . . . a professor in a neighboring literary institution" who was sanctified after listening to the testimony of a timid wife of a minister. "Never," he said, "did I see the simplicity of the way to be saved from all sin, as by hearing the simple testimony of Mrs. _____."[32] Besides holding the Tuesday Meeting in her home, Mrs. Palmer was careful to promote "social meetings" for the relation of experience whenever she held revival meetings. She also devoted a section of the *Guide to Holiness* each month to publishing the testimonies given at the Tuesday Meeting in an effort to widen their influence.[33]

While her practice of holding social meetings and publishing books of testimonies shows that Mrs. Palmer thought that experience was a powerful way to discover theological truth, her explicit teaching warns of its dangers. If experience were not tested against the standard of the Bible, it could lead to false conclusions. Mrs. Palmer blamed much of her early confusion about her spiritual state on "the fault of taking the feelings and experience of others as a standard for my own, in place of going to the word of the Lord."[34] Especially when she heard others speak of their assurance of pardon or of their reception of sanctification, she was convinced that they had been given some "luminous" revelation that "constrained [them] *irresistibly* to believe." Because she had received no such revelation, she became uncertain and depressed about her spiritual state.[35] Only when Phoebe resolved to disregard her feelings and to take the Bible as her authority, did she begin to make progress in her spiritual life.[36] She thus concluded that God was "persuasively directing her mind away from the uncertain traditions and example of the fallible creature, to the only INFALLIBLE STANDARD—the ONE STANDARD of the only wise God," that is, the Bible.[37] She was fond of repeating that the Bible must be the Christian's authority and not the experiences of fallible men.[38]

The irony of Mrs. Palmer's position about experience is that experience taught her that Scripture is superior to experience. She seems to be trapped in the logical *cul de sac* of arguing on the basis of experience that experience may not always be valid. Like reasoning to the conclusion that we may not trust reason, this way of thinking leads to absurdity. Phoebe Palmer's position, however, is not absurd. True, experience did lead her to Scripture, but her reliance on Scripture was not dependent on her experience. When Phoebe learned that she could not depend on experience, she turned to the Scripture for her authority. Convinced of its divine origin, she accepted its truth as the axiom of her existence and began to rebuild the structure of her faith on this foundation. It was as if she had been following a greenhorn guide through some unknown territory. The guide often misled her, and finally they both became hopelessly lost. The guide then admitted that the task was too difficult for him and pulled a map from his pocket. "You can't always trust me," he confessed, "but you can trust this map." Phoebe was not so foolish to trust the map on the word of the unreliable guide, but when she saw for herself the signature of the chief surveyor on it, she decided to follow its directions.

Mrs. Palmer was careful to subordinate experience to Scripture and reason because of the ill effect their inversion had had on her own life and also because of a new doctrine that arose among some of her followers. She had taught the traditional Wesleyan doctrine of two distinct "works of grace": justification and sanctification. Some of her followers, however, claimed to have experienced another work of grace beyond sanctification.[39] In its quietistic form, taught by Thomas Upham, this doctrine holds that this "third work of grace" annihilates the human will and produces a holy indifference in which the heart is free from all personal desires and passions: "We have no pleasure of our own; we have no desires of our own; we have no will of our own."[40] Temptation therefore loses all its appeal, and only the will of God has any attraction for the Christian in this state. The heart of the perfected one will harbor no desire that does not come from God. Thus Satan can no longer subtly seduce the one who had gone beyond sanctification by placing unholy longings in the heart. Instead, he "must come boldly up and make his attack face to face, as he did in the temptation of the blessed Savior." And Satan may expect similar results, Upham implies.[41]

Mrs. Palmer learned of Upham's ideas from an article he wrote entitled "Divine Guidance." She disagreed vigorously with his idea of the death of the will. She reported that reading the article pained her heart and made her head ache so severely that she took several sittings to finish the reading. Evidently she had not known of Upham's views until she read this article in the spring of 1851, but the concept of a work beyond sanctification which annihilates the human will appeared in both his earlier books on holiness.[42]

The antinomian form of this doctrine, taught by some unnamed disciples of Phoebe Palmer, began with Upham's assertion that every desire in the perfected Christian's heart comes from God. They went on to argue that sin is impossible because the believer is united with God. If sin is no longer possible, ordinary spiritual discipline is no longer necessary. Because every desire comes from God, anything that attracts the believer is right. Thus the believer is free to do anything she or he desires. If such a Christian feels an attraction for an action which breaks one of the Ten Commandments, that believer could take the desired action, confident that God is leading into "sin" for his own greater glory and that he actually approves of the deed.[43]

Mrs. Palmer pronounced her anathema on both forms of the further-work-of-grace doctrine. In response to Upham's published views, she wrote the professor and his wife a personal letter, gently pointing out the errors she thought he had made. The gravamen was that he had gone beyond Scripture in speaking about the death of the will. She inquired, "Now, where does the Bible speak of 'the *death* of the will'?"[44] Scripture gives no instance of one who experienced this level of spirituality; even Jesus himself had a human will which was never dead, but always "in subjection to the will of His Father." Mrs. Palmer knew that one of Upham's sources for the doctrine of the death of the will was the writings of the Roman Catholic mystics, such as Madame Guyon and Archbishop Fenelon.[45] She argued that the experience of these writers is suspect, because of their neglect of the Bible. Those who look to the mystics, instead of to the Bible, for guidance "have missed the mark," she said. She was equally suspicious about private revelations from God as another source of this new doctrine: "The Holy Spirit never takes us *beyond* the written Word." Citing the traditional proof text for the closing of the canon, Revelation 22:18, "If any man shall *add* unto these things, God shall add unto him the plagues written in this book," she argued that the Holy Spirit no longer gives authoritative revelations. Because Satan can transform himself into an angel of light (2 Cor. 11:14), one must test every experience against the standard of Scripture. "How exceedingly dangerous," she warned, "not to bring every new phase in experience to the law and the testimony." Besides all this, Phoebe was most concerned that Upham's quietistic form of the third blessing would lead others to accept the doctrine in its antinomian form.[46]

Professor Upham does not appear to have been totally convinced by Mrs. Palmer's arguments. A later edition of his work on Madame Guyon carries unchanged the provocative statement that every desire of a perfected person comes from God.[47] Whether Upham was unable or unwilling to change the text of this treatment of the annihilation of the will in this book, he evidently modified his ideas about temptation. A few years after Phoebe Palmer wrote to him opposing his views on the death of the will, she cited his opinion against those who taught the third-work doctrine in its antinomian form.

Some of those who had been led into the second work of grace under Mrs. Palmer's ministry later returned and attempted to lead her on to the next step. When these erstwhile disciples claimed they were free from Satan's touch, she quoted Upham: *"He now assaults thee, by not assaulting thee,* and knows that he shall conquer when *thou fallest asleep."*[48] Her argument against these misguided followers was the same one she used against Upham's ideas, but now she stated it more forcefully and publicly. The further-work teachers held that they did not need stated seasons of prayer, instruction from human teachers, or reminders of ordinary Christian duties, because their spirits were entirely one with God. In reply, Phoebe pointed to the biblical injunctions about prayer, instruction, and obedience, urging her opponents to test themselves by Scripture. They taught that one who relies on the Bible is still in a lower state and cannot appreciate the "holy liberty which the Spirit gives to those who are made free indeed." Mrs. Palmer answered this argument with the reminder that Satan transforms himself into an angel of light and so Christians must test the spirits (1 John 4:1) to see if they come from God. Her would-be teachers inquired whether she would be willing to sin if God required it. She responded, "No! no! no! . . . God never wanted any one to sin," and pronounced this a "doctrine of devils." She concluded that all of the Holy Spirit's teachings are found in the Bible and that every article of belief needs explicit scriptural foundation:

> For anyone to imagine, that the Holy Spirit will lead him into a state, beyond where the teachings of the WORD may be specially needful, or lead him into a state or a belief, for which an explicit "thus saith the Lord," may not be given is erroneous. And wherever such a device has obtained, whether among ministry or laity, we fearlessly, in the name of the Lord, pronounce it a device of Satan.[49]

Here is an apparent contradiction of Phoebe Palmer's theology of experience. On the one hand her practice shows that she valued experience, but on the other hand her teaching warns against being misled by experience, especially in the matters of sanctification and works beyond it. What then made the difference between a good experience and a bad experience? When may one trust an experience and when must one ignore it? Why do some experiences strangely warm the heart and others strongly ache the head?

The difference between good and bad experience for Phoebe Palmer is not the difference between the rational and the nonrational, nor is it between the ordinary and the mystical. If an experience had a precedent in Scripture, and if its content did not contradict the Bible's teaching, she might accept it as a valid message from God. For example, she was sure that God spoke with his children through dreams and visions, and such communications were an important part of her spiritual life.[50] As a thirteen-year-old she had a dream that assured her of God's love, and other significant dreams and visions continued to occur at critical junctures throughout her adult life.[51] Dreams and visions, however, must not be taken at face value. Because Satan may speak through these means, every communication must be tested by the Bible: "To the law and to the testimony: if they speak not according to this word, it is because there is no light in them" (Isa. 8:20).[52] If the content of the dream or vision reinforced some biblical truth, the dream came from God; if it contradicted the Scriptures, it came from Satan. When the message did not directly relate to the Bible, the task of discernment was more difficult. "Some dreams are manifestly foolish" and may be disregarded, but others should be considered in the light of their circumstances.[53]

Sometimes the circumstances led Phoebe to trust her dreams. Near the end of Mrs. Palmer's life a friend wrote her about a dream announcing Jesus' imminent return. Phoebe had been too busy to give much attention to eschatology, so she prayed that if her friend's dream were correct, the Lord would confirm the message. Shortly after that prayer Mrs. Palmer had a dream herself in which she saw the Lord return. Because the dream followed the prayer so quickly, Phoebe concluded that she should trust its message.[54] At other times the circumstances led her to dismiss her dreams. In 1838 Phoebe had a dream that informed her that she would die soon. The next day she was faced with a decision about the long-term future, so she asked the Lord to let her know if the dream had been correct. If she were to die soon, she wanted the Lord to deepen the impression the dream had made. If not, then let the Lord take the impression away, she prayed. From that moment the dream began to seem unreal, and Phoebe concluded from this circumstance that the dream's message was not correct.[55]

Phoebe Palmer considered her spiritual impressions a valuable source of divine guidance. She urged her readers to give "the most minute attention to impressions," and gave examples of how the Spirit had guided by this means.[56] Especially if they were repeated should one obey them.[57] Like dreams and visions, however, impressions could be misleading. The believer should test them by the Scriptures, and if still not sure whether they came from God, should go to some experienced Christian for help in understanding what they mean.[58]

Tradition

Because she read about dreams, visions, and impressions in the Bible, Mrs. Palmer could accept these mystical experiences as valid communications from God. But her reaction to Upham and to those who would have led her into a further work of grace showed she was suspicious of most other kinds of mysticism. There were, however, five other experiences of extrabiblical mysticism which she seemed to accept without question. The first was the sense of close approach and even union with God which she felt on "the day of days."[59] A second nonbiblical mystical experience was a dream in which she had died and was being judged.[60] Another was the "near communion and distinctness of perception of the persons of the Trinity" which she recorded in her diary on September 9, 1838.[61] The fourth was going to heaven in a vision and seeing the mansion that was prepared for her, and the fifth was the regular communion with her mother through dreams which she experienced for years after Mrs. Worrall's death.[62]

This was the woman who taught: "Think no experience desirable, however luminous, [except] as you may have a 'Thus saith the Lord' for it," yet she publicized these five spiritual experiences for which she had no scriptural precedent.[63] How could she accept and publicize these extrabiblical experiences? Why could she believe the Lord had given her these experiences, when she disbelieved that he could have performed a further work of grace?

For some reason she did not mistrust these experiences as she did the experiences of those who claimed the further work of grace. Mrs. Palmer never recognized this seeming inconsistency in her theology, so she never explained why she was prepared to accept some extrabiblical experiences while rejecting others. Although Mrs. Palmer never answered this question, she left enough data for the historian to construct a solution. The reason is not that she trusted her own experiences and mistrusted those of others. As her response to her dreams shows, she was prepared to reject her personal experience as counterfeit. The key to her acceptance of these mystical experiences is rather to be found in Mrs. Palmer's early reading. Four of the five extrabiblical experiences Mrs. Palmer reported are recorded in the journals of the early Methodist women that Phoebe Palmer knew so well; evidently their spirituality became a model for her own.

Some of the early leaders of Methodism had kept diaries in which they recorded the events of their spiritual lives. Beginning with Wesley's *Journals*, many of these works were published in the eighteenth and early nineteenth centuries. Three women were especially prominent among these diarists. They were Lady Maxwell, Mary Bosanquet Fletcher, and Hester Ann Rogers. Phoebe Palmer was familiar with the biographies of all three women.[64] Each made outstanding contributions to the Methodist movement, and each had a mystical strain.

Hester Rogers may have been the least mystical of the three, but still she recorded a dream of her judgment day. Mrs. Palmer also dreamed about her judgment day, but it would be stretching the evidence to claim a causal connection between the two women's dreams. The historian may be on firmer ground to suggest that Mrs. Rogers' devotional practice influenced the spirituality of Phoebe Palmer. Both Phoebe and her sister Sarah had been helped toward sanctification by following Hester Rogers' example of reckoning themselves dead to sin; it may be that Phoebe copied Hester's piety as well. Mrs. Rogers read the Bible on her knees and followed the schedule of reading the Old Testament in the morning, the Gospels at noon, and the Acts or Epistles at night. She also was careful to commemorate the anniversary of the day of her sanctification. Because this is exactly the practice Phoebe Palmer followed, one wonders if she did it in imitation of Hester Rogers.[65]

The experience of Mary Bosanquet Fletcher probably also encouraged Phoebe Palmer to be less distrustful of mysticism. She believed that the dead in Christ were still concerned with the "dear fellow pilgrims they have left behind" and that these departed saints come to the aid of believers still left on earth. In addition, she recorded in her journal how God communicated with her through a dream and a vision.[66]

Lady Maxwell probably influenced Phoebe Palmer's mysticism more than any other person. She once reported "a conscious union with [God]," recorded the ability to distinguish the approach of the three separate persons of the Trinity, and claimed to be often "on the borders of immortality, holding converse with its heavenly inhabitants."[67]

If it is true that Mrs. Palmer accepted certain extrabiblical mystical experiences because she had read about them in the lives of the early Methodist female saints, then this fact reveals the fourth locus of authority in her theological method. This fourth means of discovering theological truth may be called "tradition," if one remembers that it refers mainly to the experience and usages of the people called Methodists.

Phoebe Palmer never mentions tradition as a source for her theology. In fact, all of her concern is to point people to the Bible and away from merely human authority. In one letter she explicitly tells one reader not to trust even Mr. Wesley's theology but to go directly to the Scripture for herself.[68] Despite this oft-spoken insistence on the authority of Scripture alone, her reliance on Methodist tradition is shown by her acceptance of traditional Methodist mystical experiences.

Thus we have seen that Phoebe Palmer had an equivocal doctrine of experience as a part of her theological method. Where experience had biblical precedent, she accepted its authority. When she could not find an experience in the Bible, she denied its legitimacy. She denied its legitimacy, that is, except in those cases where tradition (the experience of the Methodist female saints) gave her precedent to trust her experience. Hence her problem with Upham was not so much that he claimed an extrabiblical experience but that the one he claimed was not endorsed by the pillars of early Methodism.

True, there were early Methodists who claimed to have experienced the further work of grace, but they were males, and they inevitably made trouble for John Wesley. George Bell and Thomas Maxfield taught what we have called "antinomian mysticism." They claimed that they had reached a state in which it was no longer possible for them to sin and that thus they had no further need of the disciplines of the Christian life. They went on to disparage Mr. Wesley's spiritual state and his ability as a teacher of righteousness. Consequently, Wesley was forced to remove them from his connexion.[69] It seems that extrabiblical mysticism did not form an important part of the spirituality of the men who remained loyal to Wesley. Neither John Fletcher, William Bramwell, nor

John Nelson reported the kind of mystical phenomena the leading female Methodists experienced.[70] Thus, there seems to be a line of benign mysticism running through female Methodism, while the males contract a malignant strain. Phoebe Palmer is in that line of female spirituality that runs through Hester Rogers, Mary Bosanquet Fletcher, and Lady Maxwell. Whether that same line continues through Mrs. Palmer to Amanda Smith, Frances Willard, Catharine Booth, and beyond must await further research.

INFLUENCES

Phoebe Palmer was quick to assert that the source of her theology was "Not Wesley, not Fletcher, not Finney, not Mahan, not Upham, but the Bible, the holy Bible."[71] Others dismissed her holiness teachings as a theological aberration of the Methodists, supported only by a few proof texts. In reply, she said that entire sanctification is the doctrine of the whole Bible; it "is not merely the doctrine of a sect, as some imagine, but the great crowning doctrine of the Bible; the ultimatum of all Christian ministrations, inasmuch as without it no man shall see the Lord" (Heb. 12:14).[72] Even some Methodists chided her with making holiness a hobbyhorse; she answered that she made holiness a specialty because "the God of the Bible makes it a specialty."[73]

Thus Phoebe Palmer claimed that the chief influence on her thinking, shaping both its content and emphasis, was the Bible. While this is undoubtedly true, other writings obviously had an influence on the development of Mrs. Palmer's thought. Chief among these were the writings of the Methodists, most notably John Wesley, John Fletcher, Hester Rogers, and Adam Clarke. Non-Methodists such as Finney and Mahan may have shared similar ideas, but they seem not to have been instrumental in shaping her theology.

John Wesley

The theology that Mrs. Palmer developed from the Bible, reason, experience, and tradition was largely the evangelical Anglicanism of John Wesley.[74] Her main theological contribution was to modify and popularize his doctrine of entire sanctification.[75] Wesley believed that the Bible teaches that God can do something about sin other than forgive it over and over again. He knew that the Bible says without holiness no one can see the Lord and that both the Old and New Testaments contain promises of entire sanctification. Further, he found no place in the Bible where it says that the believer can become holy only at or after death. He also reasoned that because God commands Christians to be holy and even perfect, it must be possible for them to be so. If not, then God would be commanding something which was impossible, and such a command would be an absurdity. Thus every command of God is also a promise of divine grace to enable the believer to obey.[76]

Wesley also taught that Christians experience several distinct acts of God's grace as they grow into the image of Christ. Two of these acts of grace are justification and entire sanctification. Justification occurs when a sinner is forgiven, regenerated, and made right with God. Entire sanctification happens when the carnal nature within a Christian is finally destroyed, and the believer is then enabled to love God with the whole heart, soul, mind, and strength. Entire sanctification makes Christians perfect in their love for God, but in no other way. Their hearts are so filled with the love of God that there is no room for a contrary affection. Hence they are sinless in that while in this state they do not willingly violate the known law of God. Although believers' hearts are filled with love and freed from sin, sanctified people still suffer the effects of sin on their minds and bodies. They are not free from errors in judgment or mistakes in action. Thus, they continually need the blood of Christ to cleanse them from these accidental "fallings short of the glory of God."

Like justification, sanctification is by faith and is not earned by human achievement. Entire sanctification occurs in an instant, but that instant is both preceded and followed by a gradual growth in grace. Wesley said that this experience of entire sanctification usually comes at death, but there is no reason why one cannot experience it earlier. The main reason why so few experience it before death is that so few expect or even seek it earlier. As the Wesleyan preachers proclaimed this full salvation and established Methodist societies, classes, bands, and select societies as the means of grace for attaining and retaining the promised blessing, more and more people began to seek it. As they did, many were able to testify to the experience of entire sanctification.

John Wesley's doctrine of Christian perfection was greatly opposed by many both outside and inside his societies. Those outside said entire sanctification could not happen in this life, and some inside said it could happen only gradually, and after great suffering. For a time, even his brother Charles questioned the belief in instantaneous entire sanctification by faith, but as John grew older his confidence in the doctrine grew. Near the end of his life Wesley became convinced that God had raised up the Methodists chiefly to preach entire sanctification, and his later letters often urged his itinerants to do so.[77]

Phoebe Palmer's dependence on Wesley is evident on every page of her books, and she was eager to be identified with Methodism's founder. The first line of defense for her ideas was that they were biblical, but when talking with Methodists, she quickly moved to her second point, saying that she taught nothing but what Mr. Wesley himself had maintained. She knew the Wesley corpus well and quoted from his sermons, journals, and letters to argue that she was faithful to the "old Methodist doctrine."[78]

John Fletcher

Next to John Wesley, the person who most influenced Phoebe Palmer's thinking about sanctification was John Fletcher. Mrs. Palmer was familiar with the life and work of this man, whom John Wesley picked to succeed him as the leader of the Methodists; and the addition he made to Wesley's doctrine of Christian perfection is reflected in her theology.[79] During his days at Trevecca College in the winter of 1770–71, Fletcher came to identify entire sanctification with the experience of Pentecost. He equated Christian perfection with receiving the Holy Spirit, or being "baptized with the Holy Ghost and with fire."[80] George Whitefield had earlier hinted at this equation but later abandoned it when he rejected the doctrine of entire sanctification.[81] John Wesley, of course, believed in entire sanctification, but he did not entirely agree with Fletcher's identification of the two events; he pointed out that every Christian receives the Holy Spirit at justification.[82] Wesley preferred to link entire sanctification with the fullness of the Spirit, not just its reception.[83] Under Wesley's influence, Fletcher clarified his thought and declared in his *Last Check to Antinomianism* that while receiving the Holy Spirit is what justifies a Christian, "another glorious baptism, or capital outpouring of the Spirit" is what sanctifies the believer. This sanctifying baptism, he said, is "the promise of the Father" (Acts 1:4), for which Jesus told the disciples to wait.[84] Having seen these modifications, John Wesley wrote to Fletcher, "I do not perceive . . . that there is any difference between us."[85] Mrs. Palmer followed Fletcher in his identification of entire sanctification with the Pentecost experience and then further developed the implications of this identification.

Hester Ann Roe Rogers

Hester Rogers was a friend of John and Mary Fletcher. Her autobiography contains some information about the Fletchers not available elsewhere. From her, Phoebe Palmer learned about John Fletcher's repeated loss of entire sanctification, his exhortation to reckon oneself dead to sin as a means of attaining the blessing, and perhaps his identification of holiness with the baptism of the Holy Spirit.[86] In addition to passing on Fletcher's teaching, Mrs. Rogers intensified one aspect of his thought. Fletcher followed Wesley in teaching that entire sanctification is received by faith. In his work on sanctification, he quotes and explicates Wesley through eight pages of small print, concluding, ". . . let thy faith close in with his word; ardently yet meekly embrace his promise."[87] Rogers expresses the same idea more succinctly and more personally: "I now take Thee at Thy word." Instead of embracing an impersonal promise, she spoke of sanctification as trusting a person.[88] This same intensity is present in Mrs. Palmer's thought.

Adam Clarke

Another important influence on Phoebe Palmer was the Methodist commentator Adam Clarke, whose massive edition of the Bible with notes and commentary appeared in the first two decades of the nineteenth century. Mrs. Palmer was familiar with Clarke and cited his comment on living sacrifices as an important element in her teaching on entire sanctification.[89] The passages she used to develop her "altar theology," along with the interpretation she gave to those passages, show his influence. Her exposition of the meaning of the altar incorporates Clarke's comments on Romans 12:1-2; Hebrews 13:10; and Exodus 29:37.[90]

Besides contributing to the development of Mrs. Palmer's "altar theology," Clarke's treatment of entire sanctification has four other elements which may have helped to shape Phoebe Palmer's thinking about the doctrine. First, Clarke emphasized the instantaneous element of sanctification. While both Wesley and Fletcher taught that entire sanctification is an instantaneous work, they also held that it is both preceded and followed by the gradual work of God's Spirit. Clarke was impatient with this balanced emphasis and stressed the instantaneous to the exclusion of the gradual. Along with this shift in emphasis, Clarke also implied that entire sanctification is not the culmination and goal of Christian growth but rather its precondition and proper beginning. Third,

Clarke gave greater importance to the methodology of achieving Christian perfection. While Wesley and Fletcher both told their readers how to seek perfect love, Clarke went on to add that if Christians had not experienced this blessing, it was because they had not sought it in the right way. Finally, he made more explicit the link between holiness and power, saying that when a life is saved from all sin, it can then be employed fully in the Lord's service. These four changes in nuance from the ideas taught by Wesley and Fletcher are all further developed in Mrs. Palmer's theology.[91]

Timothy Merritt

Timothy Merritt was a close friend of both Sarah Lankford and Phoebe Palmer, and a frequent visitor in their home. Sarah had read his book, *The Christian's Manual,* and a conversation with him gave her quest for sanctification an important fillip. Phoebe does not mention reading Merritt in any of her published accounts, but it is not unlikely that she read him at Sarah's urging or that Sarah told her what Merritt had written. Merritt's work is mainly a compilation of statements from Wesley and Fletcher, but he adds to their teachings the idea of making a covenant with God as a step toward obtaining sanctification. This idea of a covenant became an important element in Phoebe Palmer's teaching about entire sanctification.[92]

Asa Mahan and Charles Finney

A few months before Phoebe Palmer received the gift of entire sanctification, Asa Mahan and Charles Finney began to examine the doctrine. Mahan was the president of Oberlin College, and Finney was its leading theological professor, dividing his time between teaching in the college and preaching in the Broadway Tabernacle in New York City. During a revival meeting in October 1836, one of the school's recent graduates rose and asked, "When we look to Christ for sanctification, what degree of sanctification may we expect from him? May we look to him to be sanctified wholly, or not?" Mahan, who was leading the meeting, was surprised at the question and did not know how to answer it. He promised, however, to give it his prayerful attention.[93]

Finney was also in the meeting, and he, like Mahan, determined to learn more about sanctification. Both men went to New York that winter and spent much time praying and reading the Bible in search of an answer. The answer they found in the Scripture came to be known as "Oberlin Perfectionism." From that winter on, both Mahan and Finney taught that a person could instantaneously receive the power to will what was right. This right willing, or perfect submission to the will of God, was available as a free gift from the Lord. The gift did not guarantee perfect obedience, but it did secure consistent right intention. This doctrine, which both called "Christian perfection," was essentially the Methodist belief, the belief Phoebe Palmer came to accept and to advocate. Because Finney preached two sermons on Christian perfection in New York City during the winter of 1837, one might wonder if his ideas influenced her.[94]

While Mrs. Palmer later became close friends with Mahan and once visited Finney, it is unlikely that their ideas of Christian perfection helped to shape her doctrine of entire sanctification. Phoebe Palmer is quick to mention those who influenced her thought, but neither the published excerpts of her diary nor her later writings mention Mahan or Finney in connection with her "day of days." In the face of this lack of evidence there is no need to hypothesize some unreported contact in order to explain the likeness of their beliefs. Nothing in the teaching of the Oberlin professors was significantly different from the doctrines with which Mrs. Palmer had long been familiar in the Methodist tradition.[95] Even the identification of entire sanctification with the baptism of the Holy Spirit, which the Oberlin professors introduced into the Calvinistic denominations, probably came to Mrs. Palmer from her Methodist heritage.[96]

ENTIRE SANCTIFICATION

Like John Wesley, Phoebe Palmer taught that entire sanctification is a second distinct work of grace in which God cleanses the believer's heart of sin and fills it wholly with his love. Such heart holiness is a requirement for entry into heaven. Because God commands it, he must also supply the ability to attain it, and he gives that ability in response to the Christian's faith.[97]

Phoebe Palmer thought she was preaching holiness exactly as John Wesley had preached it, but she unconsciously modified the doctrine in six important ways. First, she followed John Fletcher in his identification of entire sanctification with the baptism of the Holy Spirit. Second, she developed Adam Clarke's suggestion and linked holiness with power. Third, like Clarke, she stressed the instantaneous elements of sanctification to the exclusion of the gradual. Fourth, again following Clarke, she taught that entire sanctification is not really the goal of the Christian life, but rather its beginning. Fifth, through her "altar theology" she reduced the attainment of sanctification to a simple three-stage process. And, sixth, she held that one needed no evidence other than the biblical text to be assured of entire sanctification.

Entire Sanctification and the Baptism of the Holy Spirit

Phoebe Palmer accepted and developed John Fletcher's identification of entire sanctification and the baptism of the Holy Spirit given at Pentecost. In her first book she compared the instantaneous sanctification of a friend with the events of Pentecost and added, "many others were baptized as suddenly at the same time [as he was]."[98] This idea continued to occur in her other early works and received fuller explication in *Promise of the Father*, published one year after the revival of 1857–58.[99] Even before the revival, Phoebe Palmer urged her hearers at a camp meeting to receive the "Pentecostal baptism."[100] With the coming of the revival, the frequency of Mrs. Palmer's use of Pentecostal language began to increase. While promoting the revival in England, the Palmers developed an order of service based on Pentecost which later became their standard pattern. They would start by leading a hymn about Pentecost, then have Dr. Palmer read and comment on Acts 2. Next Mrs. Palmer would exhort those present to be baptized with "an inward baptism of pure fire." Those wishing to receive the blessing would then come forward for a prayer service around the altar, after which they would be urged to bear testimony about what the Lord had done for them.[101]

Not only did Mrs. Palmer begin to preach more about Pentecost after the beginning of the revival of 1857–58, but she also began to report the results of her meetings in Pentecostal terms. She reported the results of her first week in Hamilton not by listing the number of saved and sanctified, but by saying, "Twenty-one souls were blessed with pardon, and several others, I trust, with the full baptism of the Holy Ghost." She went on to equate the revival with Pentecost itself: "It is that which was foretold by the prophet Joel, and of which the apostle Peter spoke, . . . furnishing a marked demonstration that the same power still continues in the church that was in the apostolic church. . . ."[102] Her use of Pentecostal language characterized her reports from England and continued after she returned to America.[103]

Donald Dayton has pointed out that the revival of 1857–58 led to an increased interest in Pentecost in the whole Evangelical movement; Mrs. Palmer's increasing use of Pentecostal language was paralleled by the practice of Baptists, Congregationalists, Presbyterians, and other Methodists.[104] He attributes the shift to a variety of cultural and theological factors. Most persuasive of his cultural arguments is his observation that the culture of the late 1850s was not as optimistic as the culture of the late 1830s had been. Immigration, urbanization, and industrialization made American society more complex, and the powers of evil, especially that of slavery, seemed more deeply entrenched than ever. Perfectionistic language was optimistic and future-oriented. It looked forward to the day when humans, by obeying God perfectly, would usher in the new age. It seemed appropriate in the heyday of Jacksonian democracy, when everyone was founding a utopia. With the dissolution of the cultural supports for the language of Christian perfection, those who held the doctrine were open to a new way to express their belief. Unlike the forward-looking perfectionistic language, Pentecostal language looked back. It called to mind a time when God had miraculously intervened to give his followers purity and power and then enabled them to turn the world upside down. Such restorationist language was more suited to a time when people felt powerless in the face of complex social problems and institutionalized evil.[105]

Besides this cultural reason for a shift to Pentecostal imagery, Dayton has also suggested a theological reason. As an interest in holiness spread beyond the Methodists, it became easier to present the doctrine in Pentecostal terms than in perfectionistic. Perfectionistic language had always been subject to misunderstanding: John Wesley himself felt constrained to spend almost as much time explaining what Christian perfection was not as he did explaining what it was.[106] Perfectionism was particularly distasteful to those in the Reformed tradition because Luther and Calvin had explicitly taught that no one achieves perfection in this life. Thus, when speaking among their spiritual heirs, evangelists found it helpful to adopt another vocabulary. In addition to this longstanding aversion to speaking of perfection, recent American events had placed the word in even worse light. In 1848 John Humphrey Noyes moved his community to Oneida, New York. Their well-publicized activities, in the name of perfectionism, caused the word to stand for heterodoxy, communism, and adultery.[107] In order to avoid confusion, another term was expedient.[108]

One may identify another factor in Phoebe Palmer's increasing use of Pentecostal language. In 1856 an English Methodist, William Arthur, published a book in New York called *The Tongue of Fire; or the True Power of Christianity*. In this immensely popular book, Arthur hints at the equation of entire sanctification with the Pentecost experience and states that if Christians would allow themselves to be baptized in the Holy Ghost, in the revival which would result, the whole world could be won for Christ.[109] Because this latter idea appears in Mrs. Palmer's writings after 1856, it is possible she was influenced by Arthur's work.[110]

An even more likely cause of Phoebe Palmer's increasing use of Pentecostal language was her study of Acts 2 in preparation for her book on women in the church. In December of 1856 she realized that the baptism of the Spirit given at Pentecost empowered and impelled its recipients to speak for Christ. Realizing that the Spirit was poured out on women as well as men, she came to see that women had the power and obligation to testify about the Lord. Over the next two years she developed this insight into a four-hundred-page book. These were the years of the revival and the years in which she began to speak more frequently about Pentecost. Evidently her own study of Scripture combined with the external influences to lead her to a greater use of Pentecostal terminology.[111]

Holiness and Power

Closely tied to Pentecostal imagery is the linkage of entire sanctification with divine power. The scriptural account of the events previous to Pentecost equates "power from on high" with the baptism of the Holy Ghost (Luke 24:49; Acts 1:4–5). John Fletcher noticed this connection but did not develop its significance. In listing nine benefits of entire sanctification, he never mentioned a greater influx of God's power.[112] Adam Clarke devoted one sentence to the idea, but Phoebe Palmer made it a central element of her teaching.[113]

Even prior to her increasing use of Pentecostal language, Mrs. Palmer had understood the connection between entire sanctification and energy in the Lord's service. Those who have been sanctified need not worry about their internal state but may give themselves wholly to the Lord's service.[114] This message became more explicit after Mrs. Palmer adopted Pentecostal imagery; she often declared, "Holiness is power."[115] She told ministers that holiness was exactly the power needed "to raise low churches," and blamed their failures on a lack of sanctification. What Peter accomplished for the Lord in five hours after Pentecost would probably have taken him five years without the baptism, she averred.[116]

Once again historical events and cultural factors may have played a role in Phoebe Palmer's increasing emphasis on the connection between holiness and power. The historical event was the revival. Mrs. Palmer believed that God had released his Pentecostal power in the revival because Christians had been seeking holiness: Wherever she went preaching holiness she saw the power poured out.[117] Conversely, the cultural factor was the declining influence of Evangelicals in the second half of the century. Despite the revival of the late 1850s, the nation was torn by war, the immigrants kept coming, and the cities grew. Even worse, many of those who thought the end of slavery would bring on "The Marriage Supper of the Lamb" lived to see that event turned into "The Great Barbeque," with most Americans left out.[118] The cultural pessimism of the late 1850s became despair in the next decade. Perhaps this sense of powerlessness made people especially hungry for Mrs. Palmer's explanation of how to get power. Thus, she was eager to preach about power because she had found it, while her listeners were eager to hear about power because they had lost it.[119]

Gradual Versus Instantaneous Sanctification

In Wesley's doctrine of Christian perfection there is a tension between sanctification as a gradual process and sanctification as an instantaneous blessing. Repeatedly Wesley said that entire sanctification came as the result of a gradual process and an instantaneous crisis. More specifically, he taught that a gradual process of growth both precedes and follows the instantaneous crisis. One of John Wesley's images for the elimination of sin from the soul is the picture of a person dying. While the life ebbs away in a gradual process, still there is an instant when the soul leaves the body. In the same way God gradually removes sin from the Christian and in an instant completes the work.[120]

Phoebe Palmer uncoupled this tension between gradual and instantaneous sanctification in Wesley's thought, placing all her emphasis on the instantaneous. As with the idea of holiness and power, she again developed a brief comment of Adam Clarke into a fundamental doctrine. The thesis of her second book is that there is a shorter way to holiness; "long waiting and struggling with the powers of darkness is not necessary" because "THERE IS A SHORTER WAY!" In fact, the shorter way is the only way.[121] She reiterated this idea in all her works, arguing for its truth from her own experience, from the words of John Wesley, and from the Scripture. She told how she had lingered just shy of holiness, waiting for deeper convictions which would enable her to ask for this grace confidently, only to find that she had been wasting her time. God did not require her to wait for the blessing. In fact, he had commanded her to possess it.[122]

What she had learned from experience, she also found in John Wesley. She quoted from his sermon "On Patience," reporting his finding that every sanctified person he knew had received the gift instantaneously, and from his sermon "The Scripture Way of Salvation" she added his words, "Certainly you may look for it now, if you believe it is by faith."[123] In addition to citing John Wesley, Mrs. Palmer strengthened her case by quoting Scripture. She used the analogy of the Exodus, pointing out that just as the Jews could have made the trip to Canaan in forty days instead of forty years, so the Christian need not wander aimlessly for years outside the promised land of holiness.[124] She quoted Matthew 11:12 about the kingdom of heaven being taken by violence, urging her readers to be bold in their quest for sanctification.[125] Most often she cited 2 Corinthians 6:2, "Now is the day of salvation," to prove her point.[126]

Having shown that one could be sanctified immediately, Phoebe Palmer went on to argue that if one could be sanctified now, one should be sanctified now. "Our privileges are duties," she taught.[127] Mrs. Palmer treated this assertion as a self-evident axiom and used it to press believers on toward their high calling: "Why not this moment, then, begin to reckon yourself dead indeed unto sin and alive to God, through our Lord Jesus Christ? Behold your present privilege-your duty! . . . Why, then, should you delay to enter? O arise with a holy boldness!"[128]

The Chronology of Sanctification

Another modification Phoebe Palmer made in the doctrine of Christian perfection was to shift the place of entire sanctification in the chronology of the Christian life. Because entire sanctification is available to every believer at this very instant, and because each Christian has a duty to receive all the blessing that God wants to bestow, no believer should tarry long at the point of justification but should quickly move on to entire sanctification. John Wesley believed the same thing, but his emphasis was different.

As early as 1739 John Wesley came to believe that Christian perfection was not the unreachable goal of the Christian life but a present possibility. He admitted that there was no reason why one may not be sanctified soon after justification and urged his hearers to expect it immediately.[129] Nevertheless, in his later writings sanctification was often presented as the goal of the Christian life.[130] Wesley wrote of sanctification as a gift usually given shortly before death as preparation for heaven.[131] In addition, Wesley asked his preachers not, "Are you perfect?" but, "Are you going on to perfection?" despite his insistence that God could sanctify the believer this instant as easily as he could in the next thousand years.[132]

Perhaps indicative of Wesley's emphasis is the relative frequency of his words about the aspiration for sanctification compared with the attainment of it. Wesley devotes only one section in his *Plain Account* to advice to those who think they have achieved Christian perfection, compared with preaching at least six different sermons urging people to aspire after it.[133] Even more telling are the verses of the hymns John Wesley prints to illustrate his teaching on sanctification. All of them speak of aspiring after holiness, but none of them speaks of having attained it. They long for the benefits of full salvation but do not testify of having received them yet.[134] Thus, while John Wesley believed that sanctification could occur early in a believer's Christian life, most of his writings and his brother's hymns present sanctification as something not yet attained, giving the impression that it is the goal of the Christian life.

Perhaps the clearest example of change in emphasis from sanctification as the goal of the Christian life to sanctification as its beginning can be seen in the differences between the hymns John Wesley directed the Methodists to use and those Phoebe Palmer wrote. John Wesley published this hymn written by his brother Charles. It is typical of those the Methodists sang about entire sanctification:

> O Jesus, at Thy feet we wait,
> Till Thou shalt bid us rise,
> Restored to our unsinning state,
> To love's sweet paradise.
>
> Saviour from sin we Thee receive,
> From all indwelling sin;
> Thy blood, we steadfastly believe,
> Shall make us thoroughly clean.
>
> Since Thou wouldst have us free from sin
> And pure as those above,
> Make haste to bring Thy nature in,
> And perfect us in love.
>
> The counsel of Thy love fulfil,
> Come quickly, gracious Lord!
> Be it according to Thy will,
> According to Thy word.
>
> According to our faith in Thee
> Let it to us be done;
> O that we all Thy face might see,
> And know as we are known!
>
> O that the perfect grace were given,
> The love diffused abroad!
> O that our hearts were all a heaven,
> Forever filled with God![135]

Note Wesley's use of the future tense, the confession that the singers are waiting to be sanctified, and the prayer that God would finish the work. In this and most other of Wesley's hymns, sanctification is a goal that the singers are still seeking, not a present attainment.

Compare Wesley's hymn to the most famous of Phoebe Palmer's songs:

> O now I see the crimson wave,
> The fountain deep and wide;
> Jesus, my Lord, mighty to save,
> Points to his wounded side.
>
> Refrain:
> The cleansing stream I see, I see!
> I plunge, and O it cleanseth me;
> O praise the Lord, it cleanseth me,
> It cleanseth me, yes, cleanseth me.
>
> I see the new creation rise,
> I hear the speaking blood;
> It speaks! polluted nature dies—
> Sinks 'neath the crimson flood.

Refrain
I rise to walk in heav'n's own light,
Above the world and sin,
With heart made pure and garments white,
And Christ enthroned within.

Refrain
Amazing grace! 'tis heav'n below,
To feel the blood applied,
And Jesus, only Jesus know,
My Jesus crucified.[136]

Here there is no prayer for cleansing and no waiting for holiness. There is no future tense in the song; everything is past or present. Now the cleansing stream is available, and now the singer is plunging and being cleansed. By the third verse, sanctification is an accomplished fact. The believer can testify to a pure heart and a sinless walk.

Another evidence that Phoebe Palmer departed from Wesley's emphasis and spoke of entire sanctification as if it were the real beginning of the Christian life is the way in which she talked about holiness. Certainly she admitted that the merely justified were true Christians, but her description of the benefits of sanctification casts doubt on the depth of that conviction. John Wesley had specifically warned his preachers against exalting sanctification by depreciating justification, but Phoebe Palmer fell into this fault.[137]

Mrs. Palmer gave several reasons why her readers should seek holiness now. The first was God's commandment. "Be ye holy," commands the Lord in Leviticus 20:7. Like any other command of God, this one must be obeyed: "God requires *present* holiness."[138] Not only must one be holy to obey the Lord, but holiness is also a requirement for being of real use to God: "Inward purity—holiness of heart—furnishes a readiness for every good work."[139] In addition, sanctification makes Christians grow in grace faster and keeps them from backsliding.[140]

According to Phoebe Palmer another benefit of sanctification is that it is the alternative to damnation. She spoke as if the choice before the believer were the choice between "holiness or hell."[141] The seed of this idea is present in John Wesley, who on the basis of Hebrews 12:14 stated that no unholy person could enter heaven. He also felt that the alternative to going on to perfection was going on to perdition.[142] Wesley, however, was careful to say that the unsanctified person was not "in a state of damnation or under the curse of God till he does attain" perfection. "No," Wesley continued, "he is in a state of grace and in favor with God as long as he believes. Neither would I say, 'If you die without it, you will perish.'" Instead, Wesley would say that God will not let one die until he makes that one holy.[143]

Phoebe Palmer was not so sure that God will sanctify every believer before death. For her, the only way to insure that one will be holy at death is to be holy in life. She said there was nothing special about death that purifies the soul. "People doubtless die in the same light in which they live," she affirmed. She believed that *"Holiness, specific holiness* is . . . an absolute necessity if we would *die* right." She expressed great anxiety for those "professors" of Christianity who will be doomed to "*disappointment*" when they awaken "in the light of eternity." So strongly did she feel on this issue that she made "it a point never to leave a place without relieving my mind on this subject." If she did not, she feared "the blood of souls would be found on my skirts."[144]

In the light of this presentation of sanctification, who would be content to remain only justified? The justified person who is not yet sanctified does not meet God's present requirement, is not insured of being holy at death and ready for heaven, is not fit for every good work, grows only slowly, and is subject to backsliding. Is this the "abundant life" Jesus promised? Who would think existence in the justified state worthy of the name "the Christian life"? Surely the Christian life proper begins at sanctification.

Melvin Dieter argues that Mrs. Palmer's change in Wesley's doctrine shows the application of "all that was America in the nineteenth century" to the preaching of the eighteenth-century divine. He points out that her upsetting of the Wesleyan balance between the gradual and the instantaneous, along with her shifting of sanctification from the goal of the Christian life to its beginning, exactly parallel the transformations Jonathan Edwards and others effected in the Puritan doctrine of conversion.[145] While John Cotton and other early American Puritans preached as if regeneration were the goal of the believer's life and minutely described the stages in the conversion process, Edwards preached that one had an "immediate duty" to repent, and Finney telescoped the stages of conversion into a single event.[146]

As correct as Dieter is to see the influence of American optimism and impatience in Phoebe Palmer's treatment of Wesleyan doctrines, there may be another explanation of the data. Not only was she applying "all that was America in the nineteenth century" to Wesley, but she was also carrying Wesleyan doctrines to their natural conclusion; she was working out their inner logic. If it is true that all Christians will eventually be sanctified, and if it is true that it is better to be sanctified than merely justified, and if it is true that God can sanctify the believer now just as easily as a thousand years from now, and if it is true that God gives sanctification in response to the believer's faith, then every Christian should be sanctified now. Wesley preached each of the protases, and he admitted the truth of the apodoses, but, as he said of others, *Non persuadebis, etiamsi persuaseris* (You will not persuade me even though you do persuade me): He was not confident of the conclusion, no matter how logical it seemed.[147] "Plain matter of fact" had convinced him that people could not merely believe and be sanctified whenever they wanted, yet the logic of his theology told him that all could be sanctified if they wanted to. He expressed the problem this way: "That every man may believe if he will I earnestly maintain, and yet that he can believe when he will I totally deny." Not knowing how to resolve the dilemma, in the end he remained content to leave it a paradox: "But there will be always something in the matter which we cannot well comprehend or explain."[148]

Phoebe Palmer's experience was different from Wesley's. Leading up to her "day of days" she followed his reasoning to its logical conclusion and then found the blessing she had been seeking. "Plain matter of fact"—that is, the experiences of other Methodists such as Hester Rogers and Mary Fletcher, and that of her sister, along with her own experience—had convinced her that people could be sanctified not only if they willed but when they willed.[149] That conviction was strengthened when she preached holiness to others and saw them find full salvation before they left the meeting. Thus both Phoebe Palmer and John Wesley agreed on three sides of the Wesleyan quadrilateral: Scripture, tradition, and reason led them to expect instantaneous entire sanctification not long after the beginning of the Christian life. But they disagreed about the fourth side, experience. Wesley's experience led him to pull back from the logic of his conclusions; Palmer's led her to preach Wesley's logical conclusions vigorously.

The Means of Sanctification

Yet another change Mrs. Palmer made in Wesley's theology was to systematize the way to seek sanctification. Once again she unhitched two contradictory elements in Wesley's thought, putting all her emphasis on the simpler, quicker element. John Wesley urged his hearers to expect instantaneous entire sanctification by faith: "Look for it then every day, every hour, every moment! Why not this hour, this moment? Certainly you may look for it now, if you believe it is by faith."[150] He had also, however, advised those seeking sanctification to "wait" for God's action

> in vigorous, universal obedience, in a zealous keeping of all the commandments, in watchfulness and painfulness, in denying ourselves, and taking up our cross daily; as well as in earnest prayer and fasting, and a close attendance upon all the ordinances of God. And if a man dream of attaining it any other way (yea, or of keeping it when it is attained, . . .), he deceiveth his own soul. It is true, we receive it by simple faith; but God does not, will not, give that faith unless we seek, it with all diligence, in the way which He hath ordained.[151]

In other words, by living the normal life of a Methodist.

In place of believing in instantaneous entire sanctification and waiting for it by practicing Wesley's generalized Christian discipline, Phoebe Palmer substituted a "shorter way" to holiness. All one needed to do was follow this simple three-step process for being sanctified: (1) entire consecration, (2) faith, and (3) testimony.[152]

Entire Consecration

The first step to entire sanctification is entire consecration, "a perfect and entire yielding up of all to Christ, an entire trust in Christ, and a continuous reliance on Christ, for all needed grace under every diversity of circumstance or experience."[153] It is a once-and-for-all surrender of "body, soul, and spirit; time, talents, and influence; and also of the dearest ties of nature, . . ." which must be reaffirmed daily.[154] It is a determination that "we give ourselves at once wholly and for ever away to [God's] service, in order that we may be unto him a peculiar people, zealous of good works, not living to ourselves . . . ."[155]

Standing in the way of entire consecration are all different kinds of sin, little and great. Phoebe Palmer listed a variety of transgressions which could keep believers from giving themselves to God. Some are obviously evil; others may seem trivial, but to Mrs. Palmer they were the symptoms of a divided heart. Her list included: a proud distaste for serving others, an indulgence in a polluting habit such as smoking or drinking alcohol, a refusal to speak for Jesus in public, an unwillingness to bear the reproach of Christ, a fear of persecution, an attachment to an unsaved fiancé, a love of ministerial reputation, a dread of evangelizing, unchristian business practices, or a fondness for the world, shown by such superfluous adornment as jewels or artificial flowers.[156] Not until all these were confessed to the Lord and repented of could the Christian hope to be sanctified.

Some of Mrs. Palmer's hearers objected that they could not be sure they had made an entire consecration. For them she had two suggestions. First, to aid the believer in reaching a complete consecration, Mrs. Palmer advised making a covenant with the Lord. She had found this helpful in her own life and even wrote out a sample for others to use. Her sample covenant is a guide to self-examination, listing the various attitudes, relationships, possessions, and desires which one is surrendering to the Lord. It also mentions ways in which the believer might have to suffer for Christ, thus enabling one to count the cost before making the transaction.[157] Second, she told them that after they had made as complete a surrender of themselves to God as they could, they should trust God to reveal any area of deficiency. Quoting Philippians 3:15, "If in any thing ye be otherwise minded, God shall reveal even this unto you," she assured the doubtful that it is God's responsibility to show them their hearts.[158]

Faith

As serious as were all the sins mentioned above, there was one sin that was such a serious obstacle to entire sanctification that Phoebe Palmer treated it in a separate step. If Christians thought they had consecrated all and yet had not received the second blessing, it showed that they were not yet completely devoted to God. As Phoebe Palmer said to one young man who was seeking holiness, "You say that you have consecrated all: but there is one thing which I know you have not laid upon the altar...." Shocked, he replied that he had no idea that he had withheld anything from the Lord. She then pointed out that before he would believe he was sanctified, he wanted some special word from God, some sign or wonder, which would attest to his sanctification. "Now, lay that will on the altar which requires signs and wonders....Give up your *will* at once and for ever, and irrespective of emotions; but, with your eye fixed on the immutable word, cry out 'Thou *dost* receive me! I am wholly thine!' "[159]

The young man's sin was unbelief. His problem was that he

wanted to have sanctification on his terms, not God's. Until he surrendered his unwillingness to believe without any evidence other than the word of God in the Bible, he could not be sanctified. The Christian must believe that God has done the work of sanctification because God's Word says he will do it. According to Mrs. Palmer, in 2 Corinthians 6:16–7:1 God promises to receive the offering of those who separate themselves from all evil through entire consecration: God says, "I will receive you," to all who separate themselves from evil and cleanse themselves from every defilement. In them holiness is perfected in the fear of God.[160] Whether or not one felt any different after devoting every area of one's life to the Lord, one must not question whether God had sanctified the heart. To doubt that one was entirely sanctified was to doubt God's Word.[161] One must not trust feelings; one must trust the written Word of God.[162]

Phoebe Palmer likened faith to accepting the validity of a will. If she were handed someone's last will and testament and found that it was in every particular strictly legal and correct, and read in it that she was the heir to the estate, she would not hesitate to avail herself of the document's provisions.[163] She also explained faith by comparing it to a bank note. "If someone owes you one hundred dollars," she asked, "but instead of giving you the gold coins, gives you a bank note for the amount, would you be disappointed? Remember, a bank note isn't money, it's just a promise to pay you money when you get to the bank." "True enough," is the reply, "but the paper of that institution is just the same with me as gold."[164] With these two examples, Mrs. Palmer conveyed the point "that a promise fully credited does in itself convey the thing promised."[165]

Faith not only plays an important role in receiving entire sanctification, it is also essential in retaining the blessing. As long as Christians do not voluntarily sin, they may be assured that they are still entirely sanctified, no matter how they feel.[166] One of Satan's favorite tricks is to cheat believers out of their sanctification by tempting them or so buffeting their emotions that they will feel that they must no longer be sanctified. In such a situation Phoebe Palmer declared, "I resolved rather to die than to doubt."[167] One brother who was not so resolute "cast away his confidence" (Heb.10:35), and quit believing he was sanctified. This was a sin and grieved the Holy Spirit. God's Word has said, ". . . If any man draw back, my soul shall have no pleasure in him" (Heb. 10:38). Thus by ceasing to believe he was sanctified, according to Mrs. Palmer, the man actually did cease to be sanctified.[168]

While doubting God's Word is unquestionably a sin, Mrs. Palmer's teaching could easily give the impression that doubting that one is currently in a sanctified state is also a sin. There is a subtle shift in the object of faith, so that one confuses trusting the veracity of God with believing something about oneself. There is a difference between believing that if one meets certain conditions God will sanctify and believing that one has met those conditions. Phoebe Palmer never spoke clearly about that difference, and much of her teaching about faith and testimony obscured it.

Testimony

The third step in the sanctification process is testimony. The work has already occurred, but it must be ratified as the believer publicly bears witness to what, on the basis of the Scripture, she or he knows God has done in the heart. While John Wesley had opined that those who received the blessing should tell other believers, Phoebe Palmer asserted the "binding nature of the obligation to profess the blessing."[169] Mrs. Palmer taught that Romans 10:9–10, which speaks of believing in the heart and confessing with the mouth, requires public profession as well as heart faith for God's work to be effective. Not to tell others is to withhold the honor due to Christ; in addition, simple gratitude requires the Christian to acknowledge what the Lord has done in the heart.[170] The sanctified also should testify because their experience is not their own; one of the reasons God gave it to them was to help others. Not to bear witness hurts others: The reason so few Methodists are sanctified is that so many ministers withhold their witness.[171]

Besides honoring Christ and helping others, testimony helps the believer. As was noted above, a refusal to testify prevents entire consecration.[172] Conversely, God often gives the emotional assurance of sanctification only after one has testified to the work. Phoebe Palmer was quick to warn people not to profess in order to obtain the blessing, or to speak before they truly believed, but she also reported that some did not feel any inward change until they had witnessed outwardly.[173] She herself reported, "In proportion as I testify of the cleansing blood to others, so does the Spirit testify in my own experience."[174]

Finally, so important is this third step that Mrs. Palmer warns those who do not confess the blessing that they will not retain it.[175] Citing the case of John Fletcher who lost holiness five times because he refused to testify about it, and, quoting John Wesley's words, she warned those who were unwilling to profess entire sanctification publicly that they would not be able to keep the blessing.[176]

One problem for Mrs. Palmer was the lack of any clear published testimony from John Wesley professing entire sanctification. People wondered how testifying to sanctification could be so important if Wesley himself never did it.[177] Phoebe Palmer's first response was the question-begging reply that he must have done it because he thought it was important: "What an inconsistency would it have involved, if Mr. Wesley, who was ever urging the attainment of the blessing of perfect love on others, and the profession of it when enjoyed, had not himself enjoyed and professed the blessing!"[178] Her second answer was to give the answer offered by Nathan Bangs. Bangs called for a volume of Wesley's letters and read the passage in which Wesley says that ten years after he had been seeking holiness, "God gave me clearer views than I had before of the way how to obtain this; namely, by faith in the Son of God."[179] Evidently for Dr. Bangs and Mrs. Palmer this equivocal statement settled the issue.

"Altar Theology"

Mrs. Palmer developed her three-step plan for achieving entire sanctification in conjunction with her "altar theology."[180] As we have already seen, she was seeking for some scriptural basis for applying 2 Corinthians 6:17, "I will receive you," to herself. She found this assurance by arguing from a catena of passages containing sacrificial imagery. In Romans 12:1-2 she read that Christians are commanded to offer themselves as sacrifices to God, in Matthew 23:19 that the altar sanctifies the gift, in Exodus 29:37 that whatever touches the altar is holy, and in Hebrews 13:10 that Christians have an altar which is more sacred than the one in the tabernacle. Following Adam Clarke, she believed that this greater altar is Christ himself.[181] From these passages Mrs. Palmer deduced that Christians who entirely consecrate themselves to Christ are presenting their bodies as living sacrifices. Christ himself is the altar on which the offering is made so as long as believers rest themselves entirely on him, their all is on the altar. Because whatever touches the altar is holy, the believers themselves are holy. Thus entire consecration guarantees entire sanctification.[182]

Evidence of Sanctification

Phoebe Palmer's sixth change in the Wesleyan doctrine of entire sanctification was to insist that the witness of the Spirit, giving assurance of full salvation, was not some subjective experience, but was the objective word of Scripture. In the *Plain Account of Christian Perfection*, Wesley had said that believers ought not to consider themselves sanctified until they had the unmistakable inner witness of the Spirit: "None therefore ought to believe that the work is done, till there is added the testimony of the Spirit, witnessing his entire sanctification, as clearly as his justification."[183] In the same work, however, he said that "the witness of sanctification is not always clear at first," that it is "sometimes stronger and sometimes fainter," and that one needs no inner witness if he has no doubt.[184]

In contrast to Wesley's equivocal view was Phoebe Palmer's teaching about the evidence of sanctification. As we have seen from her response to the young man, she believed to demand the inner witness is to question God. The Lord has said, "I will receive you," to all who offer everything to him. Those who refuse to believe God's plain word dishonor him. They cannot be sanctified and are rightly sent to hell if they persist in their unbelief.[185] Mrs. Palmer based her argument on the reasoning which led to her own sanctification. When she sought assurance that she was sanctified she remembered the Scripture, "I will receive you." When she wondered if she should believe it without any other evidence, she realized that if she had heard a voice from heaven speaking to her she would believe it. How much more then should she believe the Bible![186]

Phoebe Palmer believed that many people confuse the witness of the Spirit with their own emotions. What they expect is some deep inner stirring, some exalted feeling, or some mystical experience. Instead of these emotional upheavals, what God gives is the "internal conviction . . . that we have the grace for which we have believed." "He that believeth hath the witness in himself," Mrs. Palmer paraphrased from 1 John 5:10. She explained this verse to one friend, telling him he should trust Christ for salvation, and adding, "*When* you *do* this, the Spirit, through the revealed word, tells you that you *are* saved." Similarly, when one has laid all on the altar, and believes God's promises about sanctification, that one has the witness of the Spirit. The very believing of the Word of God is the witness of the Spirit.[187]

Phoebe Palmer once explained her idea by referring to a sacrifice presented in Old Testament times. She asked what evidence a Jew would have when he brought a sacrifice to the altar that his offering was sanctified. He knew the law of sacrifice, and if he had complied with it, he had the evidence of God's Word that the offering was accepted. In the same way, if Christians comply with the requirements in offering themselves to God, they should trust that God will keep his word and sanctify them. The Spirit speaks through the Word; if they believe the Word, they have the witness of the Spirit: "The witness comes *through* believing, not before, not after, but in the act."[188]

The doctrine of assurance was one issue that disturbed the peace of the Tuesday Meeting. On March 10, 1858, Nathan Bangs, who often led the meetings, rose trembling to state his disagreement with Mrs. Palmer in the matter of assurance. Citing Wesley, Fletcher, and the Scripture, he said that Mrs. Palmer's theory that one needs no extrascriptural evidence to claim sanctification "is not sound, is unscriptural, and anti-Wesleyan." The error is "fundamental" and "strikes at the root of experimental religion." He pointed out that while one may be sure of the scriptural promises, they "are not in themselves any evidence to *me* that I am ... sanctified; they simply declare who [is] sanctified, and give marks or evidences of the work." He urged those present who believed they were sanctified on the evidence of Scripture alone, without any inward witness, change in disposition, or emotion, to examine themselves because they may be deceiving themselves daily. He thought those who teach this doctrine are not bad people, but "their hearts are better than their heads."[189]

Bangs gave express direction that if his biography ever were published it should contain an account of the incident. Phoebe Palmer made no direct published mention of it, or of her reaction to his words. Yet shortly after his biography appeared, she published a story Bangs had told her but had been omitted from the book about him. Mrs. Palmer related that Bangs had lost the witness of sanctification and that he regained it only after he had confessed, on the basis of faith alone, that he was sanctified. Evidently she believed that this incident from his life confirmed the truth of what she taught, even if the theory Bangs espoused contradicted it.[190]

Phoebe Palmer made her doctrine of assurance hard to understand because although she usually said that the witness of the Spirit was nothing other than the voice of God in the Scripture, at times she spoke about it as if it were the emotional experience so many were seeking. In describing her own life, she repeatedly stated that her assurance was growing, and she told of seekers who returned to the altar rail two or three times because the witness that they were sanctified was not yet strong enough.[191] Her words about the value of testimony sometimes betrayed this confusion, because she told people that witnessing outwardly would strengthen the inner witness.[192] If the "witness" and the "assurance" that Phoebe Palmer spoke about on these occasions were really the objective promise in the Bible, how could it grow stronger with time, testimony, or trips to the altar? Such human actions cannot affect the validity of God's promise. What Mrs. Palmer was talking about in these instances is an emotion, an inner feeling of being accepted by God. By calling it "assurance" or "the witness" she was contradicting one of the main thrusts of her teaching. She ought to have maintained the distinction between the subjective evidence of one's own feelings and the objective evidence of God's Word. By failing to do so on many occasions she seemed to teach the absurdity that the way to get the witness was to say one already had it.

Evaluation of Mattison's Charges: How Original Was Phoebe Palmer?

Near the middle of the century Hiram Mattison began to charge that Mrs. Palmer had departed from Wesley and introduced strange doctrines into Methodism. He stated that she confused entire consecration with entire sanctification, that she made believing one was sanctified the means of being sanctified, that she urged the profession of holiness before one was sure holiness had been obtained, and that she dismissed the need for the subjective witness of the Spirit. Phoebe Palmer and her defenders replied that in everything she taught she depended on the Scripture and John Wesley.[193]

This nineteenth-century controversy raises the same issue as the twentieth-century question of the degree of originality in Mrs. Palmer's thought: To what degree was she dependent on Wesley and to what degree did she depart from him? While it is true Mattison's specific accusations show that he did not fully understand Phoebe Palmer's teachings, he was certainly correct to notice a difference between the way John Wesley had talked about entire sanctification and the way Mrs. Palmer did. One of the reasons for this difference is that Wesley was much more tolerant of ambiguity and paradox than Phoebe Palmer was. Every area of Wesley's thought, not just the doctrine of entire sanctification, is filled with balance and tension. He was a pastoral theologian, applying God's Word to different people in different ways. Thus his writings contain equivocation and apparent contradiction. When John Wesley was asked either/or questions, he usually answered, "Both/And."

Phoebe Palmer was impatient with "both/and" answers. To her they were the epitome of complex man-made theology. She loved what she thought was the simplicity of the Bible's religion. "Simplicity" was her watchword: "Everything in religion is exceedingly simple," she often asserted.[194] Thus she simplified John Wesley's doctrine of entire sanctification. She followed his main points but left out his cautions and his paradoxical elements. She uncoupled his tensions and resolved his ambiguities. She pursued the logic of his arguments beyond the point where they had led him. She strongly asserted what he had quietly expressed. The difference between their theologies is the difference between an oil portrait and a charcoal sketch. Wesley's theology is a rich mixture of subtle shades and varied hues. Many different and seemingly contradictory elements go into its composition, but the overall effect is balanced and harmonious. Mrs. Palmer's theology is different. It is a bold outline, characterized by broad strokes and stark contrasts. Simple in its conception and in its execution, it produces a striking effect. While the portrait may be more true to life, the sketch is easier to remember.

ECCLESIOLOGY

In areas other than the doctrine of entire sanctification, Phoebe Palmer did not make original contributions to theology. She believed and taught what other American Methodists of the period believed and taught.[195] The Methodists were the largest of all the denominational groups in the mid-nineteenth century, and their theology and practice influenced most of the other groups.[196] Her importance in these areas was not as a thinker but as a representative and popularizer. Thus an extended analysis of the sources of her thought, and a comparison of her work with that of other thinkers may give place to a simple explication of the ideas she shared and helped to spread.

Phoebe Palmer's thought is important in three areas of

ecclesiology. Her ministry encouraged the role of lay-people in the church and especially advocated the active role of women in ministry. These two topics will be treated in the next two chapters. Here we will discuss her thinking about ecumenism.

Although at the turn of the nineteenth century Peter Cartwright, the Methodist circuit rider, could exult over people he had rescued from the Baptists almost as much as over people he had rescued from the devil, by Phoebe Palmer's time interdenominational relations had reached a much higher plane.[197] While she recognized that the splitting of the church into the various denominations had produced some good results, her overwhelming response to the disunity of Christians was sadness, mainly because it deterred revival: "And what can be more grievous in the sight of the God of battles, whose name is LOVE, than strife and divisions among those who have been begotten together in the bowels of Christ."[198] In order not to promote disunity, she rarely answered or even acknowledged criticism in the *Guide* and tried to avoid controversy in her personal ministry.[199]

Mrs. Palmer was especially wary of sectarian chauvinism because some non-Methodists had dismissed her teachings as a denominational peculiarity.[200] She was eager to minister outside the Methodist denomination; at various times she held meetings under Moravian, Baptist, Presbyterian, Congregational, and Anglican auspices.[201] She was also quick to insist that holiness was a doctrine for all Christians, citing as evidence the love and unity felt by the people from several denominations present at the Tuesday Meeting.[202]

Mrs. Palmer once asked, "Can we doubt but there are those in all evangelical churches who by their doctrinal tenets may seem to repudiate the belief, yet at heart believe that the great salvation . . . *does* enable its possessor to live daily above the world and sin, through the power of an indwelling Christ?"[203] Later she cited the cases of Jonathan and Sarah Edwards as evidence that the answer was yes.[204] Because holiness was the "cardinal doctrine of the Bible," all Christians could unite around it.[205] She hoped that as Christians became more holy the dissensions in the church would be healed and Christendom would be empowered for world evangelism.[206] She believed this unity had already occurred in some places when holiness was preached: "Denominational barriers were annihilated, or rather swept away, by the overflowing of perfect love," she once reported.[207]

Mrs. Palmer's ecumenism, however, did not extend outside

the fold of evangelical Protestantism. She used the term "Man of Sin," knowing her readers would understand it to mean the Roman Catholic Church, and reported in the *Guide to Holiness* the killing of some Protestants by Catholics in New Caledonia. She hoped this unhappy bit of information would arm her readers against the blandishments of Father Isaac Hecker, who was trying to recommend the Roman church to American Protestants.[208] Mrs. Palmer, however, did not want to be unloving toward those who were mistaken. In one of her poems, she holds out the hope that even the pope may be saved:

> The Pope may enter paradise,
> Like any other sinner.
>
> * * *
>
> Yes, Pius IX., if he repent,
> No more his claim need borrow;
> For Christ would to his claim consent
> If he'd show godly sorrow.[209]

Another group on which Phoebe Palmer did not look with favor was the Mormons. As part of their trip to California, the Palmers stopped in Utah. There Mrs. Palmer was able to see these people for herself, as well as pick up some anti-Mormon gossip. She thought the men and women "looked like the low bred refuse of creation," yet reminded herself that "these people have souls which must forever exist in misery or joy." She was not above passing along the story that Brigham Young was in mortal terror of his latest wife. This woman demanded and got a house of her own away from the other fifteen wives, and, as Phoebe reported with ill-suppressed glee, "if he is not in due time for his meals, or otherwise crosses her inclinations, she overturns tables, breaking crockery, and by various undutiful manifestations, assures him that it is better for the peace of his house, that her will should be law." Phoebe Palmer's purpose in reporting this edifying tidbit was "to contribute my mite toward exciting a righteous indignation against a system which sets at defiance the laws of the United States, and all virtuous principle."[210]

SPIRITUALITY

Another area in which Phoebe Palmer expressed and reinforced the evangelical Protestantism of her day was spirituality. Mrs. Palmer's spirituality began with the Bible. So did her day.

Helps to Holiness

Bible Reading

Mrs. Palmer recommended rising at five each morning to begin Bible study. She felt the first hour of the day should be a time of communion with God and of reconsecration. This "holy time" should begin when one awakes with the words, "Glory to God in the highest, peace on earth, good will toward men" (Luke 2:14). Next, asking, "Lord, what wilt Thou have me to do today?" the believer should be reconsecrated to the Lord's service. Then the systematic study of the Scripture on one's knees can begin. Knowing every page of the Bible was written for the Christian's instruction, the believer should read right through the Bible, expecting God to teach something from every section. Keeping a journal is also important. There one may record insights from the Scripture as well as keep a record of God's dealing with the soul. This journal will be helpful not only to the Christian but also to others. Because nothing that involves God is "common or unclean," the insights he gives from his Word and from daily life ought to be shared. So important is the journal that Phoebe Palmer says not to keep one is "almost a sin."[211]

Mrs. Palmer realized that not everyone felt that he or she had an hour a day to devote to the "holy time." She admitted it would involve a sacrifice, but admonished, ". . . you will not wish to sacrifice to God that which costs you *nothing*" (2 Sam. 24:24). She cited the example of a working man who arose at four so he could have an hour for the "holy time" and an hour for dressing, breakfast, and travel, before arriving at work at six. She clinched her case with the story of a pioneer woman in the wilds of Michigan, living in a little shanty with half a dozen children. "What would you do with holiness . . . ?" the Tempter sneered. "What can I do without it?" the feisty woman retorted. She resolved she would rise one hour before the world would have any rightful claim on her time. Giving four to five in the morning to the Lord, she maintained a close walk with God despite a heavy load of responsibilities.[212]

Besides spending the recommended time with God in the morning, Phoebe Palmer also read a section of the Scripture at noon and another before going to bed. Thus the Bible was her first book in the morning and her last one at night. She would often read from the Old Testament in the morning, the Gospels at noon, and the Epistles in the evening. In addition, she always carried her

Bible with her so she could improve every spare moment. She publicized her devotional practices so that other Christians would imitate them and find the same benefits from them. Besides suggesting that believers read the Bible regularly and in their free moments, Mrs. Palmer also recommended that Christians edify themselves periodically from the Methodist *Book of Discipline*.[213]

Prayer

In addition to studying the Bible, Christians should also devote themselves to prayer during their "holy times." Because God says, "The very hairs of your head are all numbered" (Matt. 10:30), he cares about every aspect of the believer's life. He therefore wants the believer to bring him every concern—every concern, that is, that is at least as important as one hair.[214] Accordingly Phoebe Palmer prayed about major events, asking that people be converted, and about minor ones, asking that she be enabled to write the correct things in a letter.[215] An especially important time for prayer was just before going to bed. At that time Mrs. Palmer would review the day, evaluating her actions and reactions. Her goal was to "keep short accounts with the Lord" so that if death overtook her she would be ready for glory. This process could take more than an hour, but Phoebe Palmer found it essential.[216] Besides her stated seasons of prayer, she seemed to keep up a running dialogue with the Lord, so mindful was she of his presence.[217] Fasting was a help to effective prayer, as was the knowledge that she could pray with the authority of Jesus: "We present these petitions over the signature of Jesus," was Walter's usual ending for a time of prayer.[218]

The Sabbath

If the first hour of every day should be given to God, how much more should the first day of every week be used in his service! Sundays were consecrated to the Lord both by what Mrs. Palmer did and by what she refrained from doing. What she did on Sunday was go to church. She felt her obligation to be there was as great as the pastor's, so she was usually there for Sabbath school and morning and evening worship. The afternoon would be devoted to errands of mercy, edifying conversation, or devotional reading. What she did not do on Sunday was ordinary business or personal entertainment.[219]

Phoebe Palmer believed God blessed those who kept the Sabbath and punished those who did not. She told the story of a friend whose husband had gone to California in the gold rush of 1849. The woman had received no letters from him for a long time and was extremely worried because of the cholera epidemic there. One Saturday night her anxiety seemed unbearable. She spent most of the night in prayer, and as dawn came on Sunday, she heard the newsboy shouting, "News from California! News from California!" As she was about to buy the paper, the Spirit reminded her it was Sunday and that she must not sin against the Lord. She refrained from breaking the Sabbath by buying or selling and thereafter enjoyed a peaceful day. The next morning letters arrived from her husband, telling her not to be alarmed by any newspaper reports. He was alive and well, but the Sunday newspaper had carried an account of a man by the same name in the same town who had died of cholera. If she had desecrated the Lord's Day, she would have suffered the agony of imaginary widowhood.[220]

The Christian obeys God by giving him the first day of every week and obeys prudence by devoting to him the first day of every month. This day should be a time of praise and thanksgiving as the believer reviews how God has blessed in the intervening days.[221] New Year's Eve is another high and holy time. Following the Wesleyan custom of celebrating the new year with a watch-night service of covenant renewal, Mrs. Palmer recommended that believers review and renew their vows at this time.[222] To aid people in this process, she once wrote a song containing a New Year's resolution.[223]

Fellowship Meetings

While Phoebe Palmer practiced and recommended a daily devotional time, regular church attendance, strict Sabbath observance, and periodic days of contemplation, she had little to say about small-group fellowship meetings. Her practice indicated the importance of these meetings in her own spiritual development. She rarely missed the Tuesday Meeting and often attended class meetings, love feasts, and testimony meetings, but her advice to others rarely mentions these means of grace. She did establish and recommend "Christian Vigilance Bands" to promote the revivals she began, but these were task groups rather than growth groups. This lack is especially puzzling in view of the importance John Wesley placed on such gatherings. Perhaps Mrs. Palmer assumed that her converts would join a Methodist church and would be committed to attending a class or that they would at least attend

Hindrances to Holiness

Fancy Dress

Along with John Wesley, Phoebe Palmer believed that a significant hindrance to holiness was the desire to be fashionably dressed.[225] The problem with following the current styles is twofold: it betrays a divided heart and it wastes money. Phoebe Palmer thought she could tell at a glance exactly who were the "votaries of fashion and folly."[226] Those who wear stylish clothes show themselves to be proud because they want others to admire them.[227] They are "lovers of pleasures more than lovers of God" (2 Tim. 3:4), whose livery reveals that they are friends of the world and at enmity with God (James 4:4). Their sin is that they love eye-pleasing fashions more than the plain adornment the Bible requires and that they are afraid to dress differently from everyone else, even if God has commanded it.[228] The other aspect of the sinfulness of fashionable dress is its expense. Phoebe Palmer knew of "Christian" women who wore earrings and other jewelry costing up to five thousand dollars. Such an expenditure of the Lord's money was clearly wrong. Mrs. Palmer spoke out against such abuse of the Lord's property, calling those who did it "heathen." Quoting from Judges 8:24, "They had golden earrings because they were Ishmaelites," she said that all who wore gold or other jewelry were not true Israelites but Ishmaelites. They should purify themselves by getting rid of these "relics of heathendom" by burying them as Jacob's household buried their idols and earrings at Shechem (Gen. 35:4).[229] Mrs. Palmer once challenged her hearers to follow these directions, at least symbolically, and fifty dollars worth of jewelry was turned in to be sold. The money was given to missionary work.[230] So sensitive was Mrs. Palmer about "costly array" that once when she was given a gold watch as a gift, she exchanged it for a silver one so as not to give offense.[231]

Not only did Phoebe Palmer quote Scripture against superfluous adornment, she also had a stock of stories about the evil end of those who disobeyed the Lord in this regard. One woman of whom she had heard was a member of a fashionable church that taught that Scriptures such as "Be not conformed to this world" (Rom. 12:2) have nothing to do with dress. When reproved by a friend for her attachment to "the vanities of the world," the woman replied that her church thought this an unimportant matter. The woman became sick and realized she would die soon. As she prepared for death, she said she had absolute certainty that she was going to heaven. When the moment of death came, her friends gathered around her to witness her peaceful transition to the heavenly world. Suddenly she gave a fearful shriek and sat bolt upright on the bed, every feature distorted with terror. Horror and disappointment had transformed her countenance so that it looked indescribably fiendish. "I can't die! I won't die!" she screamed. At that moment, the minister of her fashionable church entered the room. She yelled at him, "Out of the door, thou deceiver of men!" Then she fell back and was no more.[232]

Elegant Worship

Not only were fashionable clothes a hindrance to holiness, but so were the elegant churches attended by people in those clothes. John Wesley had told his followers that they must listen to preaching on benches without backs, but in Phoebe Palmer's day the Methodist church buildings were becoming more luxurious and the church services more liturgical.[233]

Mrs. Palmer resisted these innovations. She loved a "good, neat, commodious, and dignified place of worship," but thought needlessly expensive churches were in *"ill taste."* Worse than that, they were displeasing to God. "Can it be pleasing to Him," she wondered, "that money should be taken out of His treasury to the amount of $100,000, $200,000, and even $300,000 for the purpose of fostering a taste for display . . . ?" An adequate church could be built for less than $60,000, and the surplus money given to build several churches in places that had no church. Another reason to oppose expensive churches is that they serve exactly the opposite function from that for which they were intended. Instead of being a place for the Spirit's presence, they drive him away: "Costly churches bring in their train costly worship, operatic singing, worldly, self-seeking trustees, and generally the absence of godly people, and of the precious influence of the Holy Spirit."[234]

Phoebe Palmer took issue with the costly Methodist church services as well as with the costly Methodist church buildings. She called these liturgical services "proxy worship." Only the minister kneels to pray. He is paid to do so by the church members, who sit comfortably and listen. Then there is "proxy-singing" when the orchestra and choir, all paid, and mostly unconverted, sing in order to quiet "the body and conscience" of the hearers. How different this is from the kind of worship commanded in the Bible and recommended by John Wesley![235]

Pious Amusements

Christians in Phoebe Palmer's day were not only tempted to ape the world in their dress and in their churches but also in the way they used their time. Because Mrs. Palmer had given herself entirely to the Lord, she felt grave responsibility for time he had given her. The truly committed one "feels that he has not one moment of time at his own disposal, and he dares not spend it in any pursuit but what will bear the inscription, *Holiness to the Lord*"(Exod. 28:36).[236] She therefore had little patience with those who proposed activities that did not directly benefit the Lord's kingdom. Her attitude on this issue is reflected by the scorn she poured on one family.

Phoebe Palmer knew that Lyman Beecher had been an advocate of holiness, and she became acquainted with his daughter Catharine in 1845 when they worked together in the campaign to civilize the frontier. Thus, she was grievously disappointed when Henry Ward Beecher, pastor of the influential Plymouth Congregational Church in Brooklyn, recommended the installation of bowling alleys and billiard tables in the new YMCA building. In doing so he was "prostituting" his influence and thus was no longer worthy of the title "Reverend."[237] Earlier in the year, Mrs. Palmer had editorialized against the Beecher family and their involvement in pious amusements. She reported that years ago she had seen the trouble coming when *Uncle Tom's Cabin* was first published. Blind to the effect of the book in stirring up moral outrage against slavery, Phoebe Palmer criticized it on two counts. She opposed the work because it was a novel based on fact. The mixture of fact and fiction, "truth and error," would bewilder the public mind and lead them into a mongrel religion, like that of the Samaritans, who "feared the LORD, and served their own Gods" (2 Kings 17:33). The second ill effect that she saw coming from *Uncle Tom's Cabin* was that it begot a taste for fictitious literature in "hundreds of religious families where novels had hitherto been prohibited." Thus, the wolf of fiction would sneak into the fold wearing the clothing of "pious(?) authorship."[238]

She went on to report that bad had come to worse, just as she had predicted. Now *Uncle Tom's Cabin* had been made into a play. There must be thousands of families where "professedly pious parents have been induced to attend the theater for the first time, who never would have entered one, but that the matter had been rendered seemingly tame by the fact that she who had conceived the plot, had once been known as an earnest Christian." Obviously once people have been enticed into a theater, they will keep going back, to the certain ruin of their souls. "Who would have ever thought," exclaimed Phoebe Palmer, "that the name of the author of an excellent tract on practical holiness, would one day be emblazoned in large letters on theatrical posters, by way of luring men to perdition."[239] So strongly did Mrs. Palmer feel about the theater that she quoted a minister friend who said that in going to the theater the evening when he was shot, Abraham Lincoln had departed from the "shadow of the Almighty" (Ps. 91:1), which would have protected him.[240]

Besides opposing pious novels and edifying plays because they wasted time that could be spent in the Lord's service and blurred the line between the Christian and the unholy world, Phoebe Palmer said these forms of recreation raised questions about the "competency of religion to satisfy the aspirations of the soul." If Christians really do find all they need in Jesus, why do they turn to these watered-down versions of the world's pleasures? "Are not our efforts to introduce them a mortifying confession to the world, of the mental and spiritual weakness of the Church?" What Christians need is a fresh baptism of the Holy Ghost; then "we shall no more desire these 'Pious Amusements' than the millionaire does the poor pay and hard fare of the organ grinder."[241]

Money

The fourth hindrance to holiness was increasing wealth. John Wesley had pointed out the inverse relationship between wealth and true Christianity in the church, and Phoebe Palmer echoed his concern.[242] Like Wesley, she was afraid of having rich people in the church because they drive out the Holy Spirit "who can only be cherished by the unostentatious, careful, humble, child-like dependence on God."[243] She criticized one rich church which had seven hundred dollars for a fresco, and four or five thousand for other decorations, but refused to take an offering to help raise one hundred fifty dollars to repair a missionary church. She wanted nothing to do with people who had grown rich and had trained themselves to expect luxuries: "Let us live and die with a people who have not so many artificial wants as to put up the bar against applications from necessitous churches."[244] Her kind of holiness would make no compromise with the world. It eschewed the world's fashions, the world's luxuries, the world's entertainment, and the world's attitude toward money. Mrs. Palmer's warnings about money were not "sour grapes"; first from Dr. Palmer's practice and later from Mrs. Palmer's publications, they received a large income. Because of this income they were able to offer their services as revivalists without charge and were also able to support a variety of evangelistic and benevolent enterprises.[245]

Phoebe Palmer wrote in an editorial in the *Guide to Holiness* against the compromises believers are tempted to make when they become wealthy. Citing the Lord's command not to lay up treasure on earth, she warned those whose minds were "occupied with the accumulation of earthly gains" that the "one great life-work of the Christian" is evangelism. She went on to say that bad as it is for a heathen to bow before his idol of wood, it is infinitely worse for those who call themselves Christians to "bow down to a god of their own creation, that is, money that they have hoarded up for the glorification of themselves and [their] families."[246]

ESCHATOLOGY

Adventism

Sections of the Christian church have always treasured the expectation of the "soon return of the Lord" or at least the inauguration of the Millennium. In the early 1840s there was great excitement over William Miller, whose biblical calculations had persuaded him that Jesus would return in 1843 or shortly thereafter. The speculation about the time of the Lord's return spread to the Methodists, and G. F. Cox of Portland wrote an article in *Zion's Herald* predicting the second advent. He claimed he had the "clear light of the Holy Spirit" and found not one biblical objection to the idea that the Lord would return in 1845. Mrs. Palmer wrote to Cox for further information. This letter reveals her eschatological thinking.[247]

Phoebe Palmer began by reporting that her mind had been "very seriously impressed" with this subject for the last two years. Probably she had heard of Miller, who had come to national attention in 1840. Admitting she "would love to embrace the doctrine," she inquired why he believed as he did. Warning Mr. Cox that Satan is ready to deceive us if we do not have a "Thus saith the Lord," she wondered what biblical evidence he had for his position. She closed the letter with the caution that interest in

Adventism was drawing people away from concentrating on Christ as Savior and that such eschatological speculation takes away from the church's missionary operations.[248]

No reply to this letter exists, but Mrs. Palmer continued to be interested in the Adventist movement. One of her close friends, Charles Fitch, became a prominent Millerite leader. Their friendship remained strong, at least through 1842.[249] Evidently Phoebe Palmer felt some responsibility for the Adventists, because in 1844, after Jesus did not come as Miller had said he would, she wrote to Miller urging him to tell his followers to get on with ordinary life. In an ambiguous passage she says, "Should not those lecturers, with myself, who have brought the people out under the auspices of a faith which has failed, be helpful in remanding them back. . . ?"[250] When she said, "with myself," did she mean that she, like them, had taught Adventism, or merely that they, like her, should now point out the mistake of Adventism? Most likely she meant the latter, because nothing that she published in the *Guide to Holiness* nor the *Christian Advocate and Journal* before 1845 even mentions Adventism.[251]

Despite her disenchantment with Millerite Adventism, as Phoebe Palmer grew older she became more convinced that the Lord would return soon. While she admitted that the time of the Lord's coming could not be fixed, in 1866 she wondered whether that year marked the end of history.[252] She pointed out that many commentators, including Wesley and Fletcher, believed that all the Bible's prophecies would come true between 1830 and 1880; several even settled on the year 1866. Therefore Christians should expect their Lord's return and be ready for his coming. They should hasten to spread the good news of redemption because the time is short.[253]

Mrs. Palmer's first editorial of 1867 opened the year with the gratuitous admission that the Lord did not return in 1866. Nevertheless, she knew the Lord's coming was at hand, and so she challenged her readers to do more for God in 1867 than they ever had done before. In subsequent editorials she returned to this theme, reminding believers of the Second Coming and of what they should do to be ready for it.[254]

Israel

Closely tied with her conviction that she was living in the "latter part of the last days" was Mrs. Palmer's concern for the

Jews.[255] Her study of prophecy had led her to expect a great ingathering of God's chosen people before the Messiah returned. The return of some Jews to Palestine strengthened her belief that the time of Israel's restoration was at hand. She argued that because they were seeing the fulfillment of the prophecies that Israel would return to the land, they should also expect to see the fulfillment of the prophecies that promise that Israel will accept the Messiah. Most Christians have not been aware enough of God's word to his ancient people, so they have neither prayed nor worked enough for their conversion. Mrs. Palmer worked for the conversion of the Jews by promoting the sending of Methodist missionaries to Palestine. She wrote a tract, organized committees, and gave money to the cause. In an effort to win Jews nearer home, she established a mission to New York Jews, adopted a Jewish boy, and printed a letter in the *Guide to Holiness* showing Jews that Jesus was Messiah. The boy soon returned to his parents, and neither the letter, the mission, nor the missionaries had much effect.[256]

THE IMPORTANCE OF PHOEBE PALMER'S THEOLOGY

While many of the leaders of the Methodist church were friendly toward Phoebe Palmer and lauded her ministry, some rejected her theology. The General Conference of 1852 took indirect action against her by warning Methodists against new ideas about entire sanctification:

> We advise you, however, in speaking or writing of holiness, to follow the well-sustained views and even the phraseology employed in the writings of Wesley and Fletcher, which are not superseded by the more recent writers on this subject. Avoid both new theories, new expressions, and new measures on this subject, and adhere closely to the ancient landmarks.[257]

In addition, several books and articles on sanctification written by prominent Methodists took issue with parts of her theology but never mentioned her name.[258] Others condemned her with very faint praise, like the editor who said,

> Her peculiar views of entire sanctification we never tried to understand. We doubt if we could now state, or at any time could have stated, what they were. To our mind this appeared

a matter of small moment. . . . The one fact that seemed to us admirable was that here was a Christian who *believed* the Gospel to be the power of God unto salvation, and who was resolved to make its power felt over the world.[259]

The opposition from people who overlooked her theology or sought to correct parts of it had relatively little effect. Sales of their books were small compared to the sale of Mrs. Palmer's works.[260] In addition, these writers were friendly critics. They accepted the Wesleyan doctrine that entire sanctification was attainable instantaneously by faith in this life but were not comfortable with the way Mrs. Palmer explained it. Their voices were drowned out by people in the Methodist church whose quarrel was not so much with Phoebe Palmer as with John Wesley. Some argued that sanctification was not distinct from regeneration. One of these was Samuel Franklin, a Methodist elder from Illinois. Phoebe Palmer would not allow his book on her shelf without writing a caveat in the flyleaf: "I think this a very unprofitable book. . . . I would not pronounce it tame but dangerous."[261] Others argued that entire sanctification was not attainable in this life. Daniel Whedon, who for many years edited the prestigious *Methodist Quarterly Review*, wrote of sanctification that, although theologians "cannot understand the thing we attempt to describe," nevertheless entire sanctification remains "a goal . . . set up for our holy ambition" which is "a living incitement to progressive holiness."[262] In the quarter-century after Mrs. Palmer's death, the middle ground occupied by those who believed in Wesleyan entire sanctification but differed with Mrs. Palmer was slowly eaten away. Increasingly the battle was fought between those who believed in holiness, as defined by John Wesley or Phoebe Palmer, and those who did not.[263]

The establishment and growth of the National Camp Meeting Association for the Promotion of Holiness in the early 1870s institutionalized Mrs. Palmer's view of sanctification. Headed by John S. Inskip, a close friend of the Palmers, this interdenominational organization held immensely popular camp meetings in several parts of the nation and issued tracts, journals, and songbooks to spread its views. Inskip's doctrine of sanctification was the same as Phoebe Palmer's, and when the movement adopted a statement of doctrine at the First General Holiness Assembly in 1885 they followed her teaching. During the fifteen years from the assembly to the turn of the century, when the advocates of holiness were "coming out" or being "put out" of the Methodist church, the denominations they established stood squarely on the foundation of Phoebe Palmer's interpretation of Wesley's theology. These holiness denominations, many of which merged to form the Church of the Nazarene in 1907 and 1908, adopted all six of her changes in the Wesleyan idea of Christian perfection. Her three steps to sanctification became one of the main ways to receive the second blessing, and her altar imagery helped to shape their preaching and singing. For example, Elisha Hoffman's invitation song, "Is Your All on the Altar of Sacrifice Laid?" probably written in 1873, clearly articulates Phoebe Palmer's teaching. The song still appeared in the hymnals of the Nazarene, Wesleyan, and Free Methodist churches through 1960.[264]

Phoebe Palmer is important as a theologian not only because her thought shaped the theology of the Holiness movement, but because when the Pentecostal and Charismatic movements arose out of the Holiness tradition, they took Phoebe Palmer's theology and added tongues to it.[265] Donald Dayton has argued that Oberlin Perfectionism is the "middle term" in the development of Pentecostalism, linking Methodism with the rise of the tongues movement.[266] However true that may be for those who came to Pentecostalism from traditions outside Methodism, those who came through Methodism owe much to Phoebe Palmer. Her popularization of Pentecostal language, her emphasis on immediate sanctification, her understanding of faith, and her insistence on testimony laid a firm foundation for later Pentecostal developments. Even the three steps commonly taught as a means of receiving the baptism of the Holy Spirit in most sections of the movement today are similar to the steps Mrs. Palmer taught.

Seekers for the full baptism in Pentecostalism are usually told: (1) be converted, (2) obey God fully, and (3) believe.[267] The first step, conversion, is implicit in the teaching of Phoebe Palmer. The second step, obedience, is a renunciation of all sinful practices and attitudes, and promise of future commitment. It is exactly what Mrs. Palmer means by entire consecration. Faith, the third step, means believing that God will fulfill his promise. Pentecostals teach that when faith is sufficient, God sends the baptism. Similarly, Phoebe Palmer said that God sanctifies the believer when the gift is apprehended by faith. Many Pentecostals do not mention Mrs. Palmer's third step, testimony, but the public speaking in tongues may serve the same function.

A major difference between Mrs. Palmer and most modern Pentecostals is their understanding of the role of assurance. Many Pentecostals scorn the idea that one could receive the baptism and not feel any different. For them a feeling of inner peace gives the assurance; without it one has not yet received the baptism.[268] Nevertheless, some Pentecostal teachers tell their fully consecrated hearers that God has baptized them, even if they do not feel any different. In response to their obedience, God will give the gift of tongues and other extraordinary signs to confirm their Holy Spirit baptism.[269] The affinities of this doctrine with Mrs. Palmer's are clear.

While it is unlikely that many in the Pentecostal or Charismatic movements today know about Phoebe Palmer, the situation of their theological forebears was different. They were only a generation removed from Mrs. Palmer herself, and her ideas were still being publicized through her books, through various Tuesday Meetings, and through the *Guide to Holiness*, which for three years at the turn of the century bore the title *Guide to Holiness and Pentecostal Life*. Even if they had no direct contact with Phoebe Palmer, they certainly could have imbibed her ideas from the preaching and singing of the Holiness movement.

CHAPTER SIX:
Phoebe Palmer As Revivalist

"There was about her but little of personal attractiveness. Simple in manner and plain in person and dress, even to severity, hesitant in speech and almost destitute of emotion in all her addresses and exercises," nevertheless Phoebe Palmer attracted thousands of people to hear her message.[1] Many came to her home to participate in the Tuesday Meeting; others came to hear her speak at camp meetings or church services. In addition to leading thousands of revival meetings, Mrs. Palmer articulated a clear theology of revival. She also civilized and systematized the methods of frontier Methodist revivalism, particularly the preaching of holiness and the emphasis on lay ministry, making them part of the American revival tradition.

THE TUESDAY MEETING FOR THE PROMOTION OF HOLINESS

Phoebe Palmer's career as a revivalist began when she went downstairs to a women's prayer meeting her sister Sarah was holding in the home their families shared. Soon the meeting was open to men, and Phoebe eventually took over leadership of the gathering. She called it "The Tuesday Meeting for the Promotion of Holiness." In the almost forty years between 1837 and 1874, thousands of people drawn from the leading Evangelical denominations visited her parlors. There between walls hung with the mottoes, "The Lord Our Righteousness" and "Holiness to the Lord," while the pictures of Wesley and Fletcher looked on, many professed entire sanctification. Some left to establish similar

"Tuesday Meetings," so that by 1887 they were being held in 238 places, some as far away as England, India, and New Zealand.[2] For those who could not come to the meeting in New York, Mrs. Palmer used the *Guide to Holiness* to publish detailed accounts of the testimonies given there.[3] In the Tuesday Meeting were present the most important elements of Mrs. Palmer's ministry: her stress on holiness, experience, and the Bible; the involvement of the Methodist hierarchy, laymen, and women; as well as the opposing tendencies of ecumenism and schism.

The meeting began at three o'clock on Tuesday afternoon as Dr. Palmer or Dr. Bangs read from the Scripture. Then the group sang a song. Several of the ministers present next led in prayer, and then the meeting was open for anyone to speak. One of the leaders explained the purpose and customs of the meeting. Women and men were equally encouraged to speak, and the laity was not expected to "wait for the ministry." Testimonies of God's dealing with the soul, exhortations, reports of answers to prayer, and prayer requests, along with suggestions for group prayer or song, were all welcome. Inquirers were especially requested to speak their minds freely, to tell of their past struggles, or—either by word or merely by standing—to request prayer for their sanctification. But controversy was not welcome. The meetings were "not for debate, controversy, or speechifying; but for holiness." If anyone said anything which magnified one group or belief and denigrated another, "a cold chilliness [stole] over every one present." The next ones to speak did all they could to remove the "least *tincture* of the sect, and smooth off the rough edges, and calm every rising suspicion."[4]

Many came to the meeting to find holiness. They would rise to declare their need, voice their aspirations, and ask their questions. In the midst of so many who had found what they were seeking, these inquirers would be reminded of the shorter way to sanctification, urged to make entire consecration, challenged to believe God's Word, and encouraged to confess what God had done for them. The support and sympathy of the group helped many over the final barrier to holiness, and seeing another person receive the blessing strengthened the faith of those who had already professed it.[5]

Common allegiance to the Bible brought people from many denominations together. Phoebe Palmer rejoiced to see "Methodists, Baptists, Presbyterians, Episcopalians, Quakers, United Brethren, and [messianic] Jews" gathering "with one accord." She urged her guests to forget "creeds, confessions, hair-splittings, and party distinctions" and to sit "side by side, drinking deeply of the one living fountain," the Bible. "Nothing but the spirit of this blessed book," she affirmed, "will finally extirpate a sectarian spirit."[6]

Another unifying factor was the meeting's stress on experience. Mrs. Palmer urged people not only to investigate holiness as a scriptural doctrine, but also "greatly to desire the attainment of the experience."[7] She promoted the Tuesday Meeting as "a little social circle where experimental testimony may be heard on this subject" in "unreserved fellowship."[8] Because Phoebe Palmer believed that real-life experience was worth much more than speculative theory, she encouraged people in the Tuesday Meeting to tell the story of how they experienced sanctification.[9] This strategy promoted unity because while one could quibble with someone else's theory, no one could deny someone else's experience.

The distinguished and the obscure of the nineteenth-century American Evangelical world met in the fellowship of the Tuesday Meeting. Joining Nathan Bangs and Thomas Upham in frequent attendance were Stephen Olin, president of Wesleyan University in Connecticut; John Dempster, founder of the institutions which later became Boston University and Garrett-Evangelical Seminary; Methodist bishops Edmund Janes, Leonidas Hamline, and William Taylor; along with Amanda Smith, the noted black evangelist.[10] Rubbing shoulders with them in Mrs. Palmer's crowded parlors were twenty or thirty ministers of various denominations, a number of laymen, and a crowd of godly women. Some spent the whole day getting to the meeting, coming from as far away as seventy miles.[11] Here they met "free from all imposing restraint." With "ministerial position . . . seemingly unthought of," her guests could "mingle freely in testimony on the common ground of Bible truth and Bible experience."[12] Phoebe Palmer was especially solicitous for the women present. She particularly valued their contributions. One observer noted:

> The controlling influence of Mrs. Palmer in the services gives full encouragement to any Christian women who may desire to participate; and very often some of the most thrilling, intelligent, and beautiful experiences are given by the godly women of the assembly.[13]

Although the Palmers had to build an addition to their home, and later had to move to a bigger house to accommodate the Tuesday Meeting, Mrs. Palmer steadfastly refused to move the meeting to a church building. While the informal sense of inviting a few friends into the parlor was necessarily lost when two or three hundred people attended the meeting, she wanted to do as much as she could to avoid the formality of a church service. Another reason for having the meeting in her home was that it was a safe place for those who were not from denominations noted for preaching sanctification to find out more about the doctrine. Many, especially ministers, could investigate holiness without exciting adverse comment. Most important to Phoebe Palmer, holding the meeting in her home did her part to keep holiness from being regarded as the doctrine of just one denomination. Because, according to Mrs. Palmer, "Holiness is not the distinguishing doctrine of a sect merely, but the crowning doctrine of the Bible," it was important to teach holiness in a place where people of many denominations could be identified with it.[14]

Although people from many denominations felt a strong sense of unity at the Tuesday Meeting, the solidarity was limited to those who believed that holiness really was "the crowning doctrine of the Bible." Thus, Phoebe Palmer's ecumenism also had a schismatic effect. Those for whom sanctification created such a strong bond across denominational lines were apt to feel a correspondingly weaker bond to the members of their own denominations who did not accept Mrs. Palmer's teachings. Phoebe Palmer herself was disappointed that many preachers in the Methodist church were neglecting to teach about holiness and so did not live up to their heritage.[15] She had even stronger words for those who opposed the doctrine. Calling them "troubler[s] of Israel," she compared them to the ten spies who gave the bad report about the Promised Land (Num. 13–14). Even worse, they were murderers who destroyed the souls of God's people. Mrs. Palmer cited the case of a young woman who was told that one could not attain entire sanctification in this life. If the woman had believed this false report, she might have fallen away and been damned eternally. "Where," Phoebe Palmer inquired, "might the blood of her soul been found? Would it not be on the skirts of that professor who testified that it is not the privilege of the Lord's people to be holy in the present life?" (Jer. 2:34).[16]

This tendency of the Tuesday Meeting to strengthen the commitment along theological lines and weaken it within denominational bounds showed itself in the organization John Inskip helped to found. As we have seen, Inskip was a regular attender at the Tuesday Meeting, and there met ministers of several different denominations. The National Camp Meeting Association for the Promotion of Holiness which emerged under his leadership had the same ecumenical and schismatic effects as the meeting he attended. Embracing holiness advocates from several traditions, it soon became a greater object of loyalty to its members than their own denominations.[17]

THEOLOGY OF REVIVAL

Besides leading the Tuesday Meeting in her home, Phoebe Palmer also traveled across the continent and across the ocean to speak at more than three hundred camp meetings and revival services.[18] As she participated in these meetings, and especially as she saw great blessing on her efforts in the revival of 1857–58 and its British aftermath, Mrs. Palmer worked out a theology of revival. Her thought in this area was not novel but represented an articulation of the thinking about revival which made the Methodists the fastest-growing denomination in the first half of the nineteenth century.

Because not only Mrs. Palmer's thought about revival but also many of the methods she employed in her meetings were similar to Finney's, some might think that her revivalism depended directly on his. This is not so. Instead, the reason that Phoebe Palmer's theology and methodology of revival were so similar to Finney's was that they both drew on the common source of Methodist revivalism. It is a commonplace of American religious history that Finney "Arminianized" the Reformed tradition in theology, but few realize that he "Methodistized" the Reformed tradition in revival methodology. Many still credit (or blame) him for the development of the new measures, such as the anxious bench, protracted meetings, public prayer for people by name, female participation in mixed prayer meetings, and direct, searching preaching. Richard Carwardine has pointed out that Finney was not the source of these new measures, nor was he even the first to move them from the frontier into the eastern cities. These measures originated in the frontier camp meetings and were developed by the Methodists both on the frontier and in their urban churches. All Finney did was bring the means the Methodists were using among the lower classes into the respectable

Presbyterian and Congregational churches. Because Phoebe Palmer grew up with well-developed revivalism in her own Methodist church, it was not necessary for her to go down to Finneyite Philistia to obtain the tools of revival.[19]

Phoebe Palmer was never troubled by the idea that revivals were caused by the inexplicable actions of an arbitrary Deity. Her Wesleyan doctrine of prevenient grace made it clear that God offered to every person the chance to be saved and to every church the chance to be renewed. She believed that while no human can ever do anything good by mere natural ability, God is so gracious that he never leaves anyone in the merely natural state. Christ is the light that enlightens everyone who comes into the world (John 1:9), and with that light God graciously provides the ability to turn to him.[20] Just as justification occurs when the individual turns to the Lord in repentance and faith, so revival occurs when those who profess to be Christians turn to the Lord and begin to serve him aright.

For Phoebe Palmer then, revival was "only a return to primitive Christianity untrammelled by mere human opinions and church conventionalisms"; it was "an experimental recognition of the doctrines of heart holiness, or in other words, the full baptism of the Holy Ghost, such as the 120 received on the day of Pentecost"; Pentecost itself was the first revival, and because God baptizes with the Spirit today, the church may experience Pentecost today.[21] God has established the plans for revival, and according to Mrs. Palmer, if Christians follow them, there is no reason the revival cannot begin "this hour." "TRUE REVIVALS ARE THE EFFECTS OF A LAW," she declared. All that believers need do is work according to that law, and they will see "a model revival."[22]

In Mrs. Palmer's theology human beings play an important role in advancing or retarding a revival. God is always eager to visit his people with revival power, so when revival tarries there must be some human sin that is keeping God away.[23] A church that does not have as many conversions this year as it had members last year must have an Achan in it, she reasoned (Josh. 7).[24] Phoebe Palmer once wrote to a congregation to tell them that their behavior was hindering her prayers for their revival. She believed the decree had gone forth from God's throne that they should be revived, but because they were not willing to obey the Lord, they were taking upon themselves "the awful responsibility of making that decree null and void."[25] The actions which could vacate a decree of the sovereign Lord were various: In England Mrs. Palmer had forced her hosts to remove liquor from the church basement and liquor dealers from the church vestry lest the work of God be impeded.[26] Other checks to the Spirit of God might include the prohibition of female ministry, a lack of emphasis on entire sanctification, a casual attitude about evangelism, an unwillingness to devote time and energy to the Lord's work, or a neglect of the stated means of grace, such as prayer, class, and preaching meetings.[27]

METHODOLOGY OF REVIVAL

Because God is always willing to send a revival, and because he has established a law whereby revivals work, the methods humans employ to promote the revival are very important. If they work according to God's plan, they will see results; but if they ignore the divine directions, they will be frustrated. Phoebe Palmer was convinced that God blessed her efforts because she followed his methods. Those methods were largely the methods of the Methodist frontier revivalists, civilized and organized for the urban setting.

Preaching Holiness

John Wesley was convinced that God had given the Methodists the special responsibility of preaching holiness. To him it was "the grand depositum which God has lodged with the people called Methodists; and for the sake of propagating this chiefly He appeared to have raised us up."[28] When the American Methodist church was founded at the Christmas conference in 1784, they took as their mission "to reform the continent and spread scriptural holiness through these lands."[29] The circuit riders who crisscrossed the growing nation to fulfill that mission took with them the Bible, the hymnal, and the *Discipline.* They also took with them the doctrines of free salvation, faith salvation, and full salvation.[30] Phoebe Palmer continued in this distinguished tradition, but unlike the circuit rider, she concentrated on the preaching of entire sanctification.

Mrs. Palmer preached holiness because she was convinced that sanctification was the key to revival. Others had urged that when nonbelievers were present, holiness should not be presented, and they attributed the decline in the effectiveness of camp meetings to the preaching of holiness.[31] Phoebe Palmer vigorously resisted this idea, saying that, according to Wesley and in her own experience, the more holiness was preached, the more sinners were converted.[32] She believed that people dismissed the Christian faith because they were dissatisfied with the unholy lives of many professed Christians. The way to win the unconverted, she said, was to announce the good news that believers need not be mired in sin but could live holy lives. When the Christian life was presented in its fullness, then even infidels would be attracted to it.[33]

Another reason Phoebe Palmer gave for specializing in holiness is that "judgment must begin at the house of God" (1 Peter 4:17). "An unholy membership clogs the chariot wheels of the church [Exod. 14:25], and prevents her aggressive movements"; if God were to pour out a revival and bring many into a church full of unsanctified members, who would care for those newborn Christians? God withholds his blessing until the members are willing to become "nursing fathers and mothers" (1 Thess. 2:7, 11), so that the "babes, born into the kingdom of Christ" will not "languish and die for want of the pains-taking assiduities of holy love."[34]

Sanctification not only makes members willing to be nursing fathers and mothers for baby Christians, it also motivates believers to be begetters and bearers of spiritual children. Phoebe Palmer believed that getting one person sanctified was as good as getting twenty persons saved because with holiness comes a new concern for evangelism.[35] One characteristic of those who receive full salvation is their "immediate absorption . . . in the work of soul saving." Sanctified people have a new understanding of their responsibility to those outside Christ, and they have a new "sympathy with the Saviour, whose one great life business was to seek and to save the lost" (Luke 19:10).[36]

Lay Ministry

Besides the preaching of holiness, the other characteristic of the frontier Methodists that Phoebe Palmer brought to urban revivalism was the use of laypersons in ministry. John Wesley had appointed laymen as traveling preachers and approved of women who itinerated. He used settled laypersons to lead the bands and classes he organized. When Methodism first came to America it was entirely a lay movement, with each member feeling some sense of responsibility for its ministry.[37] By the 1830s, however, the situation was different. Laypersons continued to play important roles. They itinerated, preached in their local societies, and led classes. But the problem was that the Methodists had over-methodized the ministry: They seemed to have an official position for every kind of Christian service. Some laypersons had the idea that the only way to serve the Lord was to fill a recognized position. Because there was no official position called "personal evangelist," many laypersons felt they had no responsibility in this area. Mrs. Palmer tried to reverse this trend by challenging laypersons to be more involved in evangelism and by organizing their efforts to do so.

By her example, Phoebe Palmer encouraged laypersons to be evangelists. She had dedicated herself to the work of winning souls after the death of her daughter Eliza, and her work with the tract society and other benevolent associations was an expression of that dedication.[38] She once declared, "If I have one passion above another, it is a passion for soul saving."[39] Not only did she go into the tenements and to the camp meetings to talk to people about Jesus, but she was also careful to look for every opportunity that might come her way. In her *Incidental Illustrations* she recounted several such encounters, including how she spoke to all kinds of people—from a ship's captain to the deck swabs, from a groomsman at a wedding breakfast to a woman on her death bed, and from a prosperous liquor dealer to a hopeless drunk.[40]

Theology of Lay Ministry

Besides leading by example, Phoebe Palmer also taught laypeople that they had a duty to evangelize. She felt they should be motivated by God's command, by the need of the lost, and by the promised heavenly reward. Mrs. Palmer's argument began with the biblical premise, "... Your body is the temple of the Holy Ghost which is in you, ... For ye are bought with a price: therefore glorify God in your body, and in your spirit, which are God's" (1 Cor. 6:19–20). Christians have been bought by Christ and are his servants, hence they must obey his command to bring others to him.[41] Human beings are not the only servants Christ has, but they are the only ones to whom he has entrusted the glorious responsibility of bringing the news of salvation. Angels and archangels may have supernatural powers, but "God has dispensed to [humans] the ability to do what even Gabriel may not do."[42] Therefore "SOUL SAVING is the one great work of the CHRISTIAN, whether young or old, rich or poor."[43] Christians must be willing to go to any length to win someone to Christ. Phoebe Palmer said that "any individual unwilling to circumnavigate the globe for the purposes of saving a soul . . . is unworthy of the name of Christian."[44] Not only does God command believers to spread the Good News; he also holds them accountable if they do not obey. Frequently she spoke about people who failed to evangelize as murderers, saying that in disobeying God they were staining their skirts with the blood of the lost (Jer. 2:34).[45] She also warned them that God would hold an inquest over the spirits lost through their carelessness and require this blood at their hands (Gen. 9:5; Ezek. 3:18).[46]

Another reason for telling others about Christ is the desperate plight of the unbeliever. Phoebe Palmer did not compare sinners to spiders dangling over open fires, but she did tell people "that the sinner is condemned already, and that the sentence might be executed at any moment." The lost are "rapidly verging eternity"; they stand on slippery rocks at the edge of hell, "and fiery billows roll beneath."[47] Believers must therefore "not rest night or day without warning" the unsaved of their dangerous state.[48] Satan, by means of the grim reaper, is always harvesting his crop of humans. God has given Christians brains to understand what happens to the nonbeliever. This knowledge should motivate them to work diligently to cheat the devil of his prey and to gather the harvest for Christ.[49]

In addition to obeying the Lord, saving their own souls and the souls of others, believers have another motive for trying to persuade people to become Christians. God promises to reward them richly for their efforts. The rewards begin in this life. "In about the same measure," Phoebe Palmer said, "[that] we abound in labor for the salvation of those around us, God dispenses blessing to our souls."[50] Even greater than the earthly is the heavenly reward. Phoebe Palmer believed that there would be varying degrees of reward in heaven, and that those degrees would be indicated by the number of "stars" or jewels in one's crown of life. Drawing on Daniel 12:3 and Revelation 2:10 and 12:1, she maintained that the more souls one brings to the Lord, the more stars one will have in the heavenly crown: "Who should be satisfied with a starless crown, when, after a little lingering on earth, it may be set with many brilliant stars?"[51] Mrs. Palmer similarly applied Jesus' words about laying up treasure in heaven (Matt. 6:20) and his words about bearing fruit (John 15:8) to evangelism, telling a story of a boy who had brought fifty-five friends to Christ before he died of tuberculosis in his fifteenth year. She then urged her readers, "Resolve that the one great business of life shall be to glorify God, by laying up much treasure in heaven."[52]

Organization of Lay Ministry

Phoebe Palmer did not just tell people they should be involved in evangelism; rather, she showed them how to organize their efforts. Mrs. Palmer knew that nothing important is accomplished without a well-thought-out system, so it was her desire "to *methodize* the great work of the world's conversion."[53] Because revival is an attack against Satan, she said it requires at least as much planning and preparation as a battle between nations.[54] Weighty matters require ponderous thought and effort. Because one soul is worth more than the entire universe, everything else the Christian does is merely an avocation compared with the "one work to which all else must be subservient." Because it required such great effort and such careful thought, Mrs. Palmer said, "This revival work is a business; it is the business to which we have devoted our lives."[55]

In seeking to "methodize" the conversion of the world, Phoebe and Walter Palmer developed a plan of campaign which they followed in most of their revival meetings. This plan had its origin in the ideas about revival which Mrs. Palmer published in the *Christian Advocate and Journal* in the spring of 1857. Seeing her method work so successfully in the revival of 1857–58 convinced her that she was following the Lord's pattern, and she stuck to it through the end of her life, modifying it only by the addition of Pentecostal terminology at the beginning of their British trip. Of course, local conditions often made it necessary for the Palmers to change their approach, so no two series of meetings were exactly the same. The description that follows is a generalized plan drawn from the Palmers' practices over a number of years.[56]

The first step in Mrs. Palmer's plan was deciding where to go. From the time of their well-publicized campaign in Newcastle in 1859 until the end of Phoebe Palmer's life the couple had so many invitations to hold services that they could not fulfill all of them. They did not always go to the largest or most promising areas, but to those places where they felt they were wanted most.[57] The way Mrs. Palmer determined how much people wanted them to come was by their willingness to comply with the conditions she specified before accepting an invitation.

The first condition Phoebe Palmer laid down was that they had to be invited by "*official* invitation, yes, *official* invitation, urgent and unanimous."[58] This condition prevented a holiness minority in a congregation from inviting the Palmers without the knowledge or over the opposition of the pastor. Phoebe Palmer was always careful to honor ministers. She called them "ambassadors of the King of Kings." She also said that criticizing them violated the commandment, "Touch not mine anointed" (1 Chron. 16:22), and led people to hell.[59] While she could be very critical of ministers in general, she refrained from speaking ill of any individual and urged her readers to pray for their preacher instead of criticizing him.[60] Because of her high view of the pastoral office, Mrs. Palmer would not hold meetings where the minister was not a strong supporter of holiness, and she was always careful to share leadership of the meetings with the local pastor.[61] Another reason for working closely with the minister was that he was the key to the continuance of the revival after the Palmers left. As a "captain of Israel," he was expected to teach the congregation "the arts of holy warfare" and to organize the warriors for the assaults on Satan's strongholds.[62] Because of this cooperation with the local minister, many churches continued to see revival after the Palmers had moved on to another location.[63]

The second condition was that the people in the church should be willing to make as great a sacrifice for the revival as the Palmers were making. She pointed out that Dr. Palmer had given up his medical practice to engage in this ministry. Likewise the people of the church, for the short time the Palmers would be in town, should "devote their time and energies very largely to the work." It was not the Palmers' job to bring on the revival; they went only as helpers, to be co-laborers with people who were determined to "harvest souls for the kingdom." Specifically, at least fifty of the members must pledge themselves to do their best to bring one new person to the meetings every day. The church must also guarantee that there would be enough counselors to pray at the altar with those who came forward, that there would be secretaries to take down the names of the inquirers, and that each of these seekers would later be visited by "minute men and women" who, on a moment's notice, would go to the inquirer's home or place of business.[64]

After deciding where to go and arriving on the scene, the Palmers would next preach the possibility and duty of entire sanctification to those in the church.[65] According to their usual custom, the meeting would open with singing and then a prayer by the minister. Walter would then give the Bible reading, interspersing explanatory comments with the text of Scripture. Then Phoebe would rise to exhort.[66] Though she said her voice was soft, she could speak to more than two thousand people for almost an hour without weariness.[67] The people listened carefully; this is what they had been waiting for. As one woman reported after leaving a meeting in which both Walter and Phoebe spoke: "A man has been here, and he preaches, and his wife exhorts, and the wife is the best [sic] of the two."[68] The woman probably felt that way because Walter preached and Phoebe told stories. Because God revealed his truth through "types, historical narratives, and emblems," Mrs. Palmer chose to simplify spiritual realities and to make "them tangible to the understanding of the humble" by telling stories.[69]

Sometimes her stories had dramatic effects. One preacher reported how she took her hearers through wild swings of emotion:

> We never saw our dear Sister P. used in so remarkable a manner, as on the first day after their arrival, to drag to light the inmost recesses of men's hearts and minds, and to depict sin in its hideous forms. We alternately shouted and laughed and wept, and wept and laughed again. Soon every device of the enemy was overthrown. . . . Holiness to the Lord became the general watchword.[70]

As the minister admitted, however, Phoebe Palmer's talks were not usually so emotional. Other reports of her speeches emphasize her calmness, deliberateness, and logic. Her earnestness was evident to all, and at times "her entire nature sway[ed] under the pressure" of her compassion for souls. In these times "her words, action, countenance disclose the struggle that is within. Her eye, not naturally large, almost closes. Her hands clasp . . . [as] she 'darts a prayer to heaven.'" Then a holy boldness overcame her and she spoke with power.[71]

Sometimes Mrs. Palmer spoke for twenty minutes and sometimes for an hour.[72] On the first night of a series of meetings her message would usually be that Pentecost is a model revival and that it may be duplicated whenever believers seek the full baptism of the Holy Ghost. She would then go on to say that if believers were baptized with the Holy Ghost and with fire, the world would then be convicted. Most Christians are not so baptized only because they have not sought the blessing through entire consecration, faith, and testimony. Next Phoebe Palmer would challenge all who resolved to seek the baptism to rise, indicating their determination to the Lord. Finally, she invariably concluded this section of the meeting by inviting people forward to the altar, where they could pray for the promised blessing.[73]

The purpose of the altar service was "gathering the fruit" that had ripened during the preaching.[74] It was a time for people to solidify the commitments they had made by openly presenting themselves in front of the congregation. This altar service was so important that the Palmers more than once changed the interior architecture of a church to provide space for it.[75] Both the Palmers, along with other leaders in the church, took an active part in praying with seekers, giving counsel, and listening to testimony. At times Mrs. Palmer went into the congregation seated in the nave or even up into the galleries to persuade people to come to the altar.[76]

While the focus of the altar service was on the individual seeker, at times the whole group would be asked to give its attention to one person who was having a particularly hard time "praying through." All would then join in beseeching the Lord, aiding the sister or brother to obtain the sought-for blessing. At other times those at the altar would be called to hear the testimony of one whose petition had been granted. Then those who had already received sanctification could rejoice with the newly blessed believer, and those who had not yet obtained holiness could be encouraged in their quest. Phoebe Palmer often reported that the power of the Holy Spirit was evident at such times, and once recorded that people were slain in the Spirit: "We saw it possible to be baptized with a baptism beyond what we are able physically to bear."[77] She did not, however, encourage emotionalism. Usually her meetings were free "from extravagancies, and disorderly and fanatical demonstrations."[78] One reporter noted her ability to control the emotional tone of a meeting:

> [She] could manage a large meeting with perfect ease, and wonderful effect. In the midst of excitement, while many of her sex were wild with transport, her complete self-possession and poise were wonderful. When the tendency was to extravagance and violent demonstration she could check the tornado, and do it almost insensibly to the congregation.[79]

As most of the seekers began to find what they sought, the focus of the meeting would shift from prayer to testimony. The Palmers would question the people at the altar rail, asking them to explain what the Lord had done for them.[80] This practice provided the opportunity for the seekers to give the testimony that was so important to being sanctified.[81] Then, as the people were leaving the altar, they would give their names to the recording secretaries.[82]

Besides devoting the first service to encouraging Christians to be sanctified, the Palmers also held other meetings for this purpose later in the campaign. Once they held a "Believing Meeting" in which all who had made an entire consecration but had received no assurance that they were sanctified resolved to put their wills on the altar. All resolved to take God at his word and to believe that he had sanctified them "irrespective of emotion or *sensible* demonstration."[83] At another time the Palmers led some new converts in making a covenant of sanctification with the Lord.[84] Their usual pattern, however, was to hold a meeting in the afternoon for those who wished to be sanctified and had not received the blessing in the first service.[85]

After leading believers into the blessing of entire sanctification, the Palmers took the next step of getting these believers working for God. They often did this by forming "Christian Vigilance Bands." These bands were small groups of believers who bound themselves (1) to make "secular business or domestic avocations specifically subservient to the service of Christ"; (2) to spend at least one half-hour daily "in specific direct efforts to win souls for Christ"; (3) to do their best to interest other professed Christians, no matter what their denomination, in the task of evangelism; (4) to meet together weekly to pray for each other and report on their progress; and (5) to meet monthly with any other bands in the city under the guidance of a minister.[86]

Phoebe Palmer directed these lay evangelists to begin their work with prayer. Regularly believers should focus their attentions on one new person. She urged Christians to tell their friends they were praying for them, and she held prayer meetings in which the unsaved were prayed for by name.[87] Along with prayer, the Christian should talk to unbelievers about their souls. She exhorted them not to shun their unsaved friends but to try to win them for Christ.[88] If one could not find non-Christians with whom to speak, Mrs. Palmer suggested writing letters to the unconverted. If one did not have an entire half-hour to devote to evangelism, she said to divide the task into six five-minute sections. Nothing should stand in the way of this all-important work.[89]

An important part of talking to people about their souls was inviting them to the revival services. The Palmers would lead these services, aiming to bring the lost into "a saving acquaintance with Jesus."[90] Of course, they would always preach holiness, but the main focus was evangelism. As in the services aimed primarily at sanctification, these evangelistic services would end with an "altar call" in which the penitents would be invited to come forward for prayer. At this point the lay evangelists would go into action, moving about the congregation "in earnest, importunate endeavors to win their friends and neighbors over from the ranks of sin."[91] Once again, secretaries would carefully record the names of those who responded to the invitation.[92]

Phoebe Palmer thought it was especially important that people not leave the altar area until they had given their names to the secretaries and stated whether they had come forward for justification or sanctification. She said that giving one's name to the secretary encouraged people not to leave until they were sure about their commitment and God's response. It also helped the seeker to remember that she or he had made a decision. Often the Palmers would say that the "recording angel" had written the person's name in heaven, and that recording the name on earth was a symbol and reminder of the heavenly event. The church would find the secretary's list helpful for "follow-up" visits to make sure the new converts were continuing to grow in grace. In addition, people whose names were recorded were given a printed certificate commending them to the care of a particular church. Mrs. Palmer hoped that each church would appoint female as well as male secretaries to record the names on segregated lists. In this way, she said, not even the most timid woman would be discouraged from giving her name.[93]

The secretaries' lists were invaluable because they made post-conversion pastoral care possible. Phoebe Palmer asked one church how much care they would give toward obtaining a promised gift of one million dollars. Think how much "pains-taking solicitude there would be to secure that property to the church, and [to] place it beyond contingencies!" she exclaimed. She then went on to say that because each person entrusted to their care is worth much more than one million dollars, the church must provide nursing fathers and mothers to nurture that person until she or he becomes strong and able to nurse others.[94]

Phoebe Palmer hoped each of these new converts would be an instrument for reaching others. Thus the revival would continue to spread in ever-widening circles. She gave the new believers the same kind of instruction she had given to the sanctified and sent them out to work for Jesus.[95] She also told these babes in Christ how to be entirely sanctified and reported many who received the blessing within days of their conversion, pointing out that John Wesley told similar stories.[96] After 1868 the Palmers put their advice to new converts in a booklet which they distributed to people who had come forward. Called *The Parting Gift to Fellow Laborers and Young Converts*, it recapitulates Phoebe Palmer's teaching about entire sanctification, spirituality, and lay ministry.[97]

Mrs. Palmer also held meetings for special groups of people in addition to her normal evening meetings. In England she once hosted a midnight breakfast for a town's prostitutes but seems never to have repeated this practice.[98] More common were her meetings for children. She felt that the Lord had given her a special duty to hold meetings for children and often reported the conversion of large numbers of young people.[99] Children could be sanctified as well as adults, she believed, again following Wesley. In one meeting she reported a number of children between the ages of eight and fourteen who were blessed with holiness.[100]

The final step a church must take in propagating a revival, Phoebe Palmer said, is to publish the results. Thus "all the divisions of Christ's army may send up one general shout of praise to their all-conquering Lord." Not to do so is to rob God of the glory for what he has done. In reporting the triumphs one should be careful to quote accurate figures, and to include "incidents of more than ordinary interest" to "add greatly to the zest of revival reports."[101]

EVALUATION

Phoebe Palmer's importance as a revivalist comes from three contributions. Two of them are positive and one is negative. One positive contribution is that by preaching holiness she helped to balance the relative emphases on justification and on sanctification in the American church. Her second contribution is negative. While she helped to bring a much-needed balance into the American church by preaching holiness, the way in which she preached entire sanctification tended to devalue the doctrine. Her third contribution, however, was beneficial. She systematized and organized lay-people to work in urban revival campaigns. Her contribution marks the transition between the clergy-centered crusades of Charles G. Finney and the lay-oriented campaigns of D. L. Moody.

Restoring the Balance Between Justification and Sanctification

George Croft Cell has pointed out that the Reformation led men to divide the doctrines of justification and sanctification:

> The Reformation conflict cost both sides dearly. It caused good men on both sides, as fierce conflicts are bound to do, to put asunder what in the nature of Christianity belongs together, namely, the doctrine of justification by faith central to Christianity as religion and the doctrine of holiness, central to Christianity as an ethic of life.[102]

The Reformed churches began to emphasize justification by faith so much that they were in danger of teaching that it did not matter how one lives as long as one has faith. In reaction the Roman church began to emphasize sanctification so much that they were in danger of teaching that one earned one's salvation by one's holy life. Cell also notes that John Wesley strongly emphasized both justification and sanctification. Wesley brought both these elements together in a well-balanced synthesis, avoiding the extremes of both antinomianism and Pelagianism.[103]

Unfortunately, the Wesleyan synthesis was not always present in America. Although the Methodists preached sanctification, the roughness of frontier life and the richness of urban life militated against the doctrine. Before the circuit riders could get the hard-living, hard-drinking, and hard-fighting pioneers to go on to perfection, they had to get them converted. Thus they preached salvation to sinners and sanctification to the saved. Unfortunately, on the frontier there always were more of the former than the latter, so the preaching of sanctification took a back seat. In the cities during the first decades of the nineteenth century the Methodists were becoming more respectable. Nathan Bangs pointed out in 1837 that as the Methodists came up in the world, the world came up in the Methodists. Such increasing worldliness made the preaching of entire sanctification unpopular.[104]

In the Reformed tradition the situation was even worse. Richard Lovelace has argued that the first-generation Puritans so "loaded" the conversion experience that believers had to be well down the road to holiness before they would even claim to be converted. Beecher, Finney, and others reacted against this impossibly high standard for conversion by Arminianizing the doctrine, calling people to instantaneous commitment and instantaneous conversion. In so doing, Lovelace contends,

[they] disconnected sanctification from conversion and made it easy for men to enter the kingdom on the basis of simple faith and initial repentance. Having unloaded conversion, however, they failed to reinsert sanctification in its proper place in the development of the Christian life.[105]

Lovelace calls the result of this change "The Sanctification Gap" in American revivalism.[106]

Finney, who had done so much to create the problem, recognized the sanctification gap in the mid-1830s and began to preach Christian perfection in an effort to bridge it.[107] He had trivialized conversion, calling it "a change of mind," and even likening it to a vote for the Lord.[108] As a result of this kind of preaching the church was filled with people who soon fell away, or even worse, remained to lower the standard of piety in the church. In 1836 Finney admitted that of all the converts of the revivals of the previous ten years "the great body of them are a disgrace to religion."[109] Now he hoped to correct the situation by "elevat[ing] the standard of holiness in the church."[110] Phoebe Palmer also saw the sanctification gap, but she did not have to develop a new theological doctrine in order to solve the problem. She had learned from John Wesley that unless new converts were urged on to entire sanctification they would inevitably lose their fervor for Christ.[111] Thus following Wesley's advice, she preached sanctification to a church flooded with the new converts of revivalism.

Phoebe Palmer recognized that there were some unconverted people in the Methodist church. More than half of the members in the Western and Southern conferences had been admitted after professing only that they wished to "flee the wrath to come," not that they were saved.[112] The idea was to convert them in the church, but as Bishop Hamline said and Mrs. Palmer agreed, after the revivals had brought these unconverted people into the church, class meetings and the preaching of holiness were neglected and the church "sank down into worldliness."[113]

In other conferences of the Methodist church and in other denominations she visited, Phoebe Palmer saw that many who did profess conversion did not understand that being converted obligated them to a holy life in this world as well as offered them an eternal life in the next world. She once noted that "with the multitude the line of demarcation between Christians(?) and the world has been but slight."[114] She feared even more for the members of liturgical churches, whose members "partake of the

Sacrament, or in other words, they eat and drink in Christ's presence, and yet never put on the robe of spotless purity without which they can never enter heaven. . . . They are asleep in their sins, and by church ordinances are being lulled into yet deeper repose."[115]

Phoebe Palmer did not try to ascertain which of the "worldly professors" to whom she spoke were saved and which were not. Instead she accepted the low view of justification which revivalism had brought into the church and strove to remedy the malaise by administering a strong dose of sanctification. It would have been futile to tell the thousands who thought they had "got religion" at a frontier camp meeting or in an urban revival service that some of them were deceived. Rather Mrs. Palmer preached sanctification to them all, trusting that holding up God's high standard of holiness would not only lead the believers into greater blessing but would also convict the unconverted and lead them to repentance.[116] In preaching holiness she helped to remind the whole American church of its high calling and thus to bridge the sanctification gap.

Devaluation of Entire Sanctification

Although the message of holiness which Phoebe Palmer brought to the American church helped to redress the balance between justification and sanctification, some of the methods she used in her revival meetings tended to devalue the doctrine of entire sanctification. Mattison's controversy with Mrs. Palmer in the late 1840s and early 1850s centered on her writings, but it started because of one of her camp meetings. Mattison said he wrote against Phoebe Palmer because he had seen the ill effects of her revival preaching:

> I had just come from a section of country where several Churches have [sic] been torn asunder by Mrs. Palmer's views, and were bleeding at every pore; had heard of ministers shut out of churches; of strifes and divisions in many others; and the peace of a whole conference for a time, at least, destroyed. . . .[117]

Most of Mattison's published controversy with Mrs. Palmer dealt with her theology, but some of the objections he raised pertained to her methodology.[118] He objected to her practice of preaching holiness to backslidden people on two counts: First, because John Wesley discouraged it, and second, because it led them to confuse justification with sanctification.[119] In answer to the question, "In what manner should we preach sanctification?" Mattison pointed out that Wesley answered, "Scarce at all to those who are not pressing forward. To those who are, always, by way of promise; always drawing, rather than driving."[120] Phoebe Palmer ignored this advice and preached to all the unsanctified as if they were new converts. The other problem with preaching entire sanctification to churches swollen with converts from revivals is that the unconverted and the lapsed among them will be "aroused from a state of lukewarmness, and after struggling a while for entire sanctification, suddenly imagine themselves to have obtained that blessing" when in fact they have only been converted or "healed of their backslidings."[121]

The problem Mattison pointed out was exacerbated by the way in which Phoebe Palmer conducted her meetings. Even if one fully concurs with her theology, that one must wonder if the way she urged people to make immediate decisions and used group pressure to make those decisions easier did not cheapen the doctrine she taught. In Phoebe Palmer's own life the process of laying all on the altar took at least twelve months, from the time Eliza died in 1836 until the "day of days" in 1837.[122] In her meetings, however, she compressed this process of entire consecration, speaking of it as something that was merely an act of the will and could therefore be done immediately. She made entire consecration even easier by telling people that it was God's responsibility to show them any area they were holding back, and said it was sufficient to "linger a few moments" to give him time to do so.[123] In addition, she went on to tell people who felt that they were not entirely consecrated not to look at themselves and their failings but to look at Christ and his power to enable them to give all to him.[124]

In her zeal to bring people to the place of entire consecration, Phoebe Palmer could water down the commitment. She once proposed this test to a man so he could discover if his all were on the altar:

> If the world, with all its aggrandizements, its every conceivable pleasure and honor, were concentrated and placed here, on one hand, and on the other hand were placed your once-despised Saviour, who made himself of no reputation for you, with all his disreputableness, his cross and ignominy, and the question were proposed, Which would you choose? would you not spurn the world, and a thousand times sooner say, Give me Jesus—the naked Saviour and the cross?[125]

How could the man, when the question was phrased like that, claim to be a Christian, and then choose the world? Given that theoretical choice, every professing Christian would choose the Lord. According to this standard, then, all Christians are entirely consecrated. In presenting this test, Mrs. Palmer forgot that the choice between Christ and the world is usually presented in much more subtle terms. Would that the Tempter always made the alternatives so plain!

In addition to urging people to come to a quick decision about entire consecration and lowering the standards that defined it, Phoebe Palmer also used group pressure to encourage people to make the right choice. She often called on people to stand up to present themselves as candidates for a special ordination of power or to promise not to rest until endued with power from on high.[126] It probably took a higher level of sanctification to admit honestly that one might rest before receiving the power and thus to remain seated than to stand when hundreds around were making the pledge. Probably many stood either because they were swept along with the group or because they did not have the courage to reveal the truth by remaining seated.

Once Phoebe Palmer had people on their feet, it was much easier to get them to the altar. Here again, she would phrase the invitation in such a way so as to make it difficult to refuse: Who, after indicating the desire for the blessing or that the decision has been made, would refuse to come forward to claim the blessing or ratify the decision? Besides, by standing, one had made her- or himself obvious to the group of workers Mrs. Palmer encouraged to go into the congregation. There at the altar one would join a group of seekers but would also be treated individually. In this way those who went forward subjected themselves to the psychological pressure of the group combined with the personal persuasiveness of an individual counselor. With people praying, crying, and testifying all around, it would be easy to mistake the emotions induced by the group for the work of the Holy Spirit. The testimony service and the presence of the secretaries also put pressure on the seeker to sense the attainment of the longed-for blessing. The whole group was waiting for each person to testify that God had been faithful, and the secretaries barred the way of anyone who wished to slip away from the altar undetected. All of these measures combined to make it easy for the seekers to feel that they experienced the work of God when actually all that happened had a merely human cause.

Because Mrs. Palmer's revival methods were combined with her particular understanding of faith, the results could be disastrous. If after going up to the altar, testifying, and giving one's name to the secretary, one had second thoughts about the depth of the commitment or the validity of the decision, that individual would be exhorted: "Cast not away your confidence!" To doubt that God had kept his word to bestow sanctifying grace was a sin. If one had not voluntarily transgressed, one could not question one's sanctified state without incurring the displeasure of God. It is easy to imagine that many of Phoebe Palmer's hearers were caught up in the emotion of the moment, stood to their feet, went to the altar, testified, and gave their names to the secretaries, but did not experience a true work of God in their souls. These deluded believers would then quell their doubts and smother their fears by making a bold profession of holiness. If they saw evidence of wrong attitudes in their lives, they would have either to deny that these emotions were present or to deny that the feelings were sinful. The inner dialogue might sound like this:

"I'm angry."
> "But I can't be angry. Being angry is a sin and God has cleansed my heart of all sinful tempers."

"Well, maybe I've lost my sanctification."
> "Have I voluntarily chosen to sin? Did I choose to lose my temper?"

"Of course not!"
> "Then I must not cast away my confidence. I'm still sanctified. Therefore I am not angry, because anger is sin."

"But I feel angry."
> "Then this emotion, which seems like anger, must really be righteous indignation."

Hence, by combining her theology with her revival methods, Phoebe Palmer led some people who were not sanctified to insist that they were. This confusion devalued entire sanctification both for those who claimed it and for those who observed their unsanctified behavior. Certainly the "sanctified" in whom Mattison detected "pride, anger, jealousy, envy, censoriousness, [and] covetousness" were not good testimonies to the power of holiness.[127]

The methodology of the Tuesday Meeting was much less open to abuse than was the methodology of the revival service. Here again Phoebe Palmer used group pressure to induce quick decisions, but this methodology was more appropriate for the kind of person who generally came to the Tuesday Meeting. While the unconverted or backslidden were often brought to the Palmers' revival services by the corps of lay evangelists Dr. and Mrs. Palmer had trained, those who came to the Tuesday Meeting were usually in a higher spiritual state. Four different categories of people would normally be present on a Tuesday at three in the afternoon: housewives, working women, working men, and ministers. The housewives would be present because they had been there before or because they had come at the invitation of a friend who thought they would be interested in holiness. In addition to showing the level of interest that the housewives displayed, the people who worked revealed an even greater commitment because they had to take time off from work to attend the meeting. Ministers could set their own schedules, but their profession showed their interest in spiritual matters.

Thus, the people who learned Phoebe Palmer's theology at the Tuesday Meeting were often more mature than the people who heard her in the revival services. Most of them had a good idea of what sanctification was, and many had been seeking it for a long time. Some of them had served Christ for years but never had been confident of their spiritual state. Like Professor Upham, they had the faith of a servant but not the faith of a son.[128] What they needed was not more introspection, not more soul-searching, but faith. They needed a holy boldness to shift their eyes from spiritual introspection to an outward-looking trust in God. Phoebe Palmer had discovered this truth in her own life and exhorted her hearers to follow her example.

Thus, for people who were like herself, Phoebe Palmer's revival methodology did not cheapen the doctrine of entire sanctification. Since most of the people she talked with in the Tuesday Meetings week after week were like her, she became convinced that what had been good for her must be good for everyone. She forgot, however, that the people who came to the revival services and camp meetings were not all like the people who came to the Tuesday Meeting, nor were they all like herself. They all had not loved Jesus since before they could remember, nor were they carried to church as infants, nor did they read their Bibles as children. Besides having different backgrounds, some of the people in her camp meetings had different personalities. Not all shared her spiritual intensity, her sensitive conscience, or her introspective nature. Phoebe Palmer's failure to recognize that "seizing the kingdom of God by violence" (see Matt. 11:12) was not a spiritual panacea caused her to devalue the doctrine of entire sanctification for many people.

Lay Ministry

Phoebe Palmer's emphasis on lay ministry was new to American urban revivalism. Revivalism in the Reformed tradition had always been focused on the clergy. The Great Awakening depended on the preaching of ordained men, and, after it, most revival services were conducted by the local pastor, with an occasional pulpit exchange or visit from an ordained evangelist.[129] The early American Methodists had stressed lay ministry, but in the nineteenth century urban Methodists followed the same clergy-centered pattern as their Reformed brethren. On the frontier the division between clergy and laity was less important, but still the preachers, whether ordained or not, dominated the revival movement.

Charles Finney had spoken of the role of laypersons in revivals, but Mrs. Palmer was the first to organize their labors effectively. While Finney urged church members to visit the unsaved, he placed this injunction eleventh on the list of things they should do, mentioning it after the duty of paying the minister well and keeping the church clean.[130] Phoebe Palmer did not just mention lay visitation as one of a number of tasks people could undertake to help the minister. Rather, she gave lay ministry priority in her message and also organized the church members into bands to help them carry out that ministry. She saw herself not as a preacher who brought people to Christ, but as an organizer who equipped the saints for the work of evangelism.

Phoebe Palmer's emphasis on lay ministry came at a crucial time for American revivalism. With the waning of the Second Great Awakening in the mid-1830s came the passing of the time that a lone preacher could stir an entire city. Finney's triumphs had come in towns and cities with less than ten thousand people.[131] In these communities word-of-mouth could easily inform the whole populace that a spellbinding new preacher had arrived in town. As the urban communities continued to grow, however, new means had to be found to publicize a revival campaign. In addition, the increasing pluralism of the American cities made it difficult to interest all segments of the population in religion. Rochester, New York, in 1830 was a closely knit community so that when Finney converted the wife of one of the town's lawyers, he soon gained a hearing from the whole city.[132] Such "networking" was becoming impossible as Phoebe Palmer began her career as a revivalist.

Mrs. Palmer introduced organized lay evangelism to the urban setting, not because she thought it was a wise tactic in the light of changing conditions, but because she thought the Bible required it. Nevertheless it was a wise tactic, and the revival of 1857–58 demonstrated her wisdom as a revivalist even to those who were unconvinced by her theology. Whether conscious of Phoebe Palmer's work or not, Dwight L. Moody followed her practice and made the training of lay evangelists an important part of his work.[133] Her emphasis on the role of the laity helped to prepare lay-people to play a major role in urban revivalism. Mrs. Palmer's practice was one of the factors that transformed revivalism from Finney's clergy-centered campaigns in small towns to Moody's lay-oriented crusades in large cities.[134]

CHAPTER SEVEN:
Phoebe Palmer As Feminist

When a certain Dr. Butler brought his wife down from Vermont to New York City in 1855 he hoped to get her mind off holiness. She had recently made a perfect spectacle of herself by professing sanctification before their friends and neighbors in the local Congregational church. Dr. Butler's brother, who was a Congregational minister, urged the doctor to forbid his wife to say another word about her experience. He hoped to "save the family from further mortification." Butler did not feel free to muzzle his wife, but he did make sure the book which had put all these strange ideas into his wife's head, *Incidental Illustrations of the Economy of Salvation*, disappeared. Then he thought he would take her to visit the big city to promote domestic tranquility by getting her away from his brother. He hoped with a change of scenery the whole thing would blow over.

Perhaps he had not looked carefully at the title page of the offending book. There, right under the names of the publishers, Foster & Palmer, Jr., was the address of their firm, 37 Park Row, New York. Dr. Butler probably did not realize that he was bringing his wife into Phoebe Palmer's neighborhood. Mrs. Butler bided her time, and when her husband was otherwise occupied, escaped to track down Mrs. Palmer and get a new copy of the book. Upon returning to Vermont with her husband, she continued to speak about holiness. She even persuaded her brother-in-law to read the objectionable literature she had obtained in the city. Upon taking up and reading, he too was converted. Now instead of being a humiliation to the family, Mrs. Butler was a leader in the things of the Spirit.¹ Thus, through Phoebe Palmer's influence another woman was liberated.

Mrs. Butler's experience of winning a hostile male to holiness had a precedent in that of Phoebe Upham, who led her skeptical husband into the experience. Likewise her experience served as a precedent for that of Martha Inskip, whose mate was convinced by her life. There is no way to know how many other women took the lead in the spiritual lives of their families under Phoebe Palmer's influence, but if this were her only contribution to the women's rights movement she would still deserve the title "feminist."² Mrs. Palmer's claim to be an advocate for women, however, does not rest merely on the fact that women converted their husbands and brothers to holiness under her influence. Her life came at a crucial time in women's history. In the first decades of the nineteenth century, many forces were at work to restrict women's roles.³ By her thought and example, Phoebe Palmer sought to resist those forces. Her thought made the case for women's ministries in the church. Her example showed that women could speak with power, think with clarity, and act with effectiveness. In the religious sphere, she revived the Methodist tradition of female ministry and passed on that tradition to the Holiness and Pentecostal movements. In the wider sphere, her influence encouraged other feminists, notably Catherine Booth and Frances Willard.

BACKGROUND

Female ministry in the Methodist tradition began before Methodism. John Wesley's mother, Susanna, held religious services for her household in her husband's absence. With its twenty members the Wesley household was large to begin with, but when Susanna explained the Scriptures, two or three hundred villagers begged to be included in her "household prayers."⁴ Nine-year-old Jacky never forgot how God had blessed his mother's ministry. Despite his memories of his mother, in 1748, a decade after the beginning of the Methodist movement, John Wesley could write that female preaching was wrong. Citing 1 Corinthians 14:34–35 along with 1 Timothy 2:11–12, he brushed away objections to the general application of these passages as special pleading. He acknowledged that Joel 2:28 and 1 Corinthians 11:5 permit women to prophesy, but he denied that preaching and prophesying are the same thing.⁵

Of course women were allowed to speak in the bands and

classes. But what should Wesley do when the class grew to two hundred as Sarah Crosby's did? Obviously she could not speak to every one privately, so he advised her to tell them what was on her heart. In another letter he told her that short exhortations were fine, but urged her to "keep as far from what is called preaching as you can."[6]

Later, however, John Wesley changed his mind. He decided that what God was doing through the Methodists was so extraordinary that it broke the old rules. He remarked that even in Corinth where women were not permitted to speak, Paul made exceptions for the women who prophesied. In the same way, God's obvious but "extraordinary" call of women to preach forced Wesley to make exceptions to the normal church rules.[7] With the backing of Methodism's leader, women such as Ann Gilbert, Elizabeth Tonkin Collett, Elizabeth Dickenson, Sarah Mallett Boyce, Margaret Davidson, Mary Harrison, and Mary Woodhouse Holder joined Sarah Crosby and Mary Bosanquet Fletcher as "speakers of the word."[8]

Phoebe Palmer had known of the ministries of some of these women for a long time when she was invited to hear a woman preach in a nearby Methodist church. Mrs. Palmer, however, did not go, "conceiving that however well intentioned [the woman] might be, that she nevertheless might have mistaken her call." Soon after this she was invited to meet the lady preacher at a friend's house. She asked the Lord to remove her scruple against female preaching unless it came from him. The cases of Deborah (Judg. 4–5) and Huldah (2 Kings 22) leaped to mind, convincing her that the Lord did employ women to speak his word. Meeting the woman herself strengthened this conviction, as did the memory of John Wesley's encouragement of women to speak. This experience led Phoebe Palmer to conclude that the church generally had departed from its "primitive simplicity" by limiting the exercise of women's gifts.[9]

THOUGHT EXPRESSED IN *PROMISE OF THE FATHER*

Background and Thesis

The incident with the woman preacher shows that Phoebe Palmer had been thinking about women and the church for several years before she wrote *Promise of the Father*. With pardonable exaggeration she said that the question of the role of women in the church was "the most important that can, in these last days, claim the attention of the religious world." She would have written earlier, but she had hoped that someone better qualified would address the topic.[10] Then one afternoon in the Tuesday Meeting a woman rose to explain that she wanted to be sanctified. She said she knew that one of the conditions for receiving the blessing was to speak in a church meeting as the Spirit gave her utterance. But the church she attended forbade women to speak. What should she do when the will of Christ and the will of the church were in conflict?

All eyes turned to Phoebe Palmer as she stood to answer the woman's question. Citing many Scriptures, she explained that the "Head of the church" had given the "manifest order" for the women to speak. When any human organization, even the church, conflicts with Christ, one must obey God rather than man (Acts 5:29). So helpful was her answer that an elder from the church to which the woman belonged suggested that Mrs. Palmer should publish her response, and his idea was seconded by a Congregational minister.[11] Evidently Mrs. Palmer developed her thought somewhat as she committed it to writing, because the answer given that afternoon emerged as a tome of four hundred closely reasoned pages.

The central idea of the work is that with the coming of Pentecost came the obligation of all of God's servants, both male and female, to speak for Christ. In the Old Testament the Spirit came upon a few individuals for certain periods of time to empower them to prophesy, but now the prophetic Spirit indwells every believer. This indwelling Spirit not only enables every Christian to prophesy but impels each to do so. Women in the New Testament fulfilled this requirement, as did female believers until the time of Constantine. With the establishment of the Roman Catholic church, the voices of women were silenced. Only since the time when John Wesley had to admit that female preaching was owned of God, has the situation begun to be rectified, but even today the remnants of popery still obtain in some denominations. When these are swept away in a return to scriptural purity and scriptural holiness, then God will pour out a revival and "the last act in the great drama of [human] redemption will have opened."[12]

Argument

Phoebe Palmer opens her work by explaining what she is *not* discussing. Women's rights in the secular sense or even women's preaching in the church is not her topic, she claims. She agrees with the women's rights advocates in many respects and sees no objection to women voting or holding office in the government or in the church. While these are not the normal spheres of female service, still God has often chosen to thrust women into positions of great responsibility. Women like Deborah in the Bible and Queen Victoria in the nineteenth century show that God calls and equips some women to lead and even to rule. But these questions are not the focus of her book. All she hopes to prove is that a woman should not be restrained from "open[ing] her mouth in . . . prayer or speaking in the assemblies of the saints."[13]

But the objection comes "from a thousand lips": "The Head of the church forbids it." "If the Head of the church forbids it," Mrs. Palmer admits, "this settles the question beyond all controversy." The question is, Does he really forbid it? There are two main passages that seem to indicate that he does: "Let your women keep silence in the churches" (1 Cor. 14:34), and "I suffer not a woman to teach, nor usurp authority over the man" (1 Tim. 2:12).

Phoebe Palmer argues that if the first passage is to be taken literally, then no woman can join audibly in the Lord's Prayer or sing the hymns in church. Because all would admit that this would be absurd, Paul's words cannot be an absolute prohibition. From Paul's reference to the customs of the "churches of God" in 1 Corinthians 11:16, she concludes that female prophecy was practiced in other New Testament communities. The prohibition must therefore have been a local solution for local problems and not even universal in Paul's day. The local problem must have been acrimonious debates during the preaching. Such exchanges were common in the synagogues, and Paul was trying to keep them out of the church.[14]

The second passage Mrs. Palmer explains as an hendiadys, a figure of speech in which the second element modifies the first. Paul is not saying that a woman may not teach; rather his point is that women should not teach in a way that usurps a man's authority. It is not teaching which is prohibited, but the wrong kind of teaching. That women may teach if they have a right spirit is shown by 1 Corinthians 11 and 14. There Paul gives directions to women who prophesy, and "therefore recognizes the public prophesying of females." Prophecy conveys information, and conveying information is teaching. Unlike some forms of teaching, however, prophecy does not bestow any personal authority on the prophet. Thus it cannot be construed as being the usurpation of authority which Paul disallows. Another argument that women may teach rests on the case of Priscilla, who expounded the way of God more perfectly to Apollos (Acts 18:26).[15]

Having demolished the case against female speaking, Phoebe Palmer next begins to demonstrate that women have not only the right but also the obligation to speak for Christ. She had already used the Corinthian correspondence to show that some women prophesied with God's blessing. Now she returns to those passages to show that such prophesying arises "from the immediate impulse of the Holy Ghost" and is defined by Paul as that which results in "edification, and exhortation, and comfort" (1 Cor. 14:3).[16] Moving on to the account of Pentecost in Acts, she argues that the distinguishing mark of the era that began that Sunday morning is the giving of the Holy Spirit to all believers, not just to a select few. The words of Joel came true as the Spirit descended on women and men. Under the influence of the Spirit, they all spoke, and they continued to speak for Christ even when they were driven out of Jerusalem (Acts 8:3-4). Possessing the Holy Spirit makes every Christian a prophet, and each prophet must exercise the gift by speaking in a way to edify, exhort, or comfort. To prohibit female prophecy is to quench the Spirit and to restrain "the workings of this gift of power in the church." "What account will you render to the Head of the church," Phoebe Palmer asks her opponents, "for restricting the use of this endowment of power? . . . Who can tell but long since the gospel might have been preached to every creature?"[17]

Mrs. Palmer had said her goal was only to show that women should speak in church fellowship meetings, but she defines prophecy in a way that expands a woman's sphere of ministry far beyond those bounds. Having begun by broadly defining prophecy as anything prompted by the Holy Spirit that leads to "edification, and exhortation, and comfort," she then goes on to expand her definition. Quoting Revelation 19:10, "The testimony of Jesus is the spirit of prophecy," she argues that any testimony about Jesus, any recounting of what Jesus has done in a life, is prophecy.[18] Evangelism is the next area she claims as a part of prophecy. All who are endued with the gift of prophecy will "proclaim . . . Christ crucified, as far as in them lies, under all possible circumstances."[19] Leading in public prayer is another of the prophet's roles, and finally, so is preaching. Nehemiah 6:7 says, "Thou hast appointed prophets to preach." "Hence," Phoebe Palmer concludes, "prophets were preachers, and to prophesy is to preach."[20]

In her expanding definition of prophecy, she includes all the valid speaking ministries of the church. The only speaking ministry she reserves exclusively for men is "preaching in the technical sense." Preaching "in the technical sense" means preaching "taken in connection with its attendant paraphernalia, oratorical display, onerous titles, and pulpits of pedestal eminence."[21] This she reserves for any man who would want it.

Having stated her thesis that the gift of the Holy Spirit at Pentecost requires every Christian, both male and female, to speak for Christ, Mrs. Palmer spends the next 120 pages giving examples of the way God has honored the ministries of Spirit-filled women. She quotes Justin Martyr, Chrysostom, and Theophilact to demonstrate the active role of women in the ministry of the early church and backs up her exegetical points by citing Dodwell, Grotius, Wayland, Benson, Barnes, Clarke, and Taft.[22] Her modern examples of Spirit-filled women are mainly drawn from the Methodist galaxy of saints and include Susanna Wesley, Mary Bosanquet Fletcher, Mary Barrit Taft, Sarah Mallett Boyce, Sarah Crosby, and Sarah Lawrence. Drawing on her own knowledge and relying heavily on *Biographical Sketches of the Lives and Public Ministries of Various Holy Women,* by Zechariah Taft, she gives accounts of these women and even reproduces long sections from their diaries.[23]

Mrs. Palmer devotes the remainder of her book to telling her readers how they can receive the Pentecostal baptism of the Holy Spirit and have the same kind of power as the women of old. First she carefully explains her theology of entire sanctification. Then she gives extensive reports from her own ministry, especially her involvement in the recent revival, to show the validity of her theology. Finally she closes with the testimonies of several others who received the promised blessing and worked mightily for God.

Ordination

Phoebe Palmer does not discuss ordination or the administration of sacraments in *Promise of the Father*. The only mention of the issue is in a prefatory letter commending the book. In that preface, Henry Belden, a Congregational minister, objects to ordaining women or letting them teach with a minister's authority.[24] Mrs. Palmer makes no comment on this statement, either because she agrees with it or because she does not want unnecessarily to alarm her readers by disagreeing with it. Her other works show that she did not think ordination was an important issue. She once commented, "We do not reject a man-ordained ministry. They have their work to do. Neither will we reject the heaven-ordained ministry of *all* Christ's disciples."[25] Human ordination of a few men was inconsequential compared to the divine ordination of every Christian. Has not Christ said, "I have ordained you, that ye should bear much fruit" (John 15:16)? Therefore all Christians are called to "labor for souls" even if they are not all called to "the sacred desk."[26] Phoebe Palmer herself felt she needed no human ordination. She never asked for any formal license from the Methodists or for any election to orders because she had "the conviction that she was divinely commissioned and ordained by the great Head of the church for the special work which she felt impelled to do."[27]

Women's Role in the Home

Another topic to which Phoebe Palmer gave scant attention in *Promise of the Father* was the role of women in the home. She did say that women have a "legitimate sphere of action, which differs in most cases materially from that of man." She declared that it was not her aim to suggest "a change in the social or domestic relation"; at any rate, she did not feel that women "were burdened with wrong in that direction."[28] In her other writings, however, she had much to say about how a woman should fulfill the duties of wife and mother if called to that vocation.

Because of all the traveling and writing Mrs. Palmer did, some people thought that she did not have to worry about caring for her family or taking care of her house. She noted this rumor in her diary and then commented that she had the normal responsibilities of a wife and mother, plus the added work of providing hospitality for many.[29] Her schedule for Tuesday, June 6, 1848, when her youngest child was five, was typical:

> Home mission meeting this morning. A presiding Elder, and his family, from New Jersey, to dine. [Tuesday] Meeting, this afternoon. Several friends to tea, and company till quite late this evening. Added to my several meeting engagements, weekly, are the many calls for religious conversation, &c., with the domestic engagements, which of course call for a mother's attention in every family.[30]

Phoebe Palmer felt that God had specifically called her to be a wife and mother. Her ministry in those roles was as important as preaching: "The conjugal relation, with all its ministries of love, are [*sic*] just as truly ordained of God as are the ministries of the sacred desk," she said.[a] Because God had ordained her as a housewife, even mundane tasks were important. She sang the verse: "Every work I do below, I do it to the Lord."[32] She felt that the Lord cared as much about the way she did her housework as he cared about the way she studied the Bible.[33] Fortunately, this sense of the importance of the way she ran her home did not cause her to be over-scrupulous or anxious about domestic details. Before she had given all to the Lord, worry about her household had weighed her down. After she entirely consecrated herself to God's service, the Lord gave her a due sense of proportion about her duties. Thus she was able to omit some of the jobs that had burdened her, and others of them she now did with a joyful heart because she was sure the Lord had willed it.[34]

Finding holiness not only made Phoebe Palmer better able to cope with running a large household, but it also made her a better wife. After she became willing to sacrifice even her relationship with Walter, she found that her love for him became more healthy. Previously she had never been really happy unless he was with her. Now she clung to him less and was not jealous of the long hours he spent in his busy profession. Knowing that she no longer begrudged every minute that he spent away from her freed the doctor to be more effective in his work and led to an increase in the "*genuine* affection" between them.[35] That affection between them grew and deepened to her dying day. One irony, which only those unacquainted with the topsy-turvy nature of the kingdom of God will find surprising, is that by giving up Walter to the Lord, Phoebe Palmer got back much more of him than she ever expected. Because of their mutual commitment to holiness, Walter abandoned his medical practice in 1859 to work full time with Phoebe in the ministry of evangelism and publishing. Little did she know when she renounced her right to monopolize his time that the Lord would give him back to her to work side-by-side for fifteen years.

Mrs. Palmer rarely spoke about the duties of a Christian wife toward her husband. She once praised Susanna Wesley for submitting to her husband, despite being at least her husband's equal in intelligence.[36] She then went on to point out that some modern American women had become carried away by the country's republican principles and had "shipwrecked" the "peace of an entire household" by "contend[ing] the point of family jurisdiction." Phoebe Palmer felt that the Scripture was clear that the husband should be the leader and that the wife should submit to his decisions even when his choices appeared to be unwise. She did not feel, however, that such wifely submission entailed male dominance or implied female inequality.[37] She said that a family should have "a united head [where] as one in the Lord [the wife and the husband] are mutual helpers in rearing a family for the abodes of immortality."[38] Her generalized advice thus avoided the hard cases. Wives should submit to husbands like Samuel Wesley who was poor at managing money and sometimes spanked his children when they only needed a reprimand, but what a woman should do with a drunken or abusive husband, Mrs. Palmer never said.[39]

Although she did not give advice on hard cases, Mrs. Palmer did recognize that many American families did not live up to her ideal. She published statistics showing that the proportion of women who died between the ages of thirty and forty was greater in America than in Northern Europe. Her report showed that "in every decade, 95,000 females pass away who would have lived had they been born in [Northern Europe]." This and other similar "STARTLING FACTS" convinced her that God was withholding his blessing from the United States. "The great laws of human existence" were being violated in America where husbands and wives did not regard each other as equal partners and the responsibilities of marriage were not taken seriously enough. Even worse were the men who thought that women were intellectually and spiritually unimportant and should be regarded primarily as sex objects: "The idea that woman, with all her noble gifts and qualities, was formed mainly to minister to the sensuous nature of man, is wholly unworthy a place in the heart of a Christian."[40] She was convinced that God was judging American society for these sins against the family.[41]

Mrs. Palmer's case would have been more convincing if she had been able to show that American and Northern European societies differed only in regard to their families and also that European families conformed more to God's ideal. Despite its logical flaws, however, her reasoning showed that Mrs. Palmer was aware that serious abuses were occurring in American homes. She knew that not every marriage was as workable as that between Susanna and Samuel Wesley. She realized that not every household was as peaceful as the Palmer household, where, as Bishop Hamline noted, "We are a happy family. Sister P. modestly leads in everything."[42]

Just as putting the Lord first made Phoebe Palmer a better wife, so it also made her a better mother. She understood the unending demands that babies make and how caring for them can wear a woman down. She knew that many who professed sanctification earlier found themselves falling into the sins of worry, impatience, and anger when they became mothers. She realized that some believed it was impossible for a young mother to be sanctified; they had even darkly hinted that if Mrs. Palmer had small children, she would not talk so much about holiness.[43]

Mrs. Palmer, however, did have children: six of them. And she did continue to talk about holiness. Through the early deaths of three of her children she had become convinced that as a mother her first responsibility was to love the Lord.[44] She felt her remaining three children were not her own, but that the Lord had given them to her for a time, saying, "Take this child away, and nurse it for me" (Exod. 2:9).[45] Her first responsibility toward her children was to lead them to a saving knowledge of Christ, and her second was to train them to serve him.[46] She did this by devoting them as babies to the Lord, praying for them regularly, teaching them self-denial, and creating an atmosphere of love, not fear in the home.[47]

One man wrote her asking what she did to create the love and confidence he had observed in her children. Phoebe Palmer replied that she and Walter hoped to create an atmosphere of love in the home, quoting the lines, "Never take the harsher way, / When love may do the deed." They had set their children apart for the Lord's service and aimed to have "their moral and religious training all directed to this point-usefulness in the church of Christ." Each morning before the day's routine began, Mrs. Palmer would pray for each member of her household individually, pleading the promise, "I will pour out my spirit upon thy seed, and my blessing upon thine offspring" (Isa. 44:3). Of course, if her children were to grow up to be Spirit-filled Christians, Phoebe Palmer needed to be careful that they did not develop a taste for "gay society, or conformity to the world in dress, and other respects," but even these regulations needed to be administered in a way that promoted parents' authority without provoking their children to wrath (Eph. 6:4).[48]

By being very fair in their discipline, the Palmers created an attitude of love. One time the children were rough-housing indoors. They accidentally broke a vase and tore some clothes. "You do well to be angry," Mrs. Palmer thought she heard Satan say, and was tempted to speak severe words and spank the offenders. The Lord helped her to control her temper. She realized there was no ill intent, nor had the children been playing in a forbidden place, so she did not punish them.[49] Besides being eminently fair, she also found that explaining to the children that they had been set apart for special service to the Lord made it easier for them to accept discipline and to give up being like everyone else in what they did and how they dressed.[50]

The limited evidence available seems to indicate that Phoebe Palmer considered her children the most important ministry in her life. Although God had taught her not to dote on them, meeting their spiritual, emotional, and physical needs took priority over other forms of ministry for her. In 1838 she took five-year-old Sarah with her to camp meeting and reported "the concerns of my little family demanded much of my attention." The account of her labors there shows her willingness to limit her activities in order to care for those who depended on her.[51] A report from the next year shows her concern for her children's salvation. One evening before she undressed Sarah and prepared her for bed, she read her an account of a child's life written in the *Christian Advocate and Journal*. As they talked over the story, it became evident that Sarah was ready to "give her heart to Jesus." Mrs. Palmer showed great sensitivity as she talked, prayed, and sang with her daughter for the next two hours. Bedtime had long past, but she remained in her daughter's room, reading to her from the Bible until Sarah fell asleep. Phoebe said she would remember this evening "in *time* and in *eternity*, as one of the most important in my Christian history."[52]

Mrs. Palmer's plan for raising godly children seems to have worked. Visitors to their home remarked on the love and joy the family shared.[53] The family's letters show a deep affection, and even when grown, all three children remained physically and spiritually close to their parents. Phoebe Palmer collaborated in writing songs with Phoebe Knapp, her daughter, and in holding evangelistic crusades with Sarah and Elon Foster, her other daughter and son-in-law. Foster later worked with her son, Walter, in the family publishing company for some time, and Phoebe Knapp kept it in business until the end of her life.[54]

In addition to feeling responsible to God for the way she raised her children, Mrs. Palmer also felt a special duty toward the servants she employed. She thought of herself as a priest for the entire household and discharged one aspect of this role by praying regularly for her family and servants.[55] Just as God entrusted her with children "to be trained for the better country," so she felt he allowed her to have servants "to be trained as subjects of the everlasting kingdom where earthly distinctions are unknown."[56] While Satan often tempted her to speak harshly to her servants, Phoebe Palmer hoped her loving attitude would bring them to Christ.[57] She also hoped her love would be apparent in the just wages she paid.[58] Once her hope of bringing a servant to salvation kept her from firing a maid.

The woman "was in no ordinary degree a servant of the wicked one," so Mrs. Palmer decided to dismiss her. She would have given her notice immediately but decided to give her one more week of grace to see if she would change her ways. At the end of the period things had become even worse, so Phoebe decided to let her go. Before she could talk to the servant, however, a man came to see Mrs. Palmer. He was under great conviction for his sins and cried out in agony for two or three hours. Dinner time was approaching, and the unconverted maid came to the door repeatedly to summon Mrs. Palmer to the table. Not wishing to interrupt her counseling session short of the man's deliverance, she waved the maid away each time but worried about the impression the man's distress was making on her. Finally the man "prayed through" and was converted. Walter and the dinner guests came into the room. Almost beside himself with happiness, the man ran from one to the other with tears of joy flowing down his face, exclaiming, "O, bless the Lord! He *has* forgiven *all* my sins." Once again the maid appeared to repeat the dinner call. He ran up to her, grabbed her by the hand, and began to praise the Lord for his deliverance. Her stony response seemed to perplex him, and he continued to tell her what God had done for him. Later, during dinner, the maid's resistance crumbled, and she too was convicted of her sins. Phoebe volunteered to stay at home so the maid could go to church that evening; there she was soundly converted.[59]

Phoebe Palmer felt that a woman's ministry to her husband, children, and servants in the household was important enough that she should cut back on outside commitments to make time to do it well. She once wrote to a young mother, assuring her that focusing her attention on her family and away from the lost world was " 'the *right* way' for you at the present time." She was careful to add, however, when giving advice on this topic, that women needed to be careful that household cares did not displace the Lord from the primary place in their attentions, and that by good planning and "*method*" much needless work could be eliminated.[60] In addition, women who can afford it should be careful not to spend their time doing chores that servants can do for them. Phoebe Palmer commented on the case of a woman who had the ability to write, along with other talents fitting her for various kinds of ministries, but "in view of laying up treasure on earth, she permits herself to bear unaided the cares of her family." This is a mistake: first, because it misuses the talents God has given; second, because it deprives the world of the good the woman might have done; and third, because it denies work to some unemployed poor woman in the neighborhood.[61] Mrs. Palmer seems to have committed much of the work of her household to servants and perhaps relied on her sister Sarah to care for her children when she traveled. She may even have sent Walter, Jr., to boarding school for a time, but the evidence is not clear on this point.[62]

EXAMPLE AND INFLUENCE

Fully measuring the value of Mrs. Palmer's example and the extent of her influence is impossible. We do know that twelve thousand copies of her book were printed and that its main arguments were reprinted in a pamphlet ten years later.[63] We also know of her role in the lives of Catherine Booth, Frances Willard, and Amanda Smith, but there is no way of knowing how many women attended one of her meetings and went away saying, "If she can do that, so can I."[64] Nor is there any way of determining how many men reading her magazine began to wonder if they had undervalued the intellectual capacities of all women. Thus the evidence for Phoebe Palmer's influence must be subjective and impressionistic. That she addressed thousands in an age when some thought it unseemly for a woman to speak, that she wrote theological works when some thought it impossible for a woman to reason, and that she established a mission in the slums when some thought it unsafe for a woman to venture too far outside the home, we do know. To what degree she was instrumental in changing the conditions that bound women, we do not know.

There is, however, one other bit of objective data to consider. With the exception of that of Barbara Heck, women's names are not conspicuous in the annals of early American Methodism. The dangers to a woman's life and reputation made itinerating impossible on the frontier, and an antifemale attitude seems to have arisen in nineteenth-century American Methodism. In British Methodism a reaction against women set in soon after Wesley's death; perhaps this influence discouraged women's ministries even in the local societies in America. At any rate, there was not even a female class leader in New York City until 1840.[65] Phoebe Palmer's ministry went against this antifeminist current and helped to prepare the way for women preachers like Amanda Smith and Maggie Van Cott, the first woman licensed to preach in American Methodism.[66] In the Holiness movement, which Mrs. Palmer did so much to shape, women played an important leadership role, and still continue to do so. Even one hundred years after her death, 6 percent of ordained Nazarenes were women. At that time the figure in the United Methodist Church was only 1 percent.[67]

EVALUATION

Many of the modern studies of Phoebe Palmer have been done by those primarily interested in women's history. Most of the works that mention her give a synopsis of her life as an example that women made important contributions to nineteenth-century religion and society.[68] Three works specifically treat her contribution to feminism. Nancy Hardesty shows that Phoebe Palmer was a link between the revivalist and the feminist camps in the nineteenth century. She argues that Mrs. Palmer's life shows how Finneyite revivalism led to a widening of the woman's sphere. Hardesty rightly never claims that Phoebe Palmer depended on Finney for her ideas but illustrates that other women who were undoubtedly influenced by Finney had ideas similar to those of Mrs. Palmer and were involved in similar kinds of reform. She also points out that Mrs. Palmer did not carry her feminism to the same lengths as the women closer to Finney.[69]

Anne Loveland has also examined Phoebe Palmer's contribution to feminism. She concludes that Mrs. Palmer's life is an example of Keith Melder's thesis that evangelical religion contributed toward widening the woman's sphere and expanding her status.[70] Hardesty and Loveland both employ the same kind of argument. They say that in an age that repressed women, Phoebe Palmer influenced religion and society; she also argued cogently that other women should do so as well. Thus by her example and thought she expanded the woman's sphere.

Theodore Hovet sees more of a paradox in Mrs. Palmer's contribution. Writing in the prestigious *Journal of Religion*, he contends that while what he calls "Phoebe Palmer's altar phraseology" enabled nineteenth-century Christian middle-class women to create a new self-actualized identity for themselves, it also tended to limit the expression of that identity to the domestic sphere.[71] Unfortunately, he is wrong on both counts.

Hovet begins his argument by correctly pointing out that Phoebe Palmer was frustrated with the idea that one had to wait for the action of some "ill-defined outside force" before one could claim sanctification. He then begins to go wrong when he says that "she discovered that 'gracious ability' was not something injected into the individual by a supernatural force but was only the promise by God, recorded in Scripture, that holiness was attainable in this life." This misunderstanding then leads him to depict Mrs. Palmer as a latter-day Pelagius, saying she taught "holiness was . . . a condition created out of the actions of the individual." He sees her as one who opposed the supernatural, believing people could remake themselves without waiting for outside aid. He says that Phoebe Palmer "pushed the Christian life beyond the supernaturalism of concepts like the second blessing and instantaneous change," that she "left behind the emphasis in American evangelicalism on a supernatural experience as the central element in the Christian life," and that "the altar transaction was a personal decision, an 'act' which created a new self without a baptism of the spirit."[72]

In addition to claiming that Phoebe Palmer banished the experience of the supernatural from the Christian life, Hovet says that she taught women to create their own worlds. He describes her as a protoexistentialist: according to Hovet, she was one who left "behind the old self in rder to start creating a new self free from the entanglements of the world," one whose "altar phraseology described a process of self-creation which brought to life a new Christian identity which evolved through time," one who argued "that God's kingdom is . . . a spiritual reality brought forth in this world by the holiness created by individual action," and one who "introduced to evangelical Protestants a vision of spiritual freedom, a Faustian quest for knowledge and experience, and a love of the unbounded appropriate to that Romantic era and to such an individualistic culture." If Hovet is to be believed, Mrs. Palmer was religion's answer to the self-reliant individualism of Walt Whitman and to the world-creating existentialism of William James.[73]

Hovet thinks that Mrs. Palmer is a Pelagian because he does not understand her concept of prevenient grace. Just as the Calvinists thought John Wesley was teaching human ability when he urged people to be converted, so Hovet misunderstands Mrs. Palmer when she urges people to be sanctified. As an ardent Methodist, Phoebe Palmer accepted the Wesleyan doctrine of prevenient grace, believing that any good thing a person is able to do results not from natural ability but from the grace of God. Not only is salvation entirely of God, but even the human desire to be saved comes solely from him.[74] She believed that sanctification is a supernatural, gracious act of God, not something humans can do on their own. Believers can never achieve sanctification through their own natural abilities, rather it is a "gift" bestowed by "Infinite Love" by "virtue of the great price [Christ] paid for the redemption of body, soul, and spirit."[75]

Even the human resolution to devote oneself entirely to God is made possible only by his grace.[76] She asked one correspondent what prompted him to seek holiness, what helped him to grow toward it, and what enabled him to consecrate himself:

> Let me ask, brother, how were the first movings in your heart, prompting you to seek a state of holiness, induced? Was it not by the power of the *Spirit* that you were incited to take the first step toward the attainment of this grace? And now, that you have for weeks past been sustained in a state of progression toward it, have you been enabled to go forward in your own might or have you been empowered by the might of the Spirit for every progressive step? And when you were gradually brought to submit to what you felt to be an entire crucifixion of the flesh, I need not ask how you were brought to this point, for I am sure you will acknowledge the direct agency of the Holy Spirit.[77]

Here Mrs. Palmer teaches God's prevenient grace in direct opposition to the idea of natural ability.

Wesley's problem with the Calvinists was not that he thought God's grace unnecessary for salvation but that he differed with them about the extent of that grace. They said God limited his saving grace only to the elect; he taught that God's grace embraced everyone. Because Christ had already made full and sufficient atonement for the sins of all humanity, Wesley could offer pardon to all who heard him and even tell them that God had commanded them to claim it.[78] In the same way Phoebe Palmer's quarrel with those who said one had to wait long, beseeching God for the grace of sanctification, was not that she felt that God's supernatural grace was unnecessary, but that she thought they were silly to beg for what had already been promised and even commanded. "Hath he issued the command, 'Be ye holy,'" she asked, "and not given the ability, with the command, for the performance of it?"[79] In another place, she urges a friend, "Just stop *doing,* and begin to *trust Christ to do all for you,* and you are safe."[80]

Not only does Hovet misunderstand Mrs. Palmer about the supernatural, he also misinterprets her words about the role of experience in the Christian life. When Mrs. Palmer talks about walking by faith she does not mean to de-emphasize the importance of supernatural experience, but only to express her willingness to trust that God had done a supernatural work in her heart whether or not she feels any emotional change.[81] Far from leaving behind the emphasis on a supernatural experience, she made the supernatural experience of sanctification the central element in the Christian life. According to Mrs. Palmer, until believers had experienced sanctification, they were not obeying God, they were not sure of going to heaven, they were of little service on earth to God, and they were subject to backsliding.[82] For her it was really the beginning of the proper Christian life. No wonder she urged believers not to rest until they had experienced sanctification.[83]

Hovet's most puzzling mistake is his comment about creating a new self "without a baptism of the spirit." Phoebe Palmer thought the baptism of the Spirit was the most important event in the Christian life. She followed the Methodist usage of equating the baptism of the Holy Spirit with entire sanctification. Her first book makes the identification, and she used Pentecostal language more frequently after the beginning of the revival of 1857–58. The book she wrote during those years, *Promise of the Father,* explicates the idea fully, mentioning the "Baptism of the Spirit" on almost every page. For Phoebe Palmer, the new self came only *through* the baptism of the human spirit by the Holy Spirit.[84]

Hovet's interpretation of Phoebe Palmer as an existentialist, beckoning Evangelicals to a "Faustian quest for knowledge and experience" comes from a misinterpretation of her ideas about Christian growth. Because she believed that entire sanctification marked the real beginning of the Christian life, she needed to stress that one who was sanctified had not "arrived," but would keep on growing in grace. That growth would be shown by greater love for Christ and greater usefulness to others, not outlandish or mystical experiences. She was especially wary of those who claimed novel works of grace beyond sanctification.[85]

Hovet's second conclusion about Phoebe Palmer, that she gave women freedom only within the limited sphere of the home, is also erroneous. He says, "Palmer made gatherings like her Tuesday Meeting and 'testifying' the dominant mode of Christian activism."[86] Mrs. Palmer did use the Tuesday Meeting to spread her ideas, and testifying was important to her, but to say that they were the dominant mode of her activism is false. Such a statement neglects her plain teaching about the role of women in the world.

Hovet is right to say that Phoebe Palmer regarded her home as an important sphere of ministry but wrong to think that she limited herself or any other woman to that sphere. Her life did not bring the "Romantic vision of inner autonomy and unlimited personal growth to middle class women."[87] Her focus was never inward, but always outward. Phoebe Palmer taught that God sanctifies believers in order to employ them in his service, just as a carpenter sharpens his tools before using them.[88] She told one correspondent to quit focusing on his own spiritual state and to get busy for God.[89] Because many of the people she wrote for were mothers, she told them first to make sure they were in right relationship to God and then to begin to minister where they were, raising their families for the Lord. Women who did not have the responsibility of a family should go anywhere in the world they could in order to serve the Lord.[90] In the eighteenth century John Wesley taught his followers, both men and women, to think: "I look upon the world as my parish."[91] In the nineteenth century, Phoebe Palmer expressed the same idea for the women and men she influenced when she asked, "And what is the Christian's life mission? Is it not to save the world?"[92]

Not only does Hovet's statement about Phoebe Palmer's activism neglect her plain teaching, it also ignores her example. Here was a woman who crossed the ocean and then the continent to preach holiness, a woman who wrote eighteen books and edited a magazine for eleven years, a woman who founded a mission in New York's worst slum. This was not a woman who "pushed the influence of 'the world' out the domestic door and created a sacred sphere within society in which the spirit could unfold itself."[93] No, this was a woman who followed her Master out of the safety of her home, "to seek and to save the lost" (Luke 19:10).[94]

CONCLUSION

A careful study of Phoebe Palmer as feminist confirms the findings of Hardesty and Loveland that her thought and example helped to widen the field of female influence. She was a feminist in that her words and actions asserted that women had capabilities, rights, and obligations that men of the day generally denied. Unlike some other feminists of her day, her commitment to pushing back male-established boundaries did not arise from an Enlightenment understanding of natural rights but came from her Methodist heritage and from her understanding of sanctification.[95] While mildly supportive of those women who wanted political and legal reform, her aims were both narrower and broader than theirs. Her goals were narrower in that she did not treat the whole range of women's rights but focused only on the right of women to exercise all their gifts in the church. They were broader in that she believed that if sanctified women were free to exercise all their gifts in the church, the Lord would pour out such a revival that the world would be converted. Then all injustice, not just that suffered by women, would disappear.

She is therefore the foremother of today's Christian feminist who believes that God has created people for eternal relationship with himself and has liberated them from sin and death through the death and resurrection of Christ. The Christian feminist believes God has ordained the state to protect people and has instituted the church and the family to nurture and train people for right relationships with each other and with him. This kind of feminist wants to reform abuses and purify God-ordained institutions from man-made corruptions. She would see Phoebe Palmer as a pioneer and trailblazer on the path she wants to follow.

A secular feminist would see Mrs. Palmer in a very different light. One who finds Christianity, the church, and the traditional family so filled with patriarchy that they are oppressive by their very nature would see Phoebe Palmer as her polar opposite. This kind of feminist wants, not to reform existing institutions, but to replace them with something else. For her, Mrs. Palmer is a collaborator who works with the enemy to improve conditions in the prison instead of organizing the prisoners to revolt. She and Phoebe Palmer could never understand each other because they differ about the nature of the one in authority. Is he a vicious jailer or a benevolent father?

CHAPTER EIGHT:
Phoebe Palmer As Humanitarian

Phoebe Palmer was no lady. One German visitor described the idle lives of American ladies in these words:
> New York or Philadelphia ladies [would] rise at eight or nine, breakfast at ten—then . . . potter three or four hours,—then have a chat with three or four women of their set,—then walk on Broadway or Chestnut Street or go shopping,—then sit down to dinner, then potter again until 6 o'clock,—then take tea, and finally dress for a party.[1]

By this standard, Phoebe Palmer was no lady.

In the years before she devoted herself full time to revival work, Mrs. Palmer often got up before dawn to have her "holy time," and after the needs of her family were met, could usually be found on the streets of New York, hurrying to a meeting of one of her benevolent organizations or taking food, clothing, and the gospel to those in need. While other women of her class were becoming "butterflies in amber" she thought of herself as a spade in the hands of the Lord.[2]

Growing up in a comfortable middle-class home, Phoebe Palmer wanted little to do with the poor. Like other persons of breeding and taste, she felt "an inherent shrinking from mingling in common with the mass." When she surrendered herself to Christ, however, all that changed. The Lord took her will and "caused [it] to flow out upon the world through the channel of His own blessed will." This change led to a change in her feelings about the poor: "And the class of persons who heard the Saviour gladly [Mark 12:37], was the very same class to which she now most loved to minister."[3]

Mrs. Palmer's ministry to the poor was motivated by a concern to save their souls. Because souls live in bodies and their fates are determined by decisions made by minds, Mrs. Palmer was concerned that those bodies be fed and clothed and that those minds be educated and freed from the influence of alcohol. The best way to insure that people have adequate food, clothing, and education is not to dole these things out, but to get people jobs. To hold jobs people must be sober and honest. The best way to make people sober and honest is to save their souls. Thus a concern for the inner person leads to a concern for the outer person and a concern for the outer person leads to a concern for the inner person: The work of salvation is a benevolent cycle. Phoebe Palmer sought to aid in both phases of that cycle.

Besides saving the souls of the poor, another motive that Phoebe Palmer had for helping them was the desire to save her own soul. To her had been entrusted the Good News of salvation; to withhold it was tantamount to murder. In addition she was a steward of God's wealth; she would be called to account for the way she had used his resources. The final motive which encouraged her to minister to the poor was her clear sense that God would prosper everything she undertook at his leading. Others might become discouraged at the emotional or financial cost of ministering to the poor, or feel that the tendency to backslide made all efforts futile. Mrs. Palmer, however, felt she had God's word that her work would not be wasted. This confidence, along with the other two motives, led her to support early efforts to improve the lot of the impoverished and to share in establishing a mission which helped to set the pattern for urban welfare work for the next fifty years.

MOTIVES

Saving Their Souls

Phoebe Palmer believed that all people are made in the image of God. Inside each person is a "gem of priceless value," a soul, but few people recognize their worth. Instead they hide their value. Mrs. Palmer conjured the picture of a drunk: he clothes his body in "soiled and tattered garments" and wears a broken hat. He benumbs his senses with the intoxicating cup. He bends low instead of walking upright. He lives like a beast. "His manliness of form, his intellect, his precious soul, made in the image of God, are well-nigh lost from human vision—buried beneath the rubbish of sin," she concluded.[4]

Phoebe Palmer went on to say that Jesus sees the man's worth. He has purchased him with his own blood. To him this soul is worth more than the universe. It is a gem that the Savior has willed should deck his crown and shine forever. In order to claim this soul Jesus came down from heaven. During his time on earth, he was so eager to reach people that he often did not have time to eat. Because Jesus values this soul so much, so must Phoebe Palmer. She, too, must seek and save the lost (Luke 19:10). But to rescue people like the man she has pictured is hard work: "Seeking implies *research, labor.* Research, aye, wearing labor may be needful, before we find these precious gems, so nearly lost amid the devastations of sin."[5]

Because Jesus was especially concerned for the poor during his earthly ministry, Christians now should also be likewise concerned. The Lord might have chosen his followers from "kingly palaces, halls of science, [or] schools for theology," but instead he chose common people.[6] He still chooses the common people and "is ever closely with those who, at his bidding, work low in the vale of humility."[7] The great and the wise of earth may not see the work, but "a ministering angel from the eternal city [is] present . . . to write down the name of the agent employed, on the pages of immortality."[8]

Saving Her Soul

In addition to the reward of laboring alongside Jesus to recover jewels buried in the rubbish of sin, Phoebe Palmer was also motivated to work among the poor by the desire to save her own soul. Like any other Christian, she would be blood-guilty if she withheld the message of salvation, but a special sense of stewardship drove her to seek out the needy. God had entrusted her with the task of being his agent. Thus she must know his will and then do it.

God's Concern for the Poor

The Bible revealed to Phoebe Palmer that God wills that the poor be cared for and treated justly. Jesus' example showed how important the poor are to God, and his teachings underscored the point. "We speak of the poor as objects of God's special regard, for He presents them as such," Mrs. Palmer wrote in an annual report of the Female Assistance Society. She went on to say that in serving the poor, she was really serving Christ:

... we may no more know Christ after the flesh, yet ... we hear our once lowly Redeemer say, Inasmuch as ye have done it unto one of the least of these my brethren, ye have done it unto me [Matt. 25:40]. To search out these objects of divine solicitude—to visit Christ in his members, and to raise the erring poor out of the dust, and after making their earthly condition better, to direct their wandering feet to the heavenly fold, has been the work of this Society.[9]

Stewardship of Time

Part of doing her Master's will was using her time wisely. She keenly felt how quickly time passes away. Using Wesley's image, she said her life is like an arrow shot from eternity to eternity.[10] Her goal was to fill every moment of her brief life with service for the Lord.[11] Time is a "solemn trust" from the Lord. It is not one's own; it is a gift from God, and he will demand an accounting of its use: "It is a most valuable and divine bestowment, intrusted by the moment, and for the most exalted purposes, and for which the heavenly Giver will require his *own* with *usury*."[12]

Because time is so precious, the believer cannot afford to let even an hour pass "without making its mark on eternity."[13] Mrs. Palmer reported the story of a pastor who was offered a free sightseeing trip to Europe as an example of one who knew the value of time. He declined because it would take too much time away from his calling.[14] If people should not have time for free trips to Europe, then they certainly should not waste time in reading novels or other trivial pursuits.[15] Phoebe Palmer felt that not "one moment of time [was] at [her] own disposal," and "dare[d] not spend it in any pursuit but what will bear the inscription, '*Holiness to the Lord.*'"[16]

Stewardship of Money

Besides giving Christians time to use in his service, God also gives them money. His purpose in giving material possessions is to train people for the world to come and to test people's faithfulness in this world. Some he appoints to be poor. If they "occupy faithfully" until he returns (Luke 19:13), he will make them "*heaven's nobility.*" Others he has made rich. Their duty is to distribute God's wealth and share it with others. If they do so, he will make them spiritually rich.[17]

Phoebe Palmer knew she was rich. In speaking about the rich and the poor, she said "us" and "them." Walter's medical practice had prospered; as early as 1834 he owned five parcels of land in New York City.[18] Mrs. Palmer felt God had called her and her husband to manage wisely the wealth he had bestowed upon them. Surprisingly for one who spoke so much about Pentecost, she rejected the contention that modern Christians should imitate the apostolic church and have all things in common. She strongly affirmed that all she had belonged to the Lord, but she was convinced that the Lord did not want her to liquidate her holdings as those in the Jerusalem church had done. She did not rely on the biblical argument that the Pauline churches were not communalistic, but instead pointed to Abraham, David, and Joseph of Arimathea, who all were wealthy. Then she made the somewhat illogical statement that if wealthy Christians gave away all their capital, they would no longer be able to give away the income from that capital. What she said was true, but she failed to recognize that in giving capital to the church, one would at the same time be giving all the future income from that capital. Apparently she felt that God had called the wealthy to be trustees of His wealth and that to give away all of one's wealth at once would be wrong, since it would be giving up one's role as a trustee.[19] Another reason to keep one's capital is that God wants representatives at all levels of society. God chooses whom he will place in each station, and to leave that station "deforms [God's arrangement] by evident unseemliness."[20]

In the mouth of a less ingenuous woman such rationalizations could easily become hypocrisy. Mrs. Palmer, however, sincerely believed that just as God had placed some Christians in Caesar's household (Phil. 4:22), so he had placed her in her social position.[21] The issue for her was not how much money one has but how one uses that money. She felt that God had given her money and with it the command to use it to serve the poor. The needy are God's *"chosen* ones" and the rich are their *"servants."*[22] God has given rich Christians enough money to meet all of the needs in the world. The degree to which they accomplish that task is the measure of their faithfulness.[23]

Walter and Phoebe Palmer tried to be faithful stewards of God's money. At first they gave on impulse, when their hearts were moved by a stirring appeal. They generally gave about as much as their friends did, even though most of their friends had more money than they. As time went on Phoebe became dissatisfied with this arrangement. It was not systematic enough, she said. She wanted to organize their giving by giving a tenth. Walter said that he thought they were already giving a tenth, but Phoebe wanted to make sure. She set aside a box which she called the Lord's treasury. Into it went one-tenth of all the money they received. As they began to follow this plan, they found that they were giving more, but also that they were better off because their income was rising.[24]

It would have been easy to find many things that they suddenly needed because they could now afford them, but they agreed that as their income went up their standard of giving, not their standard of living, would rise. Another temptation would be to invest their new surplus income. They were determined not to lay up for themselves treasure on earth, so they decided to give more.[25] They reasoned that money that is invested can be lost in a depression but money that is given away always pays rich dividends.[26] The seriousness with which the Palmers took this commitment to a simple lifestyle is evident from their defensiveness in justifying their use of money. When they moved to bigger houses in 1865 and in 1870, they were careful to point out that they needed the space for the Tuesday Meeting.[27] When writing about her trip to Florida in February of 1874, Phoebe Palmer anticipated that her readers would question the propriety of spending the time and presumably also the money on what looked suspiciously like a vacation. She answered that even Jesus sometimes got away from the crowd and once commanded his disciples, "Come ye yourselves apart into a desert place, and rest a while" (Mark 6:31).[28] By 1848 the Palmers were rich enough to contemplate giving away a fifth of their income and began looking forward to the time when all of their earnings could be devoted to God. This happy situation came about when Dr. Palmer sold his practice and bought the *Guide to Holiness*. They used the income from the magazine and from Mrs. Palmer's books to support themselves while they engaged in full-time unpaid revival work.[29]

Just as the Palmers had more invitations to speak than they had time to fill, so they had more appeals for funds than they had money to give. They therefore had to think through their priorities before they contributed. In listing the demands on their charity, Mrs. Palmer first mentioned "our own" poor and then the immigrant. Next there were the churches the Palmers attended, and most of these were in debt.[30] All these appeals the Palmers considered a good investment of the Lord's money. What was not a good investment, Mrs. Palmer said, was giving money to people who themselves were not willing to give. In a letter explaining why the Palmers would not give money to a certain congregation she wrote that the church was not sacrificing enough. "Yes, your church is suffering from debt," she said, "but you people are also suffering from penuriousness. Your church poverty is self-imposed. While you know the excellency of the Gospel, you are unwilling to give enough from your own means to support its ministry."[31]

Many of the church people in the Palmers' social circle did not take their obligation to serve the poor as seriously as did Walter and Phoebe. Observing their behavior and reading her Bible convinced Mrs. Palmer that "covetousness [is] the chief obstacle to the religious prosperity of thousands."[32] She illustrated her point by telling the story of a man who had promised the Lord to tithe. He was then making three hundred dollars a year and supporting his mother and sister. He kept his vow and lived comfortably. Then he got a raise to five hundred dollars a year. He continued to tithe and lived still more comfortably. By steps, his employers raised his salary to twelve hundred dollars a year. He began to wonder if by tithing he was giving too much. His friends with similar incomes were not giving as much as he. Maybe he ought to begin to give less and save more because his mother was not getting any younger. A friend advised him to follow this course, and he began to divert the Lord's money into his own savings. Mrs. Palmer concluded the story of this unwise young man with the words, "He soon made 'shipwreck of faith and a good conscience'" (1 Tim. 1:19).[33]

Even when the lives of covetous people did not result in obvious spiritual shipwreck, Phoebe Palmer was sure such people were in serious trouble. She said laying up treasure on earth is as sinful as theft or murder, and described the sin as she saw it in one of her friends.[34] She went into great detail, perhaps so the man could identify himself, but certainly so her hearers could look for it in themselves. Mrs. Palmer described him as her "rich poor friend." He was rich in this world but poor toward God. An early sign of his sin was discontent with his house and neighbors. He had moved to a bigger house in a nicer neighborhood where he would no longer be reminded of his "former ordinary estate." Another symptom was his preoccupation with business and investments. He was too busy to read his Bible or to pray, so he was never reminded of his duty to give as the Lord prospered him. Without these divine reminders he naturally began to spend his money on his splendid mansion and his servants, as well as other items of "mere worldly display." He thought nothing of spending five hundred dollars on his home, wardrobe, or entertainment, but rarely gave even fifty dollars "toward sustaining the poor and friendless, and the various institutions of Christianity." When he did give anything, it was only so others would notice his generosity. He spent money freely to make his children shine in this world but not to make them shine in heaven. Not surprisingly, they cared little for religion. Phoebe Palmer wanted nothing to do with this former friend. She would not even "sanction his costly entertainments by [her] presence." They were "unbecoming to the simplicity of the Gospel of Christ, and beneath [her] dignity in view of [her] high and holy calling."[35]

Much more to Mrs. Palmer's liking was her "poor rich friend." She and her husband ran a little grocery store. They could not afford to hire any help, so they both worked day and night to make ends meet. In the midst of her work, however, she found time to talk with her customers about their souls, and many were born again as a result of her efforts. Mrs. Palmer's friend took time away from her work to visit the poor and needy, and she helped them out of the tithe she scrupulously set aside for the Lord's work.[36] Having friends like these two convinced Mrs. Palmer that "more faith, proportionately, may be found among the poorer class in [the] community, than among the rich."[37] Rich people could be saved, Phoebe Palmer admitted, but only if "they will give up the world and come down to the foot of the cross." "But," she lamented, "Alas! how many would rather risk their all for eternity than to bow their neck to the yoke of the meek and lowly!"[38]

Although she was rich, Phoebe Palmer was confident that she had given up the world and come down to the foot of the cross. She recognized that she had a tendency to be proud and to value worldly distinctions, but when the Lord purified her heart, He taught her "lessons in humility." Only after her soul was "purified wholly from earthly dross" did she see, "as God sees, the utter insignificance of prideful positions, soaring intellects, worldly reputation, and a score of other pigmy matters, so highly prized by men, and so often an abomination to God."[39] She showed her egalitarian spirit when she wrote her rebuke in an earl's guest book, and in the comments she made about the injustices suffered by the poor in England.[40] Closer to home, she was always careful to pay her servants fairly and treat them with dignity and kindness.[41] She was saddened when she saw those who professed holiness "indulging in manifestations indicative of fancied superiority of intellect or position."[42] At times, however, Phoebe Palmer seems to have forgotten that class distinctions mean nothing to the sanctified. On their voyage to England they traveled first class but mingled with those in steerage. Having found real fellowship with these poorer travelers, she congratulated herself for her willingness to condescend to them. Her unquestioning acceptance of her privilege and her self-righteous attitude show that she was probably not as sanctified as she imagined.[43]

Labor in the Lord

In addition to wishing to save the souls of the poor and her own soul, another force powerfully motivated Phoebe Palmer's ministry to the needy: her conviction of success. Mrs. Palmer well knew that "God does not impart his blessings to us for our own exclusive enjoyment."[44] She knew her role on earth was to work for God. At the time of her sanctification she had felt that her sense of commitment to the Lord's work was as great as if God had sent her spirit from heaven to earth on a special mission. Two years later that impression was confirmed when she fell very ill. Breathing was difficult, and she felt the approach of death. As she lingered for hours in this critical condition, the Scripture came to mind, "For all things are yours, whether . . . life or death, or things present, or things to come; all are yours" (1 Cor. 3:21b–22). She felt the Lord giving her the choice between life and death. She knew that to live meant to "forego the felicities of heaven for many long years of sojourning below" but decided that for the sake of Walter, the children, and any souls that she might point toward holiness, she chose to remain on earth and work. At once she knew that she would recover, and from that time she rapidly became better.[45]

The conviction that she was on earth to labor for the Lord gave Phoebe Palmer the confidence to work hard for Him. "The purposes of our redemption," she said, "remain unanswered unless we are unto God a peculiar people, *zealous* of good works" (Titus 2:14). Her zealousness in good works was augmented by her assurance that God would bless everything she attempted. Before her sanctification she would often wonder about her motives and doubt whether God would bless her work if she were doing it, partly at least, for selfish reasons. She was "hinder[ed] and perplex[ed]," questioning whether her actions would make any eternal difference. Realizing that human effort counts for nothing unless God establishes it, she wondered if the Lord would "own" her deeds. She was discouraged by the idea that after all her hard work and sacrifice, her efforts might be wasted because she had acted with impure intentions. After her sanctification, however, came the realization that her motives were pure. All her works would be "wrought *in God*," and therefore carry his blessing. None of her efforts would be wasted. Relying on the promise in 1 Corinthians 15:58, she felt a stimulus "urg[ing her] onward to greater and still greater efforts!" Like the Corinthians, she began to be "always abounding in the work of the Lord" because she knew her "labor in the Lord was not in vain."[46]

Relying on the Word of God that her labors would never be in vain gave Phoebe Palmer a determined confidence in all her work. She once answered a letter from a stranger, who though a minister, asked her advice about his prayer life. Upon proofreading her letter, she felt the tone of her answer was not gentle enough and was tempted not to send the letter. Then she remembered that she had specifically asked the Lord to tell her what to write. Did she not believe that when she had asked for the Lord's help, He would give it? Just because the letter took a different tone than she had anticipated was no reason to cast away her confidence that God had guided her pen. Recognizing that "this [was] an old temptation of the adversary with me," she mailed the letter, smugly contemplating the victory she had just won over "the principalities and powers . . . arrayed to withstand" her. Not only was the letter helpful to its recipient, but others thought it so useful that two newspapers reprinted it.[47]

On another occasion Phoebe Palmer was tempted to think she was not in the right place at the right time. Just before arriving at the Lake Side Campground in Ohio, she was informed by some "prominent persons in authority" that holiness had been preached there last year and that the message had fallen on hard ground. She began to wonder if she had made the right choice in coming to Lake Side instead of going to one of the other camp meetings that had invited her. She resolved not to doubt God's guidance: "But though the adversary would have had us yield to the impression that we had mistaken our way, we *dared* not doubt the Lord had as ever directed our steps." She preached holiness in the confidence that God had brought her to this place for his special purpose. At least one hundred people professed entire sanctification, and the *Western Christian Advocate* crowed, "Lake Side Camp-meeting of 1874 has gone into history as one of the most successful and profitable of meetings."[48]

While arming Phoebe Palmer with confident determination, her idea that God would bless all that she did also had some negative results. When the results of her meetings were less than she expected, she could not simply say that she had misjudged the needs of the people or had not delivered her message in the right way. Instead, because she knew she was doing the Lord's will, she knew there must be an Achan in the camp who was preventing God's blessing. Three years after the end of the Civil War she was disappointed that the citizens of New Orleans did not respond warmly enough to the Yankee lady who came talking about perfect love. Because she could not say that her journey came too soon for wounds to have healed, she had to say that the ministers of the Southern Methodist church were not humble enough.[49] Likewise, when rain hampered the progress of a camp meeting in West Virginia, she absolved both herself and the Lord, blaming the organizers for not having a bigger tent.[50] Probably the worst example of the tendency of her self-confidence to become self-righteousness was her controversy with Mattison. Perhaps if she had been less confident of her own infallibility, she would have been able to defuse the crisis. As it happened, this series of increasingly nasty exchanges between Mattison and the Palmers did nothing to enhance the reputation for holiness of either side.[51]

THE FIVE POINTS MISSION

While it was not an unmixed blessing, Phoebe Palmer's confidence that her labor in the Lord was not in vain probably led to the establishment of the Five Points Mission. Ever since the day of her father's funeral in 1847 she was determined that the Ladies' Home Missionary Society would begin a mission in the heart of New York's worst neighborhood. They turned a deaf ear to her pleas for three years, telling that others had failed there in the past. The failure of others made no difference to Mrs. Palmer when she was convinced that the Lord was guiding her, so she would not give up. Finally, worn down by her persistence and encouraged by her pledge of one hundred dollars, they agreed to start the work.[52]

Background

The nature of the poverty Mrs. Palmer faced at Five Points was different from the kind of poverty New York had known when Phoebe was a girl. Back then people generally agreed that there were two kinds of poverty. One was the temporary hardship caused by unemployment during the low phases of the business cycle, and the other was the chronic need of the dependent and the infirm. People also agreed that nothing could be done to eliminate the sources of poverty. Each year winter put an end to the shipping industry, throwing thousands of sailors, shipwrights, stevedores, and cartmen out of work. No one could change the seasons or find other employment for these men in the seaport town. Nor could anyone prevent fathers from dying, accidents from happening, or people from getting old. Although no one could eliminate these causes of poverty, New Yorkers could do something to help the victims. By 1815 they had established a network of public and private societies to feed the hungry, aid the widow and orphan, and care for the sick and insane.[53]

By the late 1840s, when Phoebe Palmer first began exploring the Five Points, it was obvious that the older societies were no longer capable of meeting the needs of the poor. The city had more than tripled in size; most of the growth came from the 500,000 immigrants who had landed in New York since 1820. Those who had resources were able to push further inland, but the poorest remained in the city. They hoped to find jobs as stevedores, day laborers, or cartmen. They could afford only the cheapest housing and had to live near their work. Thus they crowded together with their compatriots, turning some of New York's neighborhoods into slums. The Five Points was the best known of these areas. The city's Fresh Water Pond had been located there, but by 1821 squatters had settled around it and tanners had polluted the waters with the carcasses of dead animals. The city government filled in the Pond and tried to encourage people to build nice houses on the reclaimed land. The new land remained wet, however, and people feared that it bred disease. Cheap housing was put up for freed blacks and for Irish immigrants, and five thousand people crowded into the area's one hundred houses. No fashionable shops were there, nor business offices, nor churches. A brewery dominated the neighborhood, and sixty-nine of the dwellings housed grog shops.[54]

Respectable people simply ignored the neighborhood, but they could not ignore the cholera epidemics which first started in the Five Points. Doctors and other public health workers had to go into the area, and soon reports of the conditions began to appear in print.[55] One daily paper reported a visit in this way:

The under part, or basement of the building, is even still worse on the southwest corner; in a lower room, not more than fifteen feet square, *twenty-six* human beings reside. A man could scarcely stand erect in it; two men were sitting by the blaze of a few sticks when our company entered; women lay on a mass of filthy, unsightly rags in the corner—sick, feeble, and emaciated; six or seven children were in various [positions] about the corner; an old table covered with a few broken dishes; two women were peeling potatoes, and actually pulling off the skins with their finger nails; the smoke and stench of the room was so suffocating that it could not be long endured, and the announcement that, in addition to the misfortune of poverty, they had the measles to boot, started most of our party in a precipitate retreat from the premises.[56]

Reports of conditions like these convinced some New Yorkers that they could no longer think of poverty in traditional terms. The poor at Five Points and in other slums, by their sheer numbers and desperate need, nullified the traditional means of charitable support. Something new had to be done.[57]

Under the influence of *laissez-faire* economists and the Second Great Awakening, something new was being done. By the 1840s the city mission had arisen to battle urban poverty. The primary goal of these societies was to win individuals to Christ, but they found that in order to achieve their goal they needed to improve the lot of the poor. The traditional thinking about poverty and the measures that should be taken to alleviate it had been done mainly in secular terms. While the early philanthropists were usually devout Christians, they thought of the needy primarily as people with economic rather than spiritual problems. God himself had allowed, if not ordained, the conditions that created poverty, and no guilt was attached to being poor. Who would blame a stevedore for not finding work when winter put an end to the arrival of ships from Europe?[58]

Although a number of societies existed in 1815 to care for those afflicted by the traditional causes of poverty, within two years signs appeared that these philanthropic groups could not care for all the poor in New York. So overwhelming was the demand for relief in 1817 that the city council stopped most contributions to charitable organizations, saying that these groups stimulated pauperism by destroying self-reliance.[59] The reasoning of the aldermen was symptomatic of a change that was occurring in the thinking of many philanthropists. Spurred on by the writings of

British thinkers such as Thomas Malthus and David Ricardo, New Yorkers increasingly came to believe that the poor contributed much to their own misery. The vices the humanitarians observed in the growing slums were evidence of moral weakness and obviously contributed to poverty. Giving the needy the necessities of life encouraged them to continue the behavior that led them into poverty. Thus, many substantial citizens came to believe that the poor needed to be reformed as well as relieved.[60]

The coming of the early-nineteenth-century revivals strengthened the conviction that the poor had spiritual needs as well as material. With the ascendancy of Methodism, and of an increasingly Arminianized Calvinism, Christians began to believe that they could and must evangelize the world. They formed missionary, Bible, tract, and Sunday school societies. Their goal was to Christianize the world, and, for some of them at least, the world included the urban poor. As these eager Christians went into the tenements and slums in search of souls, they found that poverty was a great hindrance to godliness, and so they began to battle poverty. Thus, between 1815 and 1830 humanitarian relief became inextricably linked to evangelism and moral reform.[61]

The rise of immigrant poverty strengthened the conviction of the city mission societies that conversion was the real solution to the problem of poverty. Most of the poor were German and Irish immigrants, and most of the immigrants were Roman Catholic. Most of the poor Roman Catholic immigrants were also intemperate. If only they could be converted, they would gain earthly prosperity as well as a heavenly reward. Conversion would give them the power to say no to drink; it would also make them thrifty and prudent. They could then get jobs, save their earnings, and escape from the slums. The city missions were convinced that they were offering both temporal and eternal salvation.[62]

The Tract Society

The New York City Tract Society was the first permanent city mission. Founded in 1827, the society sought to evangelize the entire city by taking tracts to every dwelling and leading the receptive to Christ. Soon after its formation, however, it began to narrow its scope and expand its ministry. It focused its concern on the poor, and began to take food, medicine, and clothing along with the gospel.[63] Whether as a part of this organization or of another tract society, Phoebe Palmer's personal ministry reflected this change. The obvious physical needs of the people she visited called for more than a spiritual response. So along with her tracts, she gave out food, clothing, and money.[64]

The Female Assistance Society

Along with visiting for the tract society, Phoebe Palmer also visited for the Female Assistance Society and later served as one of its officers. Founded in 1813, this group had as its primary purpose the alleviation of need; conversion was its secondary goal. Following the pattern established in 1797 by Isabella Graham and the Society for the Relief of Poor Widows with Small Children, the Female Assistance Society was composed of a number of "managers" who both raised money and distributed help to the poor. Each manager was responsible to visit the families in an assigned area, to determine their needs, and to take them the food, clothing, fuel, or medicine they required. Of course the manager was expected to do what she could for promoting the spiritual life of the people she visited. She was also responsible to promote the work of the society by soliciting contributions and enrolling new members. Each officer had the duties of a manager and also helped to keep the society functioning by paying its bills, handling its correspondence, writing its reports, or running its meetings.[65]

Ministry

Working with the tract society and the Female Assistance Society brought Phoebe Palmer into contact with the poor of New York's slums. Another society to which she belonged was charged with planting churches. The goals of these societies came together in her mind as she traveled to the cemetery in her father's funeral procession, perhaps passing near the Five Points. After several years of agitation, the Ladies' Home Missionary Society of the Methodist Episcopal Church finally agreed to begin a work at Five Points.[66]

Walter and Phoebe Palmer went over the neighborhood several times looking for a suitable place to begin the mission.[67] The New York Conference of the Methodist Church appointed one of its members, Louis Pease, as a missionary to be supported by the Ladies' Home Missionary Society, and work was begun in a twenty-by-forty-foot room at the corner of Little Water and Cross streets. Two hundred people attended the first meeting, and a Sunday school was established. The mission had two main goals: "Rescuing children from filth and beggary and ignorance, and all the discipline of hell, and starting them in a course of usefulness and respectability," and "recovering the daughters of vice to a life of virtuous industry and good report."[68]

Pease soon found that any positive effects of a Sunday school were undone by the education in vice and crime the children were given during the other six days of the week, so he began a day school. Many who came to hear the preacher came in a state of intoxication, thus "preaching fell on besotted ears in vain." Pease began to hold temperance meetings. In the first year one thousand signed the pledge not to drink, and many were able to keep their promise. The missionary also found that "all his instructions and warnings" to the prostitutes were "presently strangled in the slime of foul thoughts, or in the grasp of inexorable necessity." The women to whom he preached had no other way to support themselves. "Give us work and wages!" they cried. "Do but give us some other master than the devil, and we will serve him." In answer to their pleas, he took some of the women into his own home, giving them food and clothing so they would no longer be forced to earn money through their old profession. He then applied to the Ladies' Home Missionary Society, but with curious blindness, they said their charter forbade them to engage in charitable activity. Any action he took would be at his own responsibility and charge. Nevertheless, Pease found a manufacturer of shirts who would give his piece work to the women who wanted a new way of life, so he announced from the pulpit that he would turn the chapel into a workroom from Monday to Saturday. Twenty women were waiting at the door when he openedit the next morning at 7:00, and fifteen more joined them the first day.[69]

Even if the women earned a decent wage during the day, they still were tempted to earn quick money in their old surroundings at night. Pease realized that they needed a "clean and modest home; an unpolluted place of refreshment and rest." Unfortunately there were no rooms to be rented; the owners were making too much money by renting them out as brothels. With the cooperation of courts, however, and with a little heavy-handed help from an Irish cop who exceeded his commission slightly, "several . . . houses were . . . swept of their human vermin, and labelled 'To Let.'" Pease rented two of these houses, moved his family into them, and took in thirty women. These "women" were really only teenage girls who knew no other form of existence. They regarded Pease and his wife as father and mother.[70]

Once again the women of the Missionary Society thought

Pease had made a mistake. Some of the directors visited him to tell him he should not involve himself in the affairs of the world but should preach the gospel instead. Pease maintained that it was useless to preach repentance to people who have to sin or starve and told the women that as long as he held the religious services that they had commissioned, they had no right to tell him how to use his free time.[71] Eventually this disagreement led to a parting of the ways, and Pease founded the Five Points House of Industry. The Ladies' Home Missionary Society asked the New York Conference to send them another missionary, and soon there were two institutions striving to help the poor at Five Points. For a year the relations between the two organizations were amicable, but sadly, as time went on, the competition between the two organizations was not limited to seeing which could do the most for the poor, but spilled over into the area of fund raising. The women of the Missionary Society claimed that Pease had slandered them, and to show that they knew what slander was, called him "an infidel, a socialist, a communist, and a Fourierist."[72]

The new missionary, Mr. Luckey, got along with the women in the Missionary Society much better than Mr. Pease had. Under his leadership some of the programs Pease had suggested were implemented. Perhaps Luckey was more persuasive in his presentation or perhaps the women finally saw the wisdom of the ideas Pease had proposed. Under Luckey's leadership another day school was founded, scores of men and women were given work, and destitute children were adopted by responsible families.[73] As the mission reached more and more people, Mr. Luckey saw that they needed a bigger facility. The officers of the society met with their male advisory committee, which included Walter Palmer, to discuss the possibility of a bigger building. The second directress, Mrs. C. R. Duel, suggested that they buy the "Old Brewery" and replace it with a mission house. The men laughed at the idea, but the woman pressed her case:

> She *urged*, and then *pled* that that lazar-house of crime and wickedness might be secured, believing its very demolition would, in itself, prove a missionary operation, inhabited as it was, by hundreds of the most depraved of all the earth and justly named the "Head-quarters of Satan."[74]

The committee listened to her appeal and voted to investigate buying the property. It was subsequently purchased for sixteen thousand dollars, the money being raised mainly by public subscription, and was demolished in December of 1852. By June of 1853, the new mission house was ready for use.[75]

This new mission house had been built at a cost of thirty-six thousand dollars. It was a substantial five-story building, built of brick and standing twenty-five feet across and forty-five feet deep. In it was a chapel that would seat five hundred persons. This chapel was used for three services on Sunday and three other evening services during the week. Next to the chapel were a suite of apartments that served as a parsonage for the missionary and his family. On the floors above the chapel were twenty three-room apartments where "poor and deserving" families could live for five dollars a month. On the floor beneath the chapel was a school room, fitted up with "handsome desks, one for each pupil." Another school room for the infant school, as well as bathrooms used for getting the children clean enough for class occupied the rest of that floor.[76] Later the mission added more school rooms at the rear of the building, and school attendance rose to six hundred pupils. The society also built a four-story addition at the side of the mission, increasing its street frontage greatly. This addition housed an office and a room for the managers, as well as rooms for the making, storing, and distribution of clothing. The mission also established a library and reported that eighty to one hundred young men used it every evening.[77]

In its first six months of operation in its new building the mission began a Methodist class meeting which enrolled 30 adults, as well as day and Sunday schools for 160 children. It distributed about ten thousand garments and pieces of bedding but had to warn contributors not to send garments made of blue denim for the little girls because it looked too much like "poor house" clothing. On Thanksgiving Day the women of the Missionary Society put on a party for the school children and other residents of the Five Points, feeding between two and three hundred people. Each school child was then presented with a new pair of shoes and other necessary clothing.[78] By 1859 the mission had 916 students enrolled in the school and an average daily attendance of 248. That year they also reported sending 481 orphans or other destitute children to adoptive homes in the country and giving out 13,000 garments, 250 hats, and 792 pairs of shoes. Unfortunately, they also ran a deficit of nearly four thousand dollars.[79]

Missing from most of the reports of the Five Points Mission is an account of sound conversions. Although people said that the Five Points area was no longer dangerous and had become as safe as any other part of the city, and although the death rate had fallen from fifty-five per thousand to ten per thousand, still the goal of the mission would not be achieved until many of the Five Pointers had been born again.[80] During the second year in the new location, Mr. Luckey had organized a Methodist church with ten converts, but it did not survive.[81] Evidently the Roman Catholic inhabitants of the Five Points were not enthusiastic about becoming Protestants.

Early in its existence the mission experienced difficulties with the Roman church. Some Catholic parents filed suits charging that the missionaries kidnapped their children to send them to Protestant homes in the country. Other parents said they would rather see their children grow up to be beggars than to have them go to a Protestant school. The mission workers counterattacked by claiming that the Romanists cared about the inhabitants of the slum only at birth and death. They had to admit that the Five Pointers themselves preferred this kind of religion because it enabled them to live in sin and still be assured of eternal life. Roman Catholic priests were active in resisting what they saw as the Protestant effort to steal souls through food, clothing, and education. They established a church in the neighborhood and began a Sunday school. It was even reported that they refused to give last rites to any who had accepted help from the mission.[82]

The women of the mission set out to win over these hostile objects of their benevolence. They hoped that the Five Pointers would see their love and wonder about its source:

> For ladies, whose circumstances in life placed them beyond the necessity of even seeing such misery as theirs to leave their comfortable homes, seek the wretched in their filthy abodes, relieve their wants, exhort them to a better course of life, pray with the sick and dying, caring for their half-naked and famishing little ones, was strange.[83]

Besides benevolence the women also employed a more direct approach. On at least one occasion they requested Father Gavazzi, a converted Roman Catholic priest from Europe, to speak to the children at their Thanksgiving banquet. He told his recently fed listeners to "study and love your Bible" because "there is no other catechism so good to make Christians." He went on to warn the children that "If you were Roman Catholics, as they are in my country, in Spain, in Mexico, you would be slaves."[84]

Some of the people at Five Points responded either to the love or to the preaching, but many did not. After almost twenty years of operation, no Methodist church existed in the neighborhood, and the mission had "practically cease[d] from the direct work of soul saving."[85] It had become the eleventh largest of the city's three hundred religious and secular benevolent societies.[86] Everyone admitted that "as a *charitable* and *reformatory* institution it is doing a good work, especially among the children," but the real purpose of the mission was to convert people.[87] Critics pointed out that the church had poured a large amount of money into the mission and hinted that better results might have been obtained if the money had gone to establish Sunday schools and churches in other places.[88] Evidently the members of the society paid some attention to these criticisms, for one of their later reports indicated that one hundred people attended a Methodist class meeting at the mission each week, and a "large number" of them gave "evidence of conversion." Despite this hopeful sign, the overwhelmingly humanitarian character which the institution had assumed was evident in that only two sentences in the report treated spiritual matters.[89]

After her active involvement in the founding of the mission, Phoebe Palmer's role in it becomes unclear. She was third directress of the Ladies' Home Missionary Society when the mission was founded, and she moved up to second directress sometime after 1853.[90] Given the close connection between the Missionary Society and the mission at Five Points, and given the women's insistence that they did the missionary work themselves and did not merely send "hirelings," it seems reasonable to assume that she closely identified herself with the work and policies of the mission.[91] Three factors kept this conclusion from approaching a certainty: first, the absence of reports of visits in the Five Points in the printed letters and journal entries; second, the increasing number of camp meetings and revival services Mrs. Palmer conducted during the 1850s; and third, the fact that she was listed as second directress even in the years that she was in Britain.[92]

The first factor may be explained by remembering that Wheatley printed Mrs. Palmer's letters and journal entries to illustrate the point he was making about her. Before he discussed her role in the Five Points Mission he had already printed several letters and journal entries to show that she visited the poor. There was no need to make that point again in his later section on the mission.[93] The second factor, increased travel, does not necessarily mean that Mrs. Palmer was not active with the mission during the times she was in New York. Her children were growing older and probably required less of her attention, so perhaps she had more time to give to the work at Five Points than before. The third factor, absentee directorship, seems to be the most weighty. If Phoebe Palmer could be second directress of an organization in New York when she was in England, she obviously was not involved in its day-to-day affairs. When she left for Britain in 1859, however, Mrs. Palmer did not know that she would be away for four years. Evidently she planned to resume her role in the organization. Her resignation from the post in 1864 shows that she did not regard her office as merely an honorary position. When she no longer had time to serve the Missionary Society because of her work with the *Guide to Holiness* and with revival meetings, she resigned from her position.[94] In the absence of any other information, it seems logical to assume that Phoebe Palmer agreed with the policies of the Ladies' Home Missionary Society in the decade between 1849 and 1859. She thus may be seen as a woman whose primary concern was evangelistic but whose close involvement with the poor themselves led her, albeit unwillingly, to the conclusion that humanitarian relief was a prerequisite for saving souls.

OTHER HUMANITARIAN EFFORTS

Temperance

Besides visiting the poor to try to convert them, to take them food, clothing, and fuel, and to persuade them to let their children go to school, Phoebe Palmer also tried to get people to take the temperance pledge. In the first year of their work at Five Points, she and the other workers induced one thousand people to sign a pledge, promising to abstain from alcohol.[95] Mrs. Palmer did not join any of the organizations who made temperance their primary aim, but she sympathized with their goals. In England she spoke out against believers who were "bowing down to Bacchus" and tried to rid the churches of any involvement with the liquor trade.[96] Near the end of her life she editorialized in favor of the women's temperance movement, saying, "God is on their side."[97]

Slavery

Phoebe Palmer's concern for the slave led her to support the efforts of the Colonization Society in the 1830s. Besides seeking the good of the slave, she also hoped to spare the United States from the wrath of God which was sure to come if the blacks were not freed.[99] When it became obvious that colonization would not work, however, she did not become an abolitionist. She also tried to resist the tendency of other advocates of holiness to identify themselves with abolition. B. T. Roberts, who had claimed sanctification under her ministry, was an ardent champion both of entire sanctification and of abolition. He was disappointed that other teachers of holiness did not join him in his activities for the slaves and spoke with great bitterness about attending a holiness meeting in which a friend was silenced when he introduced the topic of abolition.[100] He may have been speaking of the Tuesday Meeting. Phoebe Palmer was quick to stifle any controversy in that meeting, especially anything that smacked of politics. She felt that interest in politics diverted Christians from their real business of promoting revivals.[101] Perhaps she hoped that a revival of holiness would sweep the land, inducing the slave holders to free their captives. When the Civil War came, however, she saw it as God's punishment on the South for the sin of slavery and felt that God would not give the North victory unless it fought to emancipate the slaves.[102]

EVALUATION

Phoebe Palmer's motives for humanitarian work were to save other people's souls and her own. She was encouraged in her efforts by the belief that God would prosper anything she attempted under his leadership. The study of her motives helps confirm Rosenberg's findings about the overwhelmingly evangelistic motivation of those who worked with the poor in the middle years of the nineteenth century. Beginning with evangelistic motives, she soon saw the necessity of giving food and covering along with the gospel and helped to establish a mission to bring physical and spiritual necessities to New York's worst neighborhood. Phoebe Palmer's ministry and the ministry of the institution she helped to found show the progression that Rosenberg found in most other mid-nineteenth-century religious efforts to help the poor. Beginning with almost a purely evangelistic motive, these organizations came increasingly to concentrate on humanitarian aid.[103] This progression shows that Mohl is wrong to give the impression that mid-century philanthropists thought the poor needed tracts more than they needed food.[104] A detailed study of Mrs. Palmer's involvement with the poor also supplies further evidence that Timothy Smith, Donald Dayton, and Norris Magnuson are correct in asserting the connection between revivalistic, evangelical religion and social concern.[105] Her humanitarian work is a counterexample to the contentions of Hopkins and May that the beginnings of social concern in American Christianity should be traced to the early Unitarians or to the late-nineteenth-century preachers of the social gospel, and is a direct contradiction to Cole's statement that the "Don Quixotes of the Five Points" devoted too much attention to rescuing fallen women, and not enough to relieving poverty.[106]

Thus Phoebe Palmer's work shows how concern for the soul led to concern for the body, and how interest in individual salvation led to interest in social improvement. Her humanitarian efforts also show the transition that occurred in the nineteenth century from visiting the poor to living among them. The societies that Phoebe Palmer joined in the 1840s tried to help the poor from outside. They organized upper- and middle-class people to go into the slums, help the poor, and then return to their comfortable homes. In 1850 Louis Pease saw that his ministry would be more effective if instead of merely visiting the poor, he incarnated his concern by living among them and having them live in his home. The women of the Missionary Society at first resisted this innovation but later accepted the principle and built apartments for the preacher and the poor in the new mission house at Five Points. Now instead of merely visiting the slums to preach to the people or to give them things, believers had established a Christian presence. By moving into the slums the workers became more available to the poor and more vulnerable to the ills the needy suffered. William Booth made the same discovery when he decided to move his family into the slums of East London in 1865.[107] Jeremiah McAuley and Samuel Hopkins Hadley lived in the rescue missions they established in New York's worst areas in the 1870s and 1880s.[108] Their pioneering work paved the way for Jane Addams to begin her settlement house in Chicago in 1899.[109] Phoebe Palmer never moved out of her comfortable home to live in the slum, but the organization she helped to direct played an important role in changing the way the church helped the poor.

Conclusion

Phoebe Palmer's life spanned eight decades of the nineteenth century. During that time she made a profound impact on theology, revivalism, feminism, and humanitarianism. She hoped that her life would be well balanced or, as she said, "symmetrical," and would thus display the "beauty of holiness."

Phoebe Palmer's father had been converted in England under John Wesley's preaching, and he set up a staunch Methodist home when he emigrated to America. As a child, Phoebe embraced her parents' Methodist faith and remained true to it all her life. In 1827 she married Walter Clarke Palmer, a physician and a leader in the local Methodist church. The turning point in Mrs. Palmer's life came at 9:00 in the evening of July 26, 1837, when she experienced "entire sanctification." Three of her children had died in infancy. As she grieved over her loss, Phoebe Palmer became convinced that God had taken her children because she had loved them too much and because she was spending too much time on them. She resolved that she would surrender to God everything she held dear, promising that she would never murmur at any step of obedience he required. She also resolved that the time she would have spent with her children would henceforth be dedicated to the Lord's service. She thought of her commitment as the "living sacrifice" God required, and she became convinced that God had accepted her offering. She then realized that what had happened to her was the entire sanctification her Methodist heritage had taught her to expect.

The remaining thirty-seven years of her life would see the implications of that evening worked out as she devoted herself entirely to God. She began her career as a theologian by penning religious verse, then branched out to write articles and books. She got her start as a revivalist by filling in for her husband at a Methodist class meeting, and eventually she crossed the continent and the Atlantic to preach the Good News. She started speaking at a women's prayer meeting and went on to produce a full-scale defense of women's ministries. From distributing tracts in poor neighborhoods, she moved on to the establishment of one of the nation's first settlement houses. During this time she also managed to bear and raise three other children who went into professional Christian service.

As a theologian, Phoebe Palmer simplified and popularized John Wesley's doctrine of entire sanctification by modifying it in six different ways. First, she followed John Fletcher in his identification of entire sanctification with the baptism of the Holy Spirit. Second, she developed Adam Clarke's suggestion and linked holiness with power. Third, like Clarke, she stressed the instantaneous elements of sanctification to the exclusion of the gradual. Fourth, again following Clarke, she taught that entire sanctification is not really the goal of the Christian life, but rather its beginning. Fifth, through her "altar theology," she reduced the attainment of sanctification to a simple three-stage process of entire consecration, faith, and testimony; and sixth, she held that one needed no evidence other than the biblical text to be assured of entire sanctification. Methodists, Baptists, Presbyterians, Congregationalists, and Anglicans accepted her ideas, and her thought later gave theological direction to the Holiness movement. Her emphasis on Pentecost and Holy Spirit baptism paved the way for the emergence of the Pentecostal and Charismatic movements.

As a revivalist, Mrs. Palmer spoke in more than three hundred camp meetings or revival services. She preached across North America from California to Cape Cod and from the shores of the Maritimes to the mouth of the Mississippi. In 1857 her preaching sparked a revival that brought a million converts into the American churches. In 1859 she and her husband followed the revival to the British Isles. There they led a four-year campaign in which more than 17,300 people claimed justification and several thousand others professed entire sanctification. The Palmers' efforts were part of a movement of the Spirit that brought 1.5 million people into the various churches in England, Ireland, Scotland, and Wales.

In addition to traveling to preach holiness, Mrs. Palmer led a meeting in her home to spread the doctrine. Called the "Tuesday Meeting for the Promotion of Holiness," it met for thirty-four years under her direction and continued for more than twenty years after her death. To Mrs. Palmer's parlors came Methodist bishops, missionaries, editors, and pastors to learn about entire sanctification. They were joined by theological professors and pastors from other denominations, as well as many lay-people each week. When crowds of two hundred became common, the Palmers bought a new house to accommodate them.

Besides leading more than 17,300 Britons and untold thousands of Americans to Christ, Mrs. Palmer made three other contributions to revivalism. First, her emphasis on holiness helped to remind Christians of their high calling when revivalism had flooded the church with people who were only "half converted." Second, while her teaching about sanctification brought the doctrine to the attention of many, the way in which she taught it tended to devalue the doctrine for some, leading them to believe they were entirely sanctified when they were not. Third, she civilized and systematized the methods of frontier Methodist revivalism, especially the Methodist emphasis on lay ministry. Finney had spoken of the role of the laity in revivals, but Mrs. Palmer was the first to organize her labors effectively in a city-wide effort. Her emphasis on the role of the laity helped to prepare laypeople to play a major role in urban revivalism. Mrs. Palmer's practice was one of the factors that transformed revivalism from Finney's clergy-centered campaigns in small towns to Moody's lay-oriented crusades in large cities.

Where Mrs. Palmer could not go in person, she went through her books and magazine. She wrote eighteen books of practical theology, biography, and poetry. For eleven years she edited the *Guide to Holiness* and made it one of the most popular religious periodicals of the day. The *Guide* had an international audience with subscribers in the United States, Canada, the United Kingdom, Liberia, India, and Australia.

Just by preaching and writing, Phoebe Palmer promoted the cause of women's rights. In addition she wrote a four-hundred-page book defending women's ministries. Arguing that the baptism of the Holy Spirit given at Pentecost was available to women as well as to men, she said that the filling of the Spirit obligated both men and women to speak out for Jesus. Mrs. Palmer was also a devoted wife and mother. She found time to care for her family as well as to have an active ministry by assigning routine work to servants. Her thought and example helped to widen the field of female influence. She was a feminist in that her words and actions asserted that women had capabilities, rights, and obligations that men of the day generally denied. Unlike some other feminists of her day, her commitment to pushing back male-established boundaries did not arise from an Englightenment understanding of natural rights, but came from her Methodist heritage and from her understanding of Pentecost and sanctification.

In addition to her speaking and writing, Mrs. Palmer cared for people's social and physical needs. She scoured New York's slums for children for the Sunday school, and took food, clothes, and medicine to needy families. With her husband she helped to establish a church in a poor neighborhood, and once she even paid a young mother to go to church with her! Another time the Palmers adopted a teenager whose parents had disowned him. As a member of the Methodist Ladies' Home Missionary Society, she kept agitating until the Society opened a settlement house in New York's worst slum, the Five Points. So dangerous was the area that when Charles Dickens visited it, he took two tough policemen with him! Where Dickens had been afraid to go alone, Phoebe Palmer went to show God's love to those in need. The mission house at Five Points was one of Protestantism's first efforts to meet the needs of the poor in urban America's rapidly expanding slums. Its ministry helped to set the pattern for the social action of the churches for the rest of the nineteenth century.

Phoebe Palmer's humanitarianism began as evangelistic fervor, but soon—as she saw the soul-destroying effects of urban poverty—it came to include a concern for the whole person. Her work helps to demonstrate the overwhelmingly evangelistic motivation of those who worked with the poor in the middle years of the nineteenth century. Phoebe Palmer's ministry and the ministry of the institution she helped to establish also show the progression of most other nineteenth-century religious efforts to help the poor. Beginning with almost purely evangelistic motives, various organizations came increasingly to concentrate on humanitarian aid. This progression shows that it is wrong to suppose the mid-century philanthropists thought the poor needed tracts more than they needed food. The study of Mrs. Palmer's involvement with the poor supplies further evidence of the connection between revivalistic, evangelical religion and social concern. In addition, it provides a counterexample to the contention that the beginnings of organized religious action against poverty in America should be traced solely to the early Unitarians or to the late-nineteenth-century preachers of the social gospel. Finally, her humanitarian efforts also show the transition that occurred in the nineteenth century from visiting the poor to living among them. Her pioneering work helped to break ground for the establishment of other rescue missions and settlement houses.

CONCLUSION

Phoebe Palmer's contribution to American religious history is immense. Her contributions to theology, revivalism, feminism, and humanitarianism mark her as one of the most influential American women in her century. Her achievement gives rise to the question: Where did she get her energy? Obviously having servants helped to free her from the normal routine of caring for a family. Perhaps, however, the answer lies deeper.

Phoebe Palmer knew the scriptural promise that her labor in the Lord was not in vain (1 Cor. 15:58). Because she was convinced she was entirely sanctified, she believed everything she did was a "labor in the Lord." Thus she was encouraged to attempt great things for God, knowing that in an ultimate sense, she could never fail. God had promised to crown whatever she undertook with success. Hence whatever the apparent result, whether she accomplished what she wanted or fell short, she could be sure that her labor was not wasted, but that it fulfilled God's plan. Armed with such confidence, she did not grow weary in well-doing.

It seems that entire sanctification had the same effect in Phoebe Palmer's life that justification by faith had in Luther's. In *The Freedom of a Christian* Luther argued that because Christians are justified by faith, they must not spend any energy trying to justify themselves. Freed from the impossible task of self-justification, they can give all the energy that used to go into scrupulous obedience, detailed confession, and supererogatory works to the service of the neighbor.[1] In the same way, Phoebe Palmer's doctrine of sanctification by faith freed enormous energies for the service of others. Since her "all was on the altar" she knew God accepted and empowered her. Thus all the energy that formerly went into anxious brooding about her spiritual state was now discharged in working for the betterment of others.

Phoebe Palmer, however, would have answered the question another way. She asserted, "Holiness is power."[2] She believed that just as the Holy Spirit had energized the disciples after Pentecost, so every Christian who receives the Spirit in entire sanctification will be similarly empowered. Her life, she felt, was ample demonstration of this truth.

After Mrs. Palmer died, tributes streamed in from many places. One came from R. Pearsall Smith, who said he knew of no other woman in the history of the church who had been so used of God to convert people and to build them up in holiness.

Whether this statement reveals more about Phoebe Palmer or

about Smith's knowledge of church history, is a moot point. What is clear is that Phoebe Palmer was well known at her death, while today she is almost unknown. But just as she did not care whether people thought her beautiful, so she did not aim at being famous. Indeed, she was almost saddened by her renown. She felt it would detract from her heavenly reward. She once remarked to Smith:

> ... there are others who will receive far larger rewards of faith than myself. God has given me almost to walk by sight, so constant and large have been the manifest results of my service. There are others, equally faithful to the Lord, to whom He has not shown large effects from their work of faith and labor of love [1 Thess. 1:3], and yet they have not flagged. Their crowns for faithful endurance will be above mine.[3]

Appendix A
Camp Meetings and Revival Services 1839–59

This appendix, and the next two, provide a roster of Mrs. Palmer's travels. They are the most complete listings of the places Mrs. Palmer held religious meetings. They include places mentioned in her diary, correspondence, and publications. However, they are not complete listings, because sometimes Mrs. Palmer was too sick or too busy to record all her journeys, and sometimes she reported her travels only vaguely. The locations are listed in chronological order. When a location appears twice in the same year, it means that Mrs. Palmer held two sets of meetings there.

1839
Williamsburg, N.Y.

1840
Rye, N.Y.
Williamsburg, N.Y.

1841
Hempstead Harbor, N.Y.
Burlington, N.J.
Mount Holly, N.J.
Jersey City, N.J.
Whitestown, N.J.

1842
Bethlehem, Pa.
Newburgh, N.Y.
Newark, N.J.
Ramapo Valley, N.Y.
Sing Sing, N.Y.

1843
Bridgeport, Conn.
Fairfield, Conn.

1844
Boston, Mass.
Hillsdale, N.J.
Rye, N.Y.
Sing Sing, N.Y.
Hightstown, N.J.
Trenton, N.J.
Belleville, N.J.
Bordentown, N.J.
Mount Holly, N.J.
Burlington, N.J.

1845
Sing Sing, N.Y.
Middletown, Conn.

1846
None (Sickness)

1847
Norwalk, Conn.
Philadelphia, Pa.

Sing Sing, N.Y.
Eastham, Mass.

1848
Yorkville, N.Y.
Williamsburg, N.Y.
Bow Hill, N.Y.
Vincenttown, N.J.
Fishkill, N.Y.
Rye, N.Y.
Pleasantville, N.Y.
Baltimore, Md.

1849
Sandy Hill, N.Y.
Cazenovia, N.Y.

1850
Boston, Mass.
Tully, N.Y.
Red Lion, Del.
Bustleton, Pa.
Oneida Conference Seminary, N.Y.
Springfield, Mass.
Providence, R.I.
Collins, N.Y.
Oxford, N.Y.
Norwich, N.Y.
Binghampton, N.Y.

1851
Ithaca, N.Y.
Philadelphia, Pa.
Albany, N.Y.
Walworth, N.Y.
Cardiff, N.Y.
Plymouth, N.Y.
Cuba, N.Y.
Groten, N.Y.
Spafford, N.Y.
Collins, N.Y.

1852
Red Lion, Pa.
Hillsdale, N.Y.

1853
Napanee, Ont.

1854
Theresa, N.Y.
Napanee, Ont.
Bond Head, Ont.
Martha's Vineyard, Mass.
Eastham, Mass.
Boston, Mass.

1855
Philadelphia, Pa.
Ernesttown, Ont.
Barrie, Ont.
Bond Head, Ont.
Red Lion, Pa.
Warrior's Mark, Pa.
Provincetown, Mass.
South Wilbraham, Mass.

1856
Oswego, N.Y.
Waukesha, Wis.
Millbrook, Ont.
Coburg, Ont.
Portchester, N.Y.

1857
Milford, Conn.
Brighton, Ont.
Millbrook, Ont.
Port Hope, Ont.
Montreal, Que.
St. Andrews, Que.
Kennebec, Maine
Spencertown, Ont.
Acton, Ont.
Hamilton, Ont.
London, Ont.
New York, N.Y.
Williamsburg, N.Y.
Perth Amboy, N.J.
Bedford, N.Y.
Brooklyn, N.Y.

1858
50th St., N.Y.C.
Owego, N.Y.
Binghampton, N.Y.
Union, N.Y.
Providence, R.I.
Boston, Mass.
Portland, Maine

Woodstock, N. B. Monckton, N. B
Frederickton, N. B. Sackville, N. B.
St. Johns, N. B. Boston, Mass.
Halifax, N .S.
Truro, N. S. *1859*
River John, N. S. Honesdale, Pa.
Charlottetown, P. E. I. Scranton, Pa.

Appendix B
Revival Meetings in the British Isles 1859–63

All places are in England unless otherwise indicated.

1859
London
Belfast, Ireland
Coleraine, Ireland
Bowden
Walsingham
Weardale
Newcastle
Sunderland
North Shields

1860
East Jarrow
Glasgow, Scotland
Edinburgh, Scotland
Carlisle
Penrith
Gateshead
Newport, Wight
Ryde, Wight
Cowes
Poole
Swanage
Stroud
Banbury
Lynn Regis
Banbury
Oxford

1861
Maidenhead
Winsor
Rochdale
Great Grimsby
Loughborough
Macclesfield
Ughill
Epworth
Boston
Darlington
Barnard Castle
Berwich-on-Tweed
Liverpool

1862
Madeley
Bridgend, Wales
Cardiff, Wales
Merthyr Tydfil, Wales
Abergavenney, Wales
Blaina
Aberdare, Wales
Douglas, Man
Portadown, Ireland
Woodford
Leeds
Runcorn

1863
Leeds
Walsall
Birmingham
Manchester

Nottingham
Enniskellen, Ireland
Lough
Manchester
Harpurhey

Appendix C
Camp Meetings and Revivals
1863–74

1863
Allen St. Church, N.Y.
Troy, N.Y.

1864
Troy, N.Y.
Poughkeepsie, N.Y.
Brewsters, N.Y.
Lawrence, Mass.
Boston, Mass.
Sing Sing, N.Y.
Mount Pleasant, Ia.
Peterborough, Ont.
Yarmouth, N.S.
Percy, Ont.
Pictou, Ont.

1865
Port Dover, Ont.
Grimsby, Ont.
Port Hope, Ont.

1866
Newark, N.J.
Lynn, Mass.
Saratoga, N.Y.
Upper Newton Falls, Mass.
Albion, Mich.
Morrisburg, Ont.
Brockville, Ont.
Greenbush, Ont.
Palmyra, Mich.
Ann Arbor, Mich.
Chicago, Ill.
Lima, Ind.
Adams, N.Y.

Watertown, N.Y.
Rome, N.Y.
Cleveland, Ohio

1867
St. Louis, Mo.
Leavenworth, Kans.
Kansas City, Mo.
St. Louis, Mo.
Lebanon, Ill.
New Orleans, La.
Cincinnati, Ohio
Wheeling, W.Va.
Cumberland, Md.
Erie, Pa.
Dixon, Ill.
Goshen, Ind.
Vineland, N.J.
Romeo, Mich.
Simcoe, Ont.
Grimsby, Ont.
Trenton, Ont.
St. Johnsbury, Vt.
Philadelphia, Pa.
Trenton, N.J.
Washington, D.C.
Baltimore, Md.

1868
Peel, Ont.
Goderich, Ont.
Mannheim, Pa.
Moundsville, W.Va.
Bentleyville, Pa.
Wheeling, W.Va.
Wilton, Conn.

Southport, Conn.
Centre Sandwich, N.H.
Geddes, N.Y.
Steubenville, Ohio
Pittsburgh, Pa.
Wheeling, W.Va.
Martinsville, Ohio
Zanesville, Ohio

1869
Wabash, Ind.
Buffalo, N.Y.
Attica, N.Y.
Utica, N.Y.
Decatur, Ill.
Bloomington, Ill.
Jacksonville, Ill.
Springfield, Ill.
Prince Edward Island Camp Meeting
Charlottetown, P.E.I.
St. Johns, N.B.
Dawson, Ill.
Kosta, Iowa
Maquoketa, Iowa
Baltimore, Md.
Alexandria, Va.
Indianapolis, Ind.
Fort Wayne, Ind.

1870
Corning, N.Y.
Geneva, N.Y.
Montreal, Que.
Piqua, Ohio
Geneva District Camp Meeting, N.Y.
Minnesota State Camp Meeting
Cannon's Falls, Minn.
Hastings, Minn.
Northfield, Minn.
St. Paul, Minn.
Minneapolis, Minn.
Quincy, Ill.
Southern Kansas Camp Meeting
Leavenworth, Kans.
Woodland, Calif.
Sacramento, Calif.

San Francisco, Calif.
Santa Clara, Calif.
San Jose, Calif.
Stockton, Calif.
Sacramento, Calif.

1871
Hamilton, Ont.
Toronto, Ont.
Cookstown, Ont.
Owen Sound, Ont.
Ocean Grove, N.J.
Ohio State Camp Meeting
West Virginia State Camp Meeting
Alleghany Mountain Camp Meeting
Chautauqua Lake, N.Y.
Stepney, Conn.

1872
Massena, N.Y.
Potsdam, N.Y.
Woonsocket, R.I.
Bath, N.Y.
Ohio State Camp Meeting
London District Camp Meeting, Ont.
London, Ont.

1873
Toronto, Ont.
Jackson, Mich.
Port Clinton, Ohio
Tilsonburg, Ont.
Sea Cliff, N.Y.
Ocean Grove, N.J.
Albany, N.Y.

1874
Rochester, N.Y.
Jacksonville, Fla.
New Haven, Conn.
Nova Scotia Camp Meeting
Rome Camp Meeting, N.Y.
Lake-Side Camp Meeting, Ohio
Illinois State Camp Meeting
Ohio State Camp Meeting

Appendix D
Chronology of Controversy

All the articles below appeared in the *New York Christian Advocate and Journal*. When the author used only initials or a pen name, I have indicated the true name when possible.

DATE	PAGE	AUTHOR	TITLE
11-20-51	185	Bangs	"Is It Right to Profess the Experience of Perfect Love?"
11-27-51	189	Bangs	"More Witnesses in Favor of Perfect Love"
12-4-51	193	Bangs	"Additional Testimony"
12-18-51	201	Mattison	"Professing Holiness"
1-1-52	1	Bangs	"On The Profession of Holiness"
1-8-52	5	Bangs	"On The Profession of Holiness —Scriptural Authority For It"
1-15-52	9	Bangs	"Professing Holiness"
1-22-52	13	Bangs	"Profession of Holiness"
1-29-52	17	Mattison	"Professing Holiness"
2-5-52	21	Mattison	"To Rev. Nathan Bangs, D.D."
2-12-52	25	Mattison	"To Rev. Nathan Bangs, D.D."
2-12-52	27	Palmer	"False Statement Corrected"
2-19-52	30	Editorial	"Controversy on Holiness"
2-26-52	33	Bangs	"Profession of Holiness"
2-26-52	33	Mattison	"To Rev. Nathan Bangs, D.D."
2-26-52	35	Mattison	"The 'False Statement' Shown To Be True"
3-4-52	37	Mattison	"A Parting Word with Dr. Bangs"
5-10-55	76	Bangs	"Review of *The Way From Sin to Sanctification, Holiness and Heaven* by Rev. Tobias Spicer, A.M."
6-14-55	96	Spicer	"The Witness of the Spirit"

245

DATE	PAGE	AUTHOR	TITLE
8-2-55	121	Spicer	"Self-Deception"
8-2-55	121	Mattison	"Deceived Professors of Sanctification"
9-6-55	141	Palmer	"A Voice From The Laity"
9-6-55	143	Woodriff	"On Sanctification"
9-13-55	145	A Methodist	"Entire Sanctification"
9-20-55	151	Mattison	"Deceived Professors of Sanctification"
9-20-55	152	Consistency	"Deceived Professors of Sanctification"
10-18-55	168	An Observer	"Preaching At Camp Meeting"
11-1-55	173	Palmer	"Preaching At Camp Meeting"
11-15-55	181	Palmer	"Believe That Ye Have It and Ye Have It"
11-29-55	189	Mattison	"Believe That Ye Have It and Ye Have It"
12-6-55	193	Palmer	"Coals of Fire"
12-6-55	195	Equity	"Mrs. Palmer and Her Works"
12-20-55	201	Mattison	"Believe That Ye Have It and Ye Have It"
1-3-56	3	Mattison	"Dr. Perry and The New Theology"
1-3-56	3	Perry	"Prof. Mattison vs. Mrs. Palmer"
1-10-56	5	Perry	"Prof. Mattison and His Eight Propositions"
1-24-56	13	I. Winner	"The Controversy on Holiness"

Appendix E
A Covenant of Entire Consecration

Entire Devotion to God, pp. 73-76.

"And because of all this we make a sure covenant, and write it . . . and seal unto it."—Neh. ix.38.

"Oh, happy day that seal'd my vows
To Him who merits all my love!"

In the name of the Father, Son, and Holy Ghost, I do hereby consecrate body, soul, and spirit, time, talents, influence, family, and estate—all with which I stand connected, near or remote, to be for ever, and in the most unlimited sense, THE LORD'S.

My body I lay upon Thine altar, O Lord, that it may be a temple for the Holy Spirit to dwell in. From henceforth I rely upon Thy promise, that Thou wilt live and walk in me; believing, as I now surrender myself for all coming time to Thee, that Thou condescend to enter this Thy temple, and dost from this solemn moment hallow it with Thy indwelling presence. The union is consummated! "Hallelujah to God and the Lamb forever!" With comminglings of intense yet solemn joy, and holy fear, I do at this eventful hour resolve, in the strength of the Lord Jehovah, on minute circumspection in the sustainment and adornment of my body, to indulge in only such things as may be enjoyed in the name of the Lord, and bear the legible inscription, "HOLINESS TO THE LORD."

My present and my future possessions, in family and estate, I here solemnly yield up in everlasting covenant to Thee. If sent forth as Thy servant Jacob, to commence the pilgrimage of life alone, and under discouraging circumstances; if, like him, homeless, with nought but a stone for my pillow; yet, with him, I solemnly vow, "Of all that Thou shalt give me, surely the tenth will I give unto Thee." If Thou wilt, or hast already intrusted me with children, I hereby take upon myself the solemn obligation to train them for Thee. I resolve that my training shall be in view of fitting them for the self-sacrificing service of God, and laying up treasure in Heaven, rather than in view of fitting them to make a display in the world, and lay up treasure on earth. And I resolve, if Thou givest "power to get wealth," I will still continue to regard this vow, in relation to my family, as sacredly binding as at the present hour, and will of my greater abundance "lay in store" proportionately for charities, and the evangelization of the world *according* as God hath prospered me.

Believing the Scriptures are a sufficient rule for my faith and practice, because "*all* Scripture is given by inspiration of God, and is profitable for doctrine, for reproof, for correction, and for instruction in righteousness;" I resolve that I will search the Scriptures daily on my knees (unless circumstances of health prevent), as in the more immediate presence of God; and that my faith and my duties shall be regulated by the unadulterated WORD OF GOD, rather than by the opinions of men in regard to that Word; and that no impressions in relation to doctrine or duties shall be regarded as coming from God unless the said doctrine or duty be plainly taught in the Holy Scriptures.

And now, "O Lord, the great and dreadful God, keeping the covenant and mercy to them that love Him and to them that keep His commandments," confessing that I am utterly unable to keep one of the least of Thy commandments, unless endued with power from on high, I hereby covenant to *trust in Thee* for the needful aid of Thy Spirit. Thou dost now behold my entire being presented to Thee a living sacrifice. Already is the offering laid upon Thine altar. I call heaven and earth, God the Father, Son and Spirit, the spirits of just men made perfect, and the innumerable company of angels now encamped around me, to witness this solemn act of entire, absolute, irrevocable renunciation of sin and self! Yes, my all *is* upon Thine altar. O God, Father of our Lord and Saviour Jesus Christ, behold the offering! By the hallowing fires of burning love, let it be consumed! Let the purifying, consuming energies of the Holy Spirit now penetrate soul and body, and cause every power of body and mind to ascend in ceaseless flames of love and praise, a living sacrifice. O Christ, Thou dost accept the sacrifice, and through Thy meritorious life and death, the infinite efficacy of the Blood of everlasting covenant, Thou dost accept me as Thine for ever, and dost present me before the throne of the Father without spot:

> "No more I stagger at Thy word,
> Or doubt Thy truth which cannot move."

Thou dost condescend to espouse me to Thyself in the bonds of an everlasting covenant in all things well ordered and sure, and from henceforth all my interests in time and eternity are blended in everlasting oneness with the Father and with His Jesus Christ, my fellowship is with the triune Deity, my citizenship in Heaven! And now, O Lord, I will hold fast the *profession* of this my faith before Thee, before angels, and before men. The exceeding great and precious promises upon which I have here laid hold, have been *given me* on condition of my complying with the terms thereunto annexed. Through the power of Thy Spirit alone I have complied with the conditions laid down in Thy Word upon which Thou dost promise to enter into these covenant engagements with me; and now, before angels and men, I will declare my faith in Thee as my covenant-keeping God. And as I solemnly purpose that I would sooner die than break my covenant engagements with Thee, so will I, in obedience to the command of God, hold fast the *profession* of my faith unwaveringly, in face of an accusing enemy and an accusing world. And this I will through Thy grace do, irrespective of my emotions, resolved that my faith in God shall not depend on my uncertain emotions. Now, O God, my covenant engagements are before Thee. Thou hast registered them on the pages of eternity. Already they have been ratified before the throne in the name of the triune Deity, Father, Son, and Spirit. Trusting in Thee to keep me that I may never break from Thee by violating this my solemn covenant, I hereunto set my hand and seal, on this ____ day of _____, 18 __.

Notes on the Sources

1. References to some frequently cited works appear only in abbreviated form. An alphabetical list of these abbreviations follows:

    BH — *Beauty of Holiness and Sabbath Miscellany*

    BP — Hughes, George. *The Beloved Physician: Walter C. Palmer M.D., and His Sun-lit Journey to the Celestial City.* New York: Palmer & Hughes, 1884.

    CA&J — *New York Christian Advocate and Journal*

    ED — Palmer, Phoebe. *Entire Devotion to God.* 14th ed. New York: n.p., 1853; reprint, Salem, Ohio: Schmul, 1979. Originally published as *Present to My Christian Friend on Entire Devotion to God.*

    EWM — Harmon, Nolan B., ed. *The Encyclopedia of World Methodism.* Nashville: United Methodist Publishing House, 1974.

    F&E — Palmer, Phoebe. *Faith and Its Effects: or, Fragments from my Portfolio.* New York: Joseph Longking, 1852.

    FY — [Palmer, Phoebe]. *Four Years in the Old World: Comprising the Travels, Incidents, and Evangelistic Labors of Dr. and Mrs. Palmer in England, Ireland, Scotland, and Wales.* 3d ed. New York: Foster & Palmer, Jr., 1866.

    GTH — *Guide to Holiness*

    Hamline — Palmer, Walter C. *Life and Letters of Leonidas L. Hamline, D.D., Late one of the Bishops of the*

	Methodist Episcopal Church. New York: Carlton & Porter, 1866.
II	Palmer, Phoebe. *Incidental Illustrations of the Economy of Salvation, Its Doctrines and Duties.* New York: Foster & Palmer, Jr., 1855.
J. W. Journal	Curnock, Nehemiah, ed. *The Journal of the Rev. John Wesley, A.M.* 8 vols. London: Epworth, 1906–1916; reprint, Grand Rapids: Zondervan, 1986– .
J. W. Letters	Telford, John, ed. *The Letters of the Rev. John Wesley, A.M.* 8 vols. London: Epworth, 1931.
J. W. Works	Jackson, Thomas, ed. *The Works of John Wesley.* 14 vols., 3d ed. London: Wesleyan Methodist Book Room, 1872; reprint, Grand Rapids: Baker, 1979.
Letters	Letters to Walter and Phoebe Palmer. New York Public Library, Methodist Episcopal Church Records Collection, catalog nos. 460–61.
LHMS	Ladies' Home Missionary Society of the Methodist Episcopal Church
LL	Wheatley, Richard. *The Life and Letters of Mrs. Phoebe Palmer.* New York: W. C. Palmer, Jr., 1876.
LR	*Ladies' Repository*
MG	Palmer, Phoebe. *A Mother's Gift; or, A Wreath for My Darlings.* New York: Walter C. Palmer, Jr., 1875.
NHM	Townsend, W. J., H. B. Workman, and George Eayrs, eds. *A New History of Methodism.* 2 vols. London: Hodder and Stoughton, 1909.
PF	Palmer, Phoebe. *Promise of the Father; or, A Neglected Speciality of the Last Days.* Boston: H. V. Degen, 1859; reprint, Salem, Ohio: Schmul, 1981.

PG	[Palmer, Phoebe]. *The Parting Gift to Fellow Laborers and Young Converts.* New York: Walter C. Palmer [1869].
Records	Allen Street Methodist Episcopal Church records. New York Public Library, Methodist Episcopal Church Records Collection, catalog nos. 138a–52, 156, 161, 168–72.
RR	Palmer, Phoebe. *Some Account of the Recent Revival in the North of England and Glasgow.* Manchester: W. Bremner [1860].
SLP	Roche, John. *The Life of Mrs. Sarah A. Lankford Palmer, Who for Sixty Years Was the Able Teacher of Entire Holiness.* New York: George Hughes and Company, 1898.
SP	J. Boynton. *Sanctification Practical: A Book for the Times.* New York: Foster and Palmer, Jr., 1867.
TM1	Hughes, George. *Fragrant Memories of The Tuesday Meeting and its Fifty Years' Work for Jesus.* New York: Palmer & Hughes, 1886.
TM2	Hughes, George. *Fragrant Memories of The Tuesday Meeting and the Guide to Holiness, and Their Fifty Years' Work for Jesus.* New York: Palmer & Hughes, 1886 [1889]; microfiche, El Segundo, Calif.: American Theological Libraries Association Board of Microtext, 1981.
WOH	Palmer, Phoebe. *The Way of Holiness with Notes by the Way; Being A Narrative of Religious Experience Resulting from a Determination to be a Bible Christian.* 2d ed. New York: G. Lane & C. B. Tippett, 1845.
ZH	*Zion's Herald*

2. The *Guide to Holiness*, edited by Mrs. Palmer from 1864 to her death in 1874, bore several names. Founded by Timothy Merritt in 1839, it was called the *Guide to Christian Perfection* until 1846. From then it was called the *Guide to Holiness* until the Palmers bought it and merged it with the *Beauty of Holiness*

and Sabbath Miscellany in 1864. This new combined magazine was given the inelegant title, *Guide to, and Beauty of Holiness and Revival Miscellany*. The title was streamlined in 1867 to *Guide to Holiness and Revival Miscellany*, a title it bore until Sarah Lankford Palmer died in 1896. From then until the fall of 1901 it was called *Guide to Holiness and Pentecostal Life*, and ended its career as the *Consecrated Life and Guide to Holiness* in December of that year. For ease of reference I will refer to this magazine as the *Guide to Holiness* throughout. From its beginning until July of 1844 each volume covered a full year, beginning in July. Thus citations of volumes 1–5 will include both years. From volume 6 on, each volume had only six issues. Volume 7 began in January, 1845, and volume 8 began in July of that year. This practice of having two volumes a year was maintained throughout the life of the publication. Two other points might cause confusion. One is that volume 48 (July 1865) is also called new series volume 3. The two previous volumes are not called new series 1 and 2 but after 1865 most volumes have both numbers. I will refer to the volumes by their old series number, even when that number is not printed on the magazine. The other confusing thing about the numbering of the volumes is that sometimes the volume numbers listed on the issues themselves are wrong. For example, the January issue of 1882 says it is volume 79, when it is actually part of volume 81. In these cases I will cite the correct volume number. Unfortunately these kinds of editorial lapses were not uncommon in the Palmers' work. Volume 49 for 1866 apologizes on page 95 for mislaying a manuscript, and volumes 58 and 59 in 1870 and 1871 print the same editorial twice within six months (pages 183 and 182 respectively). Mrs. Palmer once even included the same illustrative story twice in one of her books. See *Faith and Its Effects*, pp. 57, 198. The string of Theseus that will guide the reader through this confusing labyrinth of volumes and years is to locate each reference by its year. Most collections of the *Guide to Holiness* are books bound according to year. After 1844 each binding contains at least one year. Because in these books the monthly issues are not separated, it does one little good to know the month in which the article the reader seeks appeared. However, the page numbers do increase sequentially throughout each volume, and the odd-numbered volumes are for the first half of the year (January to June) and the even-numbered volumes are for the second half of the year (July to

December). Thus, if one wishes to verify a reference that is cited "*GTH* 81 (1882): 16," the reader should find the book containing the volumes for 1882, note that since 81 is an odd number it refers to the first half of the year, and find page 16 at the beginning of the book.

3. When the *Guide to Holiness* is cited, and the article has been written by someone outside the Palmer family, the author's name will appear in parentheses after the page number. Articles written by Walter C. Palmer will have (WCP) after them, and those by Sarah Lankford Palmer will have (SLP). Phoebe Palmer is the author of the citations that have no other author indicated.

4. After Phoebe's death in 1874, the editors of the *Guide to Holiness* continued to print articles she had written, along with some of her letters and diaries. Unfortunately they rarely gave the dates of composition for these works. These posthumous writings will therefore be cited in the same way as Mrs. Palmer's other contributions to the *Guide to Holiness*. Thus one of her undated letters, obviously written before her death in 1874, but not published until 1882 will be cited: "*GTH* 81 (1882): 151."

5. Wheatley's biography consists mainly of excerpts from Phoebe Palmer's diaries and letters. Where he has reproduced these materials and named his source, I will first cite his source and then the page number in Wheatley. If he is obviously quoting Mrs. Palmer but has not identified whether the source is a letter or the diary, I will assume it is the diary. Sometimes he gives the complete date, and other times only the month or the year. When I do not give the complete date for a diary entry or a letter, it is because Wheatley has not supplied this information. Thus the diary entry of July 29, 1836, quoted by Wheatley on pages 30–32, will be cited: "Diary, July 29, 1836; *LL*, pp. 30–32." But the account of the visit of Dr. and Mrs. Bradley reported on page 246 can only be cited: "Diary, 1849; *LL*, p. 246." A citation of a section in Wheatley which is not the work of Mrs. Palmer will be indicated by the abbreviation *LL* and the page number alone.

6. Sarah Worrall married Thomas Lankford in 1831. He died in 1873. Walter Palmer became a widower in 1874. Walter and Sarah married each other in 1876. Any textual references to

Sarah Worrall Lankford Palmer will refer to her by the name that is proper for the time to which reference is made. In the notes she will be Sarah Lankford Palmer throughout.

7. Mrs. Palmer and other writers are often inconsistent in their capitalization of pronouns when referring to God. In quotations I will follow their usage exactly, but will not note these inconsistencies with *sic*.

8. Mrs. Palmer often cites Scripture. If she is quoting it, I will follow her quotation, even if it differs from that of the Authorized Version which she normally used. I will not indicate any deviations from the AV with *sic* unless the variant is significant to the interpretation of the text, but I will give the reference for the passage to which she refers.

9. When illustrating elements of Phoebe Palmer's thought, I will often quote from a number of sources written at different times without drawing special attention to the various dates the works were written. This practice is legitimate because Mrs. Palmer's thought shows little, if any, development or change over the years. Many of the things she wrote in her books in the 1840s and 1850s were repeated in the *Guide to Holiness* in the 1860s and 1870s. Another reason for not being overly careful about the dates of composition for her works is that she constantly reissued them unchanged throughout her lifetime. For example, *The Way of Holiness*, written in 1843, was still being offered for sale by the Palmers in 1872. Thus it is not illegitimate to conclude that it still represented her thought. In the few cases where her ideas changed, I will note the dates that are important.

Notes

INTRODUCTION

1. *GTH* 31 (1857): 2 (Degen and Gorham).
2. *II*, p. 203.
3. J. Edwin Orr, *The Second Evangelical Awakening in Britain* (London: Marshall, Morgan & Scott, 1949), pp. 5, 14–15, 36.
4. W. H. Boole, as reported in *GTH* 66 (1874): 178 (WCP).
5. John A. Roche, "Mrs. Phoebe Palmer," *LR* 26 (1866): 65–70.
6. *LL*.
7. *BP; SLP*.
8. *TM1; TM2*.
9. Matthew Simpson, ed., *Cyclopedia of Methodism*, rev. ed. (Philadelphia: Louis H. Everts, 1880), pp. 691–92.
10. John L. Peters, *Christian Perfection and American Methodism* (New York: Abingdon, 1956).
11. Ernest Wall, "I Commend unto You Phoebe," *Religion in Life* 26 (Summer 1957): 396–408; Timothy L. Smith, *Revivalism and Social Reform: American Protestantism on the Eve of the Civil War* (Nashville: Abingdon, 1957; reprint with a new afterword by the author, Baltimore: Johns Hopkins University Press, 1980).

CHAPTER ONE

1. *GTH* 66 (1874): 42–43; *LL*, pp. 13–14. John Wesley recorded visits to Bradford on July 23–24, 1784, and April 23, 1786, but none between those dates. There is a possibility that Wheatley, who reports this event as occurring during Worrall's fourteenth year, means that Worrall was fourteen, instead of thirteen at the time. Because Worrall was fourteen from November 1785 to November 1786, his first acquaintance with Wesley could have occurred during the April visit that Wesley records. According to Wesley, however, he preached only one Sunday night in Bradford, and then left for Halifax. A similar problem exists in assuming Worrall heard Wesley in 1784: Wesley was in Bradford at 5:00 in the morning on July 24, but his text was Matthew 22:29: "Ye do err, not knowing the scriptures, nor the power of God." Another problem is that Worrall was only twelve at the time. Rather than supposing that Wheatley was wrong about the year, and that either Worrall or Wesley was wrong about the time of day or the text, it is easier to suppose that Wesley did not record the visit on which Worrall first heard him preach. For Wesley's visits to Bradford, see *J. W. Journals*, 7:4d, 157.

2. John A. Roche, "Mrs. Phoebe Palmer," *LR* 26 (1866): 65.
3. *LL*, pp. 15–16; *SLP*, p. 17.
4. *LL*, p. 16; *SLP*, pp. 17–18.
5. Diary, May 18, 1825, *LL*, p. 20.
6. *LL*, pp. 16–17.
7. *GTH* 1 (1839–40): 126.
8. *F&E*, pp. 62–63.
9. *LL*, p. 17.
10. Diary, Aug. 12, 1827, *LL*, p. 23.
11. *F&E*, pp. 63–64; *GTH* 1 (1839–40): 126.
12. *LL*, p. 18. The "altar" to which Phoebe refers was a railing which stood between the pulpit and the first rank of pews in the church. The origin of the term goes back to pre-Reformation England. The communion table was then called the altar because there the priest offered the sacrifice of the mass. The railing that separated the altar from the nave was called the altar rail. It had two functions: theologically it was a fence to keep the people away from the holy place, and practically it was a support at which to kneel when receiving communion. The Reformation changed the name of the altar to the communion table and dropped the theological function of the railing, but retained the railing itself because of its practical function. Somewhat inconsistently, the Anglican Reformers also retained its pre-Reformation name. American Methodists borrowed this Anglican terminology, but once again the function of the altar rail was transformed. Along with using the railing as a place to receive communion, they also began to use it as a place to pray. This practice of coming forward for prayer originated around 1797 when Valentine Cook, a Methodist itinerant, set up a mourner's bench between the preacher's stand and the congregation at a camp meeting. Instead of merely dropping to their knees when convicted, the penitents would come forward to kneel at the mourner's bench. This clever innovation became popular at the frontier revival services and was adopted by urban Methodists during the first decade of the nineteenth century. The main things for which Methodists were urged to pray were justification and sanctification, both of which involve giving oneself up to God. Because much of this prayer occurred at the altar rail, it was natural to associate the ideas of giving oneself to God with presenting a sacrifice at an altar. Thus the railing part of the name was forgotten, and the place where the offering occurred was called the altar. The name of the place remained almost the same, although it had a new theological significance. See Matthew Simpson, ed., *Cyclopedia of Methodism*, rev. ed. (Philadelphia: Louis H. Everts, 1880), p. 253; Richard Carwardine, *Transatlantic Revivalism: Popular Evangelicalism in Britain and America, 1790–1865*, Contributions in American History, no. 75 (Westport, Conn.: Greenwood, 1978), p. 13.
13. *F&E*, pp. 64–65. See also *GTH* 1 (1839–40): 126.
14. *LL*, p. 19.
15. *SLP*, pp. 18, 40; Abel Stevens, *Life and Times of Nathan Bangs, D.D.* (New York: Carlton & Porter, 1863), p. 350; *LL*, p. 18.
16. *GTH* 66 (1874): 161 (WCP).
17. For Bramwell, see *BH* 14 (1863): 35. Bramwell (1759–1818) became a Methodist itinerant in 1786 and was a noted revival preacher. See James Sigston, *Memoir of the Life and Ministry of Mr. William Bramwell, Lately an Itinerant Methodist Preacher: With Extracts from His Interesting and Extensive Correspondence*, 3d American ed. (New York: J. Emory and B. Waugh for the Methodist

Episcopal Church, 1830); and *EWM*, s.v. "Bramwell, William," by N. P. Goldhawk. For Mrs. Fletcher, see *GTH* 43 (1863): 82-83. Mrs. Fletcher (1739-1815) was a Methodist who ran a school and home for orphans, then married John Fletcher and shared his pastoral duties. See Henry Moore, *The Life of Mrs. Mary Fletcher, Consort and Relict of the Rev. John Fletcher, Vicar of Madeley, Salop. Compiled from Her Journal, and Other Authentic Documents* (New York: J. Emory and B. Waugh for the Methodist Episcopal Church, 1830); and *EWM*, s.v. "Fletcher, Mary Bosanquet," by John Kent. For Mrs. Rogers, see *FY*, p. 28. Mrs. Rogers (1756-94) was a friend of John Wesley and a Methodist class leader. Her religious writings were widely read in nineteenth-century Methodism. See Hester Ann Rogers, *An Account of the Experience of Hester Ann Rogers; Written by Herself. To Which Is Added, Spiritual Letters; Calculated to Illustrate and Enforce Holiness of Heart. Also, A Sermon, Preached on the Occasion of Her Death, October 26, 1794, by the Rev. Thomas Coke, L.L.D. With an Appendix, Written by Her Husband; and Containing Selections Transcribed from Her Manuscript Journals* (New York: S. & D. A. Forbes, 1830); and *EWM*, s.v. "Rogers, Hester Ann Roe," by John A. Vickers. For Nancy Cutler, see *FY*, pp. 449-50. Ann Cutler (1759-94), known as Nancy or "Praying Nanny," besides her ministry of prayer also itinerated and led band and class meetings. Phoebe Palmer knew of her from William Bramwell, *A Short Account of the Life and Death of Ann Cutler* (Leeds: Newsom, 1798). See also Earl Kent Brown, *Women of Mr. Wesley's Methodism*, Studies in Women and Religion, vol. 11 (New York: Edwin Mellen, 1983), pp. 21-22, 98, 241. For Fletcher, see *F&E*, p. 209; and *GTH* 41 (1862): 119. John Fletcher (1729-85) was the vicar of Madely (Madeley). Shortly before Fletcher's untimely death he was designated by John Wesley to succeed him as the leader of the Methodists. See Joseph Benson, *The Life of the Rev. John W. de la Flechere: Compiled from the Narrative of Rev. Mr. Wesley; The Biographical Notes of Rev. Mr. Gilpin; From His Own Letters, and Other Authentic Documents, Many of Which Have Never Before Been Published* (New York: B. Waugh and T. Mason for the Methodist Episcopal Church, 1833); and *EWM*, s.v. "Fletcher, John William," by Kenneth Cain Kinghorn. For Nelson, see *WOH*, p. 214. Nelson (1707-74) itinerated for thirty years as a Methodist preacher. See John Nelson, *Extract from the Journal of John Nelson: Being an Account of God's Dealing with Him from His Youth to the Forty-Second Year of His Age. To Which Is Added an Account of His Death*, 16th ed. (New York: Carlton & Porter, 1856); and *EWM*, s.v. "Nelson, John," by Frank Baker. For Maxwell, see *GTH* 4 (1843): 133. Lady Maxwell (1742-1810) was an early Methodist philanthropist. See John Lancaster, *The Life of Darcy, Lady Maxwell, of Pollock; Late of Edinburgh: Compiled from Her Voluminous Diary and Correspondence, and from Other Authentic Documents* (New York: T. Mason and G. Lane for the Methodist Episcopal Church, 1837); and *EWM*, s.v. "Maxwell, D'Arcy," by Frank Baker. For Carvosso, see *GTH* 4 (1843): 133. Carvosso (1750-1834) was a farmer who became a Methodist evangelist and class leader. See William Carvosso, *The Great Efficacy of Simple Faith in the Atonement of Christ Exemplified in a Memoir of Mr. William Carvosso, Sixty years a Class Leader in the Wesleyan Methodist Connection*, ed. Benjamin Carvosso, from the 10th London ed. (New York: Lane & Tippett for the Methodist Episcopal Church, 1847); and J. Robinson Gregory and Arthur E. Gregory, "Wesleyan Methodism—The Middle Period," in *NHM*, 1:394. For Mrs. Wesley, see *F&E*, pp. 304ff. For Wesley in Walsall, see *GTH* 44 (1863): 145.

18. Diary, Aug. 12, 1827, *LL*, p. 22.
19. Ibid.
20. *GTH* 53 (1868): 5.
21. *GTH* 84 (1883): 70ff. (SLP); *BP*, p. 18.
22. Diary, Nov. 24, 1827, *LL*, p. 23.
23. *MG*, pp. 98–99. The poem goes on to anticipate that after death they will be reunited in heaven.
24. Phoebe Palmer to Stephen M. Olin, July 22, 1841, Olin Manuscript Collection, Wesleyan University Library, Middletown, Conn.; *GTH* 68 (1875): 161 (WCP).
25. Diary, Nov. 24, 1827, *LL*, pp. 23–24.
26. *SLP*, p. 18.
27. *WOH*, pp. 254–55; Diary, May 9, 1872, *LL*, p. 622. Mrs. Palmer's diary entries do not agree about the date of Alexander's birth. In the entry made in 1830, recalling the events of 1827, she says the date was September 27; but in the later entry in which she reproduces what is written on Alexander's grave stone, the date is September 28. It seems that the grave stone, which probably was inscribed within days of the death, would be more accurate than the entry made in the diary more than a year later.
28. See note 27 above.
29. Diary, Sept. 28, 1830, *LL*, p. 26. Wheatley omits the date from the first entry he quotes, but internal evidence, along with the dates of other entries, indicate the date was September 28, 1830. Mrs. Palmer expresses similar sentiments in *GTH* 1 (1839–40): 128.
30. Diary, Sept. 28, 1830, *LL*, p. 26.
31. Diary, Apr. 28, 1832, *LL*, p. 25; *GTH* 84 (1883): 71 (SLP).
32. Diary, Apr. 28, 1832, *LL*, p. 25.
33. Diary, Aug. 1835, *LL*, pp. 27–28; Allen Street Methodist Episcopal Church, "Baptisms: 1820–1839," vol. 139, Methodist Episcopal Church Records Collection, New York Public Library Manuscript Collection, New York, p. 256. Her birthdate was April 11. Note that *WOH*, p. 253, gives April 16 as Sarah's birthdate, and the Palmer family genealogy gives August 6, 1834. Because the entry in the baptismal book is clear and was presumably recorded soon after the event, it probably is correct. See Horace Wilber Palmer, "Palmer Families in America," typescript, New England Historical Genealogical Society, Boston, Mass., vol. 2, pt. 2, p. 838.
34. Isaac Newton Phelps Stokes, *The Iconography of Manhattan Island, 1498–1909*, 6 vols. (New York: Robert H. Dodd, 1915–28; reprint, New York: Arno, 1967), 2:463.
35. *GTH* 84 (1883): 71 (SLP); *SLP*, p. 31.
36. *GTH* 81 (1882): 151.
37. Ibid.
38. Ibid.
39. Ibid.; *II*, p. 120. For another account of this event see Diary, July 29, 1836, *LL*, pp. 30–32.
40. *GTH* 3 (1841–42): 8–9 (SLP). Timothy Merritt was a New England Methodist who published his work in 1825. He later moved to New York City and became an associate editor of the *New York Christian Advocate and Journal*. See Timothy Merritt, *The Christian's Manual, A Treatise on Christian Perfection; with Directions for Obtaining that State, compiled Principally from the Works of the Rev. John Wesley* (New York: T. Mason and G. Lane, 1840).

41. *SLP*, 17–18, 32–33; *TM1*, p. 5. The passage quoted from Rogers is actually her report of a sermon preached by John Fletcher. In it Fletcher says one may become alive to God, not "akin" to God as Mrs. Lankford reported. See Rogers, *An Account . . . of Hester Ann Rogers*, p. 203.

42. *SLP*, pp. 34–35.

43. *GTH* 3 (1841–42): 14 (SLP).

44. There is some confusion about when and where the first Tuesday Meeting was held. The first edition of Hughes's history says that the meetings were begun on February 9, 1836, but in a later edition he adds a section saying the meetings actually started in the summer of 1835. Roche, who wrote after Hughes's second edition, also gives August as the date. In addition, both Hughes and Roche agree that the meeting was held at 54 Rivington Street, the home of the Palmer and Lankford families. But writing in the *Guide to Holiness* in 1883, Sarah Lankford Palmer states that, while the decision to share a home was made in May 1835, the families did not actually move to 54 Rivington Street until February 1836. She also adds about the new house, "The Tuesday Meeting was here commenced." This information fits in with the fact that the fiftieth anniversary of the Tuesday Meeting was celebrated on February 9, 1886. One explanation of this confusing situation is that Hughes, and Roche, who evidently depends on him, are referring to some early meetings which eventually developed into the Tuesday Meeting. They could be speaking of the two separate prayer meetings Sarah led, or to some united meeting held before both families moved to 54 Rivington Street. These preliminary meetings are what they mean when they state that the Tuesday Meetings began in 1835. When Sarah Lankford Palmer says that the first Tuesday Meeting was held in the winter of 1836, she probably means the Tuesday Meetings that were held at *54 Rivington Street*. This explanation of the evidence does not require that any witness be wrong about the facts but assumes they meant different things when they spoke of the first Tuesday Meeting. The chronological summary and the text reflect this reconstruction of the evidence and assume Sarah Lankford Palmer's definition of the Tuesday Meeting. See *SLP*, pp. 109–10; *GTH* 84 (1883): 71 (SLP); *TM1*, pp. 3, 65; *TM2*, p. 161.

45. *LL*, p. 238.

46. *TM1*, pp. 11–12. For a further account of the Tuesday Meeting and its influence, see chap. 2, "Ministry in America," and chap. 6, "Phoebe Palmer As Revivalist."

47. The story of Mrs. Palmer's experience of sanctification appears at least four times in her writings. The stages in the process and the chronological sequence of those stages vary from account to account. The first published record is a series of letters to an otherwise unidentified Mrs. W_____, published in the first volume of the *Guide to Holiness*. See *GTH* 1 (1839–40): 125–29, 145–50, 209–14. The next to appear is a rambling account, loosely strung together to illustrate theological truths, incorporated in *The Way of Holiness*, first published in 1843. See *WOH*, pp. 20–145. The third account was published in 1848 in *Faith and Its Effects*. It is the same series of letters to Mrs. W_____, with only a few minor variations. See *F&E*, pp. 64–92. Last published but first written is Wheatley's account. In 1876 he published extracts from her diary, dated July 27, 1837, the day after the event. See Diary, July 27, 1837, *LL*, pp. 36–44. Because most of the variations among the accounts involve the order in which her thoughts occurred to her, I will not try to reconcile their differences but will attempt to provide a coherent account of the experience, drawing from all four major accounts, along with several other minor sources.

48. *TM1*, pp. 12-15.
49. Diary (prior to July 29, 1836), *LL*, p. 28.
50. *WOH*, , p. 112; Robert Philip, *Devotional Guides*, with an Introductory Essay by Albert Barnes, 2 vols. (New York: D. Appleton & Co., 1837), 1:34-35. Robert Philip was an English dissenter who wrote several small books of practical advice. These appeared in America in the early 1830s and in 1837 were collected and published in two volumes. Nowhere else in her writings does Mrs. Palmer refer to Philip or his *Guides*.
51. *WOH*, pp. 108-11.
52. Diary (prior to July 29, 1836), *LL*, p. 29.
53. Ibid., pp. 29-30.
54. *GTH* 1 (1839-40): 127.
55. Diary (prior to July 29, 1836), *LL*, p. 30.
56. Charles Wesley, "How Many Pass the Guilty Night," *Hymnal of the Methodist Episcopal Church, with Tunes* (New York: Nelson & Phillips, 1878), no. 952.
57. Diary, Jan. 3, 1837, *LL*, pp. 33-34.
58. Diary, Apr. 1837, *LL*, p. 34; *GTH* 1 (1839-40): 147.
59. *LL*, p. 35.
60. Diary, July 27, 1837, *LL*, p. 36. Carvosso, whose life she had read, recorded the beginning of his quest for sanctification with the words: "I determined to be a Bible Christian." See Carvosso, *Great Efficacy of Simple Faith*, p. 35. Carvosso probably heard the phrase from John Wesley who declared, "I am determined to be a Bible Christian, not almost, but altogether." See John Wesley, "Causes of the Inefficacy of Christianity," in *J. W. Works*, 7:287. Of course, it is not impossible that Mrs. Palmer learned the phrase directly from Wesley's sermon.
61. *WOH*, pp. 19-20.
62. Diary, July 27, 1837, *LL*, pp. 36-37.
63. *GTH* 1 (1839-40): 127.
64. Diary, July 27, 1837, *LL*, pp. 37-38.
65. *WOH*, p. 24.
66. Diary, July 27, 1837, *LL*, pp. 37-38.
67. *GTH* 1 (1839-40): 125.
68. Diary, July 27, 1837, *LL*, p. 38.
69. *TM1*, p. 111.
70. *GTH* 1 (1839-40): 128.
71. Diary, July 27, 1837, *LL*, p. 39.
72. *WOH*, pp. 30-31.
73. *F&E*, p. 71.
74. Diary, July 27, 1837, *LL*, p. 39; *GTH* 1 (1839-40): 145.
75. Diary, July 27, 1837, *LL*, p. 40.
76. "Repentance of Believers," *J. W. Works*, 5:169.
77. John Fletcher, *The Works of the Reverend John Fletcher, Late Vicar of Madeley*, vol. 2: *The Last Check to Antinomianism* (New York: Carlton & Porter, n.d.), p. 643. Fletcher says, "To promote this deep repentance, consider how many spiritual evils still haunt your breast. . . . By frequent and deep confession, drag out all these abominations." Sarah's comment was "the veil was lifted, that I might glance at the corruptions of my nature. Then I was almost overwhelmed at the sight; and, while abhorring myself, was perfectly astonished that even the

infinite love of Jesus could look on one so impure." See *GTH* 3 (1841–42): 9 (SLP).
78. *WOH*, pp. 25–26.
79. *GTH* 33 (1858): 10.
80. Diary, July 27, 1837, *LL*, p. 40.
81. Ibid., pp. 40–41.
82. Ibid., pp. 41–42.
83. Ibid. The idea of "naked" faith, that is, faith based on no other evidence than the statements in the Bible, is present in both John Fletcher and John Wesley. See Benson, *Life of the Rev. John W. de la Flechere*, p. 85; and John Wesley to Mrs. Bowman, March 4, 1786, in *J. W. Letters*, 7:322.
84. Diary, July 27, 1837, *LL*, pp. 42–43.
85. Ibid., p. 43.
86. Ibid.
87. *GTH* 1 (1839–40): 146.
88. Diary, July 27, 1837, *LL*, p. 43.
89. *GTH* 1 (1839–40): 147.
90. Ibid., p. 146.
91. Diary, July 27, 1837, *LL*, pp. 43–44. Mrs. Palmer is probably using the words of Charles Wesley's hymn, "The Promise of Sanctification," printed at the end of John Wesley's sermon, "Christian Perfection," *J. W. Works*, 6:22.
92. Ibid., p. 44. I have not been able to find the hymn from which Mrs. Palmer quotes.
93. *WOH*, p. 32.
94. *GTH* 1 (1839–40): 146.
95. Ibid., p. 147.
96. Ibid., pp. 147–48.
97. Ibid., p. 148. I have been unable to find any reference to John Fletcher's loss of sanctification in either his book on sanctification or in Benson's biography. The appendix to the life of Hester Rogers quotes a diary entry Hester made August 24, 1781, which quotes Fletcher as saying, "I received this blessing four or five times before; but I lost it by [refusing to testify to it]." Since Mrs. Palmer had read Mrs. Rogers's book, and since the passage in the *Guide to Holiness* closely matches the language about Fletcher in the diary entry, it is most likely that this passage is the ultimate source of Mrs. Palmer's information about John Fletcher. See Fletcher, *Last Check*, 2:483–669; Benson, *Life of the Rev. John W. de la Flechere*, passim; Rogers, *An Account . . . of Hester Ann Rogers*, p. 201.
98. *GTH* 1 (1839–40): 148–49. See parallel accounts of this incident and the one which follows in *F&E*, pp. 80–82, and *WOH*, pp. 127–29.
99. Ephesians 4:1 says, "I therefore, *the prisoner of the Lord*, beseech you that ye walk worthy of the vocation wherewith ye are called." The angel misquoted the portion in italics. Phoebe never states why she was so sure true angels are required to speak in quotations from the Authorized Version.
100. *GTH* 1 (1839–40): 149–50; *WOH*, p. 129. George Hughes, Walter's friend and biographer, maintains that Mrs. Palmer preceded her husband into the experience of sanctification. Mrs. Palmer's diary for July 27, 1837, which *WOH* quotes, says that he received the blessing several months before she did. I have followed Mrs. Palmer's account because it is primary and is more than forty years closer to the event. See *BP*, pp. 40–41; and *TM1*, pp. 31–32.

101. *LL*, p. 36.
102. *F&E*, p. 155.
103. *GTH* 1 (1839–40): 209–10. Mrs. Palmer seems to have forgotten her resolve never to parley with the Adversary.
104. Ibid., p. 210.
105. Mrs. Palmer gives two accounts of this event, differing only in the date assigned to it. Her first account in *GTH* 1 (1839–40): 210, dates it precisely, "Tuesday, August second, five days after receiving the witness." But August 2, 1837, was a Wednesday, and July 31, not August 2, is five days after the day of her sanctification, July 26. The second account, *F&E*, p. 84, says that it occurred on a Tuesday, six days after her sanctification. This information establishes August 1 as the correct date.
106. Mrs. Palmer states that Clarke glosses the word *living* to mean "continual." However, I have not been able to trace the source of this information. Clarke's commentary on Romans 12 does not use the word "continual," nor does he discuss this idea in his chapter on entire sanctification in his *Christian Theology*. See Adam Clarke, *The Holy Bible, Containing the Old and New Testaments. The Text Carefully Printed from the Most Correct Copies of the Present Authorized Translation, Including the Marginal Readings and Parallel Texts: With a Commentary and Critical Notes; Designed as a Help to a Better Understanding of the Sacred Writings*, Royal Octavo Stereotype Edition, 6 vols. (New York: B. Waugh and T. Mason, for the Methodist Episcopal Church, 1833), 6:131. See also Adam Clarke, *Christian Theology*, 2d ed. (New York: Lane & Scott, 1851), pp. 182–209. Perhaps she had access to some other work of Clarke in which he made such a statement. There is also a chance that her memory is incorrect. The source of the long quotation is *GTH* 1 (1839–40): 210.
107. Diary, Aug. 10, 1837, *LL*, pp. 44–45.
108. Ibid.; *WOH*, pp. 140–41; *GTH* 32 (1857): 50.
109. *GTH* 1 (1839–40): 213.

CHAPTER TWO

1. *GTH* 1 (1839–40): 127.
2. Phoebe Palmer, "Ode for the Fourth of July," "Beaming Light," "Semi-Centennial Hymns," and "Centenary Hymns," *MG*, pp. 208–9, 157–58, 146–48, 140–45.
3. Phoebe Palmer, "Hymn," *CA&J*, May 1, 1835, p. 144; Phoebe Palmer, "All is Well," *ZH*, May 20, 1835, p. 77. *Zion's Herald* copied the poem from the *New York Weekly Messenger*. Many of these early poems appeared over the pseudonym, "Shepherdess."
4. *GTH* 31 (1857): 1 (Degen and Gorham).
5. Diary, Jan. 4, 1838, *LL*, p. 174.
6. *GTH* 1 (1839–40): 125–29, 145–50, 209–14; cf. 66 (1874): 20 (WCP).
7. *GTH* 105 (1894): 35.
8. [Phoebe Palmer], *Mary, or the Young Christian* (New York: Carlton and Porter, 1841).
9. Phoebe Palmer, "The Way of Holiness," *CA&J*, Dec. 28, 1842, p. 77; *LL*, p. 480; Diary, Jan. 1, 1873, *LL*, p. 482.

10. *GTH* 4 (1842–43): 200–204. Writing in 1857, the editors of the *Guide to Holiness* say that *The Way of Holiness* was first published in 1841. The evidence from the *New York Christian Advocate and Journal* as well as a letter from Mrs. Palmer in 1843 makes it clear that Degen and Gorham are in error. See *GTH* 31 (1857): 1 (Degen and Gorham); see also Phoebe Palmer to L. L. Hamline, June 7, 1843, *LL*, p. 480.

11. *WOH*, pp. 8–10; *LL*, pp. 479–80.

12. *TM2*, p. 182.

13. *GTH* 66 (1874): 178 (W. H. Boole).

14. Phoebe Palmer to Bishop and Mrs. Hamline, Nov. 8, 1855, *LL*, pp. 494–95.

15. *GTH* 36 (1859): 89–90 (J. Wesley Lelievre); Ignotus, "Mrs. Palmer's Works in French," *BH* 11 (1860): 319.

16. *LL*, p. 480.

17. W. B. Hoyt to Phoebe Palmer, June 11, 1846, in Letters. See also *GTH* 77 (1880): 132.

18. *TM2*, p. 185; John A. Roche, "Mrs. Phoebe Palmer," *LR* 26 (February 1866): 69.

19. *ED; LL*, pp. 484–85; *GTH* 62 (1872): outside back cover for various months. This figure assumes a press run of one thousand copies for each edition. The assumption is based on the following reasoning:

1. *The Way of Holiness* and *Faith and Its Effects* went through at least fifty and forty-five editions respectively. See *GTH* 62 (1872): outside back cover for various months.

2. *The Way of Holiness* and *Faith and Its Effects* by 1886 had circulations in America of 52,000 and 47,000 respectively. See *TM2*, p. 186.

3. *Present to My Christian Friend* had gone through twenty-five editions by 1872, and the title pages of the 1857 and 1865 editions say, "25th. Thousand." See *GTH* 62 (1872): outside back cover for various months, and American Library Association, *The National Union Catalog of Pre-1956 Imprints* (London: Mansell, 1976), 439:91.

4. From this information I conclude that when Mrs. Palmer's works went through multiple editions, each edition produced one thousand copies. This assumption applies only to those books which the Palmers' publishing company was producing in 1872, i.e., *The Way of Holiness, Present to My Christian Friend, Faith and Its Effects, Incidental Illustrations, Promise of the Father,* and *Four Years in the Old World*.

20. Diary, Jan. 3, 1840, *LL*, p. 177; Phoebe Palmer, *Recollections and Gathered Fragments of Mrs. Lydia N. Cox of Williamsburg, L.I.* (New York: Piercy and Reed, 1845). The book's poor showing may be inferred from its exclusion from the list of Mrs. Palmer's works advertised in various issues of the *Guide to Holiness*.

21. *GTH* 62 (1872): outside back cover for various months.

22. Phoebe Palmer, *The Useful Disciple; or, A Narrative of Mrs. Mary Gardner* (Cincinnati: Swormstedt & Poe, 1853), pp. 7–8; *LL*, pp. 507–8. Evidently Mrs. Palmer was one of those who supported Mary Gardner financially after she became disabled. See L. A. Bailey to Phoebe Palmer, May 17, 1850, in Letters, asking Phoebe to renew her subscription for "Aunty Gardner's" support.

23. Phoebe Palmer, *Israel's Speedy Restoration and Conversion Contemplated: or, Signs of the Times in Familiar Letters* (New York: J. Gray, 1854). For a further treatment of Mrs. Palmer's eschatological beliefs, see chap. 5, "Phoebe Palmer As Theologian."

24. *II*, title page; H. W. Palmer, "Palmer Families in America," typescript, New England Historical Genealogical Society, Boston, vol. 2, pt. 2, p. 842; *SP*, title page; James Caughey, *Light in the Dark, Through the Dominions of Unbelief* (New York: W. C. Palmer, Jr., 1868), title page.

25. *II*, p. v; Diary, June 15, 1857, *LL*, pp. 156–57.

26. *GTH* 30 (1856): 64 (Degen and Gorham); 62 (1872): outside back cover for various months.

27. W. B. Hoyt to Phoebe Palmer, Nov. 1, 1845, from Liberia; [Unclear initial] Howard to W. C. Palmer, Apr. 29, 1841, from Argentina; F. B. Hibbard to Phoebe Palmer, June 14, 1853, from Palestine; R. S. Maclay to Phoebe Palmer, July 27, 1848, from China; all in Letters.

28. Diary, June 6, 1848, *LL*, p. 156.

29. Mary Jane Mills to Phoebe Palmer, May 6, 1849, in Letters.

30. See, e.g., the correspondence with R. M. Hatfield, February 2, 1841, to March 11, 1842, or with Elias Brown from 1850 to 1853. Sometimes she did not answer the letters as quickly as her correspondents thought she should. Mary Jane Mills wrote again to Mrs. Palmer on July 30 and September 19, 1849, complaining that she had not yet received an answer to her original letter. All of the above may be found in Letters.

31. *GTH* 30 (1856): 155.

32. Diary, Dec. 1856, *LL*, pp. 496–97.

33. For a complete treatment of this book, see chap. 7, "Phoebe Palmer As Feminist."

34. *PF; GTH* 62 (1872): outside back cover for various months.

35. Foster calls this work "one of the first original and comprehensive American contributions to psychology." See Frank Hugh Foster, *A Genetic History of the New England Theology* (Chicago: University of Chicago Press, 1907), p. 249.

36. Diary, Jan. 3, 1840, *LL*, pp. 239–40; *TM1*, pp. 26–27.

37. Diary, Jan. 3, 1840, *LL*, p. 239.

38. *TM1*, p. 27.

39. Ibid., p. 28; *F&E*, p. 170; *LL*, p. 238.

40. Diary, Jan. 3, 1840, *LL*, p. 241.

41. *TM1*, p. 28. When Mrs. Palmer composed her diary entry, both she and Professor Upham believed that he had experienced entire sanctification. But upon his return to Maine, he was plagued with guilt and doubt. There were several more crisis experiences during the following weeks before he received complete assurance of sanctifying grace on February 14, 1840. See Diary, Jan. 3, 1840, *LL*, p. 241; Darius Salter, "Thomas Upham and Nineteenth Century Holiness Theology" (Ph.D. diss., Drew University, 1983; microfilm, Ann Arbor: University Microfilms International, 83–17858, 1983), pp. 99–100.

42. Diary, Nov. 3, 1842, *LL*, p. 268.

43. *TM1*, p. 28; *LL*, p. 239.

44. They were *Principles of the Interior or Hidden Life, Designed Particularly for the Consideration of Those Who Are Seeking Assurance of Faith and Perfect Love* (Boston: D. S. King, 1843); and *The Life of Faith in Three Parts, Embracing Some*

of the Scriptural Principles or Doctrines of Faith, The Power or Effects of Faith in the Regulation of Man's Inward Nature, and the Relation of Faith to the Divine Guidance (Boston: Waite, Pierce and Co., 1845).

45. *SLP*, pp. 40–43; *TM1*, p. 29. Caldwell-on-the-Hudson is also called Caldwell's Landing.

46. Matthew Simpson, ed., *Cyclopedia of Methodism*, rev. ed. (Philadelphia: Louis H. Everts, 1880), pp. 85–86; Abel Stevens, *Life and Times of Nathan Bangs, D.D.* (New York: Carlton & Porter, 1863), pp. 57–59; *TM1*, p. 35.

47. Diary, June 1846 (Bishop Hamline); May 1844 (unnamed general conference delegates); 1849 (Dr. and Mrs. Bradley of the Siam Mission); Oct. 27, 1844 (three Presbyterian ministers); all cited in *LL*, pp. 244–46.

48. Diary, Dec. 15, 1857, *LL*, p. 247.

49. *LL*, p. 178; Diary, Dec. 5, 1839, *LL*, pp. 178–79. Please note that Sunday school classes for children and adolescents and class meetings for adults are different. Since both could be called classes, I will refer to them as "Sunday school class" and "class meeting" unless the context makes such differentiation unnecessary.

50. Diary, Aug. 30, 1838, *LL*, p. 178.

51. *LL*, p. 178.

52. New York Allen Street Methodist Episcopal Church, "Classes 1838–1845," vol. 151, in Records, pp. 61, 63, inside front cover.

53. Diary, July 26, 1838, *LL*, p. 177; *WOH*, p. 224. A love feast is a Methodist adaptation of the early church's *agape*. The members of the Methodist society assemble, and after singing and prayer, share a symbolic meal of bread and water. Then the participants have the opportunity to rise and tell the group what God has done in their lives, and what new resolutions they are making to serve the Lord more faithfully. The meeting usually ends with a collection for the poor. The early Methodist love feasts were private, with only those bearing tickets given by the preacher being admitted. As Mrs. Palmer's attendance at a love feast held by a Methodist society of which she was not a member shows, by the mid-nineteenth century these meetings were open. Love feast tickets are now a valuable part of Methodistica, especially those bearing the portrait of an angel who looks remarkably like John Wesley. See Simpson, *Cyclopedia*, pp. 550–51.

54. Phoebe Palmer to Bishop and Mrs. Hamline, July 30, 1846, *LL*, p. 199; Diary, 1848, *LL*, 199; *F&E*, p. 166.

55. For a fuller treatment and documentation of this episode see the section below, "Norfolk Street Church."

56. Appendix A contains a roster of the places in which Mrs. Palmer ministered during the period treated in this chapter. Because the reports of many of these visits are sketchy, and because Mrs. Palmer attended so many camp meetings that even an attempt at a full account produces the "It's-Rye-this-must-be-1840" syndrome, the narrative will mention only the highlights and representative events of these travels.

57. Phoebe Palmer to unidentified, Dec. 1838, *LL*, pp. 132–33; *WOH*, pp. 271–74.

58. Robert Guy McCutchan, *Our Hymnody: A Manual of the Methodist Hymnal* (New York: Methodist Book Concern, 1939), p. 279.

59. Diary, Jan. 3, 1840, *LL*, p. 177. This is the Lydia Cox whose biography Phoebe was later to write. A social worship meeting is one in which the participants are expected to lead in prayer, to testify, or to exhort.

60. *LL*, p. 259.

61. *GTH* 67 (1875): 11–12; see also 80 (1881): 35–36, for a parallel account.

62. Diary, after Aug. 17, 1841, *LL*, p. 259. While Mrs. Palmer often reports the number of people who professed to be saved and sanctified at the various places she held meetings, no meaningful statistics can be compiled for her American labors. Besides the obvious problem that the only true record of those saved and sanctified is the Lamb's Book of Life, a document not yet available for the historian's perusal, there are two more mundane obstacles: first, she was not the only speaker at most of these meetings, and second, even if we assume she reports only those who made decisions under her ministry alone, Mrs. Palmer neglects to mention any numbers at all for about 80 percent of the meetings she held. Thus one cannot compare the earthly impact of her ministry with Finney's or Moody's by matching the grand total of people who responded to their messages. The situation is different for her British ministry. The figures she reports from England are more complete and reliable. They will be discussed in chap. 3, "Ministry in the British Isles: 1859–63."

63. Ibid., p. 260.

64. Phoebe Palmer to Mrs. James, Dec. 1841, *LL*, p. 264.

65. *LL*, p. 265.

66. Dairy, Aug. 1842, *LL*, pp. 197–98.

67. Ibid. Mrs. Palmer is inaccurately quoting the lines of one of Charles Wesley's hymns, "Christ, From Whom All Blessings Flow." The couplet is: "Names, and sects, and parties fall: / Thou, O Christ, art all in all." See Charles Wesley, "Christ, From Whom All Blessings Flow," *Hymnal of the Methodist Episcopal Church with Tunes*, no. 806.

68. Diary, Aug. 22, 1842, *LL*, p. 266.

69. H. W. Palmer, "Palmer Families," vol. 2, pt. 2, p. 842.

70. *LL*, pp. 268–73; Diary, May 1, 1844, *LL*, p. 162; Diary, May 1844, *LL*, p. 161; Mrs. Hamline to Phoebe Palmer, Dec. 26, 1844, and Oct. 24, 1848, in Letters. Mrs. Hamline asks Phoebe to pray that she may be delivered from "endless doubtings" in the former letter, and announces that she has become "a defender of the doctrine of holiness from assault" in the latter.

71. *LL*, pp. 273–74.

72. Ibid.; Diary, 1846, *LL*, p. 90.

73. *LL*, pp. 274–79; Diary, Sept. 1848, *LL*, p. 280.

74. Diary, July 18, 1849, *LL*, p. 128.

75. *TM1*, p. 147; B. T. Roberts, "A Running Sketch," *The Earnest Christian and Golden Rule* 9 (Jan. 1865): 6; B. T. Roberts, *Why Another Sect: Containing a Review of Articles by Bishop Simpson and Others on the Free Methodist Church* (Rochester, N.Y.: "The Earnest Christian" Publishing House, 1879), p. 54. See also Benson Howard Roberts, *Benjamin Titus Roberts* (North Chili, N.Y.: "The Earnest Christian" Office, 1900), pp. 50–51; Clarence Howard Zahniser, *Earnest Christian: Life and Works of Benjamin Titus Roberts* (Circleville, Ohio: Advocate Publishing House, 1957), p. 46. Roberts, writing in 1865, said that the event occurred in 1849. Hughes reproduces a letter from Roberts, written in 1886, which adds that he was sanctified under Mrs. Palmer's ministry and confirms that the year was 1849. The biography of Roberts, written by his son from Roberts's own journal, seems to indicate that the event occurred during the summer of 1850; and Zahniser, who cites the *Earnest Christian* article mentioned

above, also places the event in 1850. I am assuming that Roberts remembered the date correctly and that his biographers are in error. The Methodist church later acknowledged that it had wronged Roberts. In 1910 the Genesee Conference, which had expelled Roberts some fifty years before, voted to restore his parchments posthumously. See Leslie R. Marston, *From Age to Age a Living Witness: A Historical Interpretation of Free Methodism's First Century* (Winona Lake, Ind.: Light and Life, 1960), p. 246.

76. Phoebe Palmer to Mrs. Hamline, Apr. 14, 1869, *LL*, p. 450.

77. Diary, *LL*, p. 283.

78. Frederic Dan Huntington, *The Monthly Religious Magazine* 14 (1855): 53, 57–58, quoted in Timothy L. Smith, *Revivalism and Social Reform: American Protestantism on the Eve of the Civil War* (Nashville: Abingdon, 1957; reprint with a new afterword by the author, Baltimore: Johns Hopkins University Press, 1980), p. 95.

79. Phoebe Palmer to Dr. Huntington, Sept. 27, 1850, *LL*, pp. 573–77.

80. Smith, *Revivalism and Social Reform*, pp. 96–108.

81. *LL*, pp. 281–98.

82. Ibid., p. 299.

83. Ibid., pp. 299–301.

84. Bishop Simpson presided over at least one of the trials of B. T. Roberts, who was later expelled from the Methodist church. The Bishop's *Cyclopedia of Methodism* gives an unfavorable and inaccurate account of the origin of the denomination Roberts later founded. See Robert D. Clark, *The Life of Matthew Simpson* (New York: Harper and Row, 1969), pp. 175–77; Simpson, *Cyclopedia*, pp. 379–80; B. T. Roberts, *Why Another Sect*, pp. 15–21; B. T. Roberts, "Secession—Bishop Simpson," *Northern Independent*, Nov. 17, 1859, cited in Marston, *From Age to Age*, p. 234.

85. Clark, *Life of Matthew Simpson*, p. 164.

86. Phoebe Palmer to Bishop and Mrs. Hamline, 1854, *LL*, p. 305.

87. Ibid., p. 306.

88. Hiram Mattison, *An Answer to Dr. Perry's Reply to the Calm Review* (New York: Miller & Holman, 1856), p. 65.

89. Phoebe Palmer to Bishop and Mrs. Hamline, Sept. 25, 1856, *LL*, pp. 312–14.

90. I have not been able to find the source of Mrs. Palmer's statistic. The net gain in membership for every year of the fifties decade is at least one thousand. See Charles C. Goss, *Statistical History of the First Century of American Methodism: with a Summary of the Origin and Present Operations of Other Denominations* (New York: Carlton & Porter, 1866), p. 110.

91. *CA&J*, Feb. 12–Mar. 12, 1857, pp. 25, 29, 33, 41. The articles appear over the name "More Anon" but are identified by *LL*, p. 554. The number 800,237 is the number of Methodists in the northern church in 1856. Mrs. Palmer expects each member to win one soul. See Goss, *Statistical History*, p. 110.

92. *LL*, p. 554. There were 6,134 Methodist elders in 1857, so almost every other minister received a copy of the pamphlet. No record has survived indicating which ministers were sent the tract, nor how they were chosen. See Goss, *Statistical History*, p. 104.

93. Phoebe Palmer to Bishop and Mrs. Hamline, Aug. 3, 1857, *LL*, p. 316.

94. Phoebe Palmer to Sarah A. Lankford, July 6, 1857, *LL*, pp. 318–22.

95. Phoebe Palmer to Mrs. Hamline, Aug. 3, 1857, *LL*, pp. 322–25.

96. Phoebe Palmer to Sarah A. Lankford, Sept. 11, 1857, *LL*, p. 327.
97. Phoebe Palmer to Sarah A. Lankford, Oct. 10, 1857, *LL*, pp. 328-30; cf. Oct. 14, 1857, *LL*, pp. 330-32; *GTH* 33 (1858): 39.
98. *GTH* 33 (1858): 39.
99. Phoebe Palmer to Bishop and Mrs. Hamline, Nov. 13, 1857, *LL*, p. 332.
100. Phoebe Palmer to Sarah A. Lankford, Oct. 10, 1857, *LL*, p. 330.
101. *CA&J*, Nov. 5, 1857, p. 185.
102. Goss, *Statistical History*, p. 110.
103. "The Great Revival," *CA&J*, May 13, 1858, p. 76; J. Edwin Orr, *The Second Evangelical Awakening in Britain* (London: Marshall, Morgan & Scott, 1949), pp. 5, 14-15, 36.
104. *LL*, p. 315.
105. Phoebe Palmer to Bishop and Mrs. Hamline, Dec. 5, 1857, *LL*, pp. 333-34.
106. Diary, Mar. 26, 1858, *LL*, p. 335; *PF*, p. 269.
107. *LL*, p. 335. Binghampton is now spelled Binghamton.
108. There are three accounts of the Palmers' labors in Eastern Canada. One consists of three letters: Walter Palmer to Bishop and Mrs. Hamline, Oct. 14, 1858; Walter Palmer to Sarah A. Lankford, Nov. 4, 1858; Phoebe Palmer to Bishop and Mrs. Hamline, Nov. 25, 1858; all of these are in *LL*, pp. 337-45. The second is *PF*, pp. 269-306. The third is a series of letters from the Palmers published in *GTH* 34 (1858): 83ff., 124ff., 174ff.
109. *LL*, p. 146.
110. Phoebe Palmer to Bishop and Mrs. Hamline, May 13, 1858 [1859], and Apr. 7, 1859, *LL*, pp. 345-47; cf. p. 203.
111. Mrs. Palmer speaks of going to her "tract district" and to her "tract meeting." See Diary, 1838, *LL*, p. 205; and Diary, Oct. 1837, *LL*, p. 207. There were several other tract societies operating in New York in the late 1830s, such as the American Tract Society and the New York City Tract Society. Mrs. Palmer could have belonged to these, but with her loyalty to Methodism, she probably supported her denominational organization.
112. Diary, 1846, *LL*, p. 208.
113. Diary, May 20, 1848, *LL*, pp. 209-10.
114. Phoebe Palmer to Bishop and Mrs. Hamline, Mar. 4, 1847, *LL*, pp. 208-9.
115. Diary, Sept. 17, *LL*, p. 212.
116. Diary, Mar. 4, 1844, *LL*, pp. 211-12. For other instances of visitation, see *GTH* 70 (1876): 76-77. There Mrs. Palmer reports upon hearing the testimony of one converted through her ministry, "I need not say that I felt myself more than a thousand times repaid for my toil in visiting the garrets and cellars of scores of such families, during the winter."
117. New York LHMS, *First Annual Report* (New York: Printed at the Conference Office, 1845), pp. 1-6. It is not clear when Mrs. Palmer became an officer of the society. She is not listed as such in this first report, but Simpson says she was one of the "first officers" of the society, and Wheatley says she was an officer in 1847. Unfortunately the reports for 1845 to 1851 are not available. The report for 1852 lists her as third directress, so sometime between 1845 and 1847 she became an officer. See Simpson, *Cyclopedia*, p. 679; *LL*, p. 224; and LHMS, *Ninth Annual Report* (New York: Printed at the Conference Office, 1853), p. 3.

118. *LL*, pp. 223-24; Simpson, *Cyclopedia*, p. 658; LHMS, *Eleventh Annual Report* (New York: 200 Mulberry Street, 1855), p. 8.
119. Phoebe Palmer to Mrs. Keene, Feb. 10, 1855; Phoebe Palmer to unidentified, n.d.; Phoebe Palmer to Bishop and Mrs. Hamline, Aug. 8 and Oct. 11, 1855; Diary, June 11, 1856; all in *LL*, pp. 227-30.
120. *GTH* 60 (1871): 55-56; Phoebe Palmer to Brother B., May 30, 1854, *LL*, pp. 192-96.
121. The Palmers' version of this story is told in *GTH* 60 (1871): 55-56; in *LL*, pp. 188-96; and in J. H. Perry, *Reply to Prof. Mattison's "Answer," Etc.; Being the Summing Up of the Case of Professor Mattison Against Mrs. Palmer* (New York: John A. Gray's Fireproof Printing Office, 1856), pp. 28-72. Mattison charged that the Palmers left the Allen Street Church when their minister preached against Mrs. Palmer's "shorter way" theology. See Hiram Mattison, *A Calm Review of Dr. Perry's Late Article in the Christian Advocate and Journal; with Several Important Papers Relating to the Controversy* (New York: John A. Gray, 1856), pp. 21, 30-31; and Mattison, *Answer*, pp. 16-36, 83-84.
122. Charles Dickens visited this establishment in 1842 and was given this explanation by a guard. He recorded the conversation in his *American Notes*. See Charles Dickens, *The Writings of Charles Dickens*, ed. Edwin Percy Whipple et al., vol. 11, *Martin Chuzzlewit and American Notes* (Boston: Houghton Mifflin, 1894), p. 434.
123. Prison Discipline Society, *Sixteenth Annual Report of the Board of Managers of the Prison Discipline Society* (Boston: The Prison Discipline Society, 1841; reprint, *Annual Reports of the Prison Discipline Society*, Boston; originally published 1826 to 1854, republished 1855 by the Society; reprint, Montclair, N.J.: Patterson Smith, 1972), 4:84.
124. Diary, Nov. 1844; Phoebe Palmer to Bishop and Mrs. Hamline, May 31, 1850; Diary, Feb. 9, 1851; Phoebe Palmer to Bishop and Mrs. Hamline, Feb. 22, 1857; all in *LL*, pp. 214-18.
125. In his report on the Tombs, Dwight mentions the risk of jail fever due to filthy conditions. See *Sixteenth Annual Report of the . . . Prison Discipline Society*, 4:84-85. Kronenberger reports a case in England where six judges went inside a prison to hold court and four of the six caught jail fever and died. Brown mentions Sarah Peters, who possibly died of jail fever two weeks after she had persuaded a condemned murderer to trust Christ for salvation. See Louis Kronenberger, *Kings and Desperate Men: Life in Eighteenth-Century England* (New York: Vintage Books, 1942), p. 95. See also Earl Kent Brown, *Women of Mr. Wesley's Methodism*, Studies in Women and Religion, vol. 11 (New York: Edwin Mellen, 1983), p. 74.
126. *LL*, pp. 484-85.
127. Diary, Oct.-Nov. 1848, *GTH* 18 (1882): 17, 75.
128. N. Vansant, *Work Here, Rest Hereafter; or, The Life and Character of Rev. Hiram Mattison, D.D.*, with an introduction by Edward Thomson (New York: N. Tibbals & Son, 1870), pp. 109-15.
129. Phoebe Palmer, "False Statement Corrected," *CA&J*, Feb. 12, 1852, p. 27; Phoebe Palmer, "Believe That Ye Have It and Ye Have It," *CA&J*, Nov. 15, 1855, p. 181; Phoebe Palmer, "Coals of Fire," *CA&J*, Dec. 6, 1855, p. 193. For a chronological listing of the dispute as it developed in the pages of the *Christian Advocate and Journal*, see Appendix D.
130. Vansant, *Work Here*, p. 115.

131. This list has been adopted from Mattison's article and has been modified only to make it clearer what the disputants were affirming and denying. See H. Mattison, "Believe," *CA&J*, Dec. 20, 1855, p. 201; and J. H. Perry, "Prof. Mattison and His Eight Propositions," *CA&J*, Jan. 10, 1856, p. 10. See also, Perry, *Reply*, pp. 3–4. George Bell and Thomas Maxfield were English Methodists who claimed to have attained Christian perfection. Bell claimed that his words came directly from God, and both felt they had nothing to learn from John Wesley. After several attempts at reconciliation, Wesley was forced to remove them from the society. See *J.W. Journals*, 4:535–5:8, for Oct. 29, 1762, to Feb. 7, 1763.

132. Mattison, *Answer*, pp. 83–86.

133. See chap. 5, "Phoebe Palmer As Theologian."

134. Phoebe Palmer to Bishop and Mrs. Hamline, Nov. 29, 1853, *LL*, pp. 93–95.

135. Vansant, *Work Here*, pp. 59–64.

136. I. Winner, "The Controversy on Holiness," *CA&J*, Jan. 24, 1856, p. 13.

137. Bishop Hamline to Dr. and Mrs. Palmer, Dec. 9, 1847, in *Hamline*, pp. 285–86. As a six year old, Sarah had professed conversion. Evidently she recommitted her life to Christ as an adolescent. See *WOH*, pp. 275–88.

138. H. W. Palmer, "Palmer Families," vol. 2, pt. 2, p. 842.

139. McCutchan, *Our Hymnody*, pp. 279–80; *National Cyclopedia of American Biography*, s.v. "Knapp, Joseph Fairchild."

140. McCutchan, *Our Hymnody*, pp. 279–80; Charles Edwin Jones, *Perfectionist Persuasion: The Holiness Movement and American Methodism, 1867–1936*, ATLA Monograph Series, no. 5 (Metuchen, N.J.: Scarecrow, 1974), p. 159. McCutchan and Jones are undoubtedly wrong to state that the Knapps were married in 1885.

141. H. W. Palmer, "Palmer Families," vol. 2, pt. 2, p. 842.

142. *F&E*, pp. 121–22.

143. H. W. Palmer, "Palmer Families," vol. 2, pt. 2, p. 842; *TM2*, p. 178; *SLP*, p. 187.

144. Phoebe Palmer to Mrs. Hamline, Apr. 30, 1874, *LL*, p. 146.

145. *TM2*, p. 178; H. W. Palmer, "Palmer Families," vol. 2, pt. 2, p. 842.

146. Diary, 1846, *LL*, p. 208; Mr. Blackwell to Dr. and Mrs. Palmer, Dec. 8, 1850, in Letters.

147. *BP*, pp. 61–63.

148. Phoebe Palmer to Bishop and Mrs. Hamline, Apr. 28, 1855; May 8, 1855; and Aug. 5, 1856, *LL*, pp. 213–14.

149. Once in 1849 all five Methodist bishops were invited to the Palmers, but only four could come. See Diary, 1849, *LL*, p. 162. More than seven delegates stayed with the Palmers during the weeks of the General Conference of 1844. See Diary, May 1, 1844, *LL*, p. 162. The Palmers' close friend Bishop Hamline convalesced there. See *Hamline*, p. 256.

150. That this happened on more than one occasion we know from *LL*, p. 220, and from a letter to the Secretary of the Home for the Friendless. See Phoebe Palmer to Mrs. Marwin, July 29, 1853, *LL*, pp. 220–21.

151. Donald G. Mathews, *Slavery and Methodism: A Chapter in American Morality, 1780–1845* (Princeton: Princeton University Press, 1965), pp. 88–96;

Douglas J. Williamson, "Wilbur Fisk and African Colonization: A 'Painful Portion' of American Methodist History," *Methodist History* 23/2 (Jan. 1985): 79-98.

152. "Redemption of Africa," *MG*, pp. 206-7. The New York State Colonization Society may have been organized as early as 1819, thus 1828 would be the earliest possible date for its ninth anniversary. See Alice Dana Adams, *The Neglected Period of Anti-Slavery in America, 1808-1831*, Radcliffe College Monographs, no. 14 (Williamston, Mass.: Corner House, 1973), pp. 105-6.

153. "Ode for the Fourth of July," *MG*, pp. 208-9; Mathews, *Slavery and Methodism*, p. 93.

154. "Colonization Cause" and "Ode for the Fourth of July," *MG*, pp. 205, 208-9.

155. "Redemption of Africa," *MG*, pp. 206-7.

156. New York Allen Street Methodist Episcopal Church, *Poor Fund Accounts, 1838-1861*, vol. 161, in Records, pp. 2-15; Diary, *LL*, p. 219. Determining when the seventeen years mentioned in this diary entry began is impossible because the item is not dated. However, it is almost certain that the board did not meet in the Palmers' house after the Palmers left for England in 1859, and it is likely that when the Palmers left the Allen Street Church in 1849 the board found another place to meet. If this reasoning is correct then the latest date for the board to begin meeting in the Palmer home is 1842, the year Walter was replaced as its treasurer. By this reasoning, the earliest date for the board to begin meeting in their home would be 1832. If one accepts the reasonable surmise that the Board of Managers would not be meeting in the Palmer home unless one of the Palmers were on the board, then the conclusion follows that the Palmers were leaders in the Benevolent Society from the early 1830s. This line of reasoning also assumes that what Phoebe calls the "Benevolent Society" and what the Records call the managers of the "Poor Fund" was the same group.

157. Kathryn Kish Skylar, *Catharine Beecher: A Study in American Domesticity* (New York: W. W. Norton and Co., 1976), pp. 168-83. The quotation is from Catharine Beecher, *The Evils Suffered by American Women and American Children: The Cause and Remedy*, p. 11, quoted in Skylar, p. 174.

158. Catharine Beecher to Phoebe Palmer, Sept. 30, 1845, in Letters.

159. Catharine Beecher to Phoebe Palmer, Nov. 19, 1845; Dec. 27, 1845; Mar. 23, 1846; and Jan. 10, 1847, all in Letters.

160. Diary, Oct. 29, 1847, *LL*, p. 219; New York Female Assistance Society, For the Relief and Religious Instruction of the Sick Poor, *Thirty-eighth Annual Report* (New York: S. W. Benedict, 1851), pp. 3, 12. Unfortunately, of the twelve reports that Mrs. Palmer wrote, this is the only one that I have been able to locate.

161. Diary, Jan. 1847, *LL*, pp. 219-20.

162. Female Assistance Society, *Twenty-third Annual Report* (New York: Howe & Bates, 1836), pp. 2-4.

163. Female Assistance Society, *Thirty-eighth Annual Report*, pp. 9-10.

164. Barbara J. Berg, *The Remembered Gate: Origins of American Feminism* (New York: Oxford University Press, 1978), pp. 182-214.

165. Phoebe Palmer to Mrs. Marwin, July 29, 1853, *LL*, pp. 220-21; Diary, Feb. 8, 1865, *LL*, p. 222; *GTH* 81 (1882): 138.

166. The development and importance of the Five Points Mission will be discussed in chap. 8, "Phoebe Palmer As Humanitarian." Here we will discuss Phoebe Palmer's involvement with it.

167. The five streets were Little-Water, Cross, Anthony, Orange, and Mulberry. See Ladies of the Mission, *The Old Brewery, and the New Mission House at the Five Points* (New York: Stringer and Townsend, 1854), pp. 31–33, 47–48.

168. Dickens, *Writings*, pp. 437–39.

169. *GTH* 68 (1875): 125; 66 (1874): 42–43; Ladies of the Mission, *Old Brewery, New Mission*, pp. 21, 55.

170. Lewis E. Jackson, *Gospel Work in New York City: A Memorial of Fifty Years in City Missions* (New York: New York City Mission, 1878), p. 304.

171. Phoebe Palmer to Joseph Hartwell, Feb. 17, 1853, *LL*, pp. 224–25.

172. The extant annual reports of the LHMS link the society and the mission in their titles. See, for instance, the report from 1876 which has as its full title *Thirty-second Annual Report of the New York Ladies' Home Missionary Society of the Methodist Episcopal Church, and Twenty-sixth of Its Labors at the Five Points*. LHMS, *Thirty-second Annual Report* (New York: C. Hyllested, Jr., 1876), p. 6.

173. *LL*, p. 224; Ladies of the Mission, *Old Brewery, New Mission*, pp. x–xi, 37–38, 55; LHMS, *Thirty-second Annual Report*, p. 7. Phoebe Palmer herself gives us no evidence that she worked in the Sunday school or visited in the homes of Five Points. She records attending meetings at the mission but no letter or diary entry which I have been able to find says, "Today I went visiting the people at Five Points." But given her background of visitation with the tract society, her early advocacy of this mission, and the society's insistence that its officers were involved in its day-to-day ministry, it seems almost inconceivable that Mrs. Palmer did not share in this labor during the first years of the mission. See Diary, Nov. 24, 1853; and Jan. 17, 1858, in *LL*, p. 227.

174. *Voice of the Old Brewery* 4/6 (June 1864): 24.

175. Diary, 1847, *LL*, pp. 231–33.

176. Ibid.; Roche, "Mrs. Phoebe Palmer," *LR* 26 (February 1866): 66.

177. *LL*, pp. 233–34.

CHAPTER THREE

1. Richard Carwardine, *Transatlantic Revivalism: Popular Evangelicalism in Britain and America, 1790–1865*, Contributions in American History, no. 75 (Westport, Conn.: Greenwood, 1978), p. 170.

2. *LL*, p. 348.

3. When referring to the family of Methodist denominations in England, I will use the term "Methodist." When referring to a specific connexion or specific local church, I will speak of the "Wesleyans" or the "Primitive Methodists," etc.

4. Carwardine, *Transatlantic Revivalism*, p. 32.

5. Ibid., p. 102.

6. George G. Smith, *The History of Methodism in Georgia and Florida, from 1785 to 1865*, p. 277, cited in Carwardine, *Transatlantic Revivalism*, p. 32.

7. Carwardine, *Transatlantic Revivalism*, pp. 169–71.

8. Ibid., pp. 11, 175.

9. Charles G. Finney, *Charles G. Finney: An Autobiography* (Old Tappan, N.J.: Revell, n.d.; originally published as *Memoirs of Charles G. Finney*, New York: Trustees of Oberlin College, 1876), pp. 386, 414, 449; Carwardine, *Transatlantic Revivalism*, pp. 73, 85, 176.

10. *FY*, p. 262.

11. Ibid., pp. 13, 19.

12. Ibid., p. 20. The sole mention of young Walter's presence is an initial in one of Phoebe's letters home. She mentions that the passengers on the ship played board games, and comments, "We took pains to draw our dear W. from witnessing these scenes, which we have regarded as worse than vain." Walter, Jr., is the obvious object of this parental solicitude. With both of the daughters married, it was natural for them to take him along to England.

13. Ibid., pp. 4, 13, 16–18, 26.

14. Ibid., pp. 20–24.

15. Ibid., pp. 16, 26, 30. See appendix B for a complete list of the places in which the Palmers held services.

16. Ibid., pp. 26–28.

17. Ibid., pp. 30–36.

18. Ibid., pp. 39–40.

19. Ibid., p. 45. The "Man of Sin" is mentioned in 2 Thessalonians 2:3. Mrs. Palmer uses the term to refer to the papacy.

20. Ibid., pp. 54–68. There is some confusion about how long the Palmers remained in Belfast. The evidence of their stay is contained in two letters printed in *Four Years in the Old World*. The first letter is dated July 26, 1859, and the second is dated June 28, 1859. Internal evidence makes it probable that the one dated June 28 was actually written after the one dated July 26. Assuming that the June 28 should actually be July 28, we may conclude that the Palmers held meetings in Belfast for about a week.

21. Ibid., pp. 84–90. Walsingham is now called Wolsingham. The events of September 1859 through April 1860 are also recorded in *Some Account of the Recent Revival in the North of England and Glasgow*. This book is a collection of letters by Mrs. Palmer and others who witnessed the revival. Most of its contents were reprinted in *Four Years in the Old World*. Because few copies of the original work are extant, when parallel passages occur I will cite only the more readily available *Four Years in the Old World* and not list the references in the other work.

22. *FY*, pp. 90–92. Mrs. Palmer may be referring to Robert Young's book, *The Importance of Prayer Meetings in Promoting the Revival of Religion* (New York: Carlton & Porter, n.d.), which appeared sometime after 1840, and, despite its title, fully explains how to promote a revival.

23. *FY*, pp. 93–120. Beginning with their ministry in Newcastle, the Palmers usually had secretaries present in each service to record the names of those who came forward to seek justification or sanctification. Upon leaving the altar rail, the person would give her or his name to the recorder and state the reason for coming forward. The pastor or other church leaders would later visit these people to find if they were continuing their spiritual growth. A beneficial side effect of making such a list is that Mrs. Palmer could report specific numbers in the letters she wrote publicizing the revival. Because of the value Mrs. Palmer placed upon them, and the care she took in their collection, as well as her strict regard for truth, the historian may accept their general accuracy. There may, however, be some overlap in the numbers Mrs. Palmer reported. Her practice was to urge the unconverted in the congregation to seek justification, and the already converted to seek sanctification. Only after one was soundly converted would Phoebe urge the pursuit of sanctification. Thus some unconverted people may have come forward to be justified at one of the Palmers' meetings and then

returned some time later as a converted person to seek sanctification. Mrs. Palmer does not record whether such a doubly blessed individual would be counted once or twice in her totals.

24. Ibid., pp. 103, 114–18.

25. Ibid., pp. 255–58. For more information on the ways in which the Palmers sought to insure that the revival continued after they departed, see chap. 6, "Phoebe Palmer As Revivalist."

26. Carwardine, *Transatlantic Revivalism*, p. 105; Melvin Easterday Dieter, *The Holiness Revival of the Nineteenth Century*, Studies in Evangelicalism, no. 1 (Metuchen, N.J.: Scarecrow, 1980), p. 60; F. de L. Booth-Tucker, *The Life of Catherine Booth, The Mother of the Salvation Army*, 2 vols. (New York: Revell, 1892), 1:381–89.

27. Booth-Tucker, *Life of Catherine Booth*, 1:343–49, 357–70.

28. *FY*, pp. 120–47; *BH* 11 (1860): 37–41.

29. *FY*, pp. 147–62. Wesley's study was originally built on the roof of the Methodist orphanage in Newcastle. When that building was remodeled it was removed to a private estate in North Shields.

30. Ibid.

31. Ibid., p. 163.

32. Ibid., pp. 171–72; Wesley records this comment on June 17, 1779. *J.W. Journals*, 6:239–40.

33. *FY*, p. 172.

34. Ibid., pp. 174–77.

35. Ibid., pp. 180–82.

36. Ibid., pp. 188–92.

37. Ibid., pp. 193–207; *RR*, pp. 110–12.

38. *RR*, p. 115; *FY*, pp. 214–46.

39. *FY*, pp. 223–25.

40. Ibid., pp. 251–68. The Evangelical Alliance was formed in London in 1846 by churchmen of several denominations, including Anglican, Methodist, Presbyterian, and Independent. Its purpose was to unite "evangelical" Christians against the growing political power of Roman Catholicism and Anglo-Catholicism. Thus when the Palmers' meetings were called the "Evangelical Alliance Revival," it meant that Evangelicals of all persuasions were participating in them.

41. *FY*, pp. 270–74.

42. *RR*, passim.

43. *FY*, p. 285; Diary, July 30, 1860, and Phoebe Palmer to Bishop and Mrs. Hamline, Aug. 20, 1860, both in *LL*, pp. 368–69.

44. *FY*, p. 305.

45. Ibid., pp. 306–13.

46. The technical difference between liquor and other forms of alcoholic beverages made little difference to Mrs. Palmer. Nor did she make a distinction between temperance and abstinence. All alcohol (except communion wine and medicine) was the tool of Satan and must be opposed. In taking this stand she went beyond Wesley himself who opposed liquor but had no objections to the moderate use of wine. When discussing alcohol I will follow Mrs. Palmer's practice and use the various terms indiscriminately. For Wesley's views on wine, see John Wesley to Dr. Gibson, Bishop of London, June 11, 1747, *J.W. Letters*, 2:285.

47. *FY*, pp. 321–28.

48. Ibid., pp. 329-32.

49. Ibid., pp. 335-44. In citing the maxim from Wesley, Mrs. Palmer is quoting from the letter inviting them to come to Stroud. The pastor who wrote the letter misquoted Wesley. The exact quotation is: "And go always, not only to those that want you, but to those who want you most." See "Minutes of Several Conversations between the Rev. Mr. Wesley and Others; from the year 1744, to the year 1789," in *J.W. Works*, 8:310. Carwardine says that in neglecting the urban areas for the smaller towns, the Palmers may have made a "tactical error." He points out that Caughey continued with success in the urban areas while the Palmers seem to have lost some of their impetus by working in out-of-the-way places. Later, however, they regained their momentum by returning to larger cities. See Carwardine, *Transatlantic Revivalism*, p. 183.

50. *FY*, pp. 345-48.
51. Ibid., pp. 346-64.
52. Ibid., pp. 365-87.
53. Ibid., pp. 387-94.
54. Ibid., pp. 394-400.
55. Ibid., pp. 395-416.
56. Ibid., pp. 411-13.
57. Ibid., pp. 418-20. Mrs. Palmer spells his name "Muhler." George Müller began his orphanage in Bristol in 1835 and later moved it to Ashley Down. He supported the enterprise entirely on unsolicited gifts, making its needs known only to God in prayer.
58. *FY*, pp. 420-22.
59. Ibid., p. 419.
60. Ibid., pp. 418-30. The chronology of this period is confusing. In a letter dated February 11, 1860, Mrs. Palmer reports their labors at Rochdale and says they have been there thirty-five days. This date must be in error because they did not arrive in Rochdale until 1861, and thirty-five days before February 11, that is, January 8, they were still in Maidenhead. The correct date for the letter from Rochdale could well be March 11, 1861. This date would give the Palmers time to finish in Windsor at the end of January, make the trip down to Poole, and begin at Rochdale on February 5, 1861. Thirty-five days later on March 11 she could have written the letter as they departed from Rochdale to begin work in Great Grimsby that evening. See ibid., pp. 398, 418, 424-25, 431, 434.
61. Ibid., pp. 431-37.
62. Ibid., pp. 437-55.
63. Ibid., pp. 455-64; *BH* 12 (1861): 331.
64. *FY*, pp. 468-82; *BH* 12 (1861): 331-32.
65. *FY*, pp. 488-95.
66. On November 8, 1861, Captain Charles Wilkes of the U.S.S. *San Jacinto*, acting without orders, intercepted and boarded the *Trent*, a British ship. Finding two Confederate diplomats aboard, one bound for London and the other for Paris, he should have brought the ship into port for adjudication. Instead he took the diplomats into custody and sent the ship on its way. The British public was angered at this violation of neutrality, and the government threatened war, mustering eight thousand troops for Canada to make good the threat. Lincoln did not want to fight the British as well as the Confederacy, so he ordered the release of the diplomats and had a note of apology sent to Her Majesty's Government.

67. *FY*, pp. 498–515; Phoebe Palmer to Bishop and Mrs. Hamline, Dec. 5, 1861, *LL*, pp. 379–80; *GTH* 41 (1862): 152.

68. Mrs. Palmer consistently refers to the village as "Madely." In Wesley's day it was "Madeley," and the modern spelling is "Madley." I will retain Mrs. Palmer's spelling.

69. *FY*, pp. 516–28

70. Ibid., pp. 528–33; *GTH* 41 (1862): 152.

71. *FY*, pp. 539–41; *GTH* 41 (1862): 153.

72. *FY*, p. 562. See chap. 5, "Phoebe Palmer As Theologian," for a further discussion of her doctrine of sanctification. Merthyr Tyvdil is now called Merthyr Tydfil.

73. *FY*, p. 562.

74. Ibid., pp. 567–74.

75. *Mona Herald*, sometime during the last week of June 1862 (ibid., p. 584).

76. *FY*, pp. 584–89; *GTH* 42 (1862): 153.

77. *FY*, pp. 589–95.

78. Ibid., pp. 596–611.

79. Weaver was a collier turned evangelist with a racy style, and Booth was at this time a free-lance revivalist. Dow had come over from America to itinerate in Ireland and England in the first decade of the nineteenth century. Called "Crazy Dow," he "cut an extraordinary figure with his long hair, thin face, flashing eyes, stooped shoulders, harsh voice, crude gestures, and unkempt dress." See *GTH* 43 (1863): 62; Y. Z., "Our English Correspondent," *CA&J*, Oct. 9, 1862, p. 321; X. Z., "Letter from England," *CA&J*, Nov. 13, 1862, p. 361; George Hughes, "Letter from England," *CA&J*, July 23, 1863, p. 233; and Carwardine, *Transatlantic Revivalism*, pp. 104–7, 184–85.

80. *FY*, pp. 611–20; Earl Kent Brown, *Women of Mr. Wesley's Methodism*, Studies in Women and Religion, vol. 11 (New York: Edwin Mellen, 1983), pp. 53–55.

81. *FY*, pp. 620–26. For the origin and development of the various branches of British Methodism, see George Eayrs, "The United Methodist Church and the Wesleyan Reform Union," and H. B. Kendall, "The Primitive Methodist Church and the Independent Methodist Churches," in *NHM*, 1:481–598.

82. *FY*, pp. 627–30. Oddly enough, no printed record of these meetings in Liverpool has survived. Mrs. Palmer wrote from Runcorn on the eve of leaving for Liverpool, but her next printed letter makes no mention of any meetings held there. Perhaps some obstacle arose and they did not hold the meetings, or maybe the account of the services was omitted when Phoebe's letters were edited for publication.

83. Phoebe Palmer, *Sweet Mary; or, A Bride Made Ready for her Lord* (London: Simpkin, Marshall, & Co., 1862).

84. *FY*, pp. 630–66.

85. *GTH* 44 (1863): 50.

86. *FY*, pp. 666–94.

87. Ibid., pp. 695–700.

CHAPTER FOUR

1. Phoebe Palmer to Bishop and Mrs. Hamline, *LL*, p. 403; *GTH* 84 (1883): 72 (SLP); *TM1*, pp. 60-61.
2. *TM2*, p. 179; *GTH* 118 (1900): 164 (Hughes); 31 (1857): 2 (Degen and Gorham).
3. *TM2*, p. 162; *GTH* 66 (1874): 20.
4. *TM2*, p. 174; *GTH* 21 (1851): 188 (King); Frank Luther Mott, *A History of American Magazines*, 5 vols. (Cambridge: Belknap Press of the Harvard University Press, 1957), 1:514.
5. *GTH* 33 (1858): 188 (Degen and Gorham). We may be confident that it was Mrs. Palmer who boosted the circulation of the *Guide*, and not the *Guide* which made Mrs. Palmer popular. Mrs. Palmer was helped in Canada by a popular magazine which printed her articles and thus gave her name recognition among the Wesleyans. That magazine was not the *Guide to Holiness*, however, but the *Christian Guardian*, which had serialized *Faith and Its Effects* beginning in 1852. See *LL*, p. 300.
6. *GTH* 33 (1858): 188 (Degen and Gorham).
7. *TM2*, p. 174.
8. *Knickerbocker* 87 (Jan. 1863), quoted in Mott, *History*, 2:6.
9. *TM2*, pp. 175-76.
10. Foster's involvement in publishing the *Guide to Holiness* is shown by the appearance of his name on the cover in 1864. See *GTH* 46 (1864): July outside front cover, which lists him as an editor. This listing continued only until 1867 when, with the new volume in July, his name does not appear. See *GTH* 53 (1867): July outside front cover. Dr. Palmer's name first appeared on the *Guide* in January 1867. The next six months carried the names of all three editors, but with the July issue only Dr. and Mrs. Palmer's names appeared. There is no evidence to reconstruct the inner-workings of the family publishing business, but the relationship remained close and warm. See *GTH* 67 (1874): 162; H. W. Palmer, "Palmer Families in America," typescript, New England Historical Genealogical Society, Boston, vol. 2, pt. 2, p. 842; Diary, Dec. 19, 1871; and Phoebe Palmer to Mrs. Hamline, Feb. 27, 1873, *LL*, pp. 167-68.
11. *TM2*, pp. 175-77.
12. Mott, *History*, 3:5; *GTH* 53 (1868): 27; 57 (1870): 186; 64 (1873): 26.
13. Mott, *History*, 2:303-4; 3:5, 66; *CA&J*, Feb. 18, 1869, p. 56; Oct. 21, 1869, p. 332. One cannot speak dogmatically about the relative popularity of late-nineteenth-century magazines. As Mott says, "It must be remembered that circulation figures of the times are highly unreliable, and practically the only sources are the occasional boasts of successful publishers." See Mott, *History*, 2:9-10. We may have relative confidence in the figures for the *Guide to Holiness* under the Palmers' leadership because of Mrs. Palmer's strict regard for truth.
14. *GTH* 66 (1874): 21; *TM2*, pp. 216-33; *GTH* 120 (1901): December issue outside front cover.
15. See the sections on the Earl of Lonsdale and on Queen Victoria in the previous chapter, as well as *FY*, pp. 403-4, on the Church of England, and pp. 535-36 on Prince Albert. Mrs. Palmer did admit, however, that in the last months of his life Prince Albert finally attained experimental piety.
16. *GTH* 62 (1872): outside back cover of various issues.
17. *Hamline*, pp. 3, 97-100, 260-61.

18. *SP;* Phoebe Palmer, ed., *Pioneer Experiences; or, The Gift of Power Received by Faith* (New York: W. C. Palmer, Jr., 1868); Phoebe Palmer, *The Parting Gift to Fellow Laborers and Young Converts* (New York: Walter C. Palmer, Jr., [1869]); Phoebe Palmer, *The Tongue of Fire on the Daughters of the Lord; Or, Questions in Relation to the Duty of the Christian Church in Regard to the Privileges of her Female Membership* (New York: W. C. Palmer, Jr., 1869). No sales figures were given for these works.

19. *MG,* "Sympathy in Bereavement," "After a Scene of Affliction," "And They Slept," "A Mother's Love," pp. 60, 73, 85, 87. James Thurber mentions his aunt's poetry in *The Thurber Carnival* (New York: Harper & Brothers, 1945), p. 33.

20. *LL,* pp. 403–11.

21. *TM1,* p. 119.

22. William McDonald and John E. Searles, *The Life of Rev. John S. Inskip, President of the National Association for the Promotion of Holiness,* pp. 150–60, quoted in Melvin Easterday Dieter, *The Holiness Revival of the Nineteenth Century,* Studies in Evangelicalism, no. 1 (Metuchen, N.J.: Scarecrow, 1980), pp. 100–101; Lawrence E. Breeze, "The Inskips: Union in Holiness," *Methodist History* 13 (July 1975): 25–45.

23. Phoebe Palmer to Sarah Lankford, Aug. 15, 1866, *LL,* pp. 425–28. The Palmers' publishing company eventually issued Mahan's book in 1870. See Asa Mahan, *Baptism of the Holy Ghost* (New York: Walter C. Palmer, Jr., 1870).

24. Frances E. Willard in S. Olin Garrison, ed., *Forty Witnesses, Covering the Whole Range of Christian Experience* (New York: Eaton & Mains, 1888), pp. 94–98.

25. Phoebe Palmer to Mrs. Hamline, Mar. 30, [1867], *LL,* pp. 439–40.

26. *GTH* 51 (1867): 149–54. This letter was reprinted in its entirety in *CA&J,* Apr. 18, 1867, p. 121.

27. *GTH* 51 (1867): 150; Phoebe Palmer to Mrs. Hamline, Mar. 30, [1867], *LL,* p. 440.

28. Phoebe Palmer to Mrs. Hamline, Nov. 20, 1867, and Dec. 13, 1867, *LL,* pp. 444–45.

29. Diary, Jan. 1, 1870, *LL,* p. 69.

30. Phoebe Palmer to Mrs. Hamline, Apr. 14, 1867, and Phoebe Palmer to Mrs. Lankford, *LL,* pp. 450–52. Evidently Mrs. Palmer is relying on hearsay in her assessment of Free Methodism. That denomination arose in Illinois when a Methodist elder, acting on advice of his bishop, expelled several members of his society without trial for the offense of attending services held by J. W. Redfield. Redfield was a Methodist local preacher who exceeded his commission from the annual conference by preaching outside his own society. Fearing that the General Conference would never sustain an action by a group of laymen against an elder and a bishop, those who had been expelled formed themselves into an independent church and took the name Free Methodist. This group later joined with those who had been expelled from the Genesee Conference to form the Free Methodist denomination in August 1860. See Wilson Thomas Hogue, *History of the Free Methodist Church of North America,* 2d ed., 2 vols. (Chicago: Free Methodist Publishing House, 1918), 1:265–82.

31. Joseph Goodwin Terrill, *The Life of Rev. John Wesley Redfield, M.D.* (Chicago: Free Methodist Publishing House, 1897), pp. 90–101.

32. *GTH* 84 (1883): 71 (SLP); Phoebe Palmer to Mrs. Hamline, Dec. 10, 1870, *LL*, pp. 150-52; *TM1*, p. 37.
33. Mrs. Palmer probably suffered from chronic glomerulonephritis, which generally has only mild symptoms at first. In time, however, the disease causes progressive, irreparable damage to the kidneys. Before the days of dialysis or kidney transplants, such damage inevitably caused death.
34. *GTH* 63 (1873): 89, 93, 120, 154; 64 (1873): 23, 27, 55, 119; 65 (1874): 24; 66 (1874): 161 (WCP).
35. *GTH* 66 (1874): 161 (WCP). Mrs. Palmer never finished this work, but it may have formed the core of Wheatley's work or been published in later years in the *Guide to Holiness* which often printed previously unpublished extracts from her diary and letters.
36. Diary, Mar. 1, 1873, *LL*, p. 507; *GTH* 77 (1880): 164.
37. J. C., "Report on Troy," *CA&J*, Jan. 28, 1864, p. 28.
38. *GTH* 56 (1869): 148; 64 (1873): 120.
39. *GTH* 48 (1865): 61-62; 64 (1873): 54.
40. *GTH* 56 (1869): 148.
41. *GTH* 51 (1867): 186; 55 (1869): supplement; 58 (1870): supplement.
42. *GTH* 65 (1874): 25, 56, 119; 66 (1874): 54, 60, 83-85, 161.
43. *GTH* 66 (1874): 161-65 (WCP).
44. Ibid.
45. Ibid., p. 167; *SLP*, pp. 161-63, 196, 212-13; *GTH* 103 (1893): outside front covers of various issues.

CHAPTER FIVE

1. *GTH* 29 (1856): 155; *II*, p. 308.
2. *GTH* 29 (1856): 155.
3. *GTH* 44 (1863): 97.
4. Albert Outler, ed., *John Wesley* (New York: Oxford University Press, 1964), p. iii.
5. Young Phoebe apostrophizes the Bible: "Henceforth I take thee as my future guide." See *GTH* 66 (1874): 161 (WCP).
6. *WOH*, p. 6.
7. *GTH* 82 (1882): 148.
8. *II*, p. 190. See also *F&E*, pp. 17, 20; *GTH* 30 (1856): 33.
9. *II*, p. 309. See also *F&E*, pp. 125, 152; *GTH* 48 (1865): 137; 51 (1867): 8; and Phoebe Palmer to Mrs. Hamline, May 22, 1848, *LL*, p. 516.
10. *F&E*, p. 126.
11. Ibid., p. 241.
12. *WOH*, p. 44; *GTH* 59 (1871): 152. See also *WOH*, p. 132; *F&E* p. 6.
13. *II*, pp. 370-71.
14. *II*, p. 309.
15. Ibid., pp. 307, vi.
16. Ibid., pp. 307-8.
17. *GTH* 63 (1873): 122.
18. *WOH*, pp. 212-14; *GTH* 75 (1897): 69; *II*, pp. 132-33. Among the human resources Phoebe Palmer mentioned using are works by Justin Martyr, Chrysostom, Theophylact, Grotius, Dodwell, Benson, Sutcliff, Cobbin, Clarke,

Wayland, Taft, and Barnes. With help from these she could do word studies in the original Hebrew and Greek. See Phoebe Palmer, *Israel's Speedy Restoration*, p. 3; *PF*, pp. 26–27, 37, 40–41, 43–44, 48, 325. Justin Martyr was a second-century Christian apologist. Chrysostom was Bishop of Constantinople in the fourth century. Theophylact (or Theophilact) was an eleventh-century Greek exegete. Hugo Grotius was a seventeenth-century Dutch Arminian whose Latin annotations on the Old Testament were published in Paris in 1664. Henry Dodwell was a seventeenth-century English nonjuror who published a work on Irenaeus in Latin in 1689. Joseph Benson was an eighteenth-century Methodist preacher whose *Commentary on the Holy Scripture* was published in London in 1848. Ingram Cobbin was an eighteenth-century English congregationalist. Adam Clarke will be discussed later in this chapter. Joseph Sutcliff(e) was a nineteenth-century Methodist whose *Commentary on the Old and New Testaments* was published in 1834. Francis Wayland was a nineteenth-century American Baptist who served as president of Brown University. Zechariah Taft published a two-volume work on women in the church, *Biographical Sketches of the Lives and Public Ministries of Various Holy Women*, between 1825 and 1828. Albert Barnes was a nineteenth-century American Presbyterian whose eleven-volume *Notes Explanatory and Practical on the New Testament* appeared between 1832 and 1853.

19. *WOH*, p. 33. See also *F&E*, pp. 105, 133; *GTH* 4 (1842–43): 75.
20. Diary, Jan. 5, 1839; *GTH* 70 (1876): 5.
21. *GTH* 51 (1867): 186.
22. *GTH* 2 (1840–1): 92.
23. *II*, pp. 135–38.
24. Augustine, *On Christian Doctrine*, preface; 1:1, 40; 2:25–40; 3:25–28.
25. *GTH* 55 (1869): 11.
26. *PF*, p. 165.
27. *WOH*, p. 52. See also *F&E*, p. 144, along with *GTH* 4 (1842–3): 74; 47 (1865): 25; and 60 (1871): 88.
28. *BH* 9 (1858): 209.
29. *Hamline*, p. 62.
30. *WOH*, p. 95.
31. *II*, p. vi.
32. Ibid., pp. 284–85.
33. See chap. 6, "Phoebe Palmer As Revivalist," for a full treatment of the Tuesday Meeting and other social meetings.
34. *F&E*, p. 67.
35. *WOH*, pp. 74–75.
36. *F&E*, p. 67. See also chap. 1.
37. *WOH*, p. 113.
38. See, e.g., *F&E*, pp. 67, 143, 319; *GTH* 1 (1839–40): 127.
39. Neither Mrs. Palmer nor her opponents refer to this experience as a "third work of grace." The phrase is merely a useful name for the concept of a further distinct work of God in the soul beyond entire sanctification. It does not refer to the gradual growth in grace after sanctification which Wesley taught, but to a quantum leap analogous to justification and to entire sanctification. I will use the phrase with this meaning in the following pages.
40. Thomas C. Upham, *Principles of the Interior or Hidden Life; Designed Particularly for the Consideration of those who are Seeking Assurance of Faith and Perfect Love*, 3d ed. (Boston: Waite, Pierce and Co., 1845), pp. 364–65.

41. Thomas C. Upham, *Life and Religious Opinions and Experience of Madame de la Mothe Guyon: Together with Some Account of the Personal History and Religious Opinions of Fenelon, Archbishop of Cambray*, 2 vols. (New York: Harper & Brothers, 1847), p. 344.

42. See Phoebe Palmer to Professor and Mrs. Upham, Apr. 30, 1851, *LL*, pp. 518–23. I have not been able to locate the article to which Mrs. Palmer refers in her letter, nor is it listed in Salter's bibliography. Upham's books, however, contain several of these passages about the extinction of the human will which would have made Mrs. Palmer's head ache if she had read them. Besides the passages quoted above, Upham speaks of the "annihilation of the will" in his second book on sanctification. There he says that the annihilation of the will allows a person "to find a passage, as it were, into God himself, and to become one with Him, in a mysterious but holy and glorious union." The one in this state has no personal desires, nor is such a one even disquieted at the worst misfortune. See Thomas C. Upham, *The Life of Faith in Three Parts, Embracing Some of the Scriptural Principles or Doctrines of Faith, the Power or Effects of Faith in the Regulation of Man's Inward Nature, and the Relation of Faith to the Divine Guidance* (Boston: Waite, Pierce and Co., 1845), pp. 210–25. See also Salter, "Thomas Upham," pp. 177–79, for a further discussion of Upham's doctrine of a work of grace beyond sanctification.

43. For the teaching of the unnamed believer, see *II*, p. 56. See also, *GTH* 65 (1874): 112–13.

44. Either Upham used the phrase "death of the will" in the article, or else the phrase is Mrs. Palmer's way of referring to the annihilation of the human will taught in Upham's earlier works. Despite the change in terminology, the concept is the same.

45. In 1847 Upham had published a study of these two. See Thomas C. Upham, *Madame Guyon*.

46. Phoebe Palmer to Professor and Mrs. Upham, *LL*, pp. 518–23.

47. Upham, *Madame Guyon*, p. 344.

48. *II*, p. 124. Once again I have not been able to locate the writing of Upham from which Mrs. Palmer quotes these words. If she is quoting him accurately and fairly, and if Upham wrote these words after 1851, then they represent a much more cautious attitude about temptation, if not a substantial change from the attitude expressed in 1845.

49. *II*, pp. 56–59, 121–33.

50. *WOH*, pp. 209–12.

51. Ibid., pp. 76–77. For instances of other dreams and visions, see p. 225; *GTH* 41 (1862): 118; 67 (1875): 14.

52. *GTH* 27 (1855): 74.

53. *GTH* 69 (1876): 47.

54. *GTH* 69 (1876): 75–77. Perhaps if Mrs. Palmer had better followed her own injunctions about testing dreams by Scripture, she would not have come to this erroneous conclusion.

55. *GTH* 69 (1876): 47; *GTH* 70 (1876): 5; *WOH*, p. 195.

56. *II*, pp. 251–54; *FY*, p. 541; see also *F&E*, p. 261.

57. *GTH* 72 (1877): 106.

58. Ibid., p. 107.

59. *GTH* 1 (1839–40): 146–47; Diary, July 27, 1837, *LL*, pp. 43–44. These passages are quoted above in chap. 1.

60. *WOH*, pp. 108-10.
61. Diary, Sept. 9, [1838], *LL*, p. 48.
62. *GTH* 41 (1862): 118; 61 (1872): 18.
63. *PG*, p. 32.
64. *FY*, p. 28; *GTH* 43 (1863): 82-83; 4 (1843-44): 133.

65. For the influence of Hester Rogers on the sanctification of Sarah Lankford and Phoebe Palmer, see chap. 1. For Mrs. Rogers's dream and devotional practice, see Hester Ann Rogers, *An Account of the Experience of Hester Ann Rogers; Written by Herself* (New York: S. & D. A. Forbes, 1830), pp. 18ff., 43, 51, 53, 196-97. For Mrs. Palmer's dream of judgment, see *WOH*, pp. 108-10, and chap. 1. For her devotional practices see the section in this chapter on spirituality.

66. Henry Moore, *The Life of Mrs. Mary Fletcher, Consort and Relict of the Rev. John Fletcher, Vicar of Madeley, Salop. Compiled from Her Journal, and Other Authentic Documents* (New York: J. Emory and B. Waugh for the Methodist Episcopal Church, 1830), pp. 174ff., 205, 236.

67. John Lancaster, *The Life of Darcy, Lady Maxwell, of Pollock; Late of Edinburgh: Compiled from Her Voluminous Diary and Correspondence, and from Other Authentic Documents* (New York: T. Mason and G. Lane for the Methodist Episcopal Church, 1837), p. 341. Lady Maxwell also spoke of union with God in terms of being assimilated into God, sinking into Jehovah, and being let into the Deity. See ibid., pp. 325, 319, 338. For the experience of the Trinity and her communion with departed saints, see his pp. 247-48. Wesley reports that besides Lady Maxwell, he knew of some others who had been able to distinguish the presence of the separate persons of the Trinity. Among them were the Marquis De Renty, Charles Perronet, Elizabeth Ritchie, and Hester Ann Roe Rogers. See John Wesley to Lady Maxwell, Aug. 8, 1788, in *J. W. Letters*, 8:83.

68. *F&E*, pp. 251-52. Of course she hastens to add that when her friend goes to the Bible for herself, she will find in it exactly what Wesley taught: "It is now no small satisfaction for me to know, that the views received, by thus carefully testing every onward movement by the law and the testimony, are so fully in accordance with Mr. Wesley's views of Bible truth."

69. John Wesley, *J. W. Journals*, 4:535-5:7.

70. At least none of the three mention such experiences in their diaries. See Joseph Benson, *The Life of the Rev. John W. de la Flechere* (New York: B. Waugh and T. Mason for the Methodist Episcopal Church, 1833), passim; James Sigston, *Memoir of the Life and Ministry of Mr. William Bramwell, Lately an Itinerant Methodist Preacher: With Extracts from His Interesting and Extensive Correspondence*, 3d American ed. (New York: J. Emory and B. Waugh for the Methodist Episcopal Church, 1830), passim; John Nelson, *Extract from the Journal of John Nelson: Being an Account of God's Dealing with Him from His Youth to the Forty-Second Year of His Age. To Which Is Added an Account of His Death*, 16th ed. (New York: Carlton & Porter, 1856), passim. Charles Perronet, a Methodist preacher, but probably never in regular connection with Wesley, did record the visitation of the three separate persons of the Trinity. Wesley mentioned the experience in a letter to Hester Ann Roe [Rogers] on Feb. 11, 1777, and one to Miss March on Apr. 26, 1777. See *J. W. Letters*, 6:253, 262-63. For Perronet, see Matthew Simpson, ed., *Cyclopedia of Methodism*, rev. ed. (Philadelphia: Louis H. Everts, 1880), p. 708.

71. The quotation does not appear in Mrs. Palmer's writings but in a report of the Tuesday Meeting cited by Hughes. However, both its content and style suggest that it is a quotation of Phoebe Palmer's words at the Tuesday Meeting. See *TM1*, p. 38.

72. *WOH*, p. 7; *II*, pp. 324, 347; *GTH* 15 (1849): 66; 29 (1856): 155; *BH* 8 (1857): 4.

73. *GTH* 55 (1869): 86.

74. Two good introductions to Wesley's thought may be found in Outler, *John Wesley*, and in Robert W. Burtner and Robert E. Chiles, eds., *John Wesley's Theology: A Collection from His Works* (Nashville: Abingdon, 1954).

75. Both Mr. Wesley and Mrs. Palmer used the terms "entire sanctification," "Christian perfection," "perfect love," "full salvation," and "holiness" interchangeably. I will follow their practice.

76. Wesley's primary work on entire sanctification is *A Plain Account of Christian Perfection* which appears in his *Works*, 11:366–445. The main secondary sources are Harald Lindstrom, *Wesley and Sanctification: A Study in the Doctrine of Salvation* (London: Epworth, 1946); Merril Elmer Gaddis, "Christian Perfectionism in America," Ph.D. diss., University of Chicago, 1929; rev. 1938; Microcard Theological Studies, vol. 2 (Chicago: The Microcard Foundation for The American Theological Library Association, 1954); George Allen Turner, *The Vision Which Transforms: Is Christian Perfection Scriptural?* (Kansas City, Mo.: Beacon Hill, 1964); and John L. Peters, *Christian Perfection and American Methodism* (New York: Abingdon, 1956).

77. John Wesley to Robert Carr Brackenbury, Sept. 15, 1790, in *J. W. Letters*, 8:238; Orville S. Walters, "The Concept of Attainment in John Wesley's Christian Perfection," *Methodist History* 10 (April 1972): 23.

78. E.g., see *II*, pp. 36–43, in which Mrs. Palmer even cites the volume and page numbers for her quotations. Wesley uses the phrase "old Methodist doctrine" to refer to entire sanctification in a letter to Samuel Bardsley, Apr. 3, 1772. See *J. W. Letters*, 5:315.

79. For references to Fletcher in Mrs. Palmer's writings see *F&E*, p. 209; *ED*, p. 31; and *GTH* 27 (1855): 107; 41 (1862): 119; 55 (1869): 87.

80. John Fletcher, *Third Check to Antinomianism*, in *The Works of the Reverend John Fletcher, Late Vicar of Madeley*, 4 vols. (New York: Carlton & Porter, n.d.), 1:160. See also Luke Tyerman, *Wesley's Designated Successor* (New York: Phillips and Hunt, 1883), p. 139; Timothy L. Smith, "How John Fletcher Became the Theologian of Wesleyan Perfectionism, 1770–1776," *Wesleyan Theological Journal* 15/1 (Spring 1980): 70; and Donald W. Dayton, "Theological Roots of Pentecostalism," Ph.D. diss., University of Chicago, 1978, pp. 56–67.

81. Timothy Smith, "George Whitefield and Wesleyan Perfectionism," *Wesleyan Theological Journal* 19/1 (Spring 1984): 65–72.

82. John Wesley to Joseph Benson, Dec. 28, 1770; and John Wesley to John Fletcher, Mar. 22, 1775, in *J. W. Letters*, 5:215; 6:146.

83. John Wesley, *A Plain Account of Christian Perfection*, in *J. W. Works*, 11:404; and John Wesley to Joseph Benson, Mar. 16, 1771, in *J. W. Letters*, 5:228–29.

84. John Fletcher, *Last Check to Antinomianism*, in *Works*, 2:630–31. Fletcher actually submitted his manuscript to both John and Charles Wesley for their corrections. See John Fletcher to Charles Wesley, May 21, 1775, in ms. "Fletcher Volume," p. 51, Coleman Collection, Methodist Archives and Re-

search Center, John Rylands Library, The University of Manchester, cited in Smith, "John Fletcher," p. 79.

85. John Wesley to John Fletcher, Aug. 18, 1775, in *J. W. Letters*, 6:175.
86. Rogers, *An Account of Hester Ann Rogers*, pp. 43, 201–3.
87. Fletcher, *Last Check to Antinomianism*, in *Works*, 2:634, 645–51.
88. Rogers, *An Account of Hester Ann Rogers*, p. 45.
89. *GTH* 1 (1839–40): 210.
90. Adam Clarke, *The Holy Bible, Containing the Old and New Testaments. The Text Carefully Printed from the Most Correct Copies of the Present Authorized Translation, Including the Marginal Readings and Parallel Texts: With a Commentary and Critical Notes; Designed as a Help to a Better Understanding of the Sacred Writings*, 6 vols. (New York: T. Mason and G. Lane, 1837), 6:136–37; 6:787; 1:453. See also the section in this chapter on Mrs. Palmer's "altar theology."
91. Clarke, *Christian Theology*, pp. 202, 205, 207–8. See Peters, *Christian Perfection*, pp. 103–6, and Dayton, "Theological Roots," pp. 79–80.
92. Timothy Merritt, *The Christian's Manual, A Treatise on Christian Perfection; with Directions for Obtaining that State, compiled Principally from the Works of the Rev. John Wesley* (New York: N. Bangs and J. Emory, 1827), p. 43.
93. Asa Mahan, *Scripture Doctrine of Christian Perfection; with other Kindred Subjects, Illustrated and Confirmed in a Series of Discourses Designed to Throw Light on the Way of Holiness*, 7th ed. (Boston: Waite, Pierce and Co., 1844), p. 188. Finney describes the incident a little differently. See Charles Grandison Finney, *Charles G. Finney: An Autobiography* (Old Tappan, N.J.: Fleming H. Revell, n.d.), pp. 350–51. See also Barbara Brown Zikmund, "Asa Mahan and Oberlin Perfectionism," Ph.D. diss., Duke University, 1969, pp. 112–28.
94. Zikmund, "Asa Mahan," p. iv; Finney, *Autobiography*, p. 340.
95. Mahan knew of Mrs. Palmer's work and termed *The Way of Holiness* second only to the Scripture in its usefulness. He visited the Palmer home, and Phoebe called him "our long-valued Christian brother." See *Hamline*, p. 232; *WOH*, pp. 8–9; and *GTH* 50 (1866): 122. For her contact with Finney, see *GTH* 52 (1867): 87.
96. Both Dayton and Smith imply that the reintroduction of Pentecostal language into the Methodist stream came from the tributaries of Oberlin. Dayton credits John Morgan of Oberlin with publicizing the non-Methodist version of the identification, and Smith shows how Finney developed similar views. Smith then goes on to argue that in 1841 under Finney's influence George Peck became the first Methodist theologian since John Fletcher to use the term "baptism of the Holy Ghost" interchangeably with "entire sanctification." Both of these analyses ignore the evidence of Pentecostal language in Methodism before 1840. Smith does not mention this phenomenon, and Dayton brushes it aside, saying that it was "usually in a more general manner without specific reference to the experience of sanctification." But Allan Coppedge has given several instances of Methodists who used Pentecostal language in specific reference to entire sanctification. In addition, Smith informs us that Fisk was sanctified under the preaching of Merritt at Wellfleet, Massachusetts, in 1819; but he does not mention that Merritt was preaching on the baptism of the Holy Ghost. Smith may be technically correct that no Methodist *theologian* between John Fletcher and George Peck identified sanctification with the baptism of the Spirit, depending on how one wants to define "theologian." But the impression that the equation of the two concepts reappeared in Methodism under Finney's influence is not accurate.

Methodist preachers were using Pentecostal language to talk about sanctification before Finney was even converted. See Dayton, "Theological Roots," pp. 85–88; Timothy L. Smith, "The Doctrine of the Sanctifying Spirit: Charles G. Finney's Synthesis of Wesleyan and Covenant Theology," *Wesleyan Theological Journal* 13 (Spring 1978): 103–6; and "Righteousness and Hope: Christian Holiness and the Millennial Vision in America, 1800–1900," *American Quarterly* 31/1 (Spring 1979): 25, 35–36; John Morgan, "The Gift of the Holy Ghost," *The Oberlin Quarterly Review* 1 (1845): 90–116; Allan Coppedge, "Entire Sanctification in Early American Methodism, 1812–1835," *Wesleyan Theological Journal* 13 (Spring 1978): 37, 44–46; Claude Holmes Thompson, "The Witness of American Methodism to the Historical Doctrine of Christian Perfection," Ph.D. thesis, Drew University, 1949, p. 538; and Joseph Holdich, *The Life of Wilber Fisk, D.D., First President of the Wesleyan University* (New York: Harper & Brothers, 1842), p. 72.

97. These ideas occur so often in Mrs. Palmer's writings that it would be foolish to attempt to list all the places they appear or even to try to cite each of the different ways she states them. Thus I will give just one instance of each point, trusting that the reader easily can find many other examples. That sanctification is distinct from justification (*II*, p. 38); that it cleanses the heart from sin and fills it with love (*II*, p. 283; *WOH*, p. 118); that one needs holiness for heaven (*F&E*, p. 349); and that God supplies the ability in response to faith (*WOH*, p. 32; *GTH* 30 [1856]: 33).

98. *WOH*, p. 185.

99. *II*, p. 75; *F&E*, p. 256; *GTH* 6 (1844): 27–28; 8 (1845): 94; 23 (1853): 176; 30 (1856): 112; and *PF*, passim.

100. Mrs. Palmer made the statement at the camp meeting in Millbrook, Ontario, on September 13, 1856. See *GTH* 32 (1857): 24–25.

101. *GTH* 44 (1863): 162 (Hughes); George Hughes, "Letter from England," *CA&J*, July 23, 1863, p. 233. See also *GTH* 55 (1869): 90; 59 (1871): 154; and 61 (1872): 58.

102. *PF*, pp. 252, 257–58.

103. See, e.g., *FY*, p. 416; and *GTH* 50 (1866): 59ff.

104. Dayton, "Theological Roots," pp. 86–89.

105. Ibid., pp. 91–93.

106. See, e.g., Wesley, *Christian Perfection*, in *J. W. Works*, 11:374–75.

107. Alice Felt Tyler, *Freedom's Ferment* (New York: Harper & Row, 1962), pp. 184–95.

108. Dayton, "Theological Roots," p. 99.

109. William Arthur, *The Tongue of Fire; or the True Power of Christianity* (New York: Harper & Brothers, 1856), pp. 48–56, 321–37. For the popularity of the work, see Dayton, "Theological Roots," p. 89.

110. *GTH* 56 (1866): 151.

111. Diary, Dec. 1856, *LL*, pp. 496–97.

112. Fletcher, *Last Check to Antinomianism*, in *Works*, 2:630–32; cf. pp. 619–25.

113. Clarke, *Christian Theology*, pp. 202.

114. See chap. 1, "Preparation for Ministry: 1807–37" and chap. 8, "Phoebe Palmer As Humanitarian."

115. See, e.g., *GTH* 33 (1858): 11 and *PG*, p. 7. She went on to say that entire sanctification was "the promised ordination of power" and that "heart

holiness and the gift of power should ever be regarded as identical." *GTH* 50 (1866): 189; 64 (1873): 24.

116. *GTH* 39 (1861): 149; 68 (1875): 43; 33 (1858): 39. She could easily tell that one of her correspondents was not sanctified. She told him he lacked success in his ministry because he went to theaters and his wife dressed fashionably.

117. Phoebe Palmer to Sarah Lankford, Oct. 10, 1857, *LL*, p. 329; *GTH* 33 (1858): 11–12; 42 (1862): 178.

118. Vernon Louis Parrington uses this phrase to describe the injustice of the Gilded Age. See Vernon Louis Parrington, *Main Currents in American Thought*, 3 vols. (New York: Harcourt, Brace and Co., 1930), 3:23–24. Timothy Smith juxtaposes the two feasts in the opening pages of his well-known book. Timothy L. Smith, *Revivalism and Social Reform: American Protestantism on the Eve of the Civil War* (Nashville: Abingdon, 1957; reprint with a new afterword by the author, Baltimore: Johns Hopkins University Press, 1980), p. 7.

119. Dayton, "Theological Roots," pp. 91–97.

120. Wesley, *Christian Perfection*, in *J. W. Works*, 11:402. See also John Wesley to John Smith, Dec. 30, 1745, and John Wesley to Charles Wesley, Sept. 1762; both in *J. W. Letters*, 2:62; 4:187.

It might be argued that the earlier tension between the gradual and the instantaneous views of perfection was resolved by Wesley himself, because his later letters increasingly emphasize the instantaneous element of entire sanctification. A careful reading of all of Wesley's letters about sanctification shows that through 1771 he mentioned both gradual and instantaneous sanctification, but beginning in 1772 he increasingly mentioned the instantaneous. In these latter letters he strongly urged his correspondents to pursue and to preach entire sanctification received instantaneously by faith. From this evidence some might conclude that the shift in emphasis from sanctification as a process to sanctification as a crisis happened not in Phoebe Palmer nor in Adam Clarke but in Wesley himself.

I believe a different construction may be placed on the data. While it is true that after 1771 John Wesley increasingly spoke about instantaneous sanctification in his letters, during those years he also continued to urge people to read his *Plain Account of Christian Perfection* in which the instantaneous and the gradual are more balanced. In addition, in 1784 he published his sermon "On Patience" in the *Arminian Magazine*. In it he states that while empirical evidence has convinced him that sanctification is usually, if not always, instantaneous, he must admit that the Scripture never settles the issue. Neither in his letters nor in his published works did he ever repudiate his earlier statements about the gradual process leading to entire sanctification; instead, he published a sermon which admitted the possibility of the gradual work, and in at least one later letter said, "salvation from inbred sin is received . . . in a moment; although it is certain there is a gradual work both preceding and following."

My reading of the evidence is that Wesley did not change his mind about the relative importance of the gradual and the instantaneous but continued to maintain a balance between them, holding that entire sanctification occurred in an instant but that the crisis of sanctification usually came after a period of growth in grace, and always prepared the believer for further growth. After 1771 he felt that Methodists were in danger of upsetting the balance by forgetting the instantaneous, so he continually emphasized that side of the truth in his letters.

See Walters, "John Wesley's Christian Perfection," pp. 22–25; John Wesley, "On Patience," in *J. W. Works*, 6:490–91. For letters after 1771 urging people to read his *Plain Account*, see John Wesley to Ann Loxdale, June 10, 1781; John Wesley to Hester Ann Roe [Rogers], Jan. 7, 1782; John Wesley to Ann Loxdale, Apr. 12, 1782, all in *J. W. Letters*, 7:66, 98, 120. For a later letter mentioning both gradual and instantaneous sanctification, see John Wesley to Ann Loxdale, July 12, 1782 (7:129). For evidence that Wesley felt the Methodists were neglecting the preaching of instantaneous perfection see John Wesley to Thomas Rankin, July 21, 1774, in *J. W. Letters*, 6:103.

121. *WOH*, pp. 17–18.

122. Ibid., pp. 18–19.

123. *II*, p. 39. Interestingly, she neglected to include his comment in the same sermon, noted above, that instantaneous sanctification is nowhere explicitly taught in the Bible. *F&E*, p. 285. The passages quoted are from John Wesley's sermons "The Scripture Way of Salvation" and "On Patience" in *J. W. Works*, 6:53, 491.

124. *WOH*, p. 100.

125. Ibid., p. 231.

126. *II*, pp. 15, 80; *GTH* 46 (1864): 103.

127. *GTH* 31 (1857): 161.

128. *F&E*, p. 97.

129. Timothy Smith, "George Whitefield and Wesleyan Perfectionism," *Wesleyan Theological Journal* 19/1 (Spring 1984): 67–68; Wesley, "The Scripture Way of Salvation," in *J. W. Works*, 6:54.

130. David L. Cubie, "Perfection in Wesley and Fletcher: Inaugural or Teleological?" *Wesleyan Theological Journal* 11 (Spring 1976): 22–37.

131. Wesley, *Christian Perfection*, in *J. W. Works*, 11:387, 423.

132. Wesley, "The Scripture Way of Salvation"; and *Minutes of Several Conversations between the Rev. Mr. Wesley and Others from the year 1744, to the year 1789*, in *J. W. Works*, 6:52; 8:325.

133. Wesley, *Christian Perfection*, in *J. W. Works*, 11:427–41. The sermons are "On Sin in Believers," "The Repentance of Believers," "The Circumcision of the Heart," "Christian Perfection," "The Scripture Way of Salvation," and "On Perfection," in *J. W. Works*, 5:144–55, 156–70, 202–11; 6:1–22, 43–53, 411–23.

134. Wesley, *Christian Perfection*, in *J. W. Works*, 11:369–70, 382, 385–87, 392–93; and Charles Wesley, "The Promise of Sanctification," in *J. W. Works*, 6:20–22.

135. Charles Wesley, "O Jesus, At Thy Feet We Wait," no. 378 in John Wesley, *The Works of John Wesley*, ed. Frank Baker, vol. 7: *A Collection of Hymns for the Use of the People called Methodists*, ed. by Franz Hildenbrandt and Oliver A. Beckerlegge with the assistance of James Dale (Oxford: Oxford University, 1983), p. 551.

136. "The Cleansing Wave," *GTH* 59 (1871): 192.

137. John Wesley, *Minutes of Some Late Conversations between the Rev. Mr. Wesley and Others*, in *J. W. Works*, 8:284.

138. *WOH*, p. 19.

139. *FY*, p. 184; *II*, p. 134.

140. *FY*, p. 174; *F&E*, p. 89.

141. Dieter coined this phrase to describe some of the excesses in the Holiness movement. He feels that others took Mrs. Palmer's doctrine and "pressed it unduly" into the stark choice between "holiness or hell." My reading of Mrs. Palmer convinces me that although she may never have used the phrase, the idea is certainly present in her speaking and writing. See Melvin Easterday Dieter, *The Holiness Revival of the Nineteenth Century*, Studies in Evangelicalism, no. 1 (Metuchen, N.J.: Scarecrow, 1980), p. 32.

142. John Wesley to Joseph Alger, Feb. 24, 1782, in *J. W. Letters*, 7:109.

143. John Wesley to Elizabeth Hardy, Apr. 5, 1758, in *J. W. Letters*, 4:10. See also Wesley, *Christian Perfection*, in *J. W. Works*, 11:338.

144. *GTH* 41 (1862): 155. See also *ED*, pp. 7-8.

145. Dieter, *Holiness Revival*, pp. 18-21.

146. Ibid., p. 18; Norman Pettit, *The Heart Prepared: Grace and Conversion in Puritan Spirituality* (New Haven: Yale University Press, 1966), pp. 86-141; Charles Grandison Finney, *Revival Lectures* (Old Tappan, N.J.: Revell, n.d.), pp. 180-81, 193.

147. Wesley, "On Patience," in *J. W. Works*, 6:490.

148. John Wesley to Mr. —, Nov. 9, 1777, in *J. W. Letters*, 6:287.

149. Both Mrs. Rogers and Mrs. Fletcher reported that sanctification came immediately after they had claimed it. See Rogers, *An Account of Hester Ann Rogers*, pp. 44-45, and Moore, *The Life of Mrs. Mary Fletcher*, pp. 35-36.

150. Wesley, "The Scripture Way of Salvation," in *J. W. Works*, 6:53.

151. Wesley, *Christian Perfection*, in *J. W. Works*, 11:402-3.

152. This formula appears scores of times in Mrs. Palmer's writings. See, e.g., *II*, p. 320; *F&E*, p. 89; or *GTH* 64 (1873): 42-43. At times she neglects to mention the third step. See *GTH* 30 (1856): 33.

153. *II*, p. 131.

154. *WOH*, pp. 86, 126.

155. *F&E*, p. 15.

156. *II*, pp. 47, 180; *WOH*, p. 96; *ED*, pp. 6-7; *F&E*, pp. 227-33; *GTH* 32 (1857): 77; 50 (1866): 44; 55 (1869): 11; 63 (1873): 121.

157. *GTH* 48 (1865): 187. See also appendix E which gives the sample covenant suggested in *Entire Devotion to God*.

158. *F&E*, pp. 124-27.

159. *GTH* 48 (1865): 159.

160. Mrs. Palmer exegetes this passage in several different works, among them, *F&E*, pp. 99, 343; *GTH* 32 (1857): 77; 48 (1865): 159.

161. *SP*, pp. 119-22.

162. *WOH*, p. 38; *II*, p. 151.

163. *F&E*, p. 342. For other instances of this image see *GTH* (1840-41): 88, and *SP*, pp. 118-22.

164. Paraphrased from *F&E*, p. 185.

165. Ibid., p. 184.

166. *GTH* 1 (1839-40): 210.

167. *F&E*, p. 78.

168. *II*, pp. 148-50.

169. Wesley, *Christian Perfection*, in *J. W. Works*, 11:397-98; *F&E*, p. 83.

170. *II*, p. 114; *GTH* 33 (1858): 121; 46 (1864): 104; *SP*, p. 128.

171. *II*, p. 335-37, 359; *F&E*, *p.* 212.

172. *F&E*, p. 233.

173. *GTH* 55 (1869): 149; *II*, pp. 191, 340. See the section on the evidence of sanctification for a discussion of the relationship between feelings and Scripture as evidence of sanctification.

174. *FY*, p. 87.

175. *II*, pp. 141, 191.

176. *II*, pp. 40–41. I have only been able to locate one the five passages in Wesley from which Mrs. Palmer quotes. It is John Wesley to Mrs. Crosby, May 2, 1767, in *J. W. Letters*, 5:46–47. However, Wesley makes the point clearly in another passage which Mrs. Palmer does not mention. See John Wesley to Ann Bolton, Dec. 29, 1770, in *J. W. Letters*, 5:215. Fletcher's experience is recorded in Rogers, *An Account of Hester Ann Rogers*, pp. 201–2.

177. Hiram Mattison, *A Calm Review of Dr. Perry's Late Article in the Christian Advocate and Journal; with Several Important Papers Relating to the Controversy* (New York: John A. Gray, 1856), pp. 19–20.

178. *SLP*, p. 138.

179. Ibid., p. 141. Bangs was reading from John Wesley to the Countess of Huntington, June 19, 1771, in *J. W. Letters*, 5:258.

180. Theodore Hovet has written a lengthy analysis of Phoebe Palmer's altar phraseology. Unfortunately his work betrays a fundamental misunderstanding of Mrs. Palmer. I will examine his arguments in chap. 7, "Phoebe Palmer As Feminist." See Theodore Hovet, "Phoebe Palmer's 'Altar Phraseology' and the Spiritual Dimensions of Woman's Sphere," The Journal of Religion 63 (July 1983): 264–80.

181. *GTH* 4 (1842–43): 81. What Clarke actually says is that in this passage the altar signifies the sacrifice on the altar and that therefore the Christians' altar is the sacrifice offered for believers, i.e., Jesus himself. Evidently Mrs. Palmer missed Clarke's subtle distinction between the altar and the sacrifice offered on the altar. She concluded that Jesus Christ is the altar upon which Christians make their sacrifices of themselves. See Adam Clarke, *The Holy Bible, Commentary*, 1837 ed., 6:787.

182. Phoebe Palmer writes about her "altar theology" in several places. The most important are *WOH*, pp. 62–67; *GTH* 46 (1864): 102–3; 82 (1882): 136–37.

183. Wesley, *Christian Perfection*, in *J. W. Works*, 11:398–99, 401–2.

184. Ibid., 11:420.

185. *WOH*, p. 67.

186. Diary, July 27, 1837, *LL*, pp. 40–41.

187. *II*, pp. 150–53.

188. *F&E*, pp. 240–43; *GTH* 55 (1869): 152–53.

189. Abel Stevens, *Life and Times of Nathan Bangs, D.D.* (New York: Carlton & Porter, 1863), pp. 396–402.

190. *SLP*, pp. 135–37.

191. *F&E*, pp. 85, 92, 244; *GTH* 39 (1861): 149.

192. *GTH* 55 (1869): 149; *II*, pp. 191, 340.

193. See chap. 2, "Ministry in America: 1838–58."

194. *II*, pp. v–vi, 285, 308, 371.

195. For an introduction to nineteenth-century American Methodist thought, see Emory Stevens Buck et al., *The History of American Methodism*, 3 vols. (New York: Abingdon, 1964); Robert E. Chiles, *Theological Transition in American Methodism: 1790–1935* (New York: Abingdon, 1965); James E.

Hamilton, "Academic Orthodoxy and the Arminianizing of American Theology," *Wesleyan Theological Journal* 9 (Spring 1974): 52-59; Thomas A. Langford, *Practical Divinity: Theology in the Wesleyan Tradition* (Nashville: Abingdon, 1983); Leland H. Scott, "Methodist Theology in America in the Nineteenth Century," Ph.D. diss., Yale University, 1954; Microcard Theological Studies, vol. 20 (Madison, Wis.: The Microcard Foundation for The American Theological Library Association, 1956); David Clark Shipley, "The Development of Theology in American Methodism in the Nineteenth Century," *The London Quarterly and Holburn Review* 134 (July 1959): 249-64.

196. Smith, *Revivalism and Social Reform*, summarizes the statistical data from several primary sources on pp. 20-23. C. C. Goen shows the influence of Methodism on other denominations. See "The Methodist Age in American Church History," *Religion in Life* 34 (1965): 562-72.

197. Peter Cartwright, *Autobiography of Peter Cartwright*, ed. W. P. Strickland (New York: Methodist Book Concern, n.d.), pp. 66-72.

198. *GTH* 44 (1863): 145; 63 (1873): 154.

199. *GTH* 65 (1874): 120; 66 (1874): 21.

200. *GTH* 29 (1856): 155.

201. *LL*, p. 265; *PF*, pp. 270-72; *FY*, pp. 329-32.

202. *GTH* 53 (1868): 7.

203. *GTH* 66 (1874): 54.

204. *GTH* 67 (1875): 180.

205. *GTH* 15 (1849): 15; *F&E*, pp. 252-53.

206. *GTH* 51 (1867): 193.

207. *GTH* 51 (1867): 93.

208. *PF*, p. 29; *GTH* 63 (1873): 91.

209. *MG*, "The Keys of St. Peter," 84.

210. *GTH* 59 (1871): 56-57.

211. *GTH* 27 (1855): 73; 28 (1855): 163; 46 (1864): 80; 49 (1866): 155; 85 (1884): 105; *PG*, p. 34; *WOH*, p. 149; *LR* 5 (1845): 57.

212. *PG*, pp. 20-21.

213. *WOH*, p. 124; *F&E*, p. 45; *PG*, pp. 40, 43; *GTH* 27 (1855): 109.

214. *WOH*, p. 94.

215. *GTH* 32 (1857): 25; 70 (1876): 183.

216. *PG*, pp. 41-42.

217. A typical incident is recorded in *II*, pp. 317-18.

218. *WOH*, 168; *LL*, p. 158.

219. *PG*, pp. 39-40; *WOH*, p. 97; *GTH* 31 (1857): 129.

220. *II*, pp. 236-37. Phoebe Palmer also related how a steamboat captain would not halt ordinary work on his ship while she was holding Sunday services in the cabin. The boat later crashed, fortunately with no loss of life. Mrs. Palmer saw the avenging hand of God in that incident.

221. *GTH* 47 (1865): 65.

222. *WOH*, pp. 88-89.

223. "Watchword for 1872," *GTH* 61 (1872): 36.

224. For John Wesley on the class meeting, see this author's "The Class Meeting: Then and Now," *Light and Life*, April 1984, pp. 18ff. For the spread of the Tuesday Meeting and the establishment of Christian Vigilance Bands, see chap. 6, "Phoebe Palmer As Revivalist."

225. See Wesley, "On Dress," in *J. W. Works*, 7:15-25.

226. *II*, p. 155.
227. *WOH*, p. 158.
228. *II*, pp. 52, 69.
229. *GTH* 66 (1874): 22, 118.
230. *GTH* 33 (1858): 39.
231. *GTH* 52 (1867): 186.
232. *ED*, pp. 58-59. See also *GTH* 61 (1872): 27; 66 (1874): 118.
233. William P. Strickland, *Genius and Mission of Methodism: Embracing What is Peculiar in Doctrine, Government, Modes of Worship*, pp. 111, 113, quoted in Charles A. Johnson, *The Frontier Camp Meeting: Religious Harvest Time* (Dallas: Southern Methodist University Press, 1955), p. 46.
234. *GTH* 53 (1868): 122-23. Mrs. Palmer reprinted the final quotation from the *Presbyterian* printed in Philadelphia.
235. *II*, pp. 286-91.
236. *ED*, p. 29.
237. *GTH* 53 (1868): 87.
238. *GTH* 53 (1868): 28.
239. Ibid., p. 29.
240. *LL*, pp. 60-61.
241. *GTH* 53 (1868): 29-30.
242. Wesley, "Causes of the Inefficacy of Christianity," in *J. W. Works*, 7:289-90.
243. *WOH*, pp. 216-17.
244. *II*, pp. 87-89.
245. Phoebe Palmer's attitude about the use of money will be discussed more fully in chap. 8, "Phoebe Palmer As Humanitarian."
246. *GTH* 52 (1867): 186.
247. Walter C. and Phoebe Palmer to Gersham F. Cox, Jan. 29, 1844, New England Methodist Historical Society Collection, Boston. The letter is signed Walter C. and Phoebe Palmer, but it is in her hand. In March 1842 a book Cox wrote on the millennium was reviewed in *Zion's Herald*, and a month later Cox wrote an article against the idea of an earthly millennium, but I have not located Cox's article in which he announces the Lord's return. See E. B. Fletcher, "G. F. Cox on the Millennium," and G. F. Cox, "Millennium—The Unanswerable Argument," in *ZH*, Mar. 9, 1842, p. 37; and Apr. 6, 1842, p. 53. Unfortunately the last digit of the year Cox mentions for the Lord's return is illegible in Mrs. Palmer's letter. Most likely it is a 5, but it could also be a 3 or an 8.
248. Walter C. and Phoebe Palmer to Gersham F. Cox, Jan. 29, 1844, New England Methodist Historical Society Collection, Boston.
249. Charles Fitch to Dr. and Mrs. Palmer, July 26, 1842, Heritage Room, Andrews University, Berrien Springs, Mich. I am indebted to C. Mervyn Maxwell of Andrews University for informing me of this letter.
250. Phoebe Palmer to William Miller, Oct. 24, 1844, in *LL*, pp. 512-13.
251. The only reason for this discussion of Mrs. Palmer's connection with Adventism is the statement in Spaulding's history of Adventism that Phoebe Palmer was an "Adventist believer." As evidence he cites the Palmers' friendship with Fitches and quotes her hymn, "Song for the Times" based on Revelation 22:20, "Surely I come quickly." The song merely says that Jesus is coming soon, and is not evidence of Adventist belief. It was not published by the Palmers until 1865, and, even if its words were composed as early as the 1840s, it does not make

Phoebe Palmer an Adventist any more than writing "Lo! He Comes with Clouds Descending" qualifies Charles Wesley for that label. For Mrs. Palmer's hymn see *GTH* 48 (165): 32. See also Arthur Whitefield Spaulding, *Origin and History of the Seventh Day Adventists*, 2 vols. (Washington, D.C.: Review & Herald, 1962), 2:135.

252. *F&E*, p. 323; *GTH* 49 (1866): 189.

253. *F&E*, p. 323.

254. See *GTH* 51 (1867): 5–6; 59 (1871): 152; 61 (1872): 25–26; 63 (1873): 122, 153.

255. *GTH* 59 (1871): 152.

256. Phoebe Palmer, *Israel's Speedy Restoration*, pp. 3–11; *GTH* 52 (1867): 172ff. See also chap. 2, "Ministry in America: 1838–58."

257. Charles Eliot et al., "Pastoral Address of the General Conference to the members of the Methodist Episcopal Church, 1852," appendix N, in *Journals of the General Conference of the Methodist Episcopal Church, Held in Boston, Mass., 1852* (New York: Carlton & Phillips, 1852), p. 160.

258. See, e.g., Randolph Sinks Foster, *Nature and Blessedness of Christian Purity*, (New York: Lane & Scott, 1851), pp. 130–38; Randolph Sinks Foster, *Christian Purity* (New York: Carlton & Lanahan, 1870) pp. 206–19; Jesse T. Peck, *The Central Idea of Christianity* (Boston: H. V. Degen, 1856), pp. 214–24.

259. *GTH* 68 (1874): 177 (WCP). Dr. Palmer does not identify this editor.

260. While there are no firm figures on the sale of the anti-Palmer books mentioned, I am basing my statement on the limited numbers of editions or republications of these works compared to the frequent reissue of Mrs. Palmer's writings.

261. Handwritten note signed by Phoebe Palmer on the flyleaf of Samuel Franklin, *A Critical Review of Wesleyan Perfection* (New York: Methodist Book Concern for the author, 1866) in the Palmer Folder, Drew University Archives Manuscript Collection, Madison, N.J.

262. Daniel D. Whedon, "The Doctrines of Methodism," *Bibliotheca Sacra* 19 (1862): 271–72.

263. Peters, *Christian Perfection*, pp. 139–80.

264. Dieter, *Holiness Revival*, pp. 98–119; Peters, *Christian Perfection*, pp. 133–50; J. Wesley Corbin, "Christian Perfection and the Evangelical Association through 1875," *Methodist History* 7 (Jan. 1969): 28–44. Hoffman was the assistant editor of the *Living Epistle*, an English-language publication supported by the Evangelical Association. The Association was one of the root denominations of the United Methodist church. I am indebted to Dr. Lawrence R. Schoenhals, member of the hymnal committee of the Free Methodist Church, for information about the career of Elisha Hoffman. His song is no. 280 in the Nazarene hymnal, *Worship in Song* (Kansas City, Mo.: Lillenas, 1972), and no. 280 in *Hymns of the Living Faith* (Winona Lake, Ind.: Light and Life, 1951).

265. While some would distinguish between the Pentecostal movement and the Charismatic movement, defining the former as that group of denominations which began in the Pentecostal experiences of Americans at the beginning of the twentieth century and using the latter to describe glossolalic movements within established denominations, I will refer to the shared elements of their theology as Pentecostalism.

266. Dayton, "Theological Roots," p. 204 and passim. See also Vinson Synan, *The Holiness-Pentecostal Movement in the United States* (Grand Rapids: Eerdmans, 1971).

267. Frederick Dale Bruner, *A Theology of the Holy Spirit: The Pentecostal Experience and the New Testament Witness* (Grand Rapids: Eerdmans, 1970), pp. 92–111.
268. Ibid.
269. Dennis and Rita Bennett, *The Holy Spirit and You: A Study-Guide to the Spirit-Filled Life* (Plainfield, N.J.: Logos International, 1971), pp. 69–70.

CHAPTER SIX

1. F. B. O. Home, "Mrs. Phoebe Palmer," *ZH*, Nov. 12, 1874, p. 361.
2. *TM1*, p. 143; "The Palmer Meeting for Holiness," *ZH*, Apr. 24, 1867, p. 65.
3. "The Tuesday Meeting" was a regular feature of the *Guide*. See, e.g., *GTH* 49 (1866): 32ff.
4. This description of the Tuesday Meeting is a composite drawn from various meetings over a number of years and reported in *PF*, pp. 226–40; *TM1*, pp. 38–42; *GTH* 50 (1866): 42; "Meeting at Dr. Palmer's," *ZH*, Aug. 15, 1872, p. 387; and *BH* 8 (1857): 112–13. Of course, some of the details changed over the years. For example, by the 1870s the meeting began at 2:30. The essence of the meeting, however, remained the same.
5. See note 4 above.
6. *PF*, pp. 226–27.
7. Ibid., p. 235.
8. Ibid.
9. *WOH*, p. 95; *GTH* 53 (1868): 158.
10. *TM1*, pp. 58, 149; Amanda Smith, *An Autobiography: The Story of the Lord's Dealings with Mrs. Amanda Smith, the Colored Evangelist*, introduction by Bishop Thoburn of India (Chicago: Meyer and Bros., 1893), pp. 119, 139, 193. William Taylor was Methodist bishop for Africa.
11. John A. Roche, "Mrs. Phoebe Palmer," *LR* 26 (1866): 69; *GTH* 48 (1865): 156.
12. *PF*, p. 235.
13. *GTH* 50 (1866): 42 (G. W. Woodruff).
14. *PF*, pp. 234–35.
15. *WOH*, pp. 215–17.
16. *GTH* 66 (1874): 135–36.
17. Melvin Easterday Dieter, *The Holiness Revival of the Nineteenth Century*, Studies in Evangelicalism, no. 1 (Metuchen, N.J.: Scarecrow, 1980), pp. 98–112; John L. Peters, *Christian Perfection and American Methodism* (New York: Abingdon, 1956), pp. 134–50. Also see chap. 4.
18. The first three appendices give a partial list of the places in which Mrs. Palmer spoke in such services.
19. See William G. McLoughlin, *Modern Revivalism: Charles Grandison Finney to Billy Graham* (New York: Ronald Press, 1959), p. 11; Richard Carwardine, "The Second Great Awakening in the Urban Centers: An Examination of Methodism and the New Measures," *Journal of American History* 59/2 (September 1972): 327–40; and *Transatlantic Revivalism: Popular Evangelicalism in Britain and America, 1790–1865*, Contributions in American History, no. 75 (Westport, Conn.: Greenwood, 1978), pp. 4–18.

20. Wesley, "On Working Out Our Own Salvation," in *J. W. Works*, 6:508-9.
21. *GTH* 32 (1857): 177; 42 (1862): 178; 46 (1864): 61.
22. *GTH* 32 (1857): 177; *GTH* 54 (1868): 28.
23. *GTH* 58 (1870): 87.
24. *BH* 6 (1855): 343.
25. *II*, pp. 198-99.
26. *FY*, pp. 321-28, 395-416. These incidents are narrated in chap. 3.
27. *PF*, pp. 158, 172; *F&E*, pp. 195-201.
28. John Wesley to Robert Carr Brackenbury, Sept. 15, 1790, in *J. W. Letters*, 8:238.
29. Thomas Ware, *Sketches of the Life and Travels of Rev. Thomas Ware*, quoted in Frederick A. Norwood, ed., *Sourcebook of American Methodism* (Nashville: Abingdon, 1982), p. 97.
30. Peters has argued that the frontier preachers concentrated on the preaching of justification to the relative neglect of the preaching of sanctification. While he is right in this contention, Coppedge and Smith have shown that some elements of Peters' case are overstated. They show that holiness was preached in all sections of Methodism around the turn of the nineteenth century. See Allan Coppedge, "Entire Sanctification in Early American Methodism: 1812-1835," *Wesleyan Theological Journal* 13 (Spring 1978): 34-50; and Timothy Smith, "The Transfer of Wesleyan Religious Culture from England to America," *Historical Bulletin of the World Methodist Historical Society* 14 (First Quarter 1985): 6-9.
31. Tobias Spicer [An Observer], "Preaching at Camp-Meetings," *CA&J*, Oct. 18, 1855, p. 168.
32. Phoebe Palmer, "Preaching At Camp-Meetings," *CA&J*, Nov. 1, 1855, p. 173.
33. *WOH*, 246; *II*, pp. 25-29.
34. *II*, pp. 84-85, 97-99. Mrs. Palmer may have borrowed the image of clogged chariot wheels from Finney. The King James Version of this passage says that the Lord "took off" chariot wheels of the Egyptians. Neither Wesley nor Clarke spoke of the wheels being clogged, but Finney once preached that a misunderstanding of the human mind by Luther and Calvin had "to the present day clogged the chariot wheels of mercy." Whether Mrs. Palmer knew of this sermon or whether the image was in common use, I have not been able to determine. See Charles G. Finney, "The New Heart" in *Sermons on Various Subjects* (New York: n.p., 1835), p. 60, quoted in McLoughlin, *Modern Revivalism*, p. 69. See also John Wesley, *Explanatory Notes Upon the Old Testament*, 4 vols. (Bristol: William Pine, 1765), 1:244; and Adam Clarke, *The Holy Bible, Containing the Old and New Testaments. The Text Carefully Printed from the Most Correct Copies of the Present Authorized Translation, Including the Marginal Readings and Parallel Texts; With a Commentary and Critical Notes; Designed as a Help to a Better Understanding of the Sacred Writings*, 6 vols. (New York: T. Mason and G. Lane for the Methodist Episcopal Church, 1837), 1:369-70.
35. *F&E*, p. 205.
36. *GTH* 24 (1853): 79-80; 52 (1867): 120.
37. Frederick Norwood entitles his chapter about the first Methodists in America "Lay Beginnings." See Frederick A. Norwood, *The Story of American Methodism* (Nashville: Abingdon, 1974), pp. 61-69.

38. *II*, p. 120. See chaps. 1 and 2.
39. *GTH* 33 (1858): 67.
40. *II*, pp. 167, 192, 211–17, 229–35, 246, 317.
41. Mrs. Palmer makes these points either explicitly or by implication in a song, "Away to the Field," printed in *GTH* 61 (1872): 68.
42. *II*, p. 62. Mrs. Palmer cites Acts 10 as evidence that angels cannot be evangelists. In that story the angel does not communicate the gospel to Cornelius, but tells him to send for Peter who will explain the Good News to him. From this story she extrapolates that no angel can be an evangelist.
43. *GTH* 49 (1866): 29.
44. *GTH* 51 (1867): 94.
45. *II*, p. 201.
46. *F&E*, p. 57; *GTH* 50 (1866): 151.
47. *F&E*, p. 57; *GTH* 24 (1853): 80.
48. *F&E*, p. 57.
49. *GTH* 46 (1864): 92.
50. *F&E*, p. 334.
51. *II*, p. 220.
52. *PG*, p. 32.
53. *GTH* 33 (1858): 65.
54. *FY*, pp. 176–77.
55. *GTH* 33 (1858): 65; 44 (1863): 51.
56. From the extant sources it is impossible to tell which of the revival practices the Palmers followed originated with Phoebe and which originated with Walter. Perhaps with a husband and wife team who worked as closely as the Palmers, it is impossible to determine who contributed which idea. In the following sections I will attribute all of the ideas behind the revival practices to Mrs. Palmer because she is the one who described what they did and the thinking behind their practices.
57. See chap. 3.
58. *GTH* 51 (1867): 94.
59. *WOH*, p. 219; *PG*, p. 38.
60. *F&E*, p. 275. For instances of general criticism of ministers see *SLP*, p. 125; *II*, pp. 76, 277; *FY*, pp. 20–21.
61. *GTH* 51 (1867): 30; *PF*, p. 298.
62. Phoebe Palmer [More Anon], "A Laity for the Times," *CA&J*, Feb. 26, 1857, p. 33; *GTH* 54 (1868): 152.
63. See the accounts of Newcastle and Madely (Madeley) in chap. 3.
64. *GTH* 51 (1867): 94–95.
65. Ibid., 122.
66. *GTH* 44 (1863): 162–63 (G. Hughes); 59 (1871): 154.
67. *BH* 12 (1861): 116.
68. *TM1*, p. 100.
69. *GTH* 29 (1856): 155.
70. *GTH* 56 (1869): 125 (E. Jones).
71. Roche, "Mrs. Phoebe Palmer," p. 67.
72. Ibid.
73. *GTH* 55 (1869): 157; 57 (1870): 120.
74. *GTH* 54 (1868): 127.
75. *FY*, pp. 175–77. See chap. 3.

76. *II*, pp. 155-58.
77. *GTH* 55 (1869): 26, 58; 56 (1869): 28; 58 (1870): 55.
78. *GTH* 55 (1869): 29 (G. M. Pierce).
79. A. Lowery, "In Memorium Mrs. Phoebe Palmer," *Advocate of Holiness* 5/6 (December 1874): 37.
80. *GTH* 41 (1862): 39.
81. See chap. 5.
82. *GTH* 55 (1869): 90-91.
83. *GTH* 34 (1858): 175.
84. *GTH* 55 (1869): 107-8.
85. *GTH* 64 (1873): 24.
86. *GTH* 57 (1870): 95-96. See also *GTH* 30 (1856): 114; 33 (1858): 65; and *FY*, pp. 256-57.
87. *PG*, p. 27; *GTH* 51 (1867): 8; 61 (1872): 58.
88. *GTH* 47 (1865): 16.
89. *GTH* 41 (1862): 57; 49 (1866): 187.
90. *GTH* 34 (1858): 85.
91. Ibid.
92. *GTH* 44 (1863): 50-51.
93. Ibid.; *GTH* 53 (1868): 60; 55 (1869): 91.
94. *GTH* 51 (1867): 95.
95. *GTH* 47 (1865): 16; 51 (1867): 92.
96. *II*, pp. 364-65; *GTH* 6 (1844): 27-28. On Sept. 8, 1765, John Wesley recorded the story which Mrs. Palmer cites, the case of Grace Paddy who was converted and sanctified within twelve hours. See Wesley, *J. W. Journals*, 5:143-44.
97. *PG*, passim.
98. *FY*, pp. 363-64.
99. *GTH* 57 (1870): 90; 63 (1873): 121.
100. *GTH* 54 (1868): 127-28; John Wesley reported the case of a twelve-year-old girl whom he believed to be entirely sanctified. See John Wesley to Ann Foard, Oct. 12, 1764, in *J. W. Letters*, 4:268.
101. *GTH* 58 (1870): 153-56.
102. George Croft Cell, *The Rediscovery of John Wesley* (New York: Henry Holt and Co., 1935; reprint, Lanham, Md.: University Press of America, 1983), pp. 341-42.
103. Ibid.
104. Peters, *Christian Perfection*, pp. 92-100. Peters quotes Bangs but does not cite his source. I have not been able to locate it. Note also that Peter Cartwright, prince of the circuit riders, often speaks of people getting saved, but rarely, if ever, speaks of them experiencing sanctification. See Cartwright, *The Autobiography of Peter Cartwright*, ed. by W. P. Strickland (New York: Methodist Book Concern, n.d.), passim.
105. Richard F. Lovelace, *Dynamics of Spiritual Life: An Evangelical Theology of Renewal* (Downers Grove, Ill.: InterVarsity, 1979), pp. 232-35.
106. Ibid.
107. McLoughlin, *Modern Revivalism*, pp. 147-48.
108. Finney, "The New Heart," cited in McLoughlin, *Modern Revivalism*, pp. 69-70.

109. McLoughlin, *Modern Revivalism*, p. 147, quotes this statement from an issue of the *New York Evangelist*, published sometime in the autumn of 1836 but gives no further information.

110. Finney, *Oberlin Evangelist*, Jan. 30, 1842, pp. 25-26, quoted in McLoughlin, *Modern Revivalism*, p. 148.

111. Mrs. Palmer printed a letter to this effect from John Wesley to Thomas Rankin, July 21, 1744, in *GTH* 63 (1873): 139. The letter appears in *J. W. Letters*, 6:103. In earlier years she had also quoted Wesley to this effect. See *GTH* 38 (1860): 86; 55 (1869): 158; and 56 (1869): 147.

112. John Wesley had established this as the only criterion for joining the Methodist societies. Remaining in the society, however, required a strict adherence to the rules he established. See Wesley, *The Nature, Design, and General Rules of the United Societies in London, Bristol, Kingswood, Newcastle-Upon-Tyne, &c.*, in *J. W. Works*, 8:270.

113. *Hamline*, p. 306.

114. *GTH* 61 (1872): 90.

115. *BH* 11 (1860): 300.

116. *WOH*, pp. 242-44; *II*, p. 25; *GTH* 14 (1848): 71.

117. Hiram Mattison, *An Answer to Dr. Perry's Reply to the Calm Review* (New York: Miller & Holman, 1856), p. 5.

118. See chap. 2 for an account of the controversy and chap. 5 for an evaluation of it.

119. Hiram Mattison, *Thoughts on Entire Sanctification* (New York: Lane & Scott, 1852), pp. 5, 20.

120. Ibid., p. 20; John Wesley, *A Plain Account of Christian Perfection*, in *J. W. Works*, 11:387.

121. Mattison, *Entire Sanctification*, p. 5.

122. See chap. 1.

123. *F&E*, pp. 124-27; *GTH* 60 (1871): 123.

124. *II*, p. 182.

125. *PF*, p. 199.

126. *GTH* 54 (1868): 126; 55 (1869): 58.

127. Mattison, *Entire Sanctification*, p. 5.

128. See chap. 2.

129. For the Great Awakening see Alan Heimert and Perry Miller, *The Great Awakening: Documents Illustrative of the Crisis and its Consequences*, The American Heritage series, no. 34 (Indianapolis: Bobbs Merrill, 1967). For later revivals see McLoughlin, *Modern Revivalism*, and Bernard A. Weisberger, *They Gathered at the River: The Story of the Great Revivalists and their Impact on America* (Boston: Little, Brown and Co., 1958).

130. Charles G. Finney, *Revival Lectures* (Old Tappan, N.J.: Revell, n.d.), pp. 250-79. One should not get the impression that Finney's exhortation went unheeded. Rosenberg has pointed out that under Finney's preaching in New York the number of lay-people who volunteered as tract distributers and lay evangelists jumped from fifty to five hundred in one year. See Carol Smith Rosenberg, *Religion and the Rise of the American City; The New York City Mission Movement, 1812-1870* (Ithaca, N.Y.: Cornell University Press, 1971), pp. 88-89.

131. McLoughlin, *Modern Revivalism*, pp. 122, 166.

132. Charles Grandison Finney. *Charles G. Finney: An Autobiography* (Old Tappan, N.J.: Revell, n.d.), p. 289.

298   THE BEAUTY OF HOLINESS

133. George Othell Hand, "Changing Emphases in American Evangelism from Colonial Times to the Present," Th.D. thesis, Southern Baptist Theological Seminary, Louisville, 1949, p. 29.
134. McLoughlin, *Modern Revivalism*, p. 166.

CHAPTER SEVEN

1. Phoebe Palmer to Bishop and Mrs. Hamline, Nov. 8, 1855, *LL*, pp. 495–96. Unfortunately, Mrs. Palmer never reveals whether Dr. Butler ever was sanctified.
2. The word "feminist" is a protean term. Here it will be used to designate one who asserts that women have rights, abilities, and obligations denied by the prevailing male culture. This chapter will argue that Mrs. Palmer was a feminist in this sense of the term.
3. Barbara Berg has argued that women were needed in colonial days to help tame the frontier. With the turn of the nineteenth century and the growth of urban life, women were less economically necessary and men felt more insecure. The male response to this crisis was to evolve the "Woman-Belle Ideal," an ideology that told women they were weak, irrational, religious, and fit only for home life. Working-class women were ignored by this ideology, and middle- and upper-class women became idle adornments, "butterflies in amber." See Barbara J. Berg, *The Remembered Gate: Origins of American Feminism* (New York: Oxford University Press, 1978), pp. 11–110.
4. Susanna Wesley to Samuel Wesley, Feb. 6, 1712, and Feb. 25, 1712, reproduced in Adam Clarke, *Memoirs of the Wesley Family; Collected Principally from Original Documents*, 2d ed., George Peck, ed. (New York: Lane & Tippett, 1848; reprint, South Bend, Ind.: World Harvest, n.d.), pp. 387–91. Clarke says his source is Dr. Whitehead who transcribed the letters from the manuscripts. Whitehead's work is John Whitehead, *The Life of the Rev. Mr. John Wesley, M.A.* (London: Stephen Couchman, 1793; Boston: Dow and Jackson, 1845). Howard Snyder, *The Radical Wesley and Patterns for Church Renewal* (Downers Grove, Ill.: InterVarsity, 1980), p. 169, is the source of this bibliographic information.
5. John Wesley to Thomas Whitehead(?), Feb. 10, 1748, in *J. W. Letters*, 2:119–20.
6. John Wesley to Sarah Crosby, Feb. 14, 1761, and Mar. 18, 1769, in *J. W. Letters*, 4:132–33; 5:130–31.
7. John Wesley to Mary Bosanquet, June 13, 1771, in *J. W. Letters*, 5:257. See also the discussion of the evolution of John Wesley's position in Earl Kent Brown, *Women of Mr. Wesley's Methodism*, Studies in Women and Religion, vol. 11 (New York: Edwin Mellen, 1983), pp. 25–28.
8. Brown, *Women*, pp. 15–25.
9. Diary, Oct. 24, 1848, *GTH* 81 (1882): 43.
10. *PF*, p. v.
11. Ibid., pp. v–vi.
12. Ibid., p. 328.
13. Ibid., pp. 1–5.
14. Ibid., pp. 5–7, 47.
15. Ibid., pp. 7–9, 48–49.
16. Ibid., pp. 8–9.

17. Ibid., pp. 14–26. Nancy Hardesty examines Phoebe Palmer's argument that women should speak because they are prophets in "Minister as Prophet? Or as Mother?" in *Women in New Worlds*, pp. 88–101, ed. by Hilah F. Thomas and Rosemary Skinner Keller, vol. 1 (Nashville: Abingdon, 1981).

18. *PF*, pp. 30–33.
19. Ibid., p. 36.
20. Ibid., pp. 42–43.
21. Ibid., p. 36.
22. Ibid., pp. 26–110. See chap. 5 for an identification of these individuals.
23. For Mrs. Wesley, see *PF*, pp. 57–58; for Mrs. Fletcher, see pp. 11, 101–8; for Mrs. Taft, see pp. 71–87; for Mrs. Boyce, see pp. 115–18; for Mrs. Crosby, see pp. 119–25; and for Sarah Lawrence, see pp. 131–38. For more information on each of these women see Brown, *Women*, passim.
24. *PF*, p. ix.
25. *GTH* 53 (1868): 122.
26. *GTH* 49 (1866): 187.
27. *GTH* 78 (1880): 75 (R. J. Andrews).
28. *PF*, pp. 1, 13.
29. Diary, June 15, 1857, *LL*, pp. 156–57.
30. Diary, June 6, 1848, *LL*, p. 156. Wheatley gives several other diary entries in the next few pages to illustrate Mrs. Palmer's hospitality and domestic responsibilities.
31. *GTH* 53 (1868): 5.
32. *WOH*, p. 92. I have not been able to trace the hymn from which this verse comes.
33. Ibid.
34. Ibid., pp. 91–93.
35. Diary, Sept. 11, 1837, *LL*, p. 47.
36. *GTH* 9 (1846): 137.
37. Ibid.
38. *GTH* 53 (1868): 153.
39. *GTH* 9 (1846): 137. Mrs. Palmer does not mention Mr. Samuel Wesley's faults as a husband and father but rather assumes her readers will be familiar with them. For his financial difficulties, see Samuel Wesley to John Sharp, Archbishop of York, Dec. 30, 1700, printed in Adam Clarke, *Wesley Family*, p. 159. For Susanna's opinion of her husband as a disciplinarian, see Susanna Wesley to John Wesley, July 24, 1732, recorded on Aug. 1, 1742, in *J. W. Journals*, 3:38. Mrs. Wesley only says that "one" did not follow her method of dealing mildly with penitent children.
40. *PF*, p. 345.
41. *GTH* 53 (1868): 153.
42. *Hamline*, p. 136.
43. *GTH* 9 (1846): 136–37.
44. See chap. 1.
45. *GTH* 50 (1866): 45.
46. *F&E*, p. 333; *WOH*, pp. 266–67.
47. *F&E*, pp. 116–17.
48. Ibid.
49. *II*, pp. 271–72.

50. Ibid.; *WOH*, pp. 266-68.
51. *II*, pp. 271-74.
52. Ibid., pp. 275-88.
53. *Hamline*, pp. 141, 261.
54. Young Phoebe wrote the music for her mother's hymn, "The Cleansing Wave," *GTH* 59 (1871): 192. See Diary (?), Jan. 1859; Phoebe Palmer to Joseph and Phoebe Knapp, June 17, 1855; Diary, Dec. 19, 1871; and Phoebe Palmer to Mrs. Hamline, Feb. 27, 1873, all in *LL*, pp. 146-47, 167-68. Also see chap. 4.
55. *WOH*, p. 87.
56. *GTH* 50 (1866): 45.
57. *II*, p. 273.
58. Diary(?), *LL*, p. 598.
59. *WOH*, pp. 161-66.
60. Ibid.; Diary, June 15, 1857, *LL*, pp. 156-57.
61. Diary, 1849, *LL*, pp. 597-98.
62. The only mention of boarding school is when the Palmers sent the Jewish boy they adopted away to school. Walter, Jr., was a teenager then, and perhaps sending sons away to school was a family practice. See Phoebe Palmer to Mrs. Hamline, Aug. 5, 1856, *LL*, pp. 213-14, as well as chap. 2.
63. See chaps. 2 and 4.
64. See chaps. 3, 4, and 6.
65. Barbara Heck was the woman who upon finding some Methodists playing cards called on Philip Embury to preach to them lest they all be damned. This action led to the formation of the first Methodist society in New York. See J. B. Wakely, *Lost Chapters Recovered from the Early History of American Methodism* (New York: printed for the author, 1858), p. 35. For British Methodism, see Brown, *Women*, pp. xv-xvi. See also chap. 2.
66. See Maggie Newton Van Cott, *The Harvest & The Reaper*, introduction by Gilbert Haven (New York: N. Tibbals & Sons, 1876). This work shows that Mrs. Van Cott was active in the Five Points Mission during the same years that Mrs. Palmer was, but it does not even mention her.
67. Nancy Ann Hardesty, " 'Your Daughters Shall Prophesy': Revivalism and Feminism in the Age of Finney," Ph.D. diss., The University of Chicago, 1976, p. 203.
68. See for example Donald W. Dayton, *Discovering An Evangelical Heritage* (New York: Harper & Row, 1976); Donald W. Dayton and Lucille S. Dayton, " 'Your Daughters Shall Prophesy': Feminism in the Holiness Movement," *Methodist History* 14 (January 1976): 67-92; Donald W. Dayton, "Women as Preachers: Evangelical Precedents," *Christianity Today*, May 23, 1975, pp. 4-7; and Nancy Hardesty, Lucille Sider Dayton, and Donald W. Dayton, "Women in the Holiness Movement," in *Women of Spirit*, Rosemary Reuther and Eleanor McLaughlin, eds. (New York: Simon and Schuster, 1979), pp. 226-54.
69. Hardesty, " 'Your Daughters,' " passim.
70. Anne C. Loveland, "Domesticity and Religion in the Antebellum Period: The Career of Phoebe Palmer," *The Historian* 39 (May 1977): 455-71. See also Keith E. Melder, *Beginnings of Sisterhood: The American Woman's Rights Movement, 1800-1840*, Studies in the Life of Women (New York: Schocken Books, 1977).
71. Theodore Hovet, "Phoebe Palmer's 'Altar Phraseology' and the Spiritual Dimensions of Woman's Sphere," *The Journal of Religion* 63 (July

1983): 264–80. Hovet uses the term "altar phraseology" to refer to all of Mrs. Palmer's theology, as if everything she believed from sanctification to domestic relations could be summed up by it. As we have seen, her altar phraseology is an important part, but only a part of her thought.

72. Ibid., pp. 267–70.
73. Ibid. The labels "Pelagius" and "protoexistentialist" are mine, but the concepts are Hovet's.
74. Wesley, "On Working Out Our Own Salvation," in *J. W. Works*, 6:509.
75. *WOH*, pp. 18–19, 21.
76. Ibid.
77. *F&E*, p. 144. Emphasis original.
78. Wesley, "On Working Out Our Own Salvation," in *J. W. Works*, 6:508–9.
79. *WOH*, pp. 19, 32. Note that here "ability" is not natural ability but a gift from God.
80. *F&E*, p. 38. Emphasis original.
81. *WOH*, p. 39.
82. Ibid., p. 19; *ED*, pp. 7–8; *FY*, p. 184; *II*, pp. 134, 174; *F&E*, p. 89. See also chap. 5.
83. *GTH* 54 (1868): 126.
84. *WOH*, p. 185; *GTH* 33 (1858): 39; *PF*, passim.
85. *GTH* 55 (1869): 24; *II*, pp. 124–30. See chap. 5.
86. Hovet, "Phoebe Palmer's 'Altar Phraseology,'" p. 275.
87. Ibid., p. 279.
88. *GTH* 66 (1874): 109.
89. William Butterfield to Phoebe Palmer, n.d., but between 1849 and 1851 in *Letters*. Butterfield had written many letters to Mrs. Palmer describing his spiritual condition. She evidently had told him to quit worrying about himself and begin to serve others, because he wrote, "I am following your advice. I am visiting daily a poor sick penitent shoemaker."
90. *II*, p. 134; *GTH* 33 (1858): 65; 53 (1868): 5.
91. John Wesley to James Hervey, Mar. 20, 1739, in *J. W. Letters*, 1:286.
92. *GTH* 55 (1868): 24.
93. Hovet, "Phoebe Palmer's 'Altar Phraseology,'" p. 274.
94. *GTH* 52 (1867): 120.
95. Alice S. Rossi, ed., *The Feminist Papers from Adams to de Beauvoir* (New York: Bantam, 1973), pp. 3–6; Hardesty, "'Your Daughters,'" p. 2.

CHAPTER EIGHT

1. Francis J. Grund, *Aristocracy in America*, 1:146, quoted in Barbara J. Berg, *The Remembered Gate: Origins of American Feminism* (New York: Oxford University Press, 1978), p. 99.
2. Berg, *Remembered Gate*, pp. 95–110; *GTH* 29 (1856): 155.
3. *ED*, p. 55.
4. *II*, pp. 210–11.
5. Ibid., p. 211.
6. Ibid., p. 377.

7. Ibid., p. 218.
8. Ibid.
9. New York Female Assistance Society, For the Relief and Religious Instruction of the Sick Poor, *Thirty-eighth Annual Report* (New York: S. W. Benedict, 1851), p. 5.
10. Diary, Jan. 9, 1868, *LL*, p. 132. Wesley compares himself to a flying arrow in his "Preface to the Sermons" printed in John Wesley, *Wesley's Standard Sermons*, ed. by Edward H. Sugden, 2 vols. (London: Epworth, 1951; reprint, Grand Rapids: Zondervan, 1986), 1:31.
11. Phoebe Palmer to unidentified, 1838, *LL*, p. 133.
12. *GTH* 49 (1866): 12.
13. Phoebe Palmer to unidentified, 1838, *LL*, p. 133.
14. *GTH* 65 (1874): 89.
15. *PG*, p. 35.
16. *ED*, p. 28. Exodus 28:36 describes the high priest as wearing a small gold plate on the front of his turban with the inscription "HOLINESS TO THE LORD."
17. *F&E*, p. 214.
18. Ibid.; H. W. Palmer, "Palmer Families in America," typescript, New England Historical Genealogical Society, Boston, vol. 2, pt. 2, p. 840.
19. *F&E*, pp. 216–18.
20. *WOH*, p. 172.
21. Ibid.
22. *F&E*, p. 214.
23. Ibid.
24. Ibid., pp. 222–24; *PG*, p. 25.
25. *F&E*, pp. 223–24; *II*, p. 86.
26. *GTH* 64 (1873): 104.
27. *GTH* 84 (1883): 71 (SLP); Phoebe Palmer to Mrs. Hamline, Dec. 10, 1870, *LL*, pp. 150–52; *TM1*, p. 37.
28. *GTH* 65 (1874): 119.
29. *F&E*, pp. 222–24; *TM2*, p. 179.
30. We know that during the time this passage was probably written, between 1848 and 1855, the Palmers were supporting both Hedding, or Seventeenth Street Church, and the Norfolk Street Church. Mrs. Palmer's use of the word "most," however, implies more than two. If Mrs. Palmer is speaking strictly, this comment reveals that they visited and supported other struggling churches without leaving any historical record of their efforts. See chap. 2.
31. *II*, pp. 85–87. The last quotation is a paraphrase of Mrs. Palmer's words.
32. *F&E*, p. 222.
33. Ibid., p. 221.
34. *GTH* 54 (1868): 152.
35. *II*, pp. 259–61.
36. Ibid., pp. 261–63.
37. Ibid., p. 379.
38. *BH* 11 (1860): 233.
39. *GTH* 57 (1870): 78.
40. *FY*, pp. 224–25, 560, 586. See chap. 3.
41. Diary(?), *LL*, p. 598; *II*, p. 273. See chap. 7.

42. *GTH* 57 (1870): 79.
43. *FY*, p. 18. See chap. 3.
44. *F&E*, p. 328.
45. *WOH*, pp. 51, 258-63.
46. *GTH* 4 (1842-43): 106-7. See also *WOH*, pp. 24, 45, 56.
47. Diary, Feb. 15, 1849, *GTH* 82 (1882): 169.
48. *GTH* 66 (1874): 84.
49. Phoebe Palmer to Mrs. Hamline, Mar. 30, 1867, *LL*, pp. 439-40.
50. *GTH* 60 (1871): 121.
51. See chap. 2.
52. *GTH* 68 (1875): 125; 66 (1874): 42-43; Ladies of the Mission, *The Old Brewery and the New Mission House of the Five Points* (New York: Stringer and Townsend, 1854),pp. 21, 55; Phoebe Palmer to Joseph Hartwell, Feb. 17, 1853, *LL*, pp. 224-25. See chap. 2.
53. Carol Smith Rosenberg, *Religion and the Rise of the American City: The New York City Mission Movement, 1812-1870* (Ithaca, N.Y.: Cornell University Press, 1971), pp. 15-29.
54. Ibid., pp. 32-36; LHMS, *Thirty-second Annual Report* (New York: C. Hyllested, Jr., 1876), p. 7.
55. Rosenberg, *Religion*, pp. 32-36.
56. Ladies of the Mission, *Old Brewery, New Mission* p. 48.
57. Rosenberg, *Religion*, p. 37.
58. Ibid., p. 43; Raymond Mohl, *Poverty in New York 1783-1825* (New York: Oxford University Press, 1971), p. 159.
59. Mohl, *Poverty*, pp. 151-52.
60. Ibid., pp. 159-69.
61. Rosenberg, *Religion*, pp. 3, 37-69. Rosenberg does not mention Methodism. Her excellent work is hindered by a concentration on the Reformed tradition. She has followed McLoughlin and seems not even to know of the existence of what was then the nation's fastest-growing denomination.
62. Ibid., pp. 8, 37-41.
63. Ibid., p. 70.
64. Diary, Mar. 4, 1844; Sept. 17 [no year given]; [no day or month given] 1846, all in *LL*, pp. 208-12. See chap. 2.
65. Female Assistance Society, *Twenty-third Annual Report* (New York: Howe & Bates, 1836), passim; Mohl, *Poverty*, pp. 148-50.
66. See chap. 2.
67. *LL*, p. 224.
68. Ladies of the Mission, *Old Brewery, New Mission*, pp. 36-38; "The Five Points House of Industry," *American Church Monthly* 3 (1858): 215-16.
69. Ladies of the Mission, *Old Brewery, New Mission*, p. 39; "Five Points House of Industry," pp. 218-20.
70. "Five Points House of Industry," pp. 220-22.
71. Ibid.
72. Rosenberg, *Religion*, pp. 231-32. Fourier was a nineteenth-century French utopian socialist.
73. Ladies of the Mission, *Old Brewery, New Mission*, p. 41.
74. Henry J. Cammann, and Hugh N. Camp, *The Charities of New York, Brooklin, and Statin Island* (New York: Hurd and Houghton, 1868), pp. 350-51; Matthew Simpson, ed., *Cyclopedia of Methodism*, rev. ed. (Philadelphia: Louis H. Everts, 1880), p. 679.

75. Ladies of the Mission, *Old Brewery, New Mission*, pp. 41–72.
76. Ibid., p. 80.
77. LHMS, *Thirty-second Annual Report*, pp. 10–11.
78. "The Five Points Mission," in *CA&J*, June 30, 1853, p. 193 [103]; Nov. 17, 1853, p. 181(?); Dec. 8, 1853, p. 193.
79. *The American Christian Record: Containing the History, Confession of Faith, and Statistics of Each Religious Denomination in the United States and Europe; A List of All Clergymen with their Post Office Addresses, Etc., Etc., Etc.* (New York: W. R. C. Clark & Meeker, 1860; Microfilm, Ann Arbor: University Microfilms, 1976; Religion in America Series, reel 2:3), p. 380.
80. "The Five Points Mission," *CA&J*, Dec. 8, 1853, p. 194; Lewis E. Jackson, *Gospel Work in New York City; a Memorial of Fifty Years in City Missions* (New York: New York City Mission, 1878), pp. 127–28. Jackson's report does not indicate the exact years to which he refers when giving the death statistics. The latter figure is an estimate; Jackson simply says that only one death was reported in twenty families. If each family consists of five persons this produces a death rate of ten per thousand.
81. Ladies of the Mission, *Old Brewery, New Mission*, pp. 76–79; "The Five Points Mission," *CA&J*, May 13, 1869, p. 148.
82. Rosenberg, *Religion*, pp. 240–42; "The Five Points Mission," *CA&J*, Oct. 13, 1853, p. 162.
83. "The Five Points Mission," *CA&J*, Oct. 13, 1853, p. 162.
84. "The Five Points Mission," *CA&J*, Dec. 8, 1853, p. 193.
85. "The Five Points Mission," *CA&J*, May 13, 1869, p. 148.
86. Lewis E. Jackson, *Walks about New York. Facts and Figures Gathered From Various Sources* (New York: New York City Mission and Tract Society, 1865), pp. 10–11.
87. "The Five Points Mission," *CA&J*, May 13, 1869, p. 148.
88. "Fragments," *CA&J*, Apr. 22, 1869, p. 124.
89. LHMS, *Thirty-second Annual Report*, pp. 6–11.
90. Cammann and Camp, *Charities*, p. 349; LHMS, *Ninth Annual Report* (New York: Printed at the Conference Office, 1853), p. 3.
91. "The Five Points Mission," *CA&J*, Oct. 13, 1853, p. 162.
92. See *Voice of the Old Brewery* 1/1 (Jan. 1861): 1; 4/6 (June 1864): 24.
93. *LL*, pp. 218–27.
94. *Voice of the Old Brewery* 4/7 (July 1864) does not list Mrs. Palmer as an officer of the Ladies' Home Missionary Society.
95. Cammann and Camp, *Charities*, p. 355.
96. *GTH* 41 (1862): 40. See also chap. 3.
97. *GTH* 65 (1874): 90, 183; 66 (1874): 23.
98. See chap. 2.
99. "Ode for the Fourth of July," *MG*, pp. 208–9.
100. Benson Howard Roberts, comp., *Holiness Teachings Compiled from the Editorial Writings of the Late Rev. Benjamin Titus Roberts* (North Chili, N.Y.: "The Earnest Christian" Publishing House, 1893; reprint, Salem, Ohio: Schmul, 1983), p. 16.
101. *WOH*, pp. 224–25.
102. Phoebe Palmer to Sarah Lankford, Sept. 29, 1862, *GTH* 42 (1862): 184; 47 (1865): 40–41.
103. Rosenberg, *Religion*, pp. 44–69, 186–224.

104. Mohl, *Poverty*, pp. 190–209, 259–65.

105. Timothy L. Smith, *Revivalism and Social Reform: American Protestantism on the Eve of the Civil War* (Nashville: Abingdon, 1957; reprint with a new afterword by the author, Baltimore: Johns Hopkins University Press, 1980), pp. 163–77; Donald W. Dayton, *Discovering An Evangelical Heritage* (New York: Harper & Row, 1976), pp. 99–119; Norris Magnuson, *Salvation in the Slums: Evangelical Social Work, 1865–1920*, ATLA Monograph Series, no. 10 (Metuchen, N.J.: Scarecrow, and The American Theological Library Association, 1977), pp. ix–xvi.

106. Charles H. Hopkins, *The Rise of the Social Gospel in American Protestantism, 1865–1900*, Yale Studies in Religious Education, no. 14 (New Haven: Yale University Press, 1940), pp. 4–23; Henry F. May, *Protestant Churches and Industrial America*, new introduction by the author (New York: Harper & Row, 1967), pp. 3–36; Charles C. Cole, Jr., *The Social Ideas of the Northern Evangelists, 1826–1860* (New York: Octagon, 1966), p. 130.

107. Magnuson, *Salvation*, pp. 2–3.

108. Ibid., pp. 9–13.

109. Jane Addams, *Twenty Years at Hull-House with Autobiographical Notes* (New York: Macmillan, 1951), pp. 89–127.

CONCLUSION

1. Martin Luther, *Selected Writings of Martin Luther*, ed. Theodore G. Tappert, vol. 2: *The Freedom of a Christian*, trans. W. A. Lambert, rev. Harold J. Grimm (Philadelphia: Fortress, 1967), pp. 37–43.

2. *GTH* 33 (1858): 11.

3. R. Pearsall Smith to Walter Palmer, Mar. 3, 1875, *GTH* 67 (1875): 144.

Primary Bibliography

Palmer Manuscripts

Palmer, Phoebe. Letter to Bishop and Mrs. H[amline], November 9, 1855. Library of Congress Manuscript Collection, Washington, D.C.
Palmer, Phoebe, and Walter C. Palmer. Letter to Gersham F. Cox, January 29, 1844. New England Methodist Historical Society Collection, Boston.
Palmer, Phoebe, and Walter C. Palmer. Letters to Stephen M. Olin. Olin Manuscript Collection. Wesleyan University, Middletown, Conn.

Palmer Publications

Boynton, J. *Sanctification Practical: A Book for the Times.* New York: Foster & Palmer, Jr., 1867.
New York Female Assistance Society, For the Relief and Religious Instruction of the Sick Poor. *Annual Report*, nos. 19–83, 1832–96 (series incomplete).
Palmer, Phoebe. *Entire Devotion to God.* 14th ed. Originally published as *Present to My Christian Friend on Entire Devotion to God.* New York: n.p., 1853. Reprint. Salem, Ohio: Schmul Publishers, 1979.
———. *Faith and Its Effects: or, Fragments from my Portfolio.* New York: Joseph Longking, Printer, 1852.
———. *Four Years in the Old World: Comprising the Travels, Incidents, and Evangelistic Labors of Dr. and Mrs. Walter Palmer in England, Ireland, Scotland, and Wales.* 3d ed. New York: Foster & Palmer, Jr., 1866.
———. *Full Salvation; Its Doctrines and Duties.* English ed. of *Incidental Illustrations.* Reprint. Salem, Ohio: Schmul Publishers, 1979.
———. *Holiness to the Lord.* New York: MacDonald & Palmer, n.d.
———. *Incidental Illustrations of the Economy of Salvation, Its Doctrines and Duties.* New York: Foster & Palmer, Jr., 1855.
———. *Israel's Speedy Restoration and Conversion Contemplated: or, Signs of the Times.* New York: John A. Gray, 1854.
———. *A Mother's Gift; or, A Wreath for my Darlings.* Introduction by Edmund S. Janes. New York: Walter C. Palmer, Jr., 1875.
———. *Mary; or, The Young Christian.* New York: Carlton & Porter, 1840.
———. *The Parting Gift to Fellow Laborers and Young Converts.* New York: Walter C. Palmer, 1869.
———. *Promise of the Father; or, A Neglected Speciality of the Last Days.* Boston: H. V. Degen, 1859. Reprint. Salem, Ohio: Schmul Publishers, 1981.
———. *Recollections and Gathered Fragments of Mrs. Lydia N. Cox of Williamsburg, L.I.* New York: Piercy and Reed, 1845.

———. *Some Account of the Recent Revival in the North of England and Glasgow.* Manchester: W. Bremner, 1860.

———. *Sweet Mary; or, A Bride Made Ready for her Lord.* London: Simpkin, Marshall, & Co., 1862.

———. *The Tongue of Fire on the Daughters of the Lord; or, Questions in Relation to the Duty of the Christian Church in Regard to the Privileges of her Female Membership.* New York: W. C. Palmer, Jr., 1869.

———. *The Useful Disciple; or, A Narrative of Mrs. Mary Gardner.* Cincinnati: Swormstedt & Poe, 1853.

———. *The Way of Holiness with Notes by the Way; Being A Narrative of Religious Experience Resulting from a Determination to be a Bible Christian.* 2d ed. New York: G. Lane & C. B. Tippett, 1845.

Palmer, Phoebe, ed. *Pioneer Experiences; or, The Gift of Power received by Faith.* Introduction by Edmund S. Janes. New York: W. C. Palmer, Jr., 1868.

Palmer, Walter C. *Life and Letters of Leonidas L. Hamline, D.D., Late one of the Bishops of the Methodist Episcopal Church.* Introductory letters by T. A. Morris, Edmund S. Janes, and E. Thompson. New York: Carlton & Porter, 1866.

Other Manuscripts

Budington, William Ives. Letter to Dr. Palmer, April 2, 1869. Budington Folder. Drew University Archives Manuscript Collection, Madison, N.J.

Fitch, Charles. Letter to Dr. and Mrs. Palmer, July 26, 1842. Charles Fitch Folder. Andrews University Heritage Room, Berrien Springs, Mich.

Methodist Episcopal Church Records Collection. Catalog nos. 138a–52, 156, 161, 168–72. Allen Street Methodist Episcopal Church. New York Public Library Manuscript Collection, New York.

Methodist Episcopal Church Records Collection. Catalog no. 335. Hedding M. E. Church, New York. New York Public Library Manuscript Collection, New York.

Methodist Episcopal Church Records Collection. Catalog nos. 460–61. Letters to Walter and Phoebe Palmer. New York Public Library Manuscript Collection, New York.

Palmer Folder. Letters to Walter and Phoebe Palmer and other manuscript and printed material. Drew University Archives Manuscript Collection, Madison, N.J.

Taylor, William. Letter to Dr. and Mrs. Palmer, January 25, 1867. Taylor Folder. Drew University Archives Manuscript Collection, Madison, N.J.

Other Publications

Abbott, Jacob J. "Boardman's Higher Christian Life." *Bibliotheca Sacra* 17 (1860): 508–34.

Addams, Jane. *Twenty Years at Hull-House with Autobiographical Notes.* New York: The Macmillan Company, 1951.

Arthur, William. *The Tongue of Fire; or the True Power of Christianity.* New York: Harper & Brothers, 1856.

Augustine, Bishop of Hippo. *On Christian Doctrine.*

Bangs, Nathan. *The Necessity, Nature, and Fruits, of Sanctification: in a Series of Letters to a Friend.* New York: Phillips & Hunt, 1851.
———. *The Present State, Prospects, and Responsibilities of the Methodist Episcopal Church.* New York: Lane & Scott, 1850.
Benson, Joseph. *The Life of the Rev. John W. de la Flechere: Compiled from the Narrative of Rev. Mr. Wesley; The Biographical Notes of Rev. Mr. Gilpin; From His Own Letters, and Other Authentic Documents, Many of Which Have Never Before Been Published.* New York: B. Waugh and T. Mason for the Methodist Episcopal Church, 1833.
Bridgeman, A. L. "A High Standard of Piety Demanded by the Times." *The Evangelical Review* 7 (1855): 364–76.
Cammann, Henry J., and Hugh N. Camp. *The Charities of New York, Brooklin, and Statin Island.* New York: Hurd and Houghton, 1868.
Cartwright, Peter. *The Autobiography of Peter Cartwright.* Edited by W. P. Strickland. New York: Methodist Book Concern, n.d.
Carvosso, William. *The Great Efficacy of Simple Faith in the Atonement of Christ Exemplified in a Memoir of Mr. William Carvosso, Sixty Years a Class Leader in the Wesleyan Methodist Connection.* Edited by [Benjamin Carvosso] from the 10th London ed. New York: Lane & Tippett for the Methodist Episcopal Church, 1847.
Caughey, James. *Arrows from My Quiver; Pointed with the Steel of Truth and Winged by Faith and Love.* Introduction by Daniel Wise. New York: W. C. Palmer, Jr., 1868.
———. *Earnest Christianity Illustrated; or, Selections from the Journal of the Rev. James Caughey.* Edited by Daniel Wise. 1st ed. Boston: J. P. Magee, 1855.
———. *Glimpses of Life in Soul-Saving; or, Selections from the Journal and Writings of the Rev. James Caughey.* Introduction by Daniel Wise. New York: W. C. Palmer, Jr., 1868.
———. *Helps to a Life of Holiness and Usefulness, or Revival Miscellanies: Containing Eleven Revival Sermons, and Thoughts on Entire Sanctification—Revival Preaching—Methods to Promote Revivals—Effects of Revival Efforts—Revivals and the Terrors of God—Revival Excitements—Revival Prayer-Meetings—Difficulties of Converts—Temptation—Infidelity—Affliction—Backsliding—Prayer—Ministerial Conflicts, Etc. Selected from the Works of The Rev. James Caughey, the Eminently Successful Revivalist.* Edited by Ralph W. Allen and Daniel Wise. Boston: James P. Magee, 1856.
———. *Light in the Dark, Through the Dominions of Unbelief.* New York: W. C. Palmer, Jr., 1868.
———. *Showers of Blessing From Clouds of Mercy; Selected from the Journal and Other Writings of the Rev. James Caughey; Containing Most Stirring Scenes and Incidents, During Great Revivals in Birmingham, Chesterfield, Macclesfield, and Other Places in England, Under His Ministry; Several of Mr. Caughey's Awakening Addresses and Sermons; Thoughts on Holiness; Notes of Personal Experience, and Observations upon Persons and Places Visited.* Boston: J. P. Magee, 1857.
———. *The Triumph of Truth, and Continental Letters and Sketches, from the Journal, Letters, and Sermons of the Rev. James Caughey, as Illustrated in Two Great Revivals in Nottingham and Lincoln, England; Containing Copius Extracts from Mr. Caughey's Journal and Letters—Several of His Awakening*

Discourses—Sermons on Sanctification—Letters on a Call to Preach—Call Defined—Encouraged—Consequences if Resisted—Directions to Paths of Usefulness—Observations on the Continent of Europe, &c. Introduction by Joseph Castle. Philadelphia: Higgins and Perkinpine, 1857.

Clarke, Adam. *Christian Theology.* Selected from his published and unpublished writings and systematically arranged: with a life of the author by Samuel Dunn. 2d ed. New York: Lane & Scott, 1851.

———. *The Holy Bible, Containing the Old and New Testaments. The Text Carefully Printed from the Most Correct Copies of the Present Authorized Translation, Including the Marginal Readings and Parallel Texts: With a Commentary and Critical Notes; Designed as a Help to a Better Understanding of the Sacred Writings.* 6 vols. New York: B. Waugh and T. Mason for the Methodist Episcopal Church, at the Conference Office, 1833.

———. *The Holy Bible, Containing the Old and New Testaments. The Text Carefully Printed from the Most Correct Copies of the Present Authorized Translation, Including the Marginal Readings and Parallel Texts: With a Commentary and Critical Notes; Designed as a Help to a Better Understanding of the Sacred Writings.* A new edition with the author's final corrections. 6 vols. New York: T. Mason and G. Lane for the Methodist Episcopal Church, 1837.

———. *Memoirs of the Wesley Family; Collected Principally from Original Documents.* 2d ed. Edited by George Peck. New York: Lane & Tippett, 1848. Reprint. South Bend, Ind.: World Harvest Press, n.d.

Dickens, Charles. *The Writings of Charles Dickens.* Edited by Edwin Percy Whipple et al. Vol. 11. *Martin Chuzzlewit and American Notes.* Boston: Houghton Mifflin Co., 1894.

Dunn, L. R. "Entire Sanctification." *Methodist Quarterly Review* (October 1867): 555–71.

Fairchild, James H. "The Doctrine of Sanctification at Oberlin." *The Congregational Quarterly* 70 (1876): 237–59.

Finney, Charles Grandison. *Charles G. Finney: An Autobiography.* Old Tappan, N.J.: Fleming H. Revell Company, n.d. Originally published as *Memoirs of Charles G. Finney.* New York: Trustees of Oberlin College, 1876.

———. *Revival Lectures.* Old Tappan, N.J.: Fleming H. Revell, n.d.

———. *Views of Sanctification.* Oberlin, Ohio: James Steele, 1840.

"Finney's Sermons on Sanctification and Mahan on Christian Perfection." *The Biblical Repertory and Princeton Review* 13 (1841): 231–49.

"The Five Points House of Industry." *American Church Monthly* 3 (1858): 209–22.

Fletcher, John. *The Works of the Reverend John Fletcher, Late Vicar of Madeley.* 4 vols. New York: Carlton & Porter, n.d.

Foster, Randolph Sinks. *Christian Purity; or, The Heritage of Faith.* New York: Carlton & Lanahan, 1870.

———. *Nature and Blessedness of Christian Purity.* New York: Lane & Scott, 1851.

Franklin, S. *A Critical Review of Wesleyan Perfection.* New York: Methodist Book Concern for the author, 1866.

Gorham, B. W. *Camp Meeting Manual.* Boston: H. V. Degen, 1854.

Hamline, Leonidas L. *Works of Rev. Leonidas L. Hamline, D.D.* Edited by F. G. Hibbard. 2 vols. Cincinnati: Hitchcock and Walden, 1869–71.

Hartwell, J. *The Old Paths: Mr. Wesley's "Thoughts on Entire Sanctification." In Reply to Rev. H. Mattison.* New York: Methodist Book Depositories, 1852.

[Jackson, Lewis E.] *Walks about New York. Facts and Figures Gathered From Various Sources.* New York: New York City Mission and Tract Society, 1865.

Ladies' Home Missionary Society of the Methodist Episcopal Church. *Annual Report,* nos. 1-32, 1844-76 (series incomplete).

Ladies of the Mission. *The Old Brewery and the New Mission House of the Five Points.* New York: Stringer and Townsend, 1854.

Lancaster, John. *The Life of Darcy, Lady Maxwell, of Pollock; Late of Edinburgh: Compiled from Her Voluminous Diary and Correspondence, and from Other Authentic Documents.* New York: T. Mason and G. Lane for the Methodist Episcopal Church, 1837.

Luther, Martin. *The Freedom of a Christian.* Translated by W. A. Lambert, revised by Harold J. Grimm, in *Selected Writings of Martin Luther.* Edited by Theodore G. Tappert. 4 vols. Philadelphia: Fortress Press, 1967.

Mahan, Asa. *Baptism of the Holy Ghost.* New York: W. C. Palmer, Jr., 1870.

———. *Scripture Doctrine of Christian Perfection; with other Kindred Subjects, Illustrated and Confirmed in a Series of Discourses Designed to Throw Light on the Way of Holiness.* 7th ed. Boston: Waite, Pierce and Co., 1844.

Mattison, Hiram. *A Calm Review of Dr. Perry's Late Article in the Christian Advocate and Journal; with Several Important Papers Relating to the Controversy.* New York: John A. Gray, 1856.

———. *An Answer to Dr. Perry's Reply to the Calm Review.* New York: Miller & Holman, 1856.

———. *Thoughts on Entire Sanctification.* New York: Lane & Scott, 1852.

Merritt, Timothy. *The Christian's Manual, A Treatise on Christian Perfection; with Directions for Obtaining that State, compiled Principally from the Works of the Rev. John Wesley.* New York: N. Bangs and J. Emory for the Methodist Episcopal Church, 1827.

Methodist Episcopal Church. *Hymnal of the Methodist Episcopal Church, with Tunes.* New York: Nelson & Phillips, 1878.

———. *Journals of the General Conference of the Methodist Episcopal Church, 1792-1936.* 24 vols. ATLA Microtext Project for the Historical Commission of the Southern Baptist Convention.

Moore, Henry. *The Life of Mrs. Mary Fletcher, Consort and Relict of the Rev. John Fletcher, Vicar of Madeley, Salop. Compiled from Her Journal, and Other Authentic Documents.* New York: J. Emory and B. Waugh for the Methodist Episcopal Church, 1830.

Morgan, John. "The Gift of the Holy Ghost." *Oberlin Quarterly Review* 1 (1845): 90-116.

Nelson, John. *Extract from the Journal of John Nelson: Being an Account of God's Dealing with Him from His Youth to the Forty-second Year of His Age. To Which Is Added an Account of His Death.* 16th ed. New York: Carlton & Porter, 1856.

Olin, Julia M. *Life and Letters of Stephen Olin, D.D., L.L.D., Late President of Wesleyan University.* 2 vols. New York: Harper & Brothers, 1853.

Peck, George. *The Life and Times of Rev. George Peck, D.D.* New York: Nelson & Phillips, 1874.

_____. *The Scripture Doctrine of Christian Perfection Stated and Defended: with a Critical and Historical Examination of the Controversy, Ancient and Modern. Also Practical Illustrations and Advices.* 10th ed. rev. New York: Carlton & Porter, 1842.

Peck, Jesse T. *The Central Idea of Christianity.* Boston: H. V. Degen, 1856.

Peck, Jesse T., et al. *Systematic Beneficence: Three Prize Essays.* New York: Carlton & Phillips, 1856.

Perry, J. H. *Reply to Prof. Mattison's "Answer," Etc.; Being the Summing up of the Case of Professor Mattison Against Mrs. Palmer.* New York: John A. Gray's Fireproof Printing Office, 1856.

Philip, Robert. *Devotional Guides.* With an Introductory Essay by Albert Barnes. 2 vols. New York: D. Appleton & Co., 1837.

Prison Discipline Society. *Sixteenth Annual Report of the Board of Managers of the Prison Discipline Society.* Boston: The Prison Discipline Society, 1841. Reprinted in *Annual Reports of the Prison Discipline Society, Boston.* Montclair, N.J.: Patterson Smith Publishing Corporation, 1972.

Roche, John A. "Mrs. Phoebe Palmer." *Ladies' Repository* 26 (February 1866), pp. 65–70.

Rogers, Hester Ann. *An Account of the Experience of Hester Ann Rogers; Written by Herself. To Which Is Added, Spiritual Letters; Calculated to Illustrate and Enforce Holiness of Heart. Also, A Sermon, Preached on the Occasion of Her Death, October 26, 1794, by the Rev. Thomas Coke, L.L.D. With an Appendix, Written by Her Husband; and Containing Selections Transcribed from Her Manuscript Journals.* New York: S. & D. A. Forbes, 1830.

Sigston, James. *Memoir of the Life and Ministry of Mr. William Bramwell, Lately an Itinerant Methodist Preacher: With Extracts from His Interesting and Extensive Correspondence.* 3d American ed. New York: J. Emory and B. Waugh for The Methodist Episcopal Church, 1830.

Stevens, Abel. *Life and Times of Nathan Bangs, D.D.* New York: Carlton & Porter, 1863.

Summers, T. O. *Holiness, A Treatise on Sanctification.* Richmond: J. Early, 1850.

_____. *Systematic Theology: A Complete Body of Wesleyan Arminian Divinity Consisting of Lectures on the Twenty-five Articles of Religion.* Edited by Jon. J. Tigert. 2 vols. Nashville: Publishing House of the Methodist Episcopal Church, South, 1888.

Upham, Thomas C. *Divine Union.* New York: Walter C. Palmer, Jr., 1870.

_____. *The Life of Faith in Three Parts, Embracing Some of the Scriptural Principles or Doctrines of Faith, The Power or Effects of Faith in the Regulation of Man's Inward Nature, and the Relation of Faith to the Divine Guidance.* Boston: Waite, Pierce and Co., 1845.

_____. *Principles of the Interior or Hidden Life; Designed Particularly for the Consideration of those who are seeking Assurance of Faith and Perfect Love.* 3d ed. Boston: Waite, Pierce and Co., 1845.

Wakely, J. B. *Lost Chapters Recovered from the Early History of American Methodism.* New York: printed for the author, 1858.

Watson, Richard. *Theological Institutes: or A View of the Evidences, Doctrines, Morals, and Institutions of Christianity. A New Edition with a Copious Index, and an Analysis by J. M'Clintock.* 26th ed. 2 vols. New York: Carlton & Lanaham, 1850.

Wesley, John. *Explanatory Notes Upon the Old Testament*. 4 vols. Bristol: William Pine, 1765.
―――. *The Journal of the Rev. John Wesley, A.M.* Edited by Nehemiah Curnock. Standard ed. 8 vols. London: Epworth Press, 1906-1916.
―――. *The Letters of the Rev. John Wesley, A.M., Sometime Fellow of Lincoln College, Oxford*. Edited by John Telford, B.A. Standard ed. 8 vols. London: Epworth Press, 1931.
―――. *Wesley's Standard Sermons*. Edited by Edward H. Sugden. Standard ed. 2 vols. London: Epworth, 1951; reprint, Grand Rapids: Zondervan, 1986.
―――. *The Works of John Wesley*. Edited by Frank Baker. Vol. 7: *A Collection of Hymns for the Use of the People called Methodists*. Edited by Franz Hildenbrandt and Oliver A. Beckerlegge with the assistance of James Dale. Oxford: Clarendon Press of the Oxford University Press, 1983.
―――. *The Works of John Wesley*. Edited by Thomas Jackson. 3d ed. 14 vols. London: Wesleyan Methodist Book Room, 1872. Reprint. Grand Rapids: Baker Book House, 1979.
Whedon, Daniel D. "The Doctrines of Methodism." *Bibliotheca Sacra* 19 (1862): 241-73.
Wood, John Allen. *Perfect Love; or Plain Things for Those Who Need Them, Concerning the Doctrine, Experience, Profession and Practice of Christian Holiness*. Philadelphia: S. D. Burlock, 1861.
Young, Robert. *The Importance of Prayer Meetings in Promoting the Revival of Religion*. New York: Carlton & Porter, n.d.

Periodicals

Advocate of Christian Holiness. Boston, 1870-75.
Advocate of Holiness & Enquirer After Truth, also called *Advocate of Holiness and the Speedy Coming of the Lord*. Worcester, Mass., and New Haven, Conn., 1850.
Beauty of Holiness and Sabbath Miscellany. Columbus, Ohio, 1853-64.
Christian Advocate and Journal. New York, 1835-75.
Guide to Holiness. Boston, New York, and Philadelphia, 1839-1901.
Ladies' Repository. Cincinnati, 1841-75.
Methodist Magazine. Baltimore, 1855-57.
Methodist Quarterly Review. New York, 1835-90.
Zion's Herald. Boston, 1835-75.

Secondary Bibliography

Bibliographic Resources

American Library Association. *The National Union Catalog of Pre-1956 Imprints.* 754 vols. London: Mansell, 1968–81.
Batsel, John David, and Lyda K. Batsel, comps. *Union List of United Methodist Serials, 1773–1973.* Evanston, Ill.: The Commission on Archives and History of the United Methodist Church, The United Methodist Librarians' Fellowship, and Garrett Theological Seminary, 1974.
Dayton, Donald W. *The American Holiness Movement: A Bibliographic Introduction.* Wilmore, Ky.: Asbury Theological Seminary, 1971.
Dickerson, G. Fay, ed. *Religion Index One: Periodicals.* Vols. 1–15. Chicago: The American Theological Library Association, 1949–82.
Guide to Social Science and Religion in Periodical Literature. 16 vols. Flint, Mich.: National Periodical Library, 1964–80.
Hand, Albert E., ed. *Religion Index Two: Multi-Author Works.* Vols. 1–9. Chicago: The American Theological Library Association, 1960–83.
Hardman, Keith J. "A Checklist of Doctoral Dissertations on Methodist, Evangelical United Brethren, and Related Subjects, 1912–1968." *Methodist History* 8 (April 1975): 38–42.
Hinding, Andrea, ed. *Women's History Sources: A Guide to the Archives and Manuscript Collections in the United States.* 2 vols. New York: R. R. Bowker Company, 1979.
Jones, Charles Edwin. *A Guide to the Study of the Holiness Movement.* ATLA Bibliography Series, no. 1. Metuchen, N.J.: The Scarecrow Press and The American Theological Library Association, 1974.
Lenhart, Thomas E., and Frederick A. Norwood. *A Checklist of Wesleyan and Methodist Studies, 1970–1975.* Evanston, Ill.: Institute for Methodist Studies and Related Movements, 1976.
Lewis, Rosalyn, ed. *United Methodist Periodical Index.* 15 vols. Nashville: The United Methodist Publishing House, 1961–77.
Norwood, Frederick A. "Methodist Historical Studies, 1930–1959." *Church History* 28 (1959): 391–417 and 29 (1960): 74–88.
———. "Wesleyan and Methodist Historical Studies, 1960–70: A Bibliographic Article." *Church History* 40 (1971): 182–99.
Palmer, Walter Charles, Jr. *Catalogue of Works on the Higher Christian Life, also General Devotional Works and Books for Sunday School Libraries.* New York: Walter C. Palmer, Jr., [1870].
Richardson, E. C., et al. *An Alphabetical Subject Index and Index Encyclopedia to Periodical Articles on Religion, 1890–1899.* New York: Charles Scribner and Sons, 1907.

Rowe, Kenneth E. *Methodist Women: A Guide to the Literature.* United Methodist Bibliography Series, no. 2. Lake Junaluska, N.C.: The General Commission on Archives and History of the United Methodist Church, 1980.

Books

Abell, Aaron Ignatius. *The Urban Impact on American Protestantism, 1865-1900.* Hamden, Conn.: Archon, 1962.
Adams, Alice Dana. *The Neglected Period of Anti-Slavery in America, 1808-1831.* Radcliffe College Monographs, no. 14. Williamston, Mass.: Corner House Publishers, 1973.
Adams, Charles. *Evangelism in the Middle of the Nineteenth Century; or an Exhibit, Descriptive and Statistical, of the Present Condition of Evangelical Religion in All Countries of the World.* Boston: Charles H. Pierce, 1851.
The American Christian Record: Containing the History, Confession of Faith, and Statistics of Each Religious Denomination in the United States and Europe; A List of All Clergymen with their Post Office Addresses, Etc., Etc., Etc. New York: W. R. C. Clark & Meeker, 1860. Microfilm. Ann Arbor: University Microfilms, 1976.
Baird, Robert. *Religion in United States of America.* Glasgow: Blackie and Son, 1844. Reprint. New York: Arno Press & The New York Times, 1969.
Bennett, Dennis, and Rita Bennett. *The Holy Spirit and You: A Study-Guide to the Spirit-Filled Life.* Plainfield, N.J.: Logos International, 1971.
Berg, Barbara J. *The Remembered Gate: Origins of American Feminism.* New York: Oxford University Press, 1978.
[Bishop, Isabella Bird]. *The Aspects of Religion in the United States of America.* London: n.p., 1859. Reprint. New York: Arno Press, 1972.
Blaikie, Alexander. *The Philosophy of Sectarianism: or, A Classified View of the Christian Sects in the United States; with Notices of their Progress and Tendencies.* 2d ed. Boston: Phillips, Sampson, and Company, 1855.
Boland, J. M. *The Problem of Methodism: Being a Review of the Residue Theory of Regeneration and the Second Change Theory of Sanctification and the Philosophy of Christian Perfection.* 3d ed. Nashville: Publishing House of the Methodist Episcopal Church, South, for the author, 1888.
Booth-Tucker, F. de L. *The Life of Catherine Booth, The Mother of the Salvation Army.* 2 vols. New York: Fleming H. Revell Company, 1892.
Brace, Charles Loring. *Gesta Christi; or, A History of Humane Progress Under Christianity.* 4th American ed. New York: Hodder and Stoughton, 1887.
Bremner, Robert. *From the Depths; The Discovery of Poverty in the United States.* New York: New York University Press, [1956].
Brown, Earl Kent. *Women of Mr. Wesley's Methodism.* Studies in Women and Religion. Vol. 11. New York: The Edwin Mellen Press, 1983.
Bruner, Frederick Dale. *A Theology of the Holy Spirit: The Pentecostal Experience and the New Testament Witness.* Grand Rapids: Wm. B. Eerdmans Publishing Co., 1970.
Buck, Emory Stevens, et al. *The History of American Methodism.* 3 vols. New York: Abingdon Press, 1964.
Burtner, Robert W., and Robert E. Chiles, *John Wesley's Theology: A Collection from his Works.* Nashville: Abingdon Press, 1954.

Cannon, William R. *The Theology of John Wesley, with Special Reference to the Doctrine of Justification.* New York: Abingdon Press, 1946.
Carter, Paul A. *The Spiritual Crisis of the Gilded Age.* DeKalb, Ill.: Northern Illinois University Press, 1971.
Carwardine, Richard. *Transatlantic Revivalism: Popular Evangelicalism in Britain and America, 1790–1865.* Contributions in American History, no. 75. Westport, Conn.: Greenwood Press, 1978.
Cell, George Croft. *The Rediscovery of John Wesley.* New York: Henry Holt and Company, 1935. Reprint. Lanham, Md.: University Press of America, 1983.
Chambers, Talbot W. *The Noon Prayer Meeting of the North Dutch Church, Fulton Street, New York: Its Origin, Character and Progress, with some of its Results.* New York: Board of Publication of the Reformed Protestant Dutch Church, 1858.
Chiles, Robert E. *Theological Transition in American Methodism: 1790–1935.* New York: Abingdon Press, 1965.
Church of the Nazarene. *Worship in Song.* Kansas City, Mo.: Lillenas Publishing Company, 1972.
Clark, Adam. *Christian Theology.*
_____. *The Holy Bible, Containing the Old and New Testaments.* 6 vols. New York: T. Mason and G. Lane, 1837.
Clark, Robert D. *The Life of Matthew Simpson.* New York: Harper & Row, 1969.
Cole, Charles C., Jr. *The Social Ideas of the Northern Evangelists, 1826–1860.* New York: Octagon Books, Inc., 1966.
Coward, S. L. C. *Entire Sanctification From 1739 to 1900.* Louisville, Ky.: Pentecostal Herald Press, 1900.
Cox, Leo George. *John Wesley's Concept of Perfection.* Kansas City, Mo.: Beacon Hill Press, 1964.
Cross, Whitney R. *The Burned-over District: The Social and Intellectual History of Enthusiastic Religion in Western New York, 1800–1850.* New York: Harper Torchbooks, 1950.
Dallimore, Arnold. *Forerunner of the Charismatic Movement: The Life of Edward Irving.* Chicago: Moody Press, 1983.
Daly, Mary. *The Church and the Second Sex.* New York: Harper & Row, 1975.
Dayton, Donald W. *Discovering An Evangelical Heritage.* New York: Harper & Row, 1976.
Dieter, Melvin Easterday. *The Holiness Revival of the Nineteenth Century.* Studies in Evangelicalism, no. 1. Metuchen, N.J.: The Scarecrow Press, 1980.
Dixon, James. *Methodism in America: with the Personal Narrative of the Author, during a Tour Through a Part of the United States and Canada.* London: printed for the author; sold by John Mason, 1849.
Douglas, Ann. *The Feminization of American Culture.* New York: Avon Books, 1977.
Drummond, Lewis A. *Charles Grandison Finney and the Birth of Modern Evangelism.* London: Hodder and Stoughton, 1983.
Dunstan, John L. *A Light to the City; 150 Years of the City Missionary Society of Boston, 1818–1966.* Boston: Beacon Press, 1966.
Ferguson, Charles W. *Organizing to Beat the Devil: Methodists and the Making of America.* Garden City, N.Y.: Doubleday & Company, 1971.

Flew, Newton R. *The Idea of Perfection in Christian Theology: An Historical Study of the Christian Ideal for the Present Life.* New York: Humanities Press, 1968.
Flexner, Eleanor. *Century of Struggle.* Rev. ed. Cambridge, Mass.: The Belknap Press of Harvard University Press, 1975.
Foster, Frank Hugh. *A Genetic History of the New England Theology.* Chicago: University of Chicago Press, 1907.
Garrison, S. Olin, ed. *Forty Witnesses, Covering the Whole Range of Christian Experience.* Introduction by C. D. Foss. New York: Eaton & Mains, 1888.
Goss, Charles C. *Statistical History of the First Century of American Methodism: with a Summary of the Origin and Present Operations of Other Denominations.* New York: Carlton & Porter, 1866.
Griffin, Clifford. *Their Brother's Keeper.* New Brunswick, N.J.: Rutgers University Press, 1960.
Hardesty, Nancy Ann. *Great Women of Faith.* Nashville: Abingdon Press, 1982.
Harkness, Georgia. *Women in Church and Society: A Historical and Theological Inquiry.* Nashville: Abingdon Press, 1972.
Hibbard, F. G. *Biography of Rev. Leonidas L. Hamline D.D., Late One of the Bishops of the Methodist Episcopal Church.* Cincinnati: Hitchcock and Walden, 1880.
Hills, A. M. *Scriptural Holiness and Keswick Teaching Compared.* Reprint. Salem, Ohio: Schmul Publishers, n.d.
Hitchcock, Edward, et al., comps. *The Power of Christian Benevolence Illustrated in the Life and Labors of Mary Lyon.* 2d ed. Northampton, Mass.: Hopkins, Bridgman, and Company, 1851.
Hogue, Wilson Thomas. *History of the Free Methodist Church of North America.* Introduction by Edward P. Hart. 2d ed. 2 vols. Chicago: The Free Methodist Publishing House, 1918.
Holdich, Joseph. *The Life of Wilber Fisk, D.D., First President of the Wesleyan University.* New York: Harper & Brothers, 1842.
Hopkins, Charles H. *The Rise of the Social Gospel in American Protestantism, 1865–1900.* Yale Studies in Religious Education, no. 14. New Haven: Yale University Press, 1940.
Hughes, George. *The Beloved Physician: Walter C. Palmer M.D., and His Sun-lit Journey to the Celestial City.* New York: Palmer & Hughes, 1884.
———. *Fragrant Memories of The Tuesday Meeting and its Fifty Years' Work for Jesus.* Introduction by W. F. Mallalieu. New York: Palmer & Hughes, 1886.
———. *Fragrant Memories of The Tuesday Meeting and the Guide to Holiness, and their Fifty Years' Work for Jesus.* Introduction to part 1 by W. F. Mallalieu and to part 2 by William Taylor. New York: Palmer & Hughes, 1886 [1889]. Microfiche. El Segundo, Calif.: Micro Publication Systems for the American Theological Libraries Association Board of Microtext, 1981.
Ingraham, S. R. *Walks of Usefulness or, Reminiscences of Mrs. Margaret Prior.* New York: American Female Reform Society, 1844.
Jackson, Lewis E. *Gospel Work in New York City; a Memorial of Fifty Years in City Missions.* New York: New York City Mission, 1878.
Johnson, Charles A. *The Frontier Camp Meeting: Religious Harvest Time.* Dallas: Southern Methodist University Press, 1955.

Johnson, James E. *The Life of Charles Grandison Finney.* Ann Arbor: University Microfilms, 1959.

Jones, Charles Edwin. *Perfectionist Persuasion: The Holiness Movement and American Methodism, 1867–1936.* ATLA Monograph Series, no. 5. Metuchen, N.J.: The Scarecrow Press, 1974.

Knox, Ronald. *Enthusiasm: A Chapter in the History of Religion with Reference to the XVII and XVIII Centuries.* New York: Oxford University Press, 1961.

Kronenberger, Louis. *Kings and Desperate Men: Life in Eighteenth-Century England.* New York: Vintage Books, 1942.

Langford, Thomas A. *Practical Divinity: Theology in the Wesleyan Tradition.* Nashville: Abingdon Press, 1983.

Leete, Frederick Deland. *Methodist Bishops: Personal Notes and Bibliography.* Nashville: Parthenon, 1948.

Lindstrom, Harald. *Wesley and Sanctification: A Study in the Doctrine of Salvation.* London: Epworth Press, 1946.

Littell, Franklin H. *From State Church to Pluralism: A Protestant Interpretation of Religion in American History.* New York: Macmillan, 1971.

Lovelace, Richard F. *Dynamics of Spiritual Life: An Evangelical Theology of Renewal.* Downers Grove, Ill.: InterVarsity Press, 1979.

McCutchan, Robert G. *Our Hymnody: A Manual of the Methodist Hymnal.* New York: Methodist Book Concern, 1939.

McDonald, William, and L. Hartsough. *Beulah Songs: A Choice Collection of Popular Hymns and Music.* Philadelphia: National Publishing Association for the Promotion of Holiness, 1881.

McLoughlin, William Gerald, Jr. *The Meaning of Henry Ward Beecher.* New York: Alfred A. Knopf, 1970.

———. *Modern Revivalism: Charles Grandison Finney to Billy Graham.* New York: The Ronald Press Company, 1959.

———, ed. *The American Evangelicals, 1800–1900.* Gloucester, Mass.: Peter Smith, 1976.

Madden, Edward H., and James E. Hamilton. *Freedom and Grace: The Life of Asa Mahan.* Studies in Evangelicalism, no. 3. Metuchen, N.J.: The Scarecrow Press, 1982.

Magnuson, Norris. *Salvation in the Slums: Evangelical Social Work, 1865–1920.* ATLA Monograph Series, no. 10. Metuchen, N.J.: The Scarecrow Press and The American Theological Library Association, 1977.

Marston, L. R. *From Age to Age a Living Witness: An Historical Interpretation of Free Methodism's First Century.* Winona Lake, Ind.: Light and Life Press, 1960.

Mathews, Donald G. *Slavery and Methodism: A Chapter in American Morality, 1780–1845.* Princeton: Princeton University Press, 1965.

Mattson, John Stanley. *Charles Grandison Finney and the Emerging Tradition of "New Measure" Revivalism.* Ann Arbor: University Microfilms, 1971.

May, Henry F. *Protestant Churches and Industrial America.* New introduction by the author. New York: Harper & Row, 1967.

Melder, Keith E. *The Beginning of the Women's Rights Movement in the United States, 1800–1840.* Ann Arbor: University Microfilms, 1964.

———. *Beginnings of Sisterhood: The American Woman's Rights Movement, 1800–1840.* Studies in the Life of Women. New York: Schocken Books, 1977.

Mohl, Raymond. *Poverty in New York 1783-1825*. New York: Oxford University Press, 1971.
Mott, Frank Luther. *Golden Multitudes: The Story of Best Sellers in the United States*. New York: The Macmillan Company, 1947.
———. *A History of American Magazines*. 5 vols. Cambridge, Mass.: The Belknap Press of the Harvard University Press, 1957-58.
Nichol, John Thomas. *Pentecostalism*. New York: Harper & Row, 1966.
Norwood, Frederick A. *The Story of American Methodism*. Nashville: Abingdon Press, 1974.
———, ed. *Sourcebook of American Methodism*. Nashville: Abingdon Press, 1982.
Orr, James Edwin. *The Second Evangelical Awakening in America*. London: Marshall, Morgan and Scott, 1955.
———. *The Second Evangelical Awakening in Britain*. London: Marshall, Morgan and Scott, 1949.
Outler, Albert C., ed. *John Wesley*. New York: Oxford University Press, 1964.
Palmer, Horace Wilber. "Palmer Families in America." Vol 2. 13 parts. Typescript. New England Historical Genealogical Society. Boston.
Parrington, Vernon Louis. *Main Currents in American Thought*. New York: Harcourt, Brace and Co., 1930.
Peters, John L. *Christian Perfection and American Methodism*. New York: Abingdon Press, 1956.
Pettit, Norman. *The Heart Prepared: Grace and Conversion in Puritan Spirituality*. New Haven: Yale University Press, 1966.
Phinney, William R. *Maggie Newton Van Cott: First Woman Licensed to Preach in the Methodist Episcopal Church*. Rye, N.Y.: The Commission on Archives and History of the New York Annual Conference of the United Methodist Church, 1969.
Reuther, Rosemary, and Eleanor McLaughlin. *Women of Spirit*. New York: Simon and Schuster, 1979.
Reuther, Rosemary Radford, and Rosemary Skinner Keller, eds. *Women and Religion in America: The Nineteenth Century*. San Francisco: Harper & Row, 1981.
Ridgaway, Henry B. *The Life of the Rev. Alfred Cookman; with Some Account of his Father The Rev. George Grimston Cookman*. With an Introduction by Randolph Sinks Foster. New York: Harper & Brothers, 1873.
Roberts, Benjamin Titus. *Pungent Truths: Being Extracts from the Writings of the Rev. Benjamin Titus Roberts, A.M., while Editor of "The Free Methodist" from 1886 to 1890*. Compiled and edited by William B. Rose. Chicago: The Free Methodist Publishing House, 1912.
———. *Why Another Sect: Containing a Review of Articles by Bishop Simpson and Others on the Free Methodist Church*. Rochester, N.Y.: "The Earnest Christian" Publishing House, 1879.
Roberts, Benson Howard. *Benjamin Titus Roberts*. North Chili, N.Y.: "The Earnest Christian" Office, 1900.
———, comp. *Holiness Teachings Compiled from the Editorial Writings of the Late Rev. Benjamin Titus Roberts*. North Chili, N.Y.: "The Earnest Christian" Publishing House, 1893. Reprint. Salem, Ohio: Schmul Publishers, 1983.
Roche, John A. *The Life of Mrs. Sarah A. Lankford Palmer Who for Sixty Years Was the Able Teacher of Entire Holiness*. Introduction by John P. Newman. New York: George Hughes and Co., 1898.

Rose, Delbert. *Vital Holiness: A Theology of Christian Experience.* 3d ed. Minneapolis: Bethany Fellowship, 1975.
Rosell, Garth. *Charles G. Finney and the Rise of the Benevolence Empire.* Ann Arbor: University Microfilms, 1971.
Rosenberg, Carol Smith. *Religion and the Rise of the American City; The New York City Mission Movement, 1812–1870.* Ithaca, N.Y.: Cornell University Press, 1971.
Rossi, Alice S., ed. *The Feminist Papers from Adams to de Beauvoir.* New York: Bantam Books, 1973.
Sandall, Robert. *The History of the Salvation Army.* Vol. 1. London: Thomas Nelson and Sons, 1947.
Schaff, Philip. *America. A Sketch of the Political, Social, and Religious Character of the United States of North America.* New York: n.p., 1855.
Simpson, Matthew, ed. *Cyclopedia of Methodism.* Rev. ed. Philadelphia: Louis H. Everts, 1880.
Skylar, Kathryn Kish. *Catherine Beecher: A Study in American Domesticity.* New York: W. W. Norton & Company, 1976.
Slatte, Howard A. *The Arminian Arm of Theology: The Theologies of John Fletcher, First Methodist Theologian, and His Precursor, James Arminius.* Washington: University Press of America, 1979.
Smith, Amanda. *An Autobiography: The Story of the Lord's Dealings with Mrs. Amanda Smith, the Colored Evangelist.* Chicago: Meyer and Bros., 1893.
Smith, Timothy L. *Revivalism and Social Reform: American Protestantism on the Eve of the Civil War.* Nashville: Abingdon Press, 1957. Reprint with a new afterword by the author. Baltimore: The Johns Hopkins University Press, 1980.
Snyder, Howard. *The Radical Wesley and Patterns for Church Renewal.* Downers Grove, Ill.: InterVarsity Press, 1980.
Spaulding, Arthur Whitefield. *Origin and History of the Seventh Day Adventists.* 2 vols. Washington, D.C.: Review & Herald Publishing Association, 1962.
Stead, Francis Herbert. *The Story of Social Christianity.* 2 vols. New York: George H. Doran, [1924].
Stevens, Abel. *History of the Methodist Episcopal Church in the United States.* 4 vols. New York: Carlton & Lanahan, 1864–67.
Stokes, I[saac] N[ewton] Phelps. *The Iconography of Manhattan Island, 1498–1909.* 6 vols. New York: Robert H. Dodd, 1915–28. Reprint. New York: Arno Press, 1967.
Sweet, William Warren. *Methodism in American History.* New York: Methodist Book Concern, 1933.
―――. *Revivalism in America: Its Origin, Growth, and Decline.* New York: Charles Scribner's Sons, 1944.
Synan, Vincent. *The Holiness-Pentecostal Movement in the United States.* Grand Rapids: Wm. B. Eerdmans Publishing Co., 1971.
Terrill, Joseph Goodwin. *The Life of Rev. John Wesley Redfield, M.D.* Chicago: Free Methodist Publishing House, 1897.
Thurber, James. *The Thurber Carnival.* New York: Harper & Brothers, 1945.
Townsend, W. J., H. B. Workman, and George Eayrs, eds. *A New History of Methodism.* 2 vols. London: Hodder and Stoughton, 1909.
Turner, George Allen. *The More Excellent Way.* Winona Lake, Ind.: Light and Life Press, 1952.

---. *The Vision Which Transforms: Is Christian Perfection Scriptural?* Kansas City, Mo.: Beacon Hill Press, 1964.
Tyerman, Luke. *The Life and Times of the Rev. John Wesley, M.A., Founder of the Methodists.* 3 vols. New York: Harper & Brothers, 1872. Reprint. New York: Burt Franklin, 1973.
---. *Wesley's Designated Successor.* New York: Phillips and Hunt, 1883.
Tyler, Alice Felt. *Freedom's Ferment.* New York: Harper & Row, 1962.
Upham, Thomas C. *Life and Religious Opinions and Experience of Madame de la Mothe Guyon.* 2 vols. New York: Harper and Brothers, 1847.
---. *Principles of the Interior or Hidden Life.* 3d ed. Boston: Waite, Pierce and Co., 1845.
Van Cott, Maggie Newton. *The Harvest & The Reaper.* Introduction by Gilbert Haven. New York: N. Tibbals & Sons, 1876.
Vansant, N. *Work Here, Rest Hereafter; or The Life and Character of Rev. Hiram Mattison, D.D.* Introduction by Edward Thomson. New York: N. Tibbals & Son, 1870.
Warfield, Benjamin B. *Perfectionism.* 2 vols. New York: Oxford University, 1931.
Weisberger, Bernard A. *They Gathered at the River: The Story of the Great Revivalists and their Impact on America.* Boston: Little, Brown and Company, 1958.
Wesleyan Church of America and Free Methodist Church of America. *Hymns of the Living Faith.* Winona Lake, Ind.: Light and Life Press, 1951.
Wheatley, Richard. *The Life and Letters of Mrs. Phoebe Palmer.* New York: W. C. Palmer, Jr., 1876.
Wilcox, Leslie D. *Be Ye Holy.* Rev. ed. Cincinnati: Revivalist Press, 1965.
Willard, Frances. *Women in the Pulpit.* Chicago: Woman's Temperance Pub. Association, 1889.
Wilson, George. *Methodist Theology vs. Methodist Theologians.* Cincinnati: Jennings and Pye, 1904.
Wright, G. Frederick. *Charles Grandison Finney.* American Religious Leaders. Boston: Houghton Mifflin Co., 1891.
Wynkoop, Mildred Bangs. *A Theology of Love.* Kansas City, Mo.: Beacon Hill Press, 1972.
Zahniser, Clarence Howard. *Earnest Christian: Life and Work of Benjamin Titus Roberts.* Circleville, Ohio: Advocate Publishing House, 1957.

Articles and Dissertations

Adams, James Truslow, ed. *Dictionary of American History.* 2d rev. ed. New York: Charles Scribner's Sons, 1946. S.v. "Trent Affair."
Arnett, William M. "The Role of the Holy Spirit in Entire Sanctification in the Writings of John Wesley." *Wesleyan Theological Journal* 14/2 (Fall 1979): 15–30.
Bassett, Paul M. "A Study in the Theology of the Early Holiness Movement." *Methodist History* 13 (April 1975): 61–84.
Bible, Ken. "The Wesleys' Hymns on Full Redemption and Pentecost: A Brief Comparison." *Wesleyan Theological Journal* 17/2 (Fall 1982): 79–87.
Bowden, Henry Warner, ed. *Dictionary of American Religious Biography.* S.v. "Palmer, Phoebe Worrall." Westport, Conn.: Greenwood, 1977.

Boylan, Anne M. "Women in Groups: An Analysis of Women's Benevolent Organizations in New York and Boston, 1797–1840." *Journal of American History* 71/3 (December 1984): 497–523.

Breeze, Lawrence E. "The Inskips: Union in Holiness." *Methodist History* 13 (July 1975): 25–45.

Carwardine, Richard. "The Second Great Awakening in the Urban Centers: An Examination of Methodism and the New Measures." *Journal of American History* 59/2 (September 1972): 327–40.

Chiles, Robert E. "Methodist Apostasy: From Free Grace to Free Will." *Religion in Life* 27 (Summer 1958): 438–49.

Coppedge, Allan. "Entire Sanctification in Early American Methodism: 1812–1835." *Wesleyan Theological Journal* 13 (Spring 1978): 34–50.

Corbin, J. Wesley. "Christian Perfection and the Evangelical Association through 1875." *Methodist History* 7 (January 1969): 28–44.

Crane, J. Townley. "Christian Perfection and the Higher Life." *Methodist Quarterly Review* 60 (October 1878): 688–714.

Cross, F. L., and E. A. Livingstone, eds. *The Oxford Dictionary of the Christian Church.* 2d ed. Oxford: Oxford University, 1983. S.v. "Evangelical Alliance."

Cubie, David L. "Perfection in Wesley and Fletcher: Inaugural or Teleological?" *Wesleyan Theological Journal* 11 (Spring 1976): 22–37.

Dayton, Donald W. "Asa Mahan and the Development of American Holiness Theology." *Wesleyan Theological Journal* 9 (Spring 1974): 60–69.

⸻. "The Doctrine of the Baptism of the Holy Spirit: Its Emergence and Significance." *Wesleyan Theological Journal* 13 (Spring 1978): 114–26.

⸻. "Theological Roots of Pentecostalism." Ph.D. diss., University of Chicago, 1978.

⸻. "Women as Preachers: Evangelical Precedents." *Christianity Today* (May 23, 1975), pp. 4–7.

Dayton, Donald W., and Lucille Dayton, " 'Your Daughters Shall Prophesy': Feminism in the Holiness Movement." *Methodist History* 14 (January 1976): 67–92.

Dieter, Melvin E. "Mother of the Movement: Phoebe Palmer." *The Sounding Board* (Winter 1984), pp. 6–7.

Douglas, J. D., ed. *New International Dictionary of the Christian Church.* Rev. ed. Grand Rapids: Zondervan, 1978. S.v. "Muller, George," by J. G. G. Norman.

Dunlop, E. Dale. "Tuesday Meetings, Camp Meetings, and Cabinet Meetings: A Perspective on the Holiness Movement in the Methodist Church in the Nineteenth Century." *Methodist History* 13 (April 1975): 85–106.

Gaddis, Merril Elmer. "Christian Perfectionism in America." Ph.D. diss., University of Chicago, 1929. Rev. 1938. Microcard Theological Studies, vol. 2. Chicago: The Microcard Foundation, for The American Theological Library Association, 1954.

Garrison, George P. "A Woman's Community in Texas." *The Charities Review of New York* (November 1893), pp. 28–46.

Goen, C. C. "The Methodist Age in American Church History." *Religion in Life* 34 (1965): 562–72.

Graves, Albert Schuyler. "Wesley's Variations in Belief, and the Influence of the Same on Methodism." *Methodist Review* 69 (March 1887): 192–211.

Grider, J. Kenneth. "Evaluation of Timothy Smith's Interpretation of Wesley." *Wesleyan Theological Journal* 15/2 (Fall 1980): 64–69.

Hamilton, James E. "Academic Orthodoxy and the Arminianizing of American Theology." *Wesleyan Theological Journal* 9 (Spring 1974): 52–59.

―――――. "Nineteenth Century Philosophy and Holiness Theology: A Study in the Thought of Asa Mahan." *Wesleyan Theological Journal* 13 (Spring 1978): 51–64.

Hand, George Othell. "Changing Emphases in American Evangelism from Colonial Times to the Present." Th.D. thesis, Southern Baptist Theological Seminary, Louisville, 1949.

Hardesty, Nancy Ann. "Minister as Prophet? Or as Mother?" In *Women in New Worlds*, pp. 88–101. Edited by Hilah F. Thomas and Rosemary Skinner Keller. Vol. 1. Nashville: Abingdon, 1981.

―――――. " 'Your Daughters Shall Prophesy': Revivalism and Feminism in the Age of Finney." Ph.D. diss., University of Chicago, 1976.

Harmon, Nolan B., ed. *Encyclopedia of World Methodism*. Nashville: United Methodist Publishing House, 1974. S.v. "Bramwell, William," by N. P. Goldhawk; "Fletcher, John William," by Kenneth Cain Kinghorn; "Fletcher, Mary Bosanquet," by John Kent; "Maxwell, D'Arcy," by Frank Baker; "Nelson, John," by Frank Baker; "Palmer, Phoebe," by C. Wesley Christman, Jr.; and "Rogers, Hester Ann Roe," by John A. Vickers.

Heimert, Alan, and Perry Miller. *The Great Awakening: Documents Illustrative of the Crisis and its Consequences*. The American Heritage series, no. 34. Indianapolis: Bobbs Merrill, 1967.

Hovet, Theodore. "Phoebe Palmer's 'Altar Phraseology' and the Spiritual Dimensions of Woman's Sphere." *The Journal of Religion* 63 (July 1983): 264–80.

Howard, Ivan. "Wesley vs. Phoebe Palmer: An Extended Controversy." *Wesleyan Theological Journal* 6 (Spring 1971): 31–40.

Hynson, Leon L. "George Whitefield and Wesleyan Perfectionism: A Response." *Wesleyan Theological Journal* 19/1 (Spring 1984): 86–90.

James, Edward T., ed. *Notable American Women, 1607–1950*. 3 vols. Cambridge, Mass.: Harvard, 1971. S.v. "Smith, Amanda Berry," by John H. Bracey, Jr.; and "Palmer, Phoebe Worrall," by W. J. McCutchen.

Johnson, James E. "Charles G. Finney and a Theology of Revivalism." *Church History* 38 (September 1969): 338–58.

Knight, John A. "John Fletcher's Influence on the Development of Wesleyan Theology in America." *Wesleyan Theological Journal* 13 (Spring 1978): 13–33.

Lewis-Newberg, Carol. "Phoebe Palmer: A Prophesying Daughter." Typescript. Dayton, Ohio: United Theological Seminary, 1979.

Loveland, Anne C. "Domesticity and Religion in the Antebellum Period: The Career of Phoebe Palmer." *The Historian* 39 (May 1977): 455–71.

M'Clintock, John, and James Strong. *Cyclopedia of Biblical, Theological, and Ecclesiastical Literature*. 12 vols. New York: Harper & Brothers, 1867. Reprint. Grand Rapids: Baker, 1968. S.v. "Benson, Joseph"; "Cobbin, Ingram"; "Dodwell, Henry"; "Grotius, Hugo"; Sutcliffe, Joseph"; "Theophylact"; "Tracts and Tract Societies," by D. P. Kidder; "Wayland, Francis."

McGonigle, Herbert. "Pneumatological Nomenclature in Early Methodism." *Wesleyan Theological Journal* 8 (Spring 1973): 61–72.

Mattke, Robert A. "The Baptism of the Holy Spirit as Related to the Work of Entire Sanctification." *Wesleyan Theological Journal* 5 (Spring 1970): 22–32.

Mitchell, Norma Taylor. "From Social to Radical Feminism: A Survey of Emerging Diversity in Methodist Women's Organizations, 1869–1974." *Methodist History* 13/3 (April 1975): 21–44.

Mitchell, T. Crichton. "Response to Dr. Timothy Smith on the Wesleys' Hymns." *Wesleyan Theological Journal* 16/2 (Fall 1981): 48–57.

National Cyclopedia of American Biography. 47 vols. New York: White, 1892–1965. S.v. "Knapp, Joseph Fairchild," and "Palmer, Walter C."

Nelson, James Melvin. "The Theological Significance of City Evangelism." Th.M. thesis, Princeton Theological Seminary, 1945.

Nicholson, Roy S. "The Holiness Emphasis in the Wesleys' Hymns." *Wesleyan Theological Journal* 5 (Spring 1970): 49–61.

Parker, Charles A. "The Camp Meeting on the Frontier and the Methodist Religious Resort in the East Before 1900." *Methodist History* 18/3 (April 1980): 179–92.

Raser, Harold E. "Phoebe Palmer: Ambassador of Holiness." *The Preachers' Magazine* (September–November 1983), pp. 20–23.

Roberts, B. T. "A Running Sketch." *The Earnest Christian and Golden Rule* 9 (January 1865): 5–8.

Salter, Darius. "Thomas Upham and Nineteenth Century Holiness Theology." Ph.D. diss., Drew University, 1983. Ann Arbor: University Microfilms, 83-17858, 1983.

Sangster, William E. "The Church's One Privation." *Religion in Life* 18 (Winter 1949): 493–502.

Schaff, Philip and D. S., eds. *New Schaff-Herzog Encyclopedia of Religious Knowledge*. 15 vols. New York: Funk and Wagnalls, 1907. Reprint. Grand Rapids: Baker, 1977. S.v. "Barnes, Albert," "Evangelical Alliance," "Payson, Edward," and "Wilberforce, Samuel."

Scott, Leland H. "Methodist Theology in America in the Nineteenth Century." Ph.D. diss., Yale University, 1954. Microcard Theological Studies, vol. 20. Madison, Wis.: The Microcard Foundation, for The American Theological Library Association, 1956.

──────. "Methodist Theology in America in the Nineteenth Century." *Religion in Life* 25 (1955–56): 87–98.

Shipley, David Clark. "The Development of Theology in American Methodism in the Nineteenth Century." *The London Quarterly and Holburn Review* 134 (July 1959): 249–64.

Smith, Timothy L. "The Doctrine of the Sanctifying Spirit: Charles G. Finney's Synthesis of Wesleyan and Covenant Theology." *Wesleyan Theological Journal* 13/1 (Spring 1978): 92–113.

──────. "George Whitefield and Wesleyan Perfectionism." *Wesleyan Theological Journal* 19/1 (Spring 1984): 63–85.

──────. "The Holy Spirit in the Hymns of the Wesleys." *Wesleyan Theological Journal* 16/2 (Fall 1981): 20–47.

──────. "How John Fletcher Became the Theologian of Wesleyan Perfectionism, 1770–1776." *Wesleyan Theological Journal* 15/1 (Spring 1980): 68–87.

―――. "Notes on the Exegesis of John Wesley's 'Explanatory Notes on the New Testament.'" *Wesleyan Theological Journal* 16/1 (Spring 1981): 107–13.
―――. "Righteousness and Hope: Christian Holiness and the Millennial Vision in America, 1800–1900." *American Quarterly* 31/1 (Spring 1979): 21–45.
―――. "The Transfer of Wesleyan Religious Culture from England to America." *Historical Bulletin of the World Methodist Historical Society* 14 (First Quarter 1985): 2–16.
Thompson, A. R., ed. *Black's Medical Dictionary.* 33d ed. Totowa, N.J.: Barnes & Noble, 1981. S.v. "Bright's Disease."
Thompson, Claude Holmes. "The Witness of American Methodism to the Historical Doctrine of Christian Perfection." Ph.D. thesis, Drew University, 1949.
Turner, George Allen. "The Baptism of the Holy Spirit in the Wesleyan Tradition." *Wesleyan Theological Journal* 14/1 (Spring 1979): 60–76.
Wall, Ernest. "I Commend unto You Phoebe." *Religion in Life* 26 (Summer 1957): 396–408.
Walters, Orville S. "The Concept of Attainment in John Wesley's Christian Perfection." *Methodist History* 10 (April 1972): 12–29.
Welter, Barbara. "The Cult of True Womanhood: 1820–1860." *American Quarterly* 18/2.1 (Summer 1966): 151–74.
―――. "The Feminization of American Religion." In *Clio's Consciousness Raised: New Perspectives on the History of Women*, pp. 137–57. Edited by Mary S. Hartman and Lois Banner. New York: Octagon Books, 1976.
White, Charles Edward. "Class Meeting: Then and Now." *Light and Life* (April 1984), pp. 18ff.
White, John Wesley. "The Influence of North American Evangelism in Great Britain between 1830 and 1914 on the Origin and Development of the Ecumenical Movement." Ph.D. thesis, Mansfield College, Oxford, 1963.
Williamson, Douglas J. "Wilbur Fisk and African Colonization: A 'Painful Portion' of American Methodist History." *Methodist History* 23/2 (January 1985): 79–98.
Wilson, J. G., and John Fiske, eds. *Appleton's Cyclopedia of American Biography.* 7 vols. New York: Appleton, 1887–1900. S.v. "Palmer, Phoebe."
Woods, David A. "The Great Hamilton Revival of 1857." Typescript. Hamilton, Ont.: 1984.
Wynkoop, Mildred Bangs. "Theological Roots of the Wesleyan Understanding of the Holy Spirit." *Wesleyan Theological Journal* 14/1 (Spring 1979): 77–98.
Zikmund, Barbara Brown. "Asa Mahan and Oberlin Perfectionism." Ph.D. diss., Duke University, 1969.

Index

Addams, Jane 229
Adventism 154–55
Albert, Prince of England 80, 94 Alcohol 73, 77, 79, 80, 81, 82, 136, 167, 208, 222, 227
Altar theology 3, 22, 23, 25, 28, 54, 86, 126, 140, 142, 158, 201
American Female Guardian Society 62
Arthur, William 128
Asbury, Francis 55
Augustine, Bishop of Hippo 109

Baker, Frank xii
Bangs, Nathan viii, ix, xi, xvi, 3, 36, 37, 140, 142, 162, 163, 178
Baptism of the Holy Spirit 126–28
Barnes, Albert 193
Beauty of Holiness and Sabbath Miscellany 93
Beecher, Catharine 61, 152
Beecher, Henry Ward 152
Beecher, Lyman 178
Bell, George 54, 119
Benson, Joseph 55, 193
Bible 2, 3, 8, 11, 12, 13, 14, 17, 24, 25, 39, 107–21, 125, 128–30, 135, 138, 139, 141–48, 150, 152, 155, 162–64, 167, 172, 184, 186, 188, 190, 195, 202, 209, 213, 215, 225
Böhler, Frederica 40
Böhler, Peter 40
Booth, Catherine 71, 72, 120, 188, 200
Boston University 163
Bowdoin College 33

Boyce, Sarah Mallett 189, 193
Bramwell, William 4, 88, 119
Buchanan, George 3

Calvin, John 105, 127
Camp meetings viii, xv, 11, 38–45, 48, 58, 69, 87, 90, 91, 92, 96, 97, 99, 100–102, 180
Cartwright, Peter 145
Carvosso, William 4, 13, 107
Carwardine, Richard 165
Caughey, James 68, 71, 88
Cell, George Croft 178
Charismatic movement xvii, 158, 159
Church of the Nazarene 158, 201
Church planting 49–52
Civil War ix, xi, xiii, 93, 98, 129, 217, 228
Clarke, Adam x, 55, 79, 120, 123–26, 128, 129, 130, 140, 193
Class meetings 4, 22, 30, 36, 37, 41, 51, 54, 79, 86, 90, 167
Cleveland, Grover 58
Cole, Charles, Jr. 229
Collet, Elizabeth Tonkin 189
Colonization 60
Committee for Promoting National Education 61
Controversies 52–58
Cookman, Alfred ix
Cotton, John 134
Covenant 16, 124, 137
Cox, G. F. 154
Cox, Lydia N. 29, 38
Creagh, Bartholomew 37, 55

INDEX

Crosby, Fanny 58
Crosby, Sarah 189, 193
Cutler, Ann 4, 83

Davidson, Margaret 189
Dayton, Donald 127, 158, 229
Dempster, John xvi, 163
Dickens, Charles 63
Dickenson, Elizabeth 189
Dieter, Melvin 134
Dodwell, Henry 193
Dow, Lorenzo 88
Dreams and visions xii, 11, 21, 22, 38, 51, 57, 116, 117, 118, 136
Duel, Mrs. C. R. 223
Dwight, Louis 52

Ecumenism 40, 48, 75, 162, 164, 165
Edwards, Jonathan 48, 134, 145
Energy 14, 20, 25, 215–17
Entire sanctification xiii, 10–26, 125–44
Eschatology 30, 116, 144–46

Female Assistance Society 61, 62, 209, 221
Feminism xiv, 32, 33, 163, 167, 187–206
Fenelon, Archbishop of Cambray 114
Finney, Charles G. 68, 120, 124, 125, 134, 165, 177–79, 185, 186, 201
Fisk, Wilbur 55
Fitch, Charles 155
Five Points Mission vii, viii, 63, 64, 65, 217–27, 229
Fletcher, John x, xiii, 4, 17, 21, 25, 84, 119, 120, 122–26, 128, 139, 142, 155, 156, 161
Fletcher, Mary Bosanquet vii, 4, 84, 118, 120, 123, 135, 189, 193
Foster, Elon 31, 48, 58, 93, 198
Foster, Sarah Palmer 7, 31, 58, 93, 198
Franklin, Samuel 157
Free Methodist Church xiii, xvi, 42, 100, 158

Gardner, Mary 30
Garrett-Evangelical Seminary 163
Gilbert, Ann 189
Godey's Lady's Book 94
Graham, Isabella 221
Grant, Ulysses S. 58, 99
Grotius, Hugo 193
Guide to Holiness xvii, 28, 58, 70, 91–94, 98, 101, 102, 103, 112, 145, 146, 154, 155, 156, 159, 162, 212, 227
Guyon, Madame de la Mothe 114

Hadley, Samuel Hopkins 229
Hamline, Leonidas L. xvi, 28, 40, 46, 52, 58, 95, 111, 163, 179, 196
Hamline Mrs. Leonidas (Melinda) 40, 46, 61, 97, 98
Hardesty, Nancy 201, 205
Harrison, Benjamin 58
Harrison, Mary 189
Harvard College 42
Haven, Gilbert 97
Heck, Barbara 200
Hecker, Isaac 146
Hoffman, Elisha 158
Holder, Mary Woodhouse 189
Holiness movement xvii, 159, 188
Holy Spirit 7, 8, 10, 12, 14–20, 23, 24, 32, 39, 52, 53, 65, 71, 73, 77, 84, 96, 97, 107–10, 114, 115, 117, 122, 123, 125, 126–28, 138, 139, 141–43, 149, 151, 153, 154, 158, 166, 167, 174, 182, 188, 190, 192, 193, 197, 203, 204
Hopkins, Charles H. 229
Hovet, Theodore 201–5
Hughes, George 94
Humanitarism xiv, 48, 49, 52, 59, 60, 207–29
Huntington, Frederic Dan 42, 43

Inskip, John xvi, 97, 157, 165, 188
Inskip, Martha 97, 188

James, William 202
Janes, Edmund S. xvi, 65, 163
Judaism 30, 50, 51, 59, 66, 156

Ladies' Home Missionary Society xvi, 217, 221–23, 226, 227
Ladies' Repository xvi, 94
Lankford, Thomas A. 7
Lanphier, Jeremiah 47
Lawrence, Sarah 193
Lay ministry 45, 47, 72, 74–76, 168–73, 185–86
Lincoln, Abraham ix, 84, 153
Love feasts 37, 38, 39, 54, 86, 92
Lovelace, Richard 178, 179
Loveland, Anne 201, 205
Luckey, Mr. (given names not supplied) 223, 225
Luther, Martin 106, 127, 216

M'Kendree, William 27
Magnuson, Norris 229
Mahan, Asa 28, 52, 97, 120, 124, 125
Malthus, Thomas 220
Mattison, Hiram 38, 52–54, 57, 58, 143, 180, 183, 217
Maxfield, Thomas 54, 119
Maxwell, Lady 4, 118–20
May, Henry F. 229
McAuley, Jeremiah 229
Melder, Keith 201
Merritt, Timothy 9, 10, 28, 37, 92, 124
Merwin, Samuel 6
Methodist Quarterly Review 36, 157
Miller, William 154, 155
Mohl, Raymond 229
Moody, D. L. 177, 186
Moravians 40
Mormons 146
Miller, George 82
Mysticism in the theology of Phoebe Palmer 112–20

National Camp Meeting for the Promotion of Holiness xvi, 97, 102, 157, 165
Nelson, John 4, 120
New York Christian Advocate and Journal viii, 27, 28, 36, 45, 47, 53, 58, 68, 92, 94, 171, 198
Noyes, John Humphrey 127

Oberlin College 28, 68, 124, 125
Olin, Stephen 55, 56, 163
Orr, J. Edwin xvi, 47

Palmer, Alexander 5
Palmer, Deborah Clarke 4
Palmer, Eliza 7, 8, 9, 11, 12, 58, 169, 181
Palmer, Miles (Jr.) 5
Palmer, Miles (Sr.) 4
Palmer, Phoebe (career)
  Benevolence 59, 210–13
  Childhood 2–4
  Children 5–8, 58–59, 198–99
  Church planting 49–52
  Class meetings 4, 22, 30, 36, 37, 41, 51, 54, 79, 86, 90, 167
  Colonization society 60
  Controversies 52–58
  Death 102–3
  Energy 14, 20, 25, 215–17
  Experience of entire sanctification 10–26
  Family background 1–2
  Foreign missions 15, 30–31, 35–36, 65–66, 96
  Itinerant ministry xiii, 11, 38–48, 58, 69, 87, 90–92, 96–102
  Local church ministry 36–38
  Marriage 4–6
  Ministry in Britain 67–90
  Publications 27–34, 43, 56, 76, 85, 92–96, 189–93
  Relief ministries 60–65
  Revival of 1857–58 45–47

Tuesday Meeting for the Promotion
    of Holiness 9–10, 34–36,
    161–64
  Visitation 48–49
Palmer, Phoebe (thought)
  Feminism xiv, 32–33, 187–206
    Background 188–89
    Family 58, 194–200
    Influence 200–206
    Ordination 193–94
  Humanitarianism xiv, 48–49, 52,
    59–60, 207–29
    Five Points Mission 217–27
    Influence 228–29
    Motives 208–17
    Slavery 27, 59–60, 99, 228
    Temperance 73, 77, 79–82, 227
  Revivalism xiii, 6–7, 38–89, 43,
    161–86
    Influence 178–86
    Lay ministry 45, 47, 72, 74, 76,
      168–73, 185–86
    Methodology 167–77
    Theology of revival 165–67
    Tuesday Meeting for the
      Promotion of Holiness
      161–64
  Theology 105–59
    Altar theology 3, 22–23, 25, 28,
      54, 86, 140, 142, 158,
      201
    Assurance 10–12, 23–24
    Baptism of the Holy Spirit
      126–28
    Bible 106–10
    Covenant 16, 124
    Ecclesiology 30, 144–46
    Ecumenism 145–46
    Entire sanctification 125–44
    Eschatology 154–56
    Experience 111–17
    Faith 137–39

Importance 156–59
    Influences 120–25
    Method 106–20
    Mysticism 112–20
    Originality 143–44
    Pentecostalism 126–29, 158–59
    Power 128–29
    Reason 110–11
    Sabbath 76, 81, 148–49
    Spirituality 146–54
    Testimony 21, 28, 139–40
    Tradition 117–20
    Wealth 150–54, 210–14
Palmer, Samuel 5, 6
Palmer, Sarah Worrall Lankford 7, 9, 10,
    11, 13, 17, 21, 34–36, 38, 40, 41,
    44, 62, 91, 92, 94, 103, 118, 124
Palmer, Walter Clarke 4–7, 15, 16, 21,
    22, 31, 36, 37, 39–41, 43–45, 47,
    51, 56, 59, 60, 65, 66, 75, 77, 84,
    88, 91, 94, 95, 99, 103, 148, 154,
    171–73, 195, 197, 199, 210, 211,
    213, 215, 221, 223
Palmer, Walter Clarke, Jr. 31, 40, 58, 59,
    68, 198, 200
Pease, Louis 221–23, 229
Pentecost 32, 122, 126–29, 158, 166,
    173, 190, 192, 193, 211
Pentecostal movement xiii, xv, 127, 158,
    159, 188
Perry, J. H. 53–57
Peters, John xi, xvii
Philip, Robert 11
Primitive Methodists 88, 89 Prison
    Ministry 52
Prostitutes 78, 177, 222

Redfield, John Wesley 100
Revivals and revivalism xiii, 6, 7, 38, 39,
    43, 45, 46, 47, 51, 57, 67–74, 76,
    77, 79–88, 91, 92, 95, 97–100,
    102, 161–86
Ricardo, David 220

Roberts, Benjamin Titus xvi, 42, 100, 228
Rogers, Hester Ann Roe vii, x, 4, 9, 25, 82, 83, 118, 120, 123, 135
Roman Catholic Church 33, 45, 53, 70, 75, 79, 146, 178, 190, 220, 225
Rosenberg, Carol Smith 228
Rutgers College 4, 58

Sabbath 76, 81, 148–49
Satan 21, 22, 23, 29, 34, 38, 64, 74, 79, 87, 114–16, 138, 154, 170–72, 182, 197, 199, 223
Simpson, Matthew 43, 44
Slavery 27, 60, 99, 228
Smith, Amanda 120, 163, 200, 201
Smith, Timothy xi, xvii, 229
Stevens, Abel ix
Stowe, Harriet Beecher 61, 152, 153

Taft, Mary Barrit 193
Taft, Zechariah 193
Taylor, William xvi, 163
Tract societies 48, 61, 65, 169, 220
Tuesday Meeting for the Promotion of Holiness viii, xvi, xvii, 9, 10, 22, 23, 33–36, 41, 91, 97, 100. 103, Ill, 112, 120, 142, 145, 149, 159, 161–65, 183, 184, 190, 194, 205, 212, 228

University of Michigan 97
Upham, Mrs. Thomas C. (Phoebe) 33, 34, 188
Upham, Thomas C. xvi, 33–36, 113–15, 117, 119 120, 163, 184, 188

Van Cott, Maggie 201
Victoria, Queen of England 76, 81, 94, 191
Victoria College 44

Wade, Dorothea 2
Wall, Earnest xvii
Watson, Thomas 55

Wayland, Francis 193
Wealth 75, 80, 94, 150–54, 210–14
Weaver, Richard 88
Wesley, Charles 121, 131, 155
Wesley, John vii, ix-xiii, xv, 1, 9, 17, 40, 55, 67, 70, 73, 78, 79, 83, 101, 106, 113, 118, 119, 121–25, 127, 129–36, 139–44, 149–53, 155–58, 161, 166–68, 176–81, 188–90, 200, 202, 203, 205, 210
Wesley, Samuel 196
Wesley, Susanna 4, 188, 193, 195, 196
Wesleyan Methodist Church (American) 158
Wesleyan Methodist Church (English) 88, 89
Wesleyan University (Conn.) 36, 163
Wheatley, Richard ix, xvii, 43
Whedon, Daniel 157
While, Nicholas 4.
Whitefield, George 122
Whitman, Walt 202
Wilberforce, Samuel 79
Willard, Frances xvi, 97, 98, 120, 188, 200
Worrall, Dorothea 2, 5, 117
Worrall, Hannah 5
Worrall, Henry 1, 2, 3, 5, 35, 64, 217
Young, Brigham 146
Young, Robert 70, 71

Zion's Herald 27, 52, 154

www.ingramcontent.com/pod-product-compliance
Lightning Source LLC
Chambersburg PA
CBHW071954220426
43662CB00009B/1121